IFIP Advances in Information and Communication Technology 527

Editor-in-Chief

Kai Rannenberg, Goethe University Frankfurt, Germany

IFIP – The International Federation for Information Processing

IFIP was founded in 1960 under the auspices of UNESCO, following the first World Computer Congress held in Paris the previous year. A federation for societies working in information processing, IFIP's aim is two-fold: to support information processing in the countries of its members and to encourage technology transfer to developing nations. As its mission statement clearly states:

> IFIP is the global non-profit federation of societies of ICT professionals that aims at achieving a worldwide professional and socially responsible development and application of information and communication technologies.

IFIP is a non-profit-making organization, run almost solely by 2500 volunteers. It operates through a number of technical committees and working groups, which organize events and publications. IFIP's events range from large international open conferences to working conferences and local seminars.

The flagship event is the IFIP World Computer Congress, at which both invited and contributed papers are presented. Contributed papers are rigorously refereed and the rejection rate is high.

As with the Congress, participation in the open conferences is open to all and papers may be invited or submitted. Again, submitted papers are stringently refereed.

The working conferences are structured differently. They are usually run by a working group and attendance is generally smaller and occasionally by invitation only. Their purpose is to create an atmosphere conducive to innovation and development. Refereeing is also rigorous and papers are subjected to extensive group discussion.

Publications arising from IFIP events vary. The papers presented at the IFIP World Computer Congress and at open conferences are published as conference proceedings, while the results of the working conferences are often published as collections of selected and edited papers.

IFIP distinguishes three types of institutional membership: Country Representative Members, Members at Large, and Associate Members. The type of organization that can apply for membership is a wide variety and includes national or international societies of individual computer scientists/ICT professionals, associations or federations of such societies, government institutions/government related organizations, national or international research institutes or consortia, universities, academies of sciences, companies, national or international associations or federations of companies.

More information about this series at http://www.springer.com/series/6102

Kecheng Liu · Keiichi Nakata
Weizi Li · Cecilia Baranauskas (Eds.)

Digitalisation, Innovation, and Transformation

18th IFIP WG 8.1 International Conference
on Informatics and Semiotics in Organisations, ICISO 2018
Reading, UK, July 16–18, 2018
Proceedings

 Springer

Editors
Kecheng Liu
University of Reading
Reading
UK

Weizi Li
University of Reading
Reading
UK

Keiichi Nakata
University of Reading
Reading
UK

Cecilia Baranauskas
State University of Campinas
Campinas
Brazil

ISSN 1868-4238   ISSN 1868-422X   (electronic)
IFIP Advances in Information and Communication Technology
ISBN 978-3-319-94540-8   ISBN 978-3-319-94541-5   (eBook)
https://doi.org/10.1007/978-3-319-94541-5

Library of Congress Control Number: 2018947432

Printed on acid-free paper

This Springer imprint is published by the registered company Springer International Publishing AG part of Springer Nature
The registered company address is: Gewerbestrasse 11, 6330 Cham, Switzerland

Preface

The 2018 edition of the International Conference on Informatics and Semiotics in Organisations (ICISO 2018) is an IFIP WG 8.1 Working Conference and part of a series of international events devoted to current research and application of informatics and semiotics in organizations (see www.orgsem.org for earlier conferences since 1995). ICISO 2018 continued the innovative work of the international research community in the development of organizational semiotics, focusing not only on theory building, but also on practical benefits gained through applications of methods and techniques derived from various organizational semiotics approaches. The conference theme, "Digitalization, innovation and transformation," allows us to consider how these three concepts are driving changes globally.

Digitalization, innovation, and transformation impact both modern businesses and organizations. Business landscapes are rapidly evolving into more dynamic environments for value-creation across a wide range of industries, such as healthcare, education, public governance, agriculture, environment, accounting, and finance. The digital transformation has been predominantly enabled by information and communication technologies (ICTs), which has in turn stimulated products and services innovation. Emerging technologies, such as IoT, artificial intelligence, robotics, virtual and augment reality, 3D printing, and blockchain, have profoundly transformed the social, economic, human-centered and organizational activity across multiple sectors. Top management has evolved from a traditional leadership approach, to a more digital leadership mindset in order to manage the innovative modern business. The digital evolution within our modern society will continue to take place and transform organizations into new forms in the foreseeable future.

Organizational semiotics, with its profound theories, methods, and techniques, provides an effective approach to explore the nature and characteristics of digitalization, innovation, and transformation within the complex business landscape. Organizational semiotics, as a discipline of the study of sign, information, and human communication within organizational contexts, guides academics and practitioners with valuable insight into actionable outcomes of human interplay among the sign-based and physical worlds.

ICISO 2018 received 38 paper submissions from 12 countries, demonstrating the success and global dimension of this conference. From the papers submitted, 30 were accepted for presentation while four were accepted as posters. These numbers show the intention of preserving a high level of quality for future editions of this conference. The papers in the proceedings are organized around four topics: (1) organizational semiotics: theory and application, (2) digital business ecosystems and value networks, (3) socially aware knowledge engineering, and (4) business intelligence and analytics.

The high quality of the papers received imposed difficult choices in the review process. To evaluate each submission, two rounds of paper review were performed by the Program Committee and reviewing panels, whose members are highly qualified researchers in the conference topic areas. Moreover, ICISO also featured a number of keynote lectures delivered by internationally recognized experts, namely, Dr. Carsten Sørensen from the Department of Management, London School of Economics and Political Science, UK, Professor Cecilia Baranauskas from the Institute of Computing, University of Campinas, Brazil, and a special contribution from Professor Ronald Stamper. These keynote lectures brought significant value to the conference.

Building an interesting and successful program for the conference required the dedicated effort of many people. We would like to express our thanks to all authors including those whose papers were not included in the program. We would also like to express our gratitude to all members of the Program Committee and additional reviewers, who helped us with their expertise and valuable time. Furthermore, we thank the invited speakers for their invaluable contributions and for taking the time to synthesize and prepare their talks.

Moreover, we thank the session chairs, whose contribution to the diversity of the program was essential. Finally, we gratefully acknowledge the professional and organizational support from the Informatics Research Centre, Henley Business School, University of Reading, UK.

July 2018

Kecheng Liu
Keiichi Nakata
Weizi Li
Cecilia Baranauskas

Organization

Conference Chairs

Kecheng Liu   University of Reading, UK
Cecilia Baranauskas   University of Campinas, Brazil

Program Chairs

Keiichi Nakata   University of Reading, UK
Weizi Li   University of Reading, UK

Publication Chairs

Lily Sun   University of Reading, UK
Florin Gheorghe Filip   Romanian Academy of Science, Romania

Organizing Chair

Weizi Li   University of Reading, UK

Publicity Chairs

Chekfoung Tan   University of West London, UK
Yu-Chun Pan   University of West London, UK

Conference Secretariat

Prince Kwame Senyo   University of Reading, UK
Siwen Liu   University of Reading, UK

Program Committee

Mona Ashok   University of Reading, UK
Joseph Barjis   Delft University of Technology, The Netherlands
Adrian Benfell   University of Portsmouth, UK
Rodrigo Bonacin   CTI Renato Archer and FACCAMP, Brazil
Mangtang Chan   City University of Hong Kong, SAR China
Pierre-Jean Charrel   University of Toulouse, France
Jose Cordeiro   EST Setubal/IPS, Portugal
Simone Diniz Junqueira   PUC-Rio, Brazil
    Barbosa
Julio Cesar Dos Reis   University of Campinas, Brazil

Yanqing Duan	University of Bedfordshire, UK
John Effah	University of Ghana Business School, Ghana
Florin Gheorghe Filip	Romanian Academy of Sciences, Romania
Joaquim Filipe	EST-Setubal/IPS, Portugal
Daniel Galarreta	CNES, France
Ricardo Gudwin	University of Campinas, Brazil
Stephen Gulliver	University of Reading, UK
Selcuk Burak Hasiloglu	Pamukkale University, Turkey
Paul Johanneson	Royal Institute of Technology, Sweden
Angela Lacerda-Nobre	ESCE-IPS, Portugal
Weizi Li	University of Reading, UK
Kecheng Liu	University of Reading, UK
Ecivaldo Matos	Universidade Federal da Bahia, Brazil
Alessio Miranda Júnior	Cefet-MG Campus Timóteo, Brazil
Keiichi Nakata	University of Reading, UK
Vânia Neris	UFSCar, Brazil
Dan Oleary	University of Southern California, USA
Stephen Opoku-Anokye	University of Reading, UK
Yu-Chun Pan	University of West London, UK
Roberto Pereira	University of Campinas, Brazil
LaraPiccolo	The Open University, UK
Simon Polovina	Sheffield Hallam University, UK
Luis Quezada	University of Santiago, Chile
Kamila Rodrigues	University of São Paulo, Brazil
Wenge Rong	Beihang University, China
Vagner Santana	University of Campinas, Brazil
Keng Siau	Missouri University of Science and Technology, USA
Lily Sun	University of Reading, UK
Chekfoung Tan	University of West London, UK
Christina Tay	Chinese Culture University, China
Jasmine Tehrani	University of Bedfordshire, UK
Hans Weigand	Tilburg University, The Netherlands
Shen Xu	King's College London, UK
Mohammad Yamin	King Abdelaziz University, Saudi Arabia
Zhijun Yan	Beijing Institute of Technology, China

Additional Reviewers

Eric Afful-Dadzie	University of Ghana Business School, Ghana
Maksim Belitski	University of Reading, UK
Michael Dzandu	University of Reading, UK
Diego Fuentealba	University of Reading, UK
Elaine C. Hayashi	University of Campinas, Brazil
Lei Hou	University of Reading, UK
Caine Jamie	Sheffield Hallam University, UK
Qi Li	University of Reading, UK

Shixiong Liu   University of Reading, UK
Anupam Nanda   University of Reading, UK
Xue Pan   University of Reading, UK

Sponsors

In cooperation with

Abstract of Keynotes

Coupling the Digital, the Physical and the Social: New Demands for Information Systems Understanding?

M. Cecilia C. Baranauskas

Institute of Computing, University of Campinas,
UNICAMP, Campinas, SP, Brazil
cecilia@ic.unicamp.br

Abstract. The computational technology has become pervasive in our lives and culture, transforming our ways of understanding and living in the world. This presence has led to changes in our relations with technology, with others and with the process of building knowledge. Technology is a human creation, thus there is no neutrality in our relationship with it: we suffer the impact of technology and, at the same time, we are responsible for the form it takes and the effects it causes. Since most of the modern computing experience is about the world we live in (people, places, and things), it makes sense to understand information systems situating them out into the world people live. In the interaction design field, there has been a move away from a perspective that treats people and computers as two separate and distinct entities toward a perspective that acknowledges the need to consider people, digital technology, and traditionally non-computational materials together as a whole, forming our experiences in and of the world. The presence of new technologies and new forms of interaction (tangible, wearable and natural interfaces), coupled with the ubiquity of computing, present challenges that require the consideration of new factors in the design of systems we are naming socio-enactive. The enactive perspective collectively understands perception, cognition, and action as essential factors in the modes of signification. In this talk, I want to provoke a reflection on changes in perspectives the design of such systems, constituted from the coupling of the digital, the physical and the social, demands. Assuming a subjectivist posture and recognizing the situational character of design, I will illustrate ideas from ongoing research Projects (Fapesp#2015/16528-0, #2015/24300-9, and CNPq#306272/2017-2), their epistemological foundations and forms that they are being experienced in different scenarios.

Digital Infrastructure Innovation Dynamics

Computing in the Small, in the Large, and at Scale

Carsten Sørensen[1,2,3]

[1] Department of Management,
London School of Economics and Political Science, UK
[2] University West, Sweden
[3] Halmstad University, Sweden
c.sorensen@lse.ac.uk

Abstract. Much data has sped through personal, local, and global data networks since Gore and Bangemann in the 1990 summarised the emergent importance of the Internet in terms of "The Information Superhighway" and "The Global Information Society". It is difficult to succinctly characterise the changes global data communications have undergone since Tim Berners-Lee published the World Wide Web standard in 1991, and the first widely available Web Browser, Mosaic, followed in 1993. This talk will discuss digital innovation dynamics based on the emergent architecture of: (1) **Computing in the small** through an expanding mobile and ubiquitous device ecology; (2) **Computing in the large** network connectivity through machine-to-machine, personal, local, and global digital infrastructures; and (3) **Computing at scale**, where powerful data-centres engage in heavy-lifting computational tasks utilising the exponential growth in processing power, reduction in storage costs, and increasingly complex capabilities. Based on this architecture, the talk will draw up some of the findings from a series of multi-year studies on the dynamics of digital infrastructures, for example, their reconfiguration as multi-sided digital platforms serving smartphone content and services. A few notes will also be forwarded on the issue of distributed consensus mechanisms on top of digital infrastructures challenging the notion of platform centrality. The talk will be aimed at a broad Information Systems audience and will for the specially interested point towards recent, co-authored papers, published in Management Information Systems Quarterly (MISQ), Information Systems Research (ISR), Journal of Management Information Systems (JMIS), Journal of Information Technology (JIT), etc.

Organisational Semiotics Viewed as an Institution: How, as a Science in the Organisational Sense, Can it Best Functions?

Ronald Stamper [1,2,3]

[1] Oxford OX3 7SL#38, UK
[2] London School of Economics and Political Science, UK
[3] University of Twente, The Netherlands
stamper.measur@gmail.com

Abstract. The English saying: "The cobbler's child is the least well-shod." reminds those skilled in any craft or profession to ensure that "their own house is in order" suggesting we might, devote a session during our own annual gathering to checking that our family members benefit from well-crafted semiosis. I lieu of the cobbler's last, we have our methods of analysis and, for a hammer and tacks, we have our specification tools. I propose, therefore to use these tools on the bench (our meeting), firstly to examine our soles and then, if necessary, to repair them and to modernise them if desirable. Of course, we shall examine our media of communication and how well or ill we use them. Channel capacity matters and so do errors and how we recognise and correct them. The syntax of each language we use for recording and testing our hypotheses and theories probably relates most strongly to our specification languages, where the semantics of the terms we use obviously deserves close attention. Finding appropriate goal will influence strongly every communication of pragmatic force directing us toward a collective body of knowledge and skills, where, at the meta-level are the knowledge of our own conduct as scientists and the body of norms and social commitments that function as the "legislation" to govern our own conduct. I shall make some proposals, pose questions and, I hope, stimulate a productive debate, which should continue during the whole meeting to generate recommendations and even plans for consolidating our work and, perhaps, improve how we do it.

Contents

Organisational Semiotics: Theory and Application

Understanding the Boundary Between Information Systems and
Organizational Semiotics: POS as Case Study   3
   Manuel Ibarra, Emerson Ñahuinlla, Wilfredo Soto, Vladimiro Ibañez,
   Angel Navarro, and Waldo Ibarra

The Role of Language in Human Information Interaction:
A Social Semiotic View   12
   Enyun Li and Yinshan Tang

Building a Socio-Technical Perspective of Community Resilience
with a Semiotic Approach   22
   Lara S. G. Piccolo, Kenny Meesters, and Shadrock Roberts

Norm-Based Abduction Process (NAP) in Developing
Information Architecture   33
   Chekfoung Tan, Sara Abdaless, and Kecheng Liu

Extending Technology Acceptance Model for Proximity Mobile Payment
via Organisational Semiotics   43
   Yu-Chun Pan, Aimee Jacobs, Chekfoung Tan, and Sanaa Askool

Towards a Semiotic-Based Approach to the Design of Therapeutic
Digital Games   53
   Paula Maia de Souza, Kamila Rios da Hora Rodrigues,
   Franco Eusébio Garcia, and Vânia Paula de Almeida Neris

Intensive Innovation: A Semiotic View   63
   Daniel Galarreta

Norm-Based Approach to Incorporate Human Factors into Clinical
Pathway: Reducing Human Error and Improving Patient Safety   73
   Jasmine Tehrani, Vaughan Michell, and Yu-Chun Pan

A Framework to Evaluate Semiotic Interoperability
for Information Sharing   83
   Shixiong Liu and Weizi Li

The Social Layer of Stampers Ladder: A Systematic Approach to the Soft
Edge of Organizational Transformations   94
   Auke J. J. van Breemen and Ralf Nieuwenhuijsen

A Hidden Power of Ontology Charts from Affordances
to Environmental States   105
   José Cordeiro

Digital Business Ecosystems and Value Networks

Exploring the Cloud Computing Loop in the Strategic Alignment Model   117
   *Belitski Maksim, Fernandez Valerie, Khalil Sabine, Weizi Li,
   and Kecheng Liu*

A Framework for Assessing the Social Impact of Interdependencies
in Digital Business Ecosystems   125
   Prince Kwame Senyo, Kecheng Liu, and John Effah

Introducing the Strategy Lifecycle: Using Ontology and Semiotics
to Interlink Strategy Design to Strategy Execution   136
   Jamie Caine and Mark von Rosing

Role of Digitisation in Enabling Co-creation of Value in KIBS Firms   145
   Mona Ashok

Cluster Nodes as a Unit for Value Co-creation: The Role of Information
Technologies in Competitiveness of the Oil and Gas Industry   155
   Vitaly Ambalov and Irina Heim

Socially Aware Knowledge Engineering

Unifying Speech and Computation   167
   Martin John Wheatman

A Framework to Support the Design of Digital Initiatives in Social Science
Based Research   177
   Stuart Moran, Sophie Berckhan, and Alison Clarke

A Metamodel for Supporting Interoperability in Heterogeneous
Ontology Networks   187
   Rodrigo Bonacin, Ivo Calado, and Julio Cesar dos Reis

Enactive Systems and Children at Hospitals: For More Socially Aware
Solutions with Improved Affectibility   197
   *Elaine C. S. Hayashi, Roberto Pereira, José Valderlei da Silva,
   and M. Cecília C. Baranauskas*

Design Practices and the SAwD Tool: Towards the Opendesign Concept   208
   *José Valderlei da Silva, Roberto Pereira, Elaine C. S. Hayashi,
   and M. Cecília C. Baranauskas*

Reformulating Requirements Modelling for Digitalisation: A Structuration
and Semiotic Informed Approach 218
  Adrian Benfell and Zoe Hoy

Getting it Right: A Model for Compliance Assessment 228
  Kwasi Dankwa and Keiichi Nakata

First Steps in Developing Tangible Artifacts for All: Enabling Ideation
and Discussion Processes.................................... 238
  Vanessa R. M. L. Maike and M. Cecília C. Baranauskas

Does It Pay to Be Socially Responsible for Construction Companies? 248
  Anupam Nanda

Business Intelligence and Analytics

Method of Operational Activities and Processes Optimization Design
in Architecture 259
  Xiaoxue Zhang, Aimin Luo, Gang Liu, and Junxian Liu

Business Intelligence Architecture Informed by Organisational Semiotics 268
  John Effah, Prince Kwame Senyo, and Stephen Opoku-Anokye

Chaotic Time Series for Copper's Price Forecast: Neural Networks
and the Discovery of Knowledge for Big Data 278
  Raúl Carrasco, Manuel Vargas, Ismael Soto, Diego Fuentealba,
  Leonardo Banguera, and Guillermo Fuertes

An Abductive Process of Developing Interactive Data Visualization:
A Case Study of Market Attractiveness Analysis.................... 289
  Qi Li and Kecheng Liu

Local Government Open Data (LGOD) Initiatives: Analysis of Trends
and Similarities Among Early Adopters 299
  Eric Afful-Dadzie and Anthony Afful-Dadzie

Poster Papers

Information Systems Governance and Industry 4.0 - Epistemology of Data
and Semiotics Methodologies of IS in Digital Ecosystems 311
  Ângela Lacerda Nobre, Rogério Duarte, and Marc Jacquinet

Value Co-creation and Local Content Development: Transformation,
Digitalization and Innovation in the Oil and Gas Industry 313
  Irina Heim

The Interplay of FDI and R&D: A Study in the Seven
Developed Countries   315
   Yutong Li

The Pattern of Foreign Direct Investment and International Trade:
A Study of 30 OECD Countries from 1981 to 2015   318
   Yutong Li

Author Index   321

Organisational Semiotics: Theory and Application

Understanding the Boundary Between Information Systems and Organizational Semiotics: POS as Case Study

Manuel Ibarra[1]([⊠]), Emerson Ñahuinlla[1], Wilfredo Soto[1],
Vladimiro Ibañez[2], Angel Navarro[3], and Waldo Ibarra[4]

[1] Micaela Bastidas National University of Apurimac, Abancay, Peru
manuelibarra@gmail.com, nahuinllal01131@gmail.com,
wilsotopal@gmail.com
[2] National University of Altiplano Puno, Puno, Peru
viqibanezquispe@gmail.com
[3] Jose Maria Arguedas National University of Apurimac, Andahuaylas, Peru
angelnr22@gmail.com
[4] San Antonio Abad National University of Cusco, Cusco, Peru
ibarrazambrano@yahoo.es

Abstract. Information systems have played an important role in organizations, especially in the business field. Organizational semiotics is one of the social technical approaches that considers information through the signs, norms or activities performed within an organization. This paper proposes a conceptual design of the boundary between information systems and organizational semiotics. To perform this task, a Point of Sale (POS) information system for a restaurant was developed as a case study in Apurimac Peru. The system allows the waiter to customize the food and drink orders. To validate this proposal three type of techniques were performed: document review, observation and interview. Also participated in the proof of concept the following people: waiter, customer, owner, cashier and cook. The collected results highlight the three layers and the morphology in the restaurant information system linked to organizational semiotics.

Keywords: Organizational semiotics · Information system · Point of Sale
Restaurant

1 Introduction

In recent years, Point of Sale (POS) information systems for restaurants have undergone interesting changes to implement various communication and information technologies to improve efficiency and customer service, among other aspects [1]. Decades ago, the restaurants used cash registers and papers with pens for annotations, now restaurants use POS terminals with touch screens and mobile devices. These changes encompass both the software and hardware that top-performing restaurants are using today to improve: customer satisfaction, business operations and increase revenues.

K. Liu et al. (Eds.): ICISO 2018, IFIP AICT 527, pp. 3–11, 2018.
https://doi.org/10.1007/978-3-319-94541-5_1

The definition of POS is a retail store, a cashier at the store, or the location where the transaction occurred. More specifically, POS often refers to the hardware and software used for checkouts - the equivalent of an electronic cash registers many years ago. POS are used in supermarkets, restaurants, hotels, stadiums, and virtually any type of retail business.

With growth in the use of mobile technology, nowadays, in the restaurants waiters can improve the food ordering using "all in one" computers with touch screens and mobile devices like tablets or cell phones. The allure of mobility, which enables tableside ordering and payment processing, may be having the greatest impact on purchase decisions, at least in table service environments [2].

According to Sarkar [3], the food ordering system, until a few years ago, was a completely manual process where a waiter used to note down orders from the customers using pen and paper, then take the orders to the kitchen, bring the food to the customer and then make the bill. Although this system was simple it required extensive investment in purchase and storage of paper, large manpower and also was prone to human errors and greater time consumption. In order to overcome these limitations in the manual systems, some systems were developed later like Personal Digital Assistant (PDA) based systems and touchable tablets restaurant management systems to automate food ordering process.

The restaurants are organizations with business that are highly prospective, because everyone has to eat and the amount of opportunities and the chance to grow are in line with the growing market. Employees and customers use signs, objects, norms and language to communicate each other, this means that they are using semiotics approach and information systems.

This article draws the relation between Information Systems and Organizational Semiotics, analyzing the objects of the ticket for Point of Sale System Information.

Section 2 of this article presents and discusses the document review; Sect. 3 explains the design and implementation of the proposed design; Sect. 4 explains the findings of the proposed design; finally, Sect. 5 describes the conclusions and future work of this research.

2   Document Review

Semiotics. Semiotics is the study of signs. Sign refers to anything that stands to someone for something else in a given context [4]. Also, it is the study of the meaning of sign processes and meaningful communication. This includes the study of signs and sign processes (semiosis), analogy, metaphor, symbolism, signification, and communication. Within the organizational semiotics literature, three forms of activities are discussed, namely substantive, communication and control [5].

Organizational Semiotics. Organizational Semiotics tries to understand organizations based on the use of all kinds of elements like: signs, texts, documents, sign-based artefacts and communication, thereby using the results of for instance psychology, sociology, economics, and information systems science as basic disciplines. One of the aims of organizational semiotics is to show what you are doing when you are trying to understand, design or change organizations in terms of the use of for instance models and metaphors. This is done in order to prevent people being trapped in the unconscious use of a specific metaphor or model type, and to make design space which is visible [6].

The Organizational Onion and Norms. The Organizational Onion categorizes Norms into three types: technical, formal and informal [5] as shown in the Fig. 1. Technical Norms represent formal norms that have been digitalized; Formal Norms are documented and bureaucratic rules or standards into the organization; and Informal Norms are unstructured and undocumented rules or standards [4].

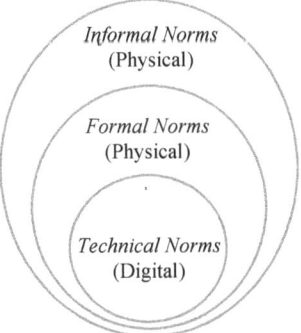

Fig. 1. The Organization Onion.

Semiotic Triangle. The study of signs must be united with the study of norms. From a triadic perspective, Peirce's version of semiotic triangle presents semantic relationship between: sign, object and interpretant [4]. Figure 2 shows that, as one interpretation, the interpretant must have knowledge or norm in order to associate the sign with the object.

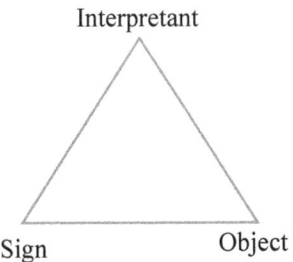

Fig. 2. The semiotic triangle

Semiotics and Information Systems. Stamper [7] has developed a semiotic framework (Fig. 3) which guides us in examining all the aspects of the signs and studying how signs are used for communication and coordination in an organizational context.

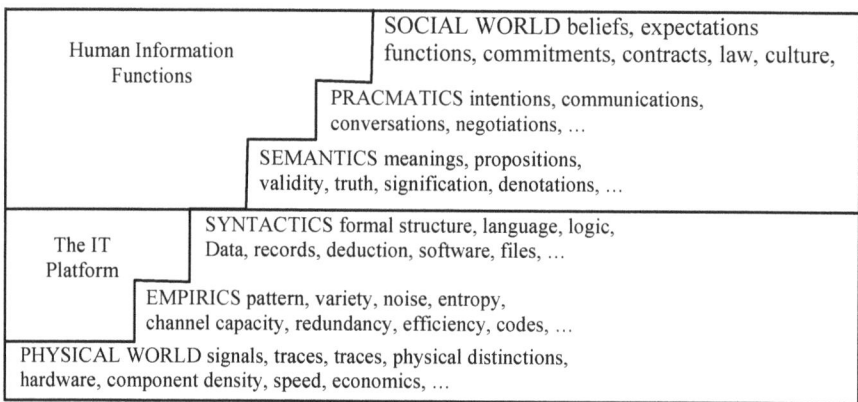

Fig. 3. The semiotic framework proposed by Stamper

Organizations have both a technical and a social dimension and their performance relies heavily on their ability to integrate both of these dimensions. From this semiotic perspective the IT platform serves the technical business operations whilst the human information functions capture the social dimension of business activities. From the semiotic perspective, an organization is essentially an information system. This is because in the organizations, information is created, stored, and processed to communicate, coordinate and to achieve the organizational objectives [8].

The organization is the whole system. Stamper [7] mention that: Within the organization, there are three categories of activities: Substantive (Organizational objectives), Communication (message passing) and Control (accomplishment of Substantive and Communication), as shown in Fig. 4. The substantive activities are governed by the assignments and tasks that are derived from the organizational objectives within a given institutional structure. Results of the actions in this category are supposed to contribute directly to the attainment of the business goals of the organization. The actions will normally result in changes physically or socially [8].

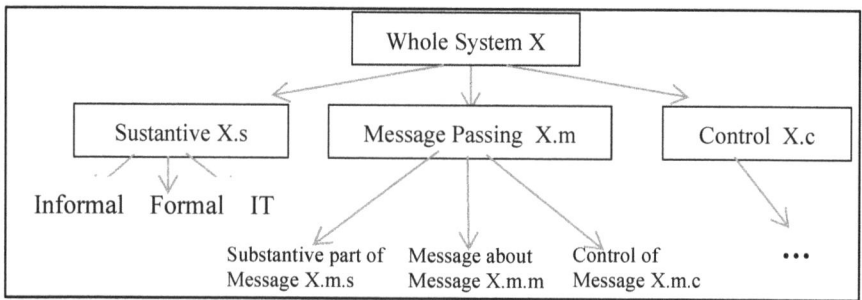

Fig. 4. System and categories of activities (morphology proposed by Stamper)

The substantive activities are carried out in three sub-systems; each depends on another and interacts with one another (Fig. 5). Informal context is represented as a subculture; Formal context is represented by defined norms or bureaucracy; and IT context automates part of the formal system. The scope of each sub-system is not always clear, and the boundary between these sub-systems can become fuzzy (therefore the dotted lines in the figure). Changing in one sub-system will definitely have impact on others. For example, re-engineering business processes will cause the need for re-design of the IT system, and vice versa [7].

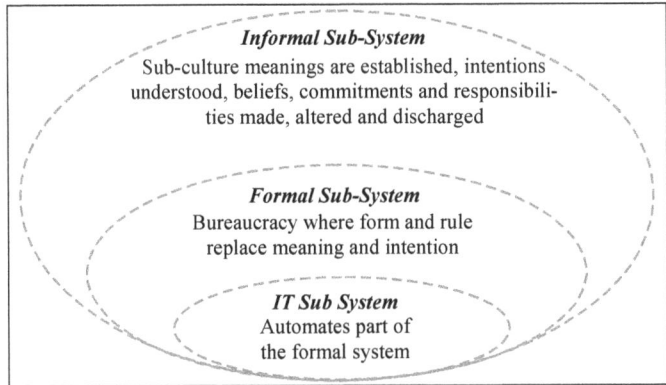

Fig. 5. Information system and organization proposed by Stamper

3   Conceptual Design

Some research papers have attempted to explain the conceptual relationship between organizational semiotics and information systems in other context such as healthcare, education and business [9–12].

For this work we used the sign-based Semiotic Communication and the System Oriented Approach of Semiotic Organization which includes Sign System Oriented Approach. Sign System Oriented Approach studies media (spoken language, texts, instruments, computer interfaces) as sign systems, and see the use of these media by people as based on systems of narration and interpretation. User interaction with media (texts, computer interfaces, instruments) is observed, as well as communication between people at work [13].

3.1   Logical Architecture for Restaurants Information System

The process (formal and informal layer) starts when the customer calls the waiter to put the food order, then the waiter communicates the order to the cook in the kitchen area, cook prepares the food and waiter takes the food to the customer. Then the data is saved to the dataset hosted in a webserver. Finally, the owner can ask by queries to the database for decision making about total amount obtained in a day.

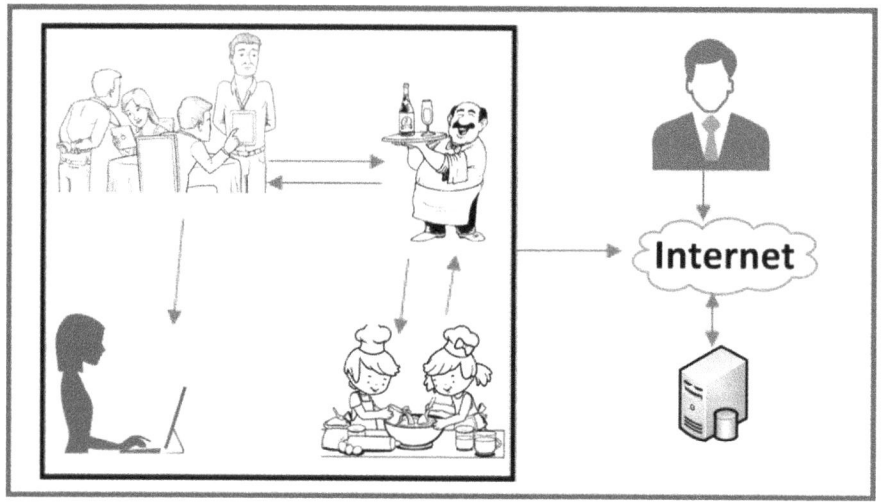

Fig. 6. Information system and organization

3.2 Methodology for This Qualitative Research

This study adopts a qualitative research approach, for this purpose we perform three types of techniques presented as follows:

(a) Theoretical and documentation review, this technique helped us to understand the main concepts of semiotics, information systems and POS, this documentation includes: papers, books, norms, internal regulations in restaurants and so forth. The results of this item are shown in theoretical section.

(b) Observation, in this case, we observed the employee's and customer's daily activities into the tableside ordering and payment processing.

(c) Interviews, we conducted semi structured interviews to three waiters, five consumers and to the owner. The interviews were conducted at "Fastworkx" Company's leader office and "Il Gato pizzas and chicken" Restaurant in Abancay-Peru, on 27–30 September 2016. The results of the interviews are shown in Table 1.

Table 1. Interviews results

Type	Question	Answer
Owner	Which are the principal rules or norms for the restaurant?	- Schedule attention is one written rule - Accounting rules, but it is done by an external worker
	What information do you need for improve decision making?	- Total amount collected in the day is important - The most requested meals also it is important. Who is my best waiter? for example is very important

(continued)

Table 1. (*continued*)

Type	Question	Answer
	Are there some informal rules for the business environment?	- Discounts and Promotions in some days of the week, for example on Tuesday because we have less customers to attend - Sometimes home delivery, but often times we don't have human resources to attend it - Customer always has the reason!
	How do you know the opinion of the customers?	- By the claims book, or sometimes by telephone calling
	How do you control de norms accomplishment in your business?	- Some accounting information is given by the POS system, but others not
Waiters	Does the POS implemented with touch screens improve your time attention to the customer?	- Of course, and we can add or delete food or drink items, now we can join tables in the system
	How is the communication with food area?	- Something important is that with the implementation of the system, we don't need to go many times to the food area (as we did before)
	How is the communication with cashier?	- The cashier can see all orders and the amounts in the computer screen
Customer	How is the communication with the customer?	- The communication is calling the waiter for food order and payment
	The time attention (before touch screen was implemented) is less than POS system was implemented?	- I think so

4 Findings

This section presents the results of the methodology applied to the analysis of the relation between information system and the semiotics. The results of the Theoretical and documentation review are shown in theoretical section.

4.1 Describing Morphology for a Restaurant Information System

The results of observation are shown in Fig. 6. Finally, the results of the interviews are summarized in the Table 2. The interview results were taken and aligned with the concepts of the theoretical section, the proposal for the Morphology of Restaurant Information System was designed, as shown in the Table 3, and also Restaurant Information System Layers are shown in the Table 1.

Table 2. Description of layers of Restaurant POS

Layer	Description	Example for restaurant
Informal	Cultural patterns norms	- Promotions - Discounts - Home delivery
Formal	Play dominant roles	- Attention to the schedule - Statistical information about consumption and earnings for decision making
Technical	IT system	- Touch screen computer and mobile devices - Ticket printer - Router - POS software - Network connectivity

4.2 Describing Morphology for Restaurant Information System

Morphology describes the Activity and Description for Restaurant POS. Table 3 shows the Morphology for POS service.

Table 3. Morphology of Restaurant POS

Activity	Description	Example for restaurant
Substantive	The objective norms	- Quality of attention to customers - Total amount earned during the day - Time for food ordering process
Communication	The interaction related norms	- Message from customer to waiter (food order) - Message from waiter to food preparation area (prepare food order) - Message from customer to cashier area (Payment for consumption)
Control	The execution related norms	- Reviewing book of claims (customer satisfaction) - Reviewing revenues (earnings)

5 Conclusions and Future Work

This paper explores the relation between organizational semiotics and information system especially in the restaurant business field. For this purpose, a Point of Sale information system was developed to compare the theoretical concepts and the practical approach. The study was conducted qualitatively by using techniques of documentation review, observation and interview. The information collected in documentation review allowed us to understand the main concepts or organizational semiotics and technical, formal and informal norms. The results obtained by the observation conducted us to know; the activities performed by the stakeholders (customer, waiter/waitress, cook, owner, and cashier); the communication between stakeholders; the business process management into the organization and the logical architecture of the Point of Sale system for restaurants. The results obtained by interview summarized the morphology for Restaurants Information System aligned with the Organizational Semiotics concepts. In future work, it is necessary to validate this proposal with other restaurants in different contexts.

References

1. Ruiz-Molina, M.E., Gil-Saura, I., Berenguer-Contri, G.: Information and communication technology as a differentiation tool in restaurants. J. Foodserv. Bus. Res. **17**(5), 410–428 (2014)
2. Bhargave, A., Jadhav, N., Joshi, A., Oke, P., Lahane, S.R.: Digital ordering system for restaurant using Android. Int. J. Sci. Res. Publ. **3**(4), 1–7 (2013)
3. Sarkar, S., Shinde, R., Thakare, P., Dhomne, N., Bhakare, K.: Integration of touch technology in restaurants using Android. Int. J. Comput. Sci. Mob. Comput. **3**(2), 721–728 (2014)
4. Stamper, R., Liu, K., Hafkamp, M., Ades, Y.: Understanding the roles of signs and norms in organizations - a semiotic approach to information systems design. Behav. Inf. Technol. **19**(1), 15–27 (2000)
5. Liu, K.: Semiotics in Information Systems Engineering. Cambridge University Press, Cambridge (2000)
6. Gazendam, K., Jorna, H.W.M., Liu, R.J.: An organizational semiotic view on interculturality and globalization. In: Round Table Workshop, Proceedings of the IASS 2004 Conference, pp. 1–11 (2004)
7. Stamper, R.K.: Signs, information, norms and systems. In: Signs of Work: Semiotics and Information Processing in Organisations, pp. 349–399 (1996)
8. Liu, K., Sun, L.: Preface: Co-design of Business and IT Systems (2002)
9. Liu, S., Liu, K., Li, W.: A multi-agent system for pervasive healthcare. In: 14th International Conference on Informatics and Semiotics in Organisation (ICISO), pp. 97–105 (2013)
10. Liu, S., Li, W., Liu, K.: Assessing pragmatic interoperability of information systems from a semiotic perspective. In: Liu, K., Gulliver, S.R., Li, W., Yu, C. (eds.) ICISO 2014. IAICT, vol. 426, pp. 32–41. Springer, Heidelberg (2014). https://doi.org/10.1007/978-3-642-55355-4_4
11. Tan, C., Liu, K.: An organisational semiotics inspired information architecture: pervasive healthcare as a case study. In: Proceedings of the 14th International Conference Informatics Semiotics Organisation, ICISO 2013. IFIP WG8.1 Working Conference, pp. 35–44 (2013)
12. de Souza Santos, M.C., da Silva Magalhães Bertãozini, B., Neris, V.P.A.: Studies in organisational semiotics: a systematic literature review. In: Baranauskas, M., Liu, K., Sun, L., Neris, V., Bonacin, R., Nakata, K. (eds.) ICISO 2016. IAICT, vol. 477, pp. 13–24. Springer, Cham (2016). https://doi.org/10.1007/978-3-319-42102-5_2
13. Ibarra, M.J., Serrano, C., Muñoz, J.C.: SIERA: improving data visualization for learning assessment in educational organisations. In: Baranauskas, M., Liu, K., Sun, L., Neris, V., Bonacin, R., Nakata, K. (eds.) ICISO 2016. IAICT, vol. 477, pp. 191–196. Springer, Cham (2016). https://doi.org/10.1007/978-3-319-42102-5_21

The Role of Language in Human Information Interaction: A Social Semiotic View

Enyun Li[(✉)] and Yinshan Tang

Information Research Centre, Business Informatics Systems and Accounting,
Henley Business School, University of Reading, Reading RG6 6UD, UK
e.li@pgr.reading.ac.uk, y.tang@henley.ac.uk

Abstract. Human information interaction is a dynamic and complex process and is affected by various factors including social and cognitive factors. This study provides a new approach to study human information interaction from a social semiotic perspective and views human information interaction as a social semiotic process. Language, as a most important information carrier, is viewed as a social semiotic system and plays a key role in human information interaction. It not only carries and stores information, but also construes information. This study analyzes the role of language in human information interaction by exploring human judgment in native language and foreign language, which implies that language affects human judgement and thinking that conducts human information activities. The effect depends on the natural logic which limits the meaning-making process of language. Language, to an extent, affects the meaning creation at information interface through which human interact with information content and process information.

Keywords: Human information interaction · Social semiotics
Language · Human judgement

1 Introduction

With the development of information digitalization, various aspects of information interaction are dramatically affected and changed, which greatly affects the design and management of information systems. Human information interaction (HII), as a part of information interaction, refers to the relationship between human actors and information content. HII is increasingly attracting scholars' interest to study all aspects of the way and process that people interact with information, aiming to create better information systems.

Most studies of HII focus on human information behavior and mainly do the analysis from psychological, cognitive and social perspectives or multiapproach views. It is still at the forming stage and needs deep study of all aspects of HII in that HII is a complex and dynamic process that integrate various elements and factors to produce information and carry out information activities. Dzandu and Tang propose a framework of HII from a semiotic perspective and divide HII into three levels—syntactic interaction, semantic interaction and pragmatic interaction, viewing semantic interaction as the center of HII which happens at an interface between human actors and

K. Liu et al. (Eds.): ICISO 2018, IFIP AICT 527, pp. 12–21, 2018.
https://doi.org/10.1007/978-3-319-94541-5_2

information content known as human information interface [8]. Dzandu also holds a viewpoint that people might have different initial trust judgement in native language and foreign language [9]. This implies that languages might affect human information activities and might affect HII through which information activities are carried out, which requires further empirical explorations. This paper attempts to analyze the role of language in HII by further studying human judgement in native language and foreign language. The study is from a social semiotic perspective which analyzes all meanings in social dimensions and views language as a social semiotic system [6], which will provide a new approach to HII.

2 Studies and Development of Human Information Interaction

HII is an emerging area and refers to the interaction between human actors and information content. With the development of modern technology and information digitalization, researchers are increasingly addressing HII and study all aspects of the way how people produce and perceive information and carry out information activities, aiming to create better information systems. HII is a complicated process involving various aspects of human communication and attracts researchers to explore all the complexity and study the affecting factors from many areas such as philosophy, psychology, sociology, linguistics and information theory. Studies addressing HII are flourishing and fruitful in many fields, e.g. human computer interaction (HCI), computer-supported cooperative work (CSCW), human factors and library and information science (LIS) [11]. HCI focuses on the study of human computer interface to develop models and theories of interaction aiming to improve HII. CSCW addresses HII when it studies information activities such as information sharing and collaborative information retrieval in the context of collaborative and cooperative work. Human factors studies address HII when they are concerned of aspects of tools used that will affect humans to get information. In LIS, one of its subject—human information behavior (HIB) pays more attention to HII, which centers on the study of human behavior of processing information in different contexts and focuses on human interaction between people and material objects in a certain environment [11].

Approaches to these studies especially of HIB which more emphasizes on HII are mainly from perspectives of psychology, social sciences or multi-approaches. The psychological approach focuses on the cognitive factors affecting information interaction within or without context. One important theory is the information-processing model of cognition which describes that thinking is limited by the linear information structure and limited processing resources [3]. Another one is the mental models which evoke researches to study HIB by focusing on human thinking conducting information behavior, simulating presumed cognitive functions and observing various information behaviors in certain environment [3]. The psychological approach addresses cognitive processes and emphasizes individual psychological variables in HII, which helps researchers propose many useful models for information behavior such as Talor's model of prenegotiation decisions, Krikelas's model of information seeking and Dervin's sense-making model and Belkin's ASK model [11]. The psychological approach emphasizing cognitive stages and processes and ignores physical environment and cultural backgrounds which are important factors that affect information behavior. Therefore, some researchers devote to studying the effect of social factors on information behavior. These studies addressing social context and employ various social theories to develop information framework, such as diffusion theory, gratification theory, social network theory, social capital theory and sociolinguistic theory. They also analyze the effect of communities on information interaction like gender, age and social classes in a group [10]. Fidel proposes a framework of cognitive work analysis (CWA) of HII employing ecological approach [11]. This approach emphasizes the effect of context and addresses cognitive factors as well and analyzes human actors' information interaction with its environment. The framework is effective in analyzing information behavior within a particular community, especially the analysis of collaborative information retrieval (CIR).

Until now, the studies addressing HII focus on the process and relevant factors affecting HIB, which greatly contributes to the development of information retrieval, human-computer interaction and digital libraries. HII is a complex and dynamic process, and the study of it is still at the forming stage and needs to explore all its complexity.

3   Language and HII

3.1   A Social Semiotic View of HII

First, it is necessary to discuss the definition of information. Scholars from different areas give different definitions with different emphasis of information. Shannon and Weaver define that information is the reduction of uncertainty addressing the function or purpose of information in information transmission [2]. Davis and Ohlson define information as processed data "that is meaningful to the recipient and is of real or perceived value in current or prospective actions or decisions" [4]. Fidel gives a similar definition viewing information as a thing that has meaning and is useful for decision making [11]. Dzandu and Tang's study on HII emphasizes that human actors interact with information by making meanings within a certain environment from a semiotic view [8]. Thus, meaning is the main concern of information and information is construed on the base of meaning processed with content within a certain environment.

HII is in nature human actors' meaning-making process with information content. The central meaning-making process takes place at a semantic interface known as human information interface through which information and meaning are transformed. All the interaction takes place within a certain social environment and is affected by various factors including social and cultural backgrounds, situational background and personal backgrounds. The information content is represented by information carriers such as words, images, sounds, colors, etc. All the information carriers are of social meaning potential from social semiotic perspective, which are called as social semiotic resources/systems. HII is human's interaction with social semiotic resources and making meanings within a certain environment. Thus, HII is in nature a social semiotic process between human actors and social semiotic resources/information content. The

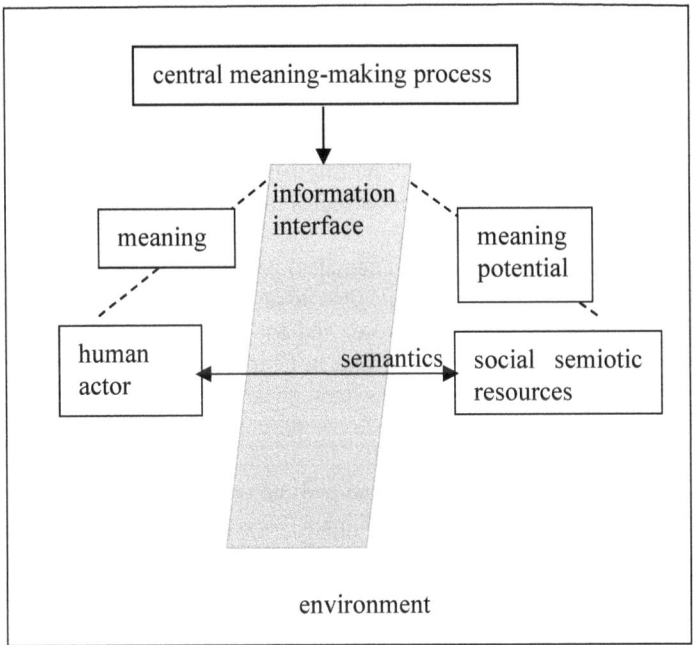

Fig. 1. A social semiotic view of HII

central concern of human information interface through which information is produced and information activities are carried out is the meaning creation (Fig. 1).

A Trial of People's Judgment in Native Language and Foreign Language

Various factors affect the meaning creation at human information interface, e.g., social environment, situational context, individual's differences. Language is a most significant information carrier although not the only one and important in storing and transmitting information. Language is viewed as a social semiotic resource and plays a key role in constituting social structures [5]. It is not only an information carrier but also an element of social and cultural environment. Thus, it is very significant in HII and communication. Dzandu describes that people might have different initial trust judgement in native language and foreign language [9]. Keysar and his team also carry out series of experiments on risk judgements among people whose native language was English and foreign language was Japanese. The experiments imply that people tend to make less risky judgment in foreign language. They attribute the results to people's different reasoning systems in different languages from psychological perspective. Dr Keysar wrote: "A foreign language provides a distancing mechanism that moves people from the immediate intuitive system to a more deliberate mode of thinking" [1]. These experiments show that human judgement might be affected by different languages. The experiments are still limited in supporting the results. There are too many factors affecting people's judgment and more empirical explorations are required.

To further test whether people have different judgements in different languages, a trial was designed with enlarged types of judgements, questions and languages. A questionnaire was used in the trial and languages are Chinese (native language) and English (foreign language). The questionnaire contained five questions about people's judgement in a certain situation including initial trust judgment, moral judgement. The original materials were in Chinese and the English version was equivalent translation. Each question was followed by likelihood scales ranging from 1 to 5 (1 = very highly likely to do, 5 = not very likely to do).

In the trial, 60 people (19 males, 41 females) participated in the experiment. Their age ranged from 20 to 40 (<20rs = 6, 20ys–30ys = 49, 30rs–39rs = 5). All participants' native language should be Chinese, and foreign language should be English. Among the participants, 30 people took part in Chinese questionnaire while the other 30 people participated in English equivalent questionnaire. Two participants were excluded from the analysis, either because the participant's foreign language was not English or the participant did not do the questionnaire at all. 52 participants were Chinese university students living in China and the other 8 participants were Chinese people living or working in UK. The participants' level of English proficiency was not tested. Questionnaires were sent to participants randomly. Participants were asked to give their judgement on the events by giving a likelihood scale and a brief explanation.

4   Results and Discussion

In the trial, the collected data was divided into two groups according to languages and was analyzed by descriptive analysis and non-parameter analysis with SPSS. According to the significance test (p value) between the two language groups which was analyzed by non-parameter analysis, except question 5 ($p = 0.10$), the results showed that the p value of other questions was less than 0.05, which demonstrated that people's judgement in native language and foreign language were significantly different.

Although the p value of question 5 was 0.10, the mean values of likelihood ratings (M value) between Chinese group and English group were different (M = 3'45 and M = 3.9 respectively). The mean likelihood ratings of questions between each group were illustrated in Fig. 2, which showed people made different judgment on the events between the two language groups. The mean values of foreign language groups (English) were higher than that of native language groups (Chinese). Question 1, 2 and 5 were about initial trust judgement. Question 3 and question 4 were about moral judgement. According to the mean values of each language group, people might tend to make more negative decisions on initial trust and moral events in a foreign language.

In the trial, the question about initial trust (question 2) is more significantly different than other questions in the language groups ($p = 0.00$), which implies that people's initial trust judgment might be more easily affected by native language and foreign language. This is consistent with the result of Dzandu's experiment. However, the results still need further experiments to test it because either the present trial or Dzandu's experiment is still limited in supporting the results. The samples are too small and the participants' backgrounds are too complicated. More variables need to be

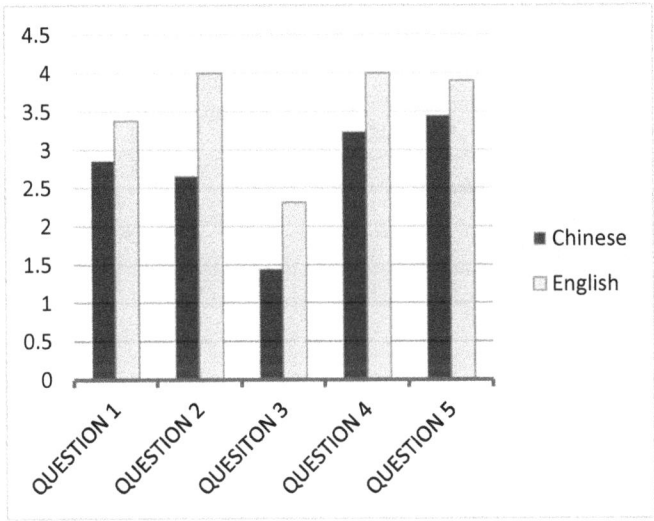

Fig. 2. Mean likelihood ratings for the groups of items by language. Native language: Chinese; Foreign language: English.

further controlled, e.g., age ranges, job backgrounds and foreign language proficiency, which would affect human judgement.

The result is consistent with Halliday's viewpoint that people have different emphasis on meanings when perceiving the same events in different languages. Language, as a social semiotic system, embodies the relations between language, meaning and functions within society, just as what Halliday describes "language is as it is because of the functions it has evolved to serve in people's lives" [5]. The functions of language are realized by the semantic system of language, which is stratified into strata consisting of phonology/morphology, lexicogrammar and semantics. The central meaning-making resource of language takes place in its lexicogrammar and semantics which are called as content plane of language. The semantic layer is the interface where experience and information are "transformed into meaning" and the lexicogrammar layer conducts "the way this transformation takes place" [6]. Different languages are different social semiotic systems and differ in their meanings, not only differing in basic units such as words, sounds and meanings but also differing in the way they are combined to make meanings. This determines the meaning-making resources and affects "what the members of the community attend to" perceive the world around them [5]. Even people who can speak two languages have "the same perception of events", but "they pay attention to different characteristics of them and so build up a rather different framework for the systematization of experience" [5]. For example, in the trial of question 3, the participants had the same perception that the situation was a kind of dilemma, either in Chinese or in English. However, participants' responses to the situation in native language and foreign language were different. Native language and foreign language as two different social semiotic systems constituting their own social

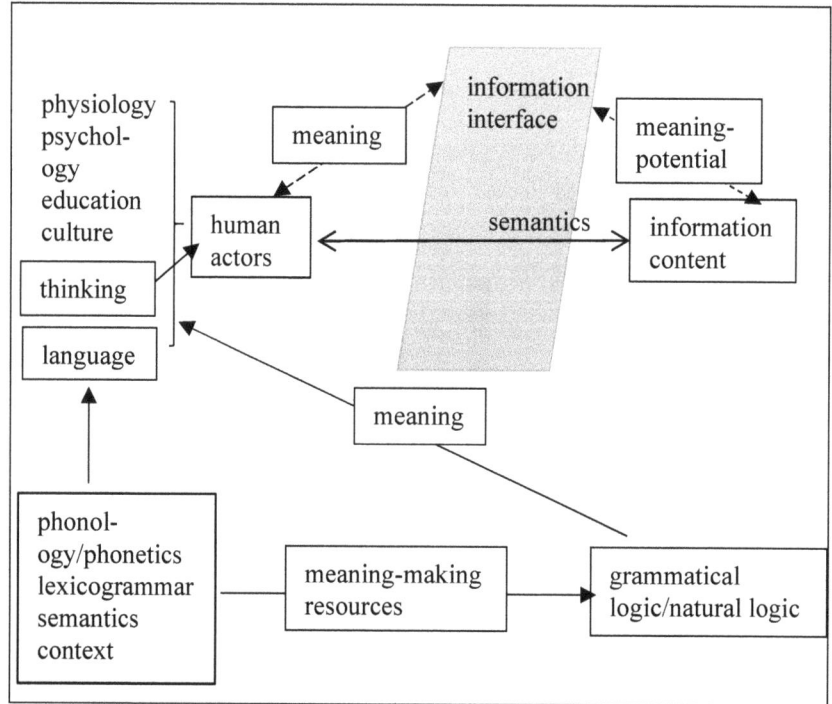

Fig. 3. Language in human information interaction

meanings have different meaning-making resources and would affect people's judgement of the world.

The study also extends Whorf hypothesis that language affects its native speaker's thinking [12]. The result of the trial implicates that human thinking is not only affected by native language but also affected by foreign language. Languages affect human thinking and the meaning-making process. Thinking is the way human mind works which conducts all human activities. In most situation, human think with language. In the process that human learn or acquire a language, the system of each language forms a meaning framework which could affect human thinking. HII refers to the relationship between human actors and information content and is in nature human's meaning-making process with information carriers. The meaning-making process takes place at an information interface through which meaning is created and information is processed, which is conducted by human thinking.

In HII, human actors' backgrounds including physiology, psychology, education, culture, cognition and language are important factors affecting human actors on making meanings and performing information activities (Fig. 3). Among these factors, language is a most significant one. It not only carries and transmit information, but also construes information by affecting human information interface and thus affects human information activities, as what showed in the trial that native language and foreign language affect human judgement and decision making in the same situation. Language, as a social semiotic system, affects human thinking on the basis of its semantic system which is stratified into phonology/phonetics (expression), lexicogrammar (wording), semantics (meaning) and context [6]. The strata of language work together to realize meaning logically, which is mainly realized on the meaning base—the three dimensions of meaning: ideational, interpersonal and textual meaning and each is realized by its grammatical system within a context. Halliday describes "Language is powered by grammatical energy" [7]. The "grammatical energy" to generate meaning mainly exist in lexicogrammar and semantics between which the realizational relationship is natural. The realization of meaning is based on the natural relationship or natural logic, which affects human thinking and meaning and creation. Thus, the effect of language on human thinking lies in the natural logic. The logic of language in nature exists in the various systems of language which influence human in choosing language items to realize meaning. The natural logic is the framework or scaffolding of meaning.

The study explores human judgment in native language and foreign language and analyzes the role of language in HII, emphasizing the central meaning-resources of language and their realization of meaning. It is meaningful for the study and development of information systems of which user, system, content are three important elements. At each level including user-system management, system-content management and user-content management, various factors affect user's information activities, among which human factors are a most important and complicated one. The study of the role of language in HII is a deep study of human elements affecting information activities through information systems. This will be helpful for the design and management of information systems, especially for communities of multilingual backgrounds which would influence human information activities. Analyzing and digitalizing the differences in languages and their effect on information activities will be greatly important for information systems management and services to reduce language barriers. For example, the appraisal systems of different languages have similar items, however, may have different positive effect and negative effect on human thinking and judgement.

This will also promote the study of natural language understanding which is a most difficult topic in artificial intelligence (AI). The study implies that human judgement and thinking is different in native language and foreign language, which is resulted from their different social semiotic systems which is of natural logic. To help a machine understand and produce natural language is to help a machine have natural language logic based on the semantic system of language in that natural logic of language lies in the systems of language. Digitalizing and analyzing the central meaning-making resources or semantic systems of different languages and the way of combination to make meanings which would affect human thinking will be a way to help machines think grammatically and act grammatically. This is also meaningful for foreign language teaching and learning in which language logic is an important topic.

The study of human judgment in native language and foreign language also extends previous related studies which are focused on human psychological process of language process. This study explores the influence of foreign language on human judgement from social semiotic perspective and emphasizes the logic of language which conducts the meaning-making re-sources of language to realize meaning that affects human judgement.

5   Conclusion

The study provides a new approach to HII by analyzing the role of language in HII from a social semiotic perspective. HII is a dynamic and complex process and is affected by various factors including social and cognitive factors. Previous studies addressing HII analyze these factors mainly from cognitive perspective or social and cultural perspective. The social semiotic study of HII view information as a subclass of meaning and HII as a social semiotic process in which human actors interact with information content and make meanings within a certain social environment. The central meaning-making process takes place through information interface between human actors and information content where information is transformed and interpreted based on the meaning base within a certain environment. Language is not only an important information carrier, but also plays a key role in construing information on the base of its semiotic system. The study analyzes the role of language by exploring human judgment in native language and foreign language, which implies that human judgment and thinking is affected by languages. Language construes meaning with its semantic systems conducted by natural logic, which affects human's meaning creation and affects human thinking, thus affecting human information interface through which meaning is created and information is transformed and interpreted.

Appendix: The 5 Questions in the Questionnaire

A: There is a person who always tries to help others but ends up making everything worse. Given that you do not know the person at all,
Question 1. What would be your first impression of this person?
Question 2. If you might work with the person, what would be your trust in the person?

B:
Question 3. How likely are you going to lift up a senior who falls over?
Question 4. Given that a ship in the sea is damaged, to save the people on the ship, you would have to push a person into the sea. How likely are you going to agree the idea?
Question 5. What would be your trust in a person who once was addicted to drug?

References

1. Keysar, B., Hayakawa, S.L., An, S.G.: The foreign-language effect: thinking in a foreign tongue reduces decision biases. Psychol. Sci. **23**(6), 1–8 (2012)
2. Shannon, C.E., Weaver, W.: The Mathematical Theory of Communication. University of Illinois Press, Urbana (1964)
3. Marchionini, G.: Human-information interaction research and development. Libr. Inf. Sci. Res. **30**, 165–174 (2008)
4. Hill, M.W.: The Impact of Information on Society: An Examination of Its Nature, Value and Usage, p. 16. K.G. Saur, Munchen (2005)
5. Halliday, M.A.K.: Language as Social Semiotic, pp. 4, 198, 199. Edward Arnold, London (1978)
6. Halliday, M.A.K., Matthiessen, C.M.I.M.: Construing Experience Through Meaning: A Language-Based Approach to Cognition, p. 604. Continuum, London (1999)
7. Halliday, M.A.K.: On grammar. In: Webster, J. (ed.) Collected Works of MAK Halliday, vol. 1, p. 387. Continuum, New York (2002)
8. Dzandu, M.D., Tang, Y.: Beneath a learning management system - understanding the human information interaction in information systems. Procedia Manufact. **3**, 1946–1952 (2015)
9. Dzandu, M.D.: Initial trust judgement in native language and foreign language. Personal Communication (2015)
10. Fidel, R., Pejtersen, A.M., Cleal, B., Bruce, H.: A multidimensional approach to the study of human information interaction: a case study of collaborative information retrieval. J. Am. Soc. Inf. Sci. Technol. **55**(11), 939–953 (2004)
11. Fidel, R.: Human Information Interaction: An Ecological Approach to Information Behavior. The MIT Press, London/Cambridge (2012)
12. Whorf, B.L.: Language, mind, and reality. In: Carroll, J.B. (ed.) Language, Thought and Reality. The MIT Press, Cambridge (1956)

Building a Socio-Technical Perspective of Community Resilience with a Semiotic Approach

Lara S. G. Piccolo[1(✉)] , Kenny Meesters[2] ,
and Shadrock Roberts[3]

[1] The Open University, Milton Keynes MK76AA, UK
lara.piccolo@open.ac.uk
[2] Delft University of Technology, 2628BX Delft, Netherlands
k.j.m.g.meesters@tudelft.nl
[3] Ushahidi, Nairobi, Kenya
shadrock@ushahidi.com

Abstract. Situated in the diversity and adversity of real-life contexts facing crisis situations, this research aims at boosting the resilience process within communities supported by digital and social technology. In this paper, eight community leaders in different parts of the world are invited to express their issues and wishes regarding the support of technology to face social challenges. Methods and artefacts based on the Organisational Semiotics (OS) and the Socially-Aware computing have been applied to analyse and consolidate this data. By providing both a systemic view of the problem and also leading to the identification of requirements, the analysis evidences some benefits of the OS-based approach to consolidate perspectives from different real-life scenarios towards building a socio-technical solution.

Keywords: Community resilience · Human-computer interaction
Crisis · Organisation semiotics · Socially-aware computing

1 Introduction

Natural catastrophes, man-made emergencies, accidents, or social issues threatening human rights are constant challenges to humans' ability to live in peace and harmony, both individually and as a society.

Coping with crisis situations and recovering from them are complex processes that may involve resources, several stakeholders, logistics and, above all, collaboration. Thus, communication and information awareness are increasingly being required in disaster management or peace-building processes [7]. The availability of digital information has been fostered by the broad adoption of technology and the willingness to share information online. Though, to be effective in supporting individuals and stakeholders' actions, a digital platform for crisis needs to reflect real-world practices of affected populations and the responders both in social and technical terms [3].

K. Liu et al. (Eds.): ICISO 2018, IFIP AICT 527, pp. 22–32, 2018.
https://doi.org/10.1007/978-3-319-94541-5_3

Ushahidi (www.ushahidi.com) is a platform that provides situational awareness in crises by enabling anyone to share geo-located information in real time. Since the violent process of the Kenyan presidential election in 2007, scenario that originated Ushahidi, this platform has been deployed in more than 159 countries and translated into more than 35 languages to support communities to recover from hurricanes, flooding, to fight against corruption, among other issues [7]. As an example, the earthquake that devastated Nepal in 2015 generated 2031 geo-located reports on the platform, 1289 of them demanding an action [16]. Figure 1 (obtained at [16]) illustrates (a) a report requesting help with water, food and shelter, and (b) aggregated reports represented on the map.

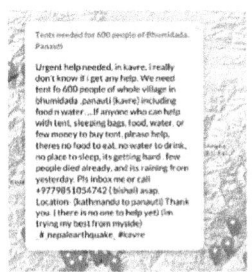 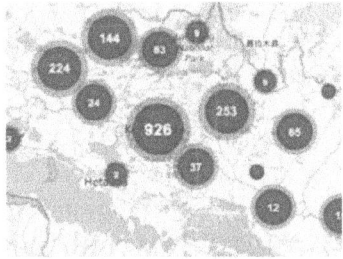

Fig. 1. Screenshots of the Ushahidi platform (a) report requesting help (b) aggregated reports plotted on a map [16]

This research aims at adding new features to Ushahidi for boosting the capacity of the platform to support community resilience. As a globally adopted tool, a socio-technical solution for Ushahidi should be capable of coping with the diversity of contexts without neglecting particularities of each scenario.

As acknowledged in the literature [3, 13], involving communities in the platform design improves their purposefulness and usability, also increases the community's awareness and adoption of such tools in times of real crises. The design is then based on the participation of communities to discuss beyond technical features or current usability issues, but to reflect towards establishing a common meaning of community resilience supported by a digital and social tool.

In this paper, the initial steps of this research are reported. Eight community leaders in different contexts have been interviewed expressing their needs and wishes related to technology to support the resilience process. The analysis of this material has been supported by methods and artefacts of the Organisational Semiotics (OS) [9, 11] revealing (i) the complexity of stakeholders involved; (ii) informational needs in technical and social aspects; (iii) key elements in a shared understanding of community resilience supported by technology.

By providing both a systemic view of the problem and the stakeholders involved, as well as leading to eliciting socio-technical requirements, this analysis evidences the benefits gained through the application of methods and techniques based on OS approaches to consolidate the diversity of perspectives.

In the next section, works related to community resilience and social platform for crisis are introduced. Then, the research method is described. The OS-based analysis is split into two sections: understanding the problem and socio-technical requirements. In the sequence, the results are discussed by building a situated perspective of community resilience, followed by the conclusion.

2   Related Works

As stated by [20], *community resilience* is an amorphous concept. In the disaster-management literature it has been defined and applied in many different ways, but commonly referring to the ability of a community to cope with emergency situations [19]. Finding systematic ways to boost resilience within communities has been a concern for governments and policymakers worldwide. Situated frameworks maps stakeholders and their roles, stages in the resilience process, tools, and practices. Examples as the United States' one [5], and the United Kingdom's in [15], which centres resilience in planning, response and recovery.

Despite the growing number of crisis-related research, the focus is usually given to responses by authorities instead to empowering citizens [18]. Less attention has been given to bottom-up approaches, especially in the recovering phase [17], justifying the need of local communities not only as information providers but as actors therein [8]. Linnell [8] lists some conditions to promote citizen participation in community resilience, such as managing voluntarism and matching needs/skills/knowledge, reinforcing the culture of collaboration, etc. In line with that, the framework in [4] suggests an approach focused on Engagement, Education, Empowerment and Encouragement (the 4 "Es"). By informing (educating), enhancing social capital (empowerment and encouragement), and connections (engagement), the author recognises social media as a potential tool to boost community resilience collectively.

Such potential has been confirmed in recent crises, so that big players have launched specific services to cope with emergencies. *Twitter Alert* broadcasts and highlights critical information to public when authoritative accounts mark Tweets as alerts. Facebook provides the *Safety Check*, for people in a disaster area to check if they/their friends are safe. And Google, through the *Crisis Map* displays many types of geographic information, such as storm paths, shelters, and power outages from a variety of sources, including official and user-generated content. Beyond these services, Houston et al. [6] analysed 15 applications for disaster situations and came up with a set of features for all the phases of an emergency, which includes mental-health support, detecting related events, discussing implications of and responsibilities for events, among others.

Initiatives like that boost resilience by offering psychosocial support, locating missing people, helping users to provide and share information, etc. However, they are not fully driven by community resilience frameworks and guidelines, which can direct the design of features to maximise support for resilience.

Towards this direction, Turoff et al. [14] state that the design of resilience information systems must consider the processes that emerge in the field and are influenced by cultural traits. The authors suggest 9 design principles including treating exception as norms, sharing information at the community level, connecting people with authorities and resources, and adaptability in assigning users' roles and profiles.

3   Method

Building on the disaster-management literature, this research understands community resilience driven by technology as 'a process of continuously enabling a broad range of actors to acquire a relevant, consistent and coherent understanding of a stressing situation, empower decision makers and trigger community engagement on response and recovery efforts, including long-term mitigation and preparation.' [3].

This particular study aims at finding what sociotechnical requirements should be considered to design a social platform to boost communities' resilience. The solution is built on real-life experiences in different scenarios. To this end, 8 community leaders were interviewed to understand: (i) the meaning of community resilience in their own contexts; (ii) how they operate in a disaster situation supported by technology; (iii) how a new technology could improve it.

The interviewees were Ushahidi users, potentially collaborating with the co-design of innovative features as the research advances. They were in Nepal, 2 in Nigeria, 2 in Indonesia and 1 in India. For privacy reasons, the identity of the communities and the interviewees have been preserved in this paper.

The social issues they fight against include securing shelter and subsistence after an earthquake, elections monitoring against corruption and violence, sexual harassment and abuse, pursuing human rights, youth empowerment, and environmental issues in urban contexts. Such diversity of actions was pursued to build a comprehensive picture considering multiple possible roles of technology.

The interviews happened by phone lasting approximately 1 h each. They were semi-structured and recorded for further analysis with the consent of the interviewee. The questions included:

- How is your organisation structured (formal/informal)?
- What is the organisation goal? Who are the users and the beneficiaries?
- Who are the main stakeholders involved to achieve this goal?
- How do you establish connections with key stakeholders?
- When would you consider the project a success?
- Can you exemplify an (big) achievement? Why was it successful?
- What are the major issues you encountered/shortcomings?
- What factors play a role in effective community engagement?
- How do you ensure that the community has adopted your project/tools?
- What is the relationship between information and a resilient community?

The analysis has been grounded on the concepts of the Socially-aware Computing [1] and the Organisational Semiotics [9, 11, 12]. The Socially-Aware Computing is an approach to design technology informed by sociocultural aspects. It relies on the involvement of stakeholders with a diversity of experiences for understanding the problem from different perspectives, also considering how the new technology is expected to impact the community [1]. The design is seen as a three-layer process considering first the informal aspects of a society (e.g. people's values, beliefs), then the formal aspects (regulations, rules, procedures), towards the construction of a technical system. The technical layer, on the other hand, impacts back on the external layers towards influencing the society. This understanding suggests that innovation risks to fail if only the technical level is considered and is not compatible with people's values, beliefs, or current regulations [1].

For translating social aspects into design elements and technical features, the Socially-aware computing is grounded on the Organisational Semiotics, an approach for understating information in a social context [9, 11, 12], based on semiotics principles by Peirce [10]. The OS artefacts applied in this analysis are part of a set called *Problem Articulation Methods* - PAM, usually helpful in the initial stage of projects when the problem definition is still vague and complex [2]. The artefacts are: (i) Stakeholders Identification Diagram [9], which enables a systemic view of the stakeholders' according to their levels of involvement, interest and expectations. (ii) Evaluation Frame [2] for revealing issues that worthy attention from the stakeholders' perspective. (iii) Semiotic Framework [9] that helps to understand the problem as an information system.

This OS-based approach has been chosen due to its capacity to deal with a diversity of meanings and perspectives, and the adequate support to transform social issues into sociotechnical requirements. The artefacts and results are described in the next sections.

4 Semiotic-Based Analysis

4.1 Stakeholders and Their Concerns

The stakeholder analysis evidences the complexity and diversity of actors involved with the socio-technical system, enabling a systemic view of the forces (expectations, concerns) from the interested parties [9]. All the interested parts mentioned by the community leaders during the interviews are represented in the layers of the Stakeholders Identification Diagram (SID) [9] (Fig. 2).

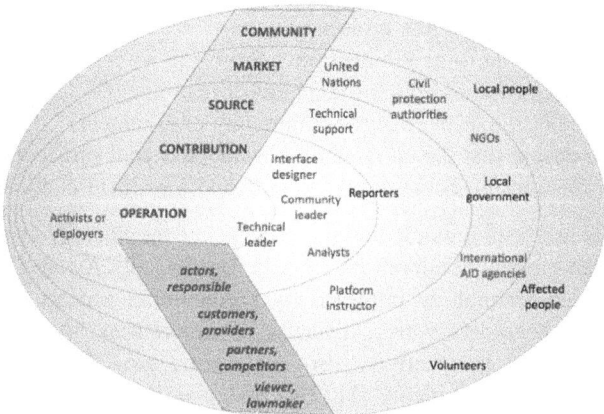

Fig. 2. Stakeholders Identification Diagram

Three main groups of stakeholders were identified: those related to the platform supply, local community members assuming distinct roles, and the responders, organisations that will act upon the information obtained through the platform. They are represented with different colours in the diagram: members of the local community are in orange, platform suppliers in purple, responders in green. Those in black are members of the society exercising different roles.

Some stakeholders are in more than one layer. The interested parts acting upon the society are in the Community layer, they are: volunteers, affected people and local people not directly affected by the crisis. Partners or competitors are placed in the Market one, such as the United Nations, other civil protection authorities, NGOs, international aid agents. Those providing any type of information, like technical support, platform instructor and reporters are in the Source, followed by those contributing more directly with the system in the Contribution layer, interface designer, community leader, analysts, and again the reporters. The stakeholders related to the technical and operational aspects are in the core, in the Operation layer. They are activists, deployers, and the technical leader, which is also in the contribution layer.

Derived from the SID, the Evaluation Frame [2] reveals stakeholders' main concerns towards the information systems, as described in Table 1 below.

Table 1. Evaluation frame

Stakeholders	Concerns
Operation level	
Activists or deployers	Create an instance of the platform efficiently
Technical leader	Provide conditions for the platform operation
Contribution level (actors, responsible)	
Technical leader	Provide platform training for the community staff
Community leaders	Engage volunteers and staff (meetings, adverts, etc.) Solve local conflicts to enable actions Assess current situation and vulnerabilities Coordinate actions connecting volunteers with locals
Analysts	Process the information provided by reporters Ensure the reliability of the information provided
Interface designer	Design an attractive and easy to use platform
Source level (customers, providers)	
Reporters	Provide impressions and reports from the field
Platform instructor	Training the technical leaders on the platform
Technical support	Ensure the platform availability
Market level (partners, competitors)	
Responders (UN, civil protection, NGOs)	Identify the most relevant issues Find the necessary information to act upon the issue

(*continued*)

Table 1. (*continued*)

Stakeholders	Concerns
Local government	Identify the most relevant issues and find the necessary information to act upon them
	Establish guidelines on how to act on the emergency
	Get prepared for next disaster and reconstruction
Community level (viewer, lawmaker)	
Affected people	Get information on the current situation
Volunteers (i.e. donors)	Offer any sort of assistance
Not affected local people	Have the necessary conditions to act as reporters

In the next step of the analysis, the focus on the stakeholders is shifted to the information, as further described.

4.2   Towards Socio-Technical Requirements

The Semiotic Framework [9] has been applied for understanding the way communities deal with information, and also to translate their current practices and wishes into socio-technical requirements. The framework considers how information operates in the six levels of a "semiotic ladder" representing the perspective of the Physical, Empirics, Syntactics, Semantics, Pragmatics, and the Social world. Issues at the three lower layers will answer questions as to how information is structured, used, transmitted, what its properties are, etc. The upper layers are concerned with the use of signs, meaning in the communication, intentions, etc. [9], evidencing the information that is related to the social environment from those that are part of the digital system.

At this stage of the analysis, all the issues pointed out in the interviews were captured, with no filtering; therefore, controversial issues pointed out by different communities are possible. In the same way, some issues may refer to Ushahidi's existing features, beyond needs and wishes.

For being in line with this research aims, Turoff's design principles [14] for a community resilience platform have also been considered in the framework. Issues that were similarly mentioned by different interviewees were grouped and prioritised for further consideration. In total, this analysis revealed 43 issues related to the social environment and 40 to the technical system. In Table 2, the most popular issues are presented as an example of the results.

Table 2. Issues mapped according to the semiotic ladder

Step/main topics	Examples of issues
Social (12 issues in total) Engagement Trust Social impact Familiarity with technology	Engaging local government and policymakers with the platform is difficult People should not be afraid of making a report due to conflicts with other stakeholders People are familiar with SMS, social media, WhatsApp, but not necessarily with Ushahidi
Pragmatics (15 issues) Community impact General communication Policymakers and government involvement	Approaching the local government is more effective with organised tasks and groups Complement the platform with physical communication (printed maps, posters, leaflets) Connect producers/consumers, donors/receivers
Semantics (16 issues) Community perception Reliability of information Policymakers perception Understanding the platform Monitoring the crisis	Complement the platform with physical meetings within the community on how to solve issues Convincing the community that the platform is meant to help, not to manipulate Check status reports with the community Ensure that every report has a response. Feedback to reporters
Syntactics (18 issues) Language Information visualisation Users' profiles, Standards Layers of information	Information should be understandable by the community, not only by humanitarian actors Bilingual system to receive reports Representing the reports in a map
Empirics (10 issues) Interoperability Reports fields	For every reported issue collect geographic coordinates, date, anonymity of the reporter, pictures, source, issue
Physical (12 issues) Offline/mobile access Audio platform Internet access issues Social media channels	Building dedicated lines with key stakeholders such as police to respond to reports quickly Allowing information to be accessible offline Voice channel for people unfamiliar with technology to create reports by phone

The more than 80 issues collected have been analysed, generating then the socio-technical requirements. In Table 3, some examples of socio-technical requirements are described, followed by the list of stakeholders most benefitted by the features. Possible solutions to the identified concerns in Table 1 also evolved to requirements.

Table 3. Examples of derived socio-technical requirements

Requirements	Most benefited stakeholders
Automatically estimate and inform the degree of reliability of the reports	Analysts and responders
Graphical evidence of the most reported issues	Responders
Offline access to reports	Community members, affected people, responders
Integration with social media (i.e. Facebook)	Reporters
Self-explanatory user interface (no training)	Reporters, community leader
Print maps	Community leader, responders

5 Situating Community Resilience

Building a situated notion of community resilience supported by technology, key elements that emerged in the analysis were mapped in the three layers informal, formal, and technical, following the metaphor of the 'Semiotic Onion' [11] (Fig. 3). People's beliefs, values and motivations are in the informal level, the elements that regulate the way people act are in the formal one, and the technical aspects are in the core. The three levels constantly influence each other from the moment the technology is conceived until its appropriation [1, 11].

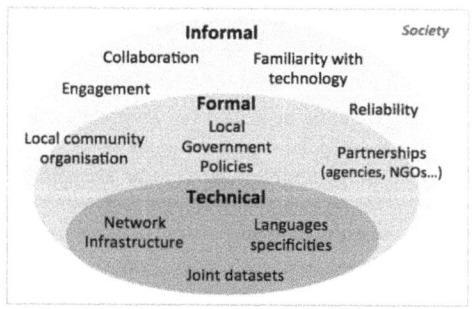

Fig. 3. Community resilience key elements

The main challenges revealed in the informal level are related to engaging local people and policymakers to adopt the technical platform. The lack of familiarity with technology or specifically with the platform were frequently cited as barriers for engagement. Still in the informal level, the platform should be perceived as trustworthy and reliable by all users and stakeholders.

The informal and formal aspects are related to the organisation of the communities, referring to the way they are structured and interact with others, and partnerships between communities, agencies, responders, NGOs, etc. These aspects differ from one scenario to another, and the platform may improve such connections and communication. Also, the platform has to be in line with local government policies, not only to be accepted by them, but also adopted for influencing decision-making.

Technically speaking, the most evidenced problems are network infrastructure, which may be precarious in some disaster situations, the desired integration with other media and communication platforms, such as WhatsApp, voice platforms and Facebook, and, finally, the challenge of dealing with different languages, which may even co-exist in the same scenario.

The analysis evidenced that engaging a community encompasses not only raising awareness of their problems and possible solutions, but also how to use the platform in technical terms.

6 Discussion and Conclusion

Translating real-life constraints of adverse environments into requirements is a crucial step of designing a platform for crisis situations. In the context of this research, is also imperative that any technical solution be adjustable to different realities in social, technical, economics, and cultural terms.

Traditional methods of software engineer may fail in supporting a system designer to build an understanding of the problem dealing with a variety of perspectives, and equality considering requirements from both social and technical angles.

The principles of meaning articulation, participation, and the reciprocal impact between society and the technical solution by the Socially-Aware approach supported building a systemic view of the problem, situating the notion of community resilience. Likewise, methods and artefacts of the Organisational Semiotics provided the necessary resources for transforming constraints, wishes and needs into socio-technical requirements, evidencing the suitability of this approach to complex contexts as emergency-related platforms.

The analysis suggested that to achieve a real social impact, the introduction of a digital platform to promote community resilience should also consider placing engagement strategies like: (i) developing digital literacy; (ii) raising the community voice (including on social media) to influence local government decisions; and (iii) involve policymakers and responders with the platform.

In terms of socio-technical features, results pointed out, for instance, ways of sharing and presenting information, integration of other communication channels and social media, and the evident need to check the validity of the information, building a trustworthy environment for affected people and responders.

This paper represents an ongoing research that aims at identifying, developing and evaluating new features for Ushahidi for boosting the potential of the platform to support a community resilience process. Next steps of this research include participatory design activities to start translating the requirements into design elements.

References

1. Baranauskas, C.: Social awareness in HCI. ACM Interact. **21**(4), 66–69 (2014)
2. Baranauskas, C., et al.: Guiding the process of requirements elicitation with a semiotic approach. In: 11th International Conference on Human-Computer Interaction, Las Vegas, pp. 100–110 (2005)
3. Comes, T., Toerjesen, S., Meesters, K.: D2.1 Requirements for boosting community resilience in crisis situation. Technical report   (2016). http://www.comrades-project.eu
4. Edwards, C.: Resilient Nation. Demos, London (2009). https://goo.gl/sEjfNs
5. Federal Emergency Management Agency (FEMA), US Department of Homeland Security: A whole community approach to emergency management: principles, themes, and pathways for action (2011). www.fema.gov/media-library/assets/documents/23781
6. Houston, J.B., et al.: Social media and disasters: a functional framework for social media use in disaster planning, response, and research. Disasters **39**, 1–22 (2015)
7. Hyman, P.: 'Peace technologies' enable eyewitness reporting when disasters strike. Commun. ACM **57**(1), 27–29 (2014)
8. Linnell, M.: Citizen response in crisis: individual and collective efforts to enhance community resilience. Hum. Technol. **10**(2), 68–94 (2014)
9. Liu, K.: Semiotics in Information Systems Engineering. Cambridge University Press, Cambridge (2000)
10. Peirce, C.S.: Collected papers. In: Hartshorne, C., Weiss, P. (eds.) 1960, vol. 1–8, Harvard University Press, Cambridge (1958)
11. Stamper, R.: Organisational semiotics: informatics without the computer? In: Information, Organisation and Technology: Studies in Organisational Semiotics. Academic Press, New York (2001)
12. Stamper, R.: Information in Business and Administrative Systems. Wiley, New York (1973)
13. Terp, S.: Evolution of the humanitarian data ecosystem. In: AAAI Conference on Artificial Intelligence (AAAI-15), Texas, USA (2015)
14. Turoff, M., et al.: The design of a dynamic emergency response management information system. J. Inf. Technol. Theor. Appl. **5**(4), 1–36 (2004)
15. United Kingdom Cabinet Office: Community Resilience Framework for Practitioners (2016). https://goo.gl/8VzFFH
16. Ushahidi. Quakemap. https://www.ushahidi.com/case-studies/quakemap
17. Vos, M., Sullivan, H.: Guest editors' introduction: community resilience in crises: technology and social media enablers. Hum. Technol. **10**(2), 61–67 (2014)
18. Wetzstein, I., et al.: Crises and social media. A meta-study on pertinent research and practice. Hum. Technol.: Interdisc. J. Hum. ICT Environ. **10**(2), 95–124 (2014)
19. Wickes, R., et al.: Community resilience research: current approaches, challenges and opportunities. In: Proceedings of the 2010 National Security Science and Innovation, pp. 62–78 (2010)
20. Patel, S.S., Rogers, M.B., Amlôt, R., Rubin, G.J.: What do we mean by 'community resilience'? A systematic literature review of how it is defined in the literature. PLOS Curr. Disasters, 1 February 2017. https://doi.org/10.1371/currents.dis.db775aff25efc5ac4f0660ad9c9f7db2. Edition 1

Norm-Based Abduction Process (NAP) in Developing Information Architecture

Chekfoung Tan[1(✉)], Sara Abdaless[2(✉)], and Kecheng Liu[3,4(✉)]

[1] School of Computing and Engineering, University of West London, London, UK
chekfoung.tan@uwl.ac.uk
[2] School of Business, London South Bank University, London, UK
abdaless@lsbu.ac.uk
[3] Informatics Research Centre, University of Reading, Reading, UK
kecheng.liu@henley.ac.uk
[4] Wuhan College, Wuhan, China

Abstract. Abduction is a logical reasoning process that allows the discovery and creation of new knowledge. However, the function of knowledge is not explicitly developed in the existing research on abduction. Developing information architecture is a scientific inquiry in a practical context as it engages multiple stakeholders. However, the current research in information architecture does not appear to be underpinned by sound theoretical foundations. This paper proposes a norm-based abduction process (NAP) where norms are seen as knowledge in developing information architecture. A case study of a UK hospital is used for illustration purposes. The key contribution of this paper is to incorporate norms in the existing abduction process, to assert abduction as the foundation of a logical reasoning process and to derive a theoretical proposition for information architecture.

Keywords: Abduction · Logical reasoning · Information architecture
Organisational semiotics

1 Introduction

The term of information architecture (IA) was coined by Richard Saul Wurman back in the mid-seventies. IA is seen as a tool to gather, organise and present information that serves a purpose [1]. Research has shown that IA did not seem to have sufficient theoretical underpinnings as it is defined based on the application context [2]. For instance, IA is referred to as the external presentation of information (e.g. the websites) or the internal organisation of information (e.g. information management) [3]. Therefore, IA can be seen as a design process or a solution for a design problem [modified from 4]. Hence, there is a need to establish a theoretical proposition for the development of IA which is in relation to its nature as a design process.

Abduction is a type of logical reasoning and it plays a vital role in design process [5]. Peirce [6] defined abduction as the process of forming explanatory proposition which starts a new idea. Peirce viewed the reasoning approach as a semiosis process.

K. Liu et al. (Eds.): ICISO 2018, IFIP AICT 527, pp. 33–42, 2018.
https://doi.org/10.1007/978-3-319-94541-5_4

Semiosis is a sense-making process which involves three universal categories (firstness, secondness and thirdness) which correspond to the three main reasoning approaches (abduction, deduction and induction). Being based on prior knowledge and preliminary data collection about the phenomenon, abduction is used to generate a theoretical proposition which is then explicated through deduction and empirically verified through induction [7]. However, the existing research on the abduction process does not develop the function of knowledge explicitly. For this reason, a new abduction process highlighting the importance of knowledge in the development of information architecture is introduced in this paper.

The aim of this paper is to propose a norm-based abduction process (NAP) in the development of IA. Norms are regarded as the interpretation of signs, or knowledge, which guides human behaviour and actions [8–10]. The notion of norms is employed to unambiguously elicit the function of knowledge in each stage of NAP. Norms emphasise the cumulative nature of knowledge in each stage of the scientific inquiry. NAP helps researchers to resolve the puzzlement based upon the prior knowledge and preliminary data collection. IA is seen as a design process for an observed problem; it is also an inquiry process which involves reasoning in deriving the artefacts. The reasoning process is complicated as it engages multiple human agents. NAP is therefore an abduction process that explicitly focusses on the use of knowledge in developing IA.

This paper is structured as follows: Sect. 2 describes the theoretical foundation of this research, Sect. 3 illustrates NAP, Sect. 4 demonstrates a practical application of NAP in developing the IA for a UK hospital. Healthcare organisations are complex and known as the world's largest and most inefficient information enterprises [11, 12], and Sect. 5 concludes the discussion of the contributions, limitations and future work on NAP as a reasoning process in developing IA.

2 Literature Review

2.1 Information Architecture

Information architecture (IA) describes the transformation of data into meaningful information for people to use [1]. IA possesses a high level map of information requirements in an organisation; it is also a design process in architecting information in order to achieve organisational benefits [13, 14]. In this section, the theories covered for developing IA are organisational semiotics (OS) and service-oriented enterprise architecture (SOEA). OS underpins the fundamental concept of signs and norms in learning the use of information in an organisation. IA plays various roles depending on the context of application [15]. SOEA offers an architectural method for designing IA as an artefact.

OS characterises an organisation as a structure of social norms and it is seen as an information system [9]. Hence, information requirements can be deduced once the norms within an organisation are identified. Norms are developed through the practical experiences of the human agents in an organisation, thus the norms have directive and prescriptive functions on the human agent's action [16]. Organisational onion (OO) categorises norms of an organisation into three layers [17]: informal, formal and technical. The informal layer refers to organisational culture, customs and values which are reflected as beliefs, habits and patterns of members in the organisation. The formal layer denotes the rules and bureaucracy to perform the organisational activities. The technical layer contains technical systems which enable actions performed in the formal and informal layers. Organisational morphology (OM) further analyses the norms embedded in each layer in substantive, communication and control perspective which guide the activities performed in an organisation [18]. Substantive norms are productivity related actions. Communication norms administer activities that involve message passing from one agent to another in order to coordinate their substantive activities. Control norms reinforce the substantive and communication activities through rules and regulation.

SOEA provides a holistic information management framework for an organisation [adapted from 19, 20]. SOEA is one of the approaches in designing IA. SOEA aims to leverage the strengths of service-oriented architecture in aligning various architectures derived from the enterprise architecture. The service-oriented concept emphasises on framing the business and IT capability in an organisation as a series of services. SOEA designs a language which is mutually understandable by the business and IT personnel. SOEA contains three layers: business layer, application layer and technical layer. The business layer offers services or products to customers through business components such as business processes and business actors. The application layer contains the application components which realise the business services. The technical layer offers technical components which realise the application services.

2.2   Abduction in Design Research

Abduction is a reasoning approach which aims to explore the data, find a pattern and suggest a plausible hypothesis [6]. The logical form of abduction is as follows: *The surprising fact, C is observed; but if A were true, C would be a matter of course; hence, there is reason to suspect that A is true.* Kovács and Spens [21] and Thagard [22] propose the abduction process based on Peirce's definition on abduction. The proposed abduction process starts with the observation of a phenomenon and simultaneously triggers a process of matching prior knowledge with the observed phenomenon. Abduction is therefore a logical reasoning process. Peirce stamped the logic of reasoning as a semiosis process. Based on the semiosis process (see Fig. 1), one can postulate that abduction takes the firstness as the starting point to generate new ideas. These ideas are in the form of theoretical propositions which suggest a possible explanation of a phenomenon. Abduction process eventually generates new knowledge. Deduction commences at the secondness which takes the existing theoretical propositions and applies them in a small number of individual cases. Induction departs from the thirdness and it uses the data gathered in a large scale to conduct empirical studies. The results obtained from the empirical experiments serve for generalisation of the proposition. The logic of reasoning is employed to answer the research questions which require an answer in a form of the respective conclusion [23].

Abduction is closely related with design science research. March [5] was the first to introduce Peirce's abduction to design. He posits "abduction is the only logical operation which introduces any new ideas; for induction does nothing but determine a

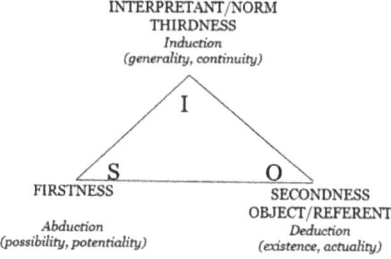

Fig. 1. Semiosis as a logical reasoning process [adapted from 6, 29–33]

value; and deduction merely evolves the necessary consequences of a pure hypothesis". Abduction is seen as a key reasoning approach in designing a solution which deals with complex problems [24]. Abduction generates better ideas over time, hence boosting creativity in problem solving [25–27]. Fischer et al. [28] propound four aspects of abduction in the design science research: (1) *validity*, ensures the design solution proposed by the theory works correctly, (2) *utility*, ascertains the design solution fulfils stakeholders' needs, (3) *generality*, reflects the design solution as a generic solution, and (4) *innovativeness*, demonstrates the new element in the design solution.

3   Norm-Based Abduction Process (NAP)

The norm-based abduction process (NAP) is a logical reasoning process that involves the use of norms (knowledge) (see Fig. 2). NAP consists of interactions (inferring, resulting or matching) between three main elements which are: (1) the human agent who is always going to have some sort of prior knowledge (A + K), (2) the sign which is referred to as S when it is representing the observed phenomenon and S$^+$ when it refers to the data collected about the phenomenon and, (3) the proposition that is referred to as P when it is the first set of propositions and P$^+$ when it is the second set of propositions after reforming the former. This relationship between A + K, S and P/P$^+$ will vary from a stage to another in NAP. Section 4 provides the description and application of each stage of NAP.

4   Case Study: NAP in Developing IA for a UK Hospital

A case study has been conducted in a UK hospital in order to demonstrate NAP in the development of IA. IA is vital for healthcare organisations in providing the right information to the right hospital staff at the right time [15]. Below is the illustration of the NAP (in reference to Fig. 1) in the development of IA for a UK hospital.

Stage 1: Identifying the Motivation of Research

NAP starts with a *puzzlement* following the observation of a problem (resulted by *signs (S)*) by the *agent*. The *agent* here refers to the researcher. The *agent* is then using the prior *knowledge (A + K)* to infer the observed problem *(the S)*. The agent noticed that

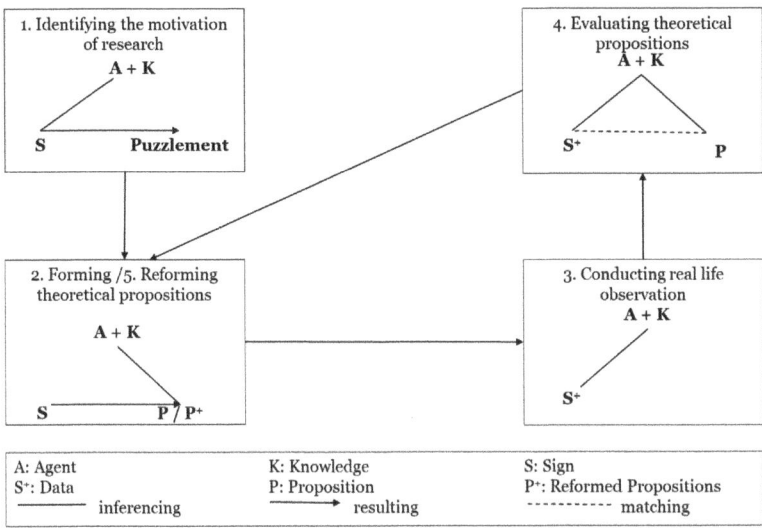

Fig. 2. Norm-based abduction process (NAP)

there were redundancy processes in creating clinical and operational reports in the hospital (the *puzzlement*) and the hospital did not opt for any architectural frameworks to address the issue of information mismanagement *(the S)*. This stage refers to the motivation of having the IA in place to better the information management practice of the hospital.

Stage 2: Forming Theoretical Propositions

The researcher *(agent)* with the prior *knowledge* on IA attempts to form the theoretical *proposition*, which is the result of the information mismanagement phenomenon *(sign)*. In this case study, IA is meant to resolve the information mismanagement issue. Therefore, the theoretical proposition is that "IA is norm centric", whereby designing and using IA to enable effective information management. Norms, in the study of OS illustrate how the information is used by the human agents in performing certain actions in an organisation [9]. Norms therefore are adopted in the development of IA. Following OO and OM [2], Fig. 3 describes the nine activity categories of norms for eliciting information requirements: *organisation.informal.substantive (o.i.s), organisation.informal.message passing (o.i.m), organisation.informal.control (o.i.c), organisation.formal.substantive (o.f.s), organisation.formal.message passing (o.f.m), organisation.formal.control (o.f.c), organisation.technical.substantive (o.t.s), organisation.technical.message passing (o.t.m),* and *organisation.technical.control (o.t.c).*

Based on this activity categorisation, information requirements are elicited in six dimensions per each activity. The dimensions are: *Who* are using the information, *What* is the content of the information, *How* information is represented, *Where* information is stored, *When* the information is needed and *Why* the information is needed in that activity. Figure 4 depicts the example of information requirements from one of the *organisational.formal.substantive (o.f.s)* activities. SOEA was employed to model the actual IA for practical use in the final stage.

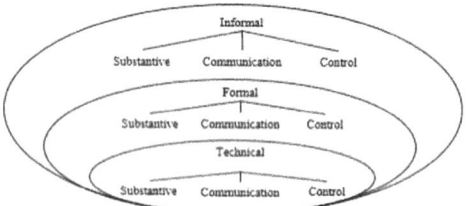

Fig. 3. Norms and activities

When	Who	What	How	Where	Why
Check-in patients	Receptionist, Clinician	Appointment details such as patient demographic information, appointment type, purpose of appointment, date and time, clinician details	Format is in the electronic patient record	Hospital correspondence letter, Electronic patient record	Ensure clinician is aware of this patient's appointment and health condition

Fig. 4. Information requirements of the 'check-in patient' activity

Stage 3: Conducting Real Life Observation

In this case study, the researcher (*agent*) with prior *knowledge* (*A* + *K*) on IA collects data in order to understand the phenomenon of information mismanagement. Data (*S⁺*) were collected through observations in two sites: (1) an outpatient clinic for gathering the information requirements by using the template as in Figs. 2 and 3, and (2) information services department in order to understand how information is processed at the backend for reporting purpose. The secondary data were collected through various documents produced by the hospital. The standard operating procedures (SOPs) were the key documentation for understanding the business activities (formal norms) and how these business activities were executed through IT systems (technical norms). In addition, the outpatient commissioning data sets (CDS) from Hospital Episode Statistics (HES) [34] were adapted to detail the information elements which construct the IA.

Stage 4: Evaluating Theoretical Propositions

The researcher (*agent*) with prior *knowledge* (*A* + K) on information architecture and experience working in the hospital is inferred by the data collected (*S⁺*) which will direct the method for data analysis. The result of the data analysis is then used to verify or refute the theoretical *proposition* (*P*) formed in stage 2, which "information architecture is norm centric". In this case study, thematic analysis was used to analyse the collected data in the outpatient clinic in stage 3. SOEA was adopted to encapsulate the collected information requirements into services. These services informed the information elements that supported the activities. As a result, there were two types of services: clinical and administrative services. The clinical services were: consultation (non-theatre procedure, elective surgical procedure), triage, advice and guidance, diagnosis (pathology, radiology), discharge and prescription. The administrative services were patient administration, referral, appointment and scheduling, payment, and information management. Descriptive analysis was adopted to analyse the collected data in the information service department. It narrated the information management processes (information collection, processing and dissemination) in the hospital. Document analysis was conducted for analysing the SOPs and CDS. This was used to detail the information elements that supported the services. Figure 5 illustrated one of the information elements for the '*radiologic diagnosis*' activity. The information architecture was a collection of information elements which can be modelled with SOEA principles. IA shows how information was collected in the business layer and processed through the application and infrastructure layer. The theoretical proposition was preliminarily evaluated through gathering feedback from the subject matter experts in the hospital. According to the subject matter experts, the proposed IA covered the information requirements for a whole department instead of a single information system view and demonstrates how information was facilitated from the business environment to the technical systems. Moreover, they found that the proposed IA had a positive contribution to addresses the issue of information mismanagement in the hospital.

Radiologic Diagnosis	
Radiology Investigation Plan Identifier	Radiology Procedure Requested Date
Diagnosis Scheme in Use	Radiology Procedure Priority
Primary Diagnosis	Radiology Latest Date
Present on Admission Indicator (Primary Diagnosis)	Radiology Procedure Earliest Date
Secondary Diagnosis	Radiology Investigation Status Reason
Radiology Service Report Urgency	Radiology Investigation Prev Indicator
Radiology Service Order Issue Time	Radiology Investigation Plan Status
Radiology Service Order Issue Date	Radiology Appointment Required
Radiology Procedure Requested Time	

Fig. 5. Information element

Stage 5: Reforming Theoretical Propositions
The researcher (*agent*) concludes the theoretical proposition (*P*) formed in stage 2 which is resulted by the information mismanagement phenomenon (*sign*) with the prior *knowledge* on information architecture and new knowledge gained from the analysed data in stage 4. In this case study, the researcher partially accepted the theoretical proposition as the evaluation result showed that the proposed information architecture in stage 2 contributes to a better information management. This case study demonstrated the initial version of the information architecture for the hospital. A new theoretical proposition (*proposition*$^+$) in stage 2 will be triggered if the proposed information architecture is no longer serving the purpose. This in turn launches the second cycle of NAP.

5   Discussions and Conclusion

This paper illustrates the norm-based abduction process (NAP) in the development of information architecture. The five stages in NAP involve prior knowledge of the human agents to perform the relative actions within the stages. Abduction is a logical reasoning that plays a role in design research and IA is seen as a design process. NAP is therefore applied in developing IA. A case study is conducted in a UK hospital to demonstrate the application of NAP in developing IA. IA is vital for healthcare organisations in ensuring the right information is provisioned to the right hospital staff at the right time. The contributions of this paper are twofold: (1) extending the existing abduction process by incorporating norms, and (2) deriving a theoretical proposition for information architecture.

The first contribution of this paper is that NAP incorporates norms in the existing abduction process such as [21, 22]. Norms are regarded to be knowledge as they are derived from the interpretation of signs by the human agents [8, 10]. NAP scrutinises the use of norms (interpretation of signs) in each stage of the abduction process in order to highlight the function of knowledge (see Sects. 3 and 4). NAP fulfils the scientific inquiry process suggested by Kuhn [35] in leading to new knowledge in the form of a new proposition, which is the result of the observation of a phenomenon. In addition, NAP adopts Popper's [36] refutation approach, where the formed proposition can be refuted by the observed facts. This encourages the agent to continue the inquiry process in order to find the best proposition resulted by the phenomenon. NAP guides the design process in producing the IA and provides a specification of the IA as an artefact. The abduction approach in NAP where knowledge is imparted in each stage of the process helps in forming the theoretical proposition for the development of IA. In a practical perspective, the abduction approach in NAP helps information professionals to apply a new idea in boosting the informatics creativity for finding ways to progress from being "*data rich and discovery poor to a state of information wealth*" [37]. NAP is iterative, and the number of NAP cycles is depending on the subjective view of the agent.

There are two limitations identified in this paper. The first limitation is that it is hard to determine when the iteration of NAP stops. It is assumed that the agent will stop when he or she believes that a best proposition has been achieved. In addition, the second limitation is that there is only one cycle of NAP presented in the case study of developing the IA. There is a need for the agent to conduct multiple cycles of NAP in order to reform the theoretical proposition until it explains or resolves, in this instance, the information mismanagement phenomenon.

As for the future work, the impact of abduction on a scientific inquiry will be explored in depth especially with the purpose of discovering and creating knowledge. In this paper, NAP consists of five stages and regards norms as a mean to understand the function of knowledge. The norms specification from OS will be incorporated in each stage of NAP for knowledge profiling at the individual level by incorporating perceptual, cognitive, evaluative, denotative and behavioural norms. In addition, NAP will be developed as a research methodology which will enable the researcher to make more informed decision on how IA should be designed. From the practical perspective, more cycles of the NAP are going to be conducted in the industry with practitioners such as information managers. This approach aims to finalise the best proposition in the process of developing IA. In addition, this will increase the validity, utility, generality, and innovativeness of the specification of the IA as an artefact.

References

1. Dillon, A., Turnbull, D.: Information architecture. In: Encyclopedia of Library and Information Science. Marcel Dekker, New York (2005)
2. Tan, C., Liu, K., White, E.: Information architecture for healthcare organizations: the case of a NHS hospital in UK. Paper Presented at the Thirty Fourth International Conference on Information Systems (ICIS 2013), Milan, Italy (2013)
3. Bryant, A., Maes, R.: The role of the information architect: conquering cognitive parochialism. All Sprouts Content Paper 96 (2008)
4. Haverty, M.: Information architecture without internal theory: an inductive design process. J. Am. Soc. Inform. Sci. Technol. **53**(10), 839–845 (2002)
5. March, L.: The logic of design. In: Cross, N. (ed.) Developments in Design Methodology, pp. 265–276. Wiley, Chichester (1984)
6. Peirce, C.S.: Collected Papers of Charles Sanders Peirce: Pragmaticisms and Pragnoaticism, Scientific Metaphysics, vol. 5–6. Belknap Press, Cambridge (1935)
7. Liu, K., Li, W.: Organisational Semiotics and Business Informatics. Routledge, Abingdon (2015)
8. Stamper, R.K.: Information systems as a social science. In: Falkenberg, E.D., Lyytinen, K., Verrijn-Stuart, A.A. (eds.) Information System Concepts: An Integrated Discipline Emerging. ITIFIP, vol. 36, pp. 1–51. Springer, Boston (2000). https://doi.org/10.1007/978-0-387-35500-9_1
9. Stamper, R., Liu, K., Hafkamp, M., Ades, Y.: Understanding the roles of signs and norms in organizations-a semiotic approach to information systems design. Behav. Inf. Technol. **19**(1), 15–27 (2000)
10. Braf, E.: Knowledge or information: what makes the difference? In: Liu, K., Clarke, R.J., Andersen, P.B., Stamper, R.K., Abou-Zeid, E.-S. (eds.) Organizational Semiotics: Evolving a Science of Information Systems, pp. 71–90. Kluwer Academic Publishers, Norwell (2002)
11. Hillestad, R., Bigelow, J., Bower, A., Girosi, F., Meili, R., Scoville, R., Taylor, R.: Can electronic medical record systems transform health care? Potential health benefits, savings, and costs. Health Aff. **24**(5), 1103–1117 (2005)
12. Martin, A., Dmitriev, D., Akeroyd, J.: A resurgence of interest in information architecture. Int. J. Inf. Manag. **30**(1), 6–12 (2010)
13. Brancheau, J.C., Wetherbe, J.C.: Information architectures: methods and practice. Inf. Process. Manag. **22**(6), 453–463 (1986)
14. Evernden, R., Evernden, E.: Information First: Integrating Knowledge and Information Architecture for Business Advantage. Elsevier Butterworth-Heinemann, Oxford (2003)
15. Tan, C., Liu, K.: An organisational semiotics inspired information architecture: pervasive healthcare as a case study. Paper presented at the 14th International Conference on Informatics and Semiotics in Organisation (ICISO), Stockholm, Sweden, 25–27 March 2013
16. Liu, K.: Semiotics in Information Systems Engineering. Cambridge University Press, Cambridge (2000)
17. Stamper, R.: Language and computer in organized behavior. In: Riet, R.P., Meersman, R.A. (eds.) Linguistic Instruments in Knowledge Engineering. Elsevier Science Inc., New York (1992)
18. Stamper, R., Liu, K., Huang, K.: Organisational morphology in re-engineering, pp. 729–737 (1994)

19. Steen, M.W., Strating, P., Lankhorst, M.M., ter Doest, H., Iacob, M.-E.: Service-oriented enterprise architecture. In: Stojanović, Z., Dahanayake, A. (eds.) Service-oriented Software System Engineering: Challenges and Practices, pp. 132–154. Idea Group Publishing, Hershey (2005)
20. Van den Hoven, J.: Data architecture: blueprints for data. Inf. Syst. Manag. 19(4), 90–92 (2003)
21. Kovács, G., Spens, K.M.: Abductive reasoning in logistics research. Int. J. Phys. Distrib. Logist. Manag. 35(2), 132–144 (2005)
22. Thagard, P.: Abductive inference: from philosophical analysis to neural mechanisms. In: Feeney, A., Heit, E. (eds.) Inductive Reasoning: Experimental, Developmental, and Computational Approaches, pp. 226–247. Cambridge University Press, Cambridge (2007)
23. Minnameier, G.: The logicality of abduction, deduction, and induction. In: Ideas in Action: Proceedings of the Applying Peirce Conference 2010, pp. 239–251. Nordic Pragmatism Network Helsinki (2010)
24. Dorst, K.: The core of 'design thinking' and its application. Des. Stud. 32(6), 521–532 (2011)
25. Gregory, R., Muntermann, J.: Theorizing in design science research: inductive versus deductive approaches. Paper presented at the Thirty Second International Conference on Information Systems (ICIS 2011), Shanghai (2011)
26. Dubois, A., Gadde, L.-E.: Systematic combining: an abductive approach to case research. J. Bus. Res. 55(7), 553–560 (2002)
27. Pauwels, P., De Meyer, R., Van Campenhout, J.: Design thinking support: information systems versus reasoning. Des. Issues 29(2), 42–59 (2013)
28. Fischer, C., Gregor, S., Aier, S.: Forms of discovery for design knowledge. Paper presented at the 20th European Conference on Information Systems (ECIS 2012), Barcelona, Spain (2012)
29. Yu, C.H.: Abduction? Deduction? Induction? Is there a logic of exploratory data analysis? Paper presented at the Annual Meeting of the American Educational Research Association, New Orleans, LA (1994)
30. Wirth, U.: What is abductive inference? In: Bouissac, P. (ed.) Encyclopedia of semiotics, pp. 1–3. Oxford University Press, Oxford (1998)
31. Staat, W.: On abduction, deduction, induction and the categories. Trans. Charles S. Peirce Soc. 29(2), 225–237 (1993)
32. Everaert-Desmedt, N.: Peirce's semiotics (2010). http://www.signosemio.com/peirce/semiotics.asp. Accessed 1 Apr 2014
33. Burks, A.W.: Peirce's theory of abduction. Philos. Sci. 13(4), 301–306 (1946)
34. HSCIS: Hospital Episode Statistics (2013). http://www.hscic.gov.uk/hes. Accessed 1 Apr 2014
35. Kuhn, T.S.: The Structure of Scientific Revolutions, vol. 2. The University of Chicago Press, Chicago (1962)
36. Popper, K.R.: Conjectures and Refutations, vol. 192. Routledge and Kegan Paul, London (1963)
37. Ross, J.M.: Informatics creativity: a role for abductive reasoning? Commun. ACM 53(2), 144–148 (2010)

Extending Technology Acceptance Model for Proximity Mobile Payment via Organisational Semiotics

Yu-Chun Pan[1]([✉]), Aimee Jacobs[2], Chekfoung Tan[1],
and Sanaa Askool[3]

[1] School of Computing and Engineering, University of West London,
London, UK
{y.pan, chekfoung.tan}@uwl.ac.uk
[2] Craig School of Business, California State University, Fresno,
Fresno, CA, USA
ajacobs@csufresno.edu
[3] Hekma School of Business, Dar Al-Hekma University,
Jeddah, Saudi Arabia
saskool@dah.edu.sa

Abstract. The growth of mobile technologies and smartphones is reshaping the individual and organisational behaviour which affect the business environment. One of the key challenges of mobile payment is how to understand and manage user expectations and technology acceptance. Therefore, to better understand mobile payment use and acceptance, we need to analyse the factors and barriers that influence technology use. The investigation uses Technology Acceptance Model in conjunction with Organisational Semiotics, a socio-technical method of design, to overcome possible limitations addressed in research. This approach offers methods that can help to develop a research model for mobile payment use focusing on technical and social aspects.

Keywords: Mobile payment · Proximity mobile payment
Technology Acceptance Model · Organisational Semiotics
Semiotics · Adoption

1 Introduction

With the widespread of mobile devices and users' appetite for convenient and timely payment, the use of proximity mobile payment (m-payment) is expected to continue to grow. According to Statista [1], the global revenue for proximity m-payment market is expected to reach 930 billion US dollars in 2018. However, according to WorldPay [2], whilst 30% of customers have used mobile devices for contactless (tap and go) payment, 75% of customers prefer to use their credit or debit cards for contactless payment in the UK. Despite the growing use, the adoption of m-payment amongst smartphone users is still relatively low [3]. Therefore, it is essential to further investigate the factors of adoption to identify the blocks as well as provide guidance to merchants on how to better encourage users to adopt m-payment.

© IFIP International Federation for Information Processing 2018
Published by Springer International Publishing AG 2018. All Rights Reserved
K. Liu et al. (Eds.): ICISO 2018, IFIP AICT 527, pp. 43–52, 2018.
https://doi.org/10.1007/978-3-319-94541-5_5

The main contribution of this paper is the development of an extended Technology Acceptance Model (TAM) for m-payment focusing on both social and technical aspects. This paper meets this aim by analysing the current research in technology acceptance and m-payment and proposing Organisational Semiotics (OS) as a suitable perspective to extend TAM.

2   Context and Motivation

Advances in technologies have introduced a wide range of features to mobile devices, which have changed user behaviours significantly. Since the early 1990s, m-payment systems have allowed people to use radio connection between their mobile devices and their mobile network providers to authorise financial transactions. M-payment is considered as a payment or economic exchange for good and/or services via mobile devices through a wireless network or communication technologies [4]. However, such m-payment systems require mobile network coverage and might not always be available. Near Field Communication (NFC) allows a contactless short-range communication facilitating data transmission between mobile devices and payment terminals. With the support of NFC, proximity m-payment allows users with compatible mobile devices to use m-payment function via their mobile phones and portable devices for financial transactions when their devices and Point of Sale (POS) terminals are within a distance of 10 cm. Proximity m-payment eliminates the need for customers to carry and use cash [5] and offers convenience and speed [6].

Since the advent of m-payment, plenty of research has identified the factors of m-payment adoption, including perceived ease of use (PEOU) [7–9], perceived usefulness (PU) [7, 9], trust [8, 10], security and risks [11], costs [12, 13], privacy [14], use context [15], culture [16], and social influence [12, 16]. TAM and its extensions have been widely applied in m-payment adoption research, as they provide a framework to understand the variables influencing intention to use. However, despite the high adoption of smartphones, the adoption of m-payment is still relatively low [3]. Previous research suggests that adoption is heavily influenced by technology itself as well as user perception of technology. Therefore, there is a need to further develop a framework that comprehensively investigates the adoption factors from a different perspective. OS provides a framework that bridges the gap between technology and people [17], and it can be used to enhance the understanding of adoption factors. The following section introduces TAM and its extensions, as well as OS.

3   Theoretical Background

The aim of this section is to explore the various theoretical models proposed for technology use and adoption. Adoption models have roots in information systems (IS), psychology [18], and sociology [19, 20]. However, many researchers ignore the social cultural aspects. Davis [19] stated that group, cultural, or social aspects of decision making, and usage are not considered very much in technology acceptance research. This research intends to bridge this gap by investigating adoption through an OS lens.

OS focuses on semiotic aspects to understand and analyse organisations as IS according to the use of signs, text and communication. The following sections provide background and context for this research through technology adoption, TAM model and extensions of TAM, and OS, respectively.

3.1 Technology Acceptance Model (TAM) and Its Extensions

TAM is used as a predictive and explanatory tool for testing user acceptance of technologies with the aim of understanding the impact of external factors on internal beliefs, attitudes, and intentions. The basis of TAM comes from Theory of Reasonable Action (TRA), which suggests the actual behaviour is an outcome of their behavioural intentions to perform the behaviour. These behavioural intentions are constructed jointly by the user's attitude toward the behaviour and subjective norms [18]. TAM was extended to include the determents of Perceived Usefulness (PU) and Perceived Ease-Of Use (PEOU) as shown in Fig. 1.

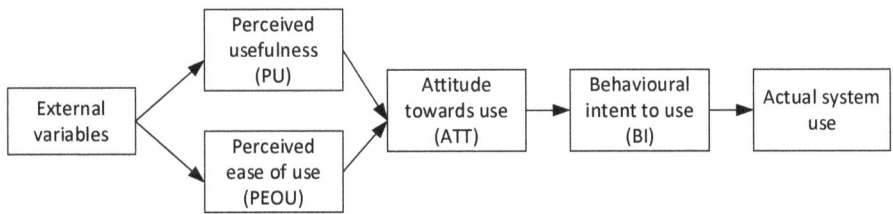

Fig. 1. Original Technology Acceptance Model (TAM)

TAM theorises that the influence of external variables will determine PU and PEOU. PU is defined by Davis [19] as the probability the user's job performance will increase given use of a specific application. PEOU pertains to how effortless the new system will be for the user. These two determinants, PU and PEOU, influence a user's attitude toward using. Both TAM and TRA propose that usage is determined by behavioural intentions, however, TAM differs in that it views intentions as being jointly determined by the person's attitude toward using the system and perceived usefulness [19]. In a recent review [21] of adoption models, researchers found that most studies using TAM either used the original TAM constructs or extended TAM by adding new predictive constructs. Perceived risks are a construct that has been proven [22] to show relevance in adoption of new technologies.

Perceived Risks (PR)
Perceived risks include two dimensions: the level of uncertainty (the likelihood of certain events happening) and the seriousness of impacts shall the events occur [23]. Before adopting new technologies, people assess the two dimensions of potential risks to determine whether they are willing to take the risks as part of their decision-making process [24]. Such potential risks could include technology and information security, privacy, financial loss and so on [25, 26]. Technology and information security has a strong influence on user intention to adopt technologies facilitating monetary

transactions [26]. Other researchers have identified several dimensions of the perceived risk in online shopping field. Zheng et al. [27] propose five dimensions: financial risk, performance risk, social risk, psychological risk, and physical risk, whereas Dai et al. [28] identify three dimensions product, financial and privacy risks.

Limitations of TAM

Bauer et al. [25] suggests that one model cannot fully explain decisions and behaviours across various technologies and adoption situations causing researchers to overlook essential determinants of decisions and action in favour of using the simplistic TAM model. TAM is further criticised for its focus on the individual user ignoring the social process of IS development and implementation and social consequences [29]. Additionally, TAM focuses on technology use, which takes away from the purpose and benefits that are trying to be achieved. Therefore, decision makers focus on the adoption of technology rather than focusing on behaviour or the combination.

TAM and other associated models of technology acceptance have been questioned [29, 30–32]. Since they do not explain why such groups of the population are more likely to adopt a technology and other groups in a population are less so, regardless of sharing similar individual characteristics; therefore, TAM could not validate across all cultures. For example, TAM was found to be valid for both the United States and Switzerland, but not for Japan due to cultural differences [33]. The impact of uncertainty avoidance was reported as the reason for the difference among participants; Japanese were classified to be high on uncertainty avoidance, and accordingly, they were less eager to adopt a new technology [33]. This research proposes the use of OS to addresses these limitations of the TAM model. OS permits a norm analysis of an organisation's socio-technical components thus identifying the salient factors for adoption of m-payment. The following section introduces OS and its methods.

3.2 Organisational Semiotics (OS)

OS applies concepts and methods of semiotics in studying an organisation [34]. Semiotics is the study of signs [35]. A sign can either be an object, an index or a symbol. An object is a sign that conveys message, an index signifies meaning derived by repeated observation, and a symbol refers to a sign associating with norms or rules [36]. An organisation is hence understood as an IS where signs are considered as information.

Scholars [37] have applied OS in extending the behavioural factors in TAM. Semiotics ladder is an OS framework that studies social and technical aspects of an IS [38]. In this research, the IS refers to the m-payment system. The technical aspect consists of three layers: *physical layer* identifies the physical carrier of storing and processing information such as the mobile devices and servers that host the mobile payment application, *empirical layer* refers to the way signs are transmitted such as the network technology and communication protocol, and *syntactic layer* relates to the sign structure and in this case, it is the design of the mobile payment application. The social aspect consists of three layers: *semantic layer*, describes the meaning of signs which in this case how information of the mobile payment system being perceived by the users, *pragmatic layer* studies how users perceive signs such as studying users' intention in using the mobile payment system, and *social layer* examines the interpretation of signs where new knowledge is created, for example, if users acknowledge the benefits of using the mobile payment system outweigh the costs (including sacrifice of privacy), this would prompt them in using the system. In OS, a norm "*is more like a field of force that makes the members of a community tend to behave or think in a certain way*" [38]. The users' behaviour can then be studied through norms [37]. In an organisation, norms are seen as all types of signs [17]. A sign can be an object, or an effect produced by an object that conveys information. Norms impact on how a user behaves that leads to perform certain actions, which will generate more signs that leads to subsequent actions. Stamper [38] proposes the Organisational Containment Analysis (OCA) to analyse norms of an organisation. OCA consists of three layers: informal, formal and technical. The informal layer refers to organisational culture, customs and values that are reflected as beliefs, habits and patterns of members within the organisation. These norms are part of the culture in the organisation, so they are usually being applied informally. The formal layer denotes the rules and bureaucracy to perform the organisational activities. The technical layer automates the norms captured in the informal and formal layer.

4 OS Perspective to TAM for Mobile Payment

According to Bagozzi [29], the social aspect is a gap in TAM research because while sometimes we seem to be acting in isolation, spontaneously, deliberatively, or in response to social pressure, we typically act interpersonally, or as agents of organisations, or collectively. Therefore, we adopt OS to analyse the acceptance of m-payment. The OS analysis of m-payment can be categorised into six distinctive layers (Fig. 2).

OCA	OSF		
Informal	Human Information Functions		**Social World**: Social influence, peer pressure, perceived risks, confidence in service providers, culture…
		Pragmatics: Time saving, convenience, accessible records, perceived advancement …
Formal		**Semantics**: Contactless financial transactions, regulations for financial transactions, service agreements, terms and conditions …	
Technical	The Platform	**Syntactics**: Design and structure of M-payment application, compatibility, security protocol, encryption, verification, user guide…	
		Empirics: NFC, transaction platform, portal, internet connectivity, connection speed and liability, archives…
	Physical World: POS terminal, mobile devices, server, cables, database…		

Fig. 2. Organisational Semiotics Framework (OSF) with Organisational Containment Analysis (OCA) for m-payment

The analysis identifies the requirements for m-payment adoption in the human information functions and the IT platform respectively. This analysis may provide the foundation for m-payment adoption development. The OCA helps to identify socio-technical factors that contribute to adoption of m-payment. Based on previous research in technology adoption and OS, we integrate the OS Ladder and OCA (Fig. 2) to propose a conceptual model for understanding m-payment acceptance (Fig. 3). The model can be explained as follows: m-payment acceptance can be evaluated in three levels, technical (technology characteristics), formal (organizational antecedents), and informal (external environment). These three levels affect the intention to use and adopt m-payment. The advantages obtained by using m-payment will either positively or negatively influence user acceptance.

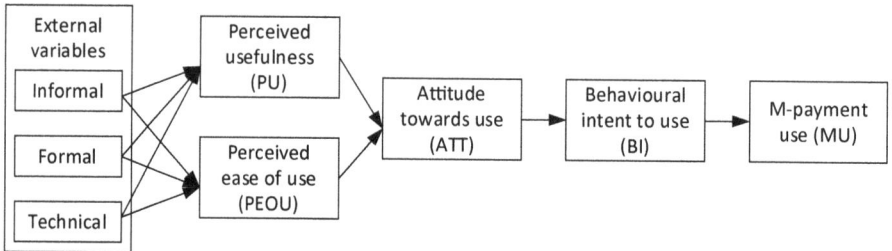

Fig. 3. Conceptual model for understanding m-payment acceptance

Factors that contribute to the adoption of m-payment include speed and convenience through contactless payments [6], which can be considered as PEOU, PU and intent to use in the informal layer. The level of perceived risks of a technology could affect the level of technology use and acceptance; where risk is perceived to be high, adopters would be less willing to adopt the technology [39]. Lwin et al. [40] concluded that consumers' concerns about security risk are one of the key factors for electronic services adoption. In the context of m-payment, users might be concerned with risks related to privacy, personal data and, transactions [25]. Therefore, whether users feel comfortable using m-payment due to security, privacy and risk concerns form key informal norms. Additionally, difficulties that users may face due to security measurements/verification and the fears that companies have not taken adequate steps to reduce transaction risks could also negatively affect transaction intentions.

The findings also identify the formal factors of costs, context of use, customers' perceived risks of privacy, personal data & transactions which should be lessened by an organisation's regulations and policies to reduce these risks. Although perceived risks and security are informal norms, the formal policies and regulations can influence users' perception of risks and security. Therefore, the service agreements provided by m-payment service providers, e.g. Google and Apple, play a key role. Technology and information security has a strong influence on user intention to adopt technologies facilitating monetary transactions [26]. Hence, the relevant regulations set by authorities to prevent users' financial loss form the formal norms for m-payment. Other formal factors also include costs, security and privacy policies, risk management policies, availability of assistance for online and mobile service.

Mobile transactions are conducted with the following technical factors; mobile devices, along with mobile technology, radio connections and wireless telecommunications. NFC and payment terminals such as POS terminals and m-payment applications are all necessary for m-payment use. Also, technologies to help ensure privacy and security should be carefully thought out. For customers to adopt m-payment all these socio-technical factors should be considered by organisations that want to implement an m-payment service. Moreover, Suh and Han [41] indicate that consumers who want to buy products or services online have concerns about security due to the vulnerabilities of website forms. Accordingly, several factors such as protection, encryption, verification, and authentication should be the antecedent of perceived security [42].

5 Discussion and Conclusion

M-payment system has empowered the digital transformation of business and has been adopted by several industries. Although this new paying method shows several advantages when compared with traditional ways, consumers have been slow to adopt. TAM has been used as a suitable user acceptance model to understand technology adoption, however, several gaps were reported such as a gap in linking technical and social factors. Therefore, the purpose of this paper is to address a TAM gap with OS as it provides a structural approach in studying organisational norms through individual behaviour. OS as a theoretical lens to examine the factors that affect adoption in technical and social levels was used to extend TAM.

The OS Ladder and OCA were used to analyse the factors that influence the adoption of mobile payment. This analysis indicates that the socio-technical factors can be considered either as enablers or inhibiters. It was found that m-payment adoption can produce the benefits of enhanced speed and convenience through contactless payments. Inhibitors may include level of perceived risks, namely risks related to security, privacy, personal data and, transactions. Other formal factors also include costs, security and privacy policies, risk management policies, availability of personal assistance for online and mobile service. Additionally, several factors such as protection, encryption, verification, and authentication should be the antecedent of perceived security in the technical layer. These factors were then used to extend TAM. The proposed conceptual model (Fig. 3) with supporting OS ladder and OCA (Fig. 2) serves as a backbone methodology for organisations who would like to implement m-payment for their customers. The research model provides a useful framework for organisations wanting to develop the infrastructure for m-payment transactions. This research enables organisations to consider the social perspective of the adoption factor in m-payment that should be taken into consideration when planning to implement such a system.

A limitation, however, is that the research framework is based on literature review without empirical studies. However, the proposed model presents the relationships between the technical and social challenges of m-payment. Future investigation will look into alternatives to OS as an extension to TAM for m-payment adoption, for example, Everitt Rogers's Technology Adoption Lifecycle. Further research can be applied to test the internal and external validity of the theoretical propositions by collecting empirical data from consumers.

In conclusion, this paper focused on the extension of TAM based on OS. The analysis highlights the requirements through the six layers in OS framework focusing on semantic, pragmatic and social aspects of m-payment without disregarding the social characteristics.

References

1. Statista: Total revenue of global mobile payment market from 2015 to 2019 (in billion U.S. dollars). https://www.statista.com/statistics/226530/mobile-payment-transaction-volume-forecast/
2. WorldPay: WorldPay Consumer Behaviour and Payments Report 2017: What's driving today's consumers? (2017)
3. Deloitte: Contactless mobile payments (finally) gain momentum (2015)
4. Liu, J., Kauffman, R.J., Ma, D.: Competition, cooperation, and regulation: understanding the evolution of the mobile payments technology ecosystem. Electron. Commer. Res. Appl. **14**, 372–391 (2015). https://doi.org/10.1016/j.elerap.2015.03.003
5. Pham, T.-T.T., Ho, J.C.: The effects of product-related, personal-related factors and attractiveness of alternatives on consumer adoption of NFC-based mobile payments. Technol. Soc. **43**, 159–172 (2015). https://doi.org/10.1016/J.TECHSOC.2015.05.004
6. Teo, A.-C., Tan, G.W.-H., Ooi, K.-B., Hew, T.-S., Yew, K.-T.: The effects of convenience and speed in m-payment. Ind. Manag. Data Syst. **115**, 311–331 (2015). https://doi.org/10.1108/IMDS-08-2014-0231
7. Kim, C., Mirusmonov, M., Lee, I.: An empirical examination of factors influencing the intention to use mobile payment. Comput. Hum. Behav. **26**, 310–322 (2010). https://doi.org/10.1016/J.CHB.2009.10.013
8. Shin, D.-H.: Modeling the interaction of users and mobile payment system: conceptual framework. Int. J. Hum. Comput. Interact. **26**, 917–940 (2010). https://doi.org/10.1080/10447318.2010.502098
9. Koenig-Lewis, N., Marquet, M., Palmer, A., Zhao, A.L.: Enjoyment and social influence: predicting mobile payment adoption. Serv. Ind. J. **35**, 537–554 (2015). https://doi.org/10.1080/02642069.2015.1043278
10. Lu, Y., Yang, S., Chau, P.Y.K., Cao, Y.: Dynamics between the trust transfer process and intention to use mobile payment services: a cross-environment perspective. Inf. Manag. **48**, 393–403 (2011). https://doi.org/10.1016/J.IM.2011.09.006
11. Arvidsson, N.: Consumer attitudes on mobile payment services – results from a proof of concept test. Int. J. Bank Mark. **32**, 150–170 (2014). https://doi.org/10.1108/IJBM-05-2013-0048
12. Hongxia, P., Xianhao, X., Weidan, L.: Drivers and barriers in the acceptance of mobile payment in China. In: 2011 International Conference on E-business and E-government (ICEE), pp. 1–4. IEEE (2011)
13. Mallat, N.: Exploring consumer adoption of mobile payments – a qualitative study. J. Strateg. Inf. Syst. **16**, 413–432 (2007). https://doi.org/10.1016/j.jsis.2007.08.001

14. Slade, E.L., Williams, M.D., Dwivedi, Y.K.: Mobile payment adoption: classification and review of the extant literature. Mark. Rev. **13**, 167–190 (2013). https://doi.org/10.1362/146934713X13699019904687
15. Mallat, N., Rossi, M., Tuunainen, V.K., Öörni, A.: The impact of use context on mobile services acceptance: the case of mobile ticketing. Inf. Manag. **46**, 190–195 (2009). https://doi.org/10.1016/J.IM.2008.11.008
16. Alalwan, A.A., Rana, N.P., Dwivedi, Y.K., Lal, B., Williams, M.D.: Adoption of mobile banking in jordan: exploring demographic differences on customers' perceptions. In: Janssen, M., Mäntymäki, M., Hidders, J., Klievink, B., Lamersdorf, W., van Loenen, B., Zuiderwijk, A. (eds.) I3E 2015. LNCS, vol. 9373, pp. 13–23. Springer, Cham (2015). https://doi.org/10.1007/978-3-319-25013-7_2
17. Stamper, R.K.: Information systems as a social science. In: Falkenberg, E.D., Lyytinen, K., Verrijn-Stuart, A.A. (eds.) Information System Concepts: An Integrated Discipline Emerging. ITIFIP, vol. 36, pp. 1–51. Springer, Boston (2000). https://doi.org/10.1007/978-0-387-35500-9_1
18. Fishbein, M., Ajzen, I.: Belief, Attitude, Intention, and Behavior: An Introduction to Theory and Research. Addison-Wesley Publishing Co., Reading (1975)
19. Davis, F.D.: Perceived usefulness, perceived ease of use, and user acceptance of information technology. MIS Q. **13**, 319 (1989). https://doi.org/10.2307/249008
20. Venkatesh, V., Davis, F.D.: A theoretical extension of the technology acceptance model: four longitudinal field studies. Manag. Sci. **46**, 186–204 (2000). https://doi.org/10.1287/mnsc.46.2.186.11926
21. Chhonker, M.S., Verma, D., Kar, A.K.: Review of technology adoption frameworks in mobile commerce. Procedia Comput. Sci. **122**, 888–895 (2017). https://doi.org/10.1016/j.procs.2017.11.451
22. Zimmer, J.C., Arsal, R.E., Al-Marzouq, M., Grover, V.: Investigating online information disclosure: effects of information relevance, trust and risk. Inf. Manag. **47**, 115–123 (2010). https://doi.org/10.1016/J.IM.2009.12.003
23. Bauer, R.: Consumer behavior as risk taking. In: Risk Taking and Information Handling in Consumer Behavior. Harvard University Press, Cambridge (1967)
24. Featherman, M.S., Pavlou, P.A.: Predicting e-services adoption: a perceived risk facets perspective. Int. J. Hum. Comput. Stud. **59**, 451–474 (2003). https://doi.org/10.1016/S1071-5819(03)00111-3
25. Bauer, H.H., Reichardt, T., Barnes, S.J., Neumann, M.M.: Driving consumer acceptance of mobile marketing: a theoretical framework and empirical study. J. Electron. Commer. Res. **6**, 181 (2005)
26. Cheng, T.C.E., Lam, D.Y.C., Yeung, A.C.L.: Adoption of internet banking: an empirical study in Hong Kong. Decis. Support Syst. **42**, 1558–1572 (2006). https://doi.org/10.1016/J.DSS.2006.01.002
27. Zheng, L., Favier, M., Huang, P., Coat, F.: Chinese consumer perceived risk and risk relievers in e-shopping for clothing. J. Electron. Commer. Res. **13**, 255 (2012)
28. Dai, B., Forsythe, S., Kwon, W.-S.: The impact of online shopping experience on risk perceptions and online purchase intentions: does product category matter? J. Electron. Commer. Res. **15**, 13 (2014)
29. Bagozzi, R.P.: The legacy of the technology acceptance model and a proposal for a paradigm shift. J. Assoc. Inf. Syst. **8**, 3 (2007)
30. Benbasat, I., Barki, H.: Quo vadis TAM? J. Assoc. Inf. Syst. **8**, 7 (2007)
31. Yousafzai, S.Y., Foxall, G.R., Pallister, J.G.: Technology acceptance: a meta-analysis of the TAM: part 1. J. Model. Manag. **2**, 251–280 (2007). https://doi.org/10.1108/17465660710834453

32. Venkatesh, V., Davis, F.D., Morris, M.G.: Dead or alive? The development, trajectory and future of technology adoption research. J. Assoc. Inf. Syst. **8**, 267–286 (2007)
33. Straub, D., Keil, M., Brenner, W.: Testing the technology acceptance model across cultures: a three country study. Inf. Manag. **33**, 1–11 (1997). https://doi.org/10.1016/S0378-7206(97)00026-8
34. Liu, K.: Semiotics in Information System Engineering. Cambridge University Press, Cambridge (2000)
35. Peirce, C.S.: Collected Papers of Charles Sanders Peirce: Pragmaticisms and Pragnoaticism, Scientific Metaphysics. Belknap Press, Cambridge (1935)
36. Stamper, R.K.: Towards a theory of information: information: mystical fluid or a subject for scientific enquiry? Comput. J. **28**, 195–199 (1985). https://doi.org/10.1093/comjnl/28.3.195
37. Al-Rajhi, M., Liu, K., Nakata, K.: A conceptual model for acceptance of information systems: an organizational semiotic perspective. In: Americas Conference on Information Systems (AMCIS), p. 348 (2010)
38. Stamper, R.K.: Organisational semiotics: informatics without the computer? In: Kecheng, L., Anderson, P.B., Stamper, R.K., Clarke, R.J. (eds.) Information, Organisation and Technology: Studies in Organisational Semiotics. Kluwer, Dordecht (2001)
39. Shoemaker, R.W., Shoaf, F.R.: Behavioral Changes in the Trial of New Products. http://www.jstor.org/stable/2488751
40. Lwin, M., Wirtz, J., Williams, J.D.: Consumer online privacy concerns and responses: a power–responsibility equilibrium perspective. J. Acad. Mark. Sci. **35**, 572–585 (2007). https://doi.org/10.1007/s11747-006-0003-3
41. Suh, B., Han, I.: The impact of customer trust and perception of security control on the acceptance of electronic commerce. Int. J. Electron. Commer. **7**, 135–161 (2003)
42. Chellappa, R.K., Pavlou, P.A.: Perceived information security, financial liability and consumer trust in electronic commerce transactions. Logist. Inf. Manag. **15**, 358–368 (2002). https://doi.org/10.1108/09576050210447046

Towards a Semiotic-Based Approach to the Design of Therapeutic Digital Games

Paula Maia de Souza$^{(\boxtimes)}$, Kamila Rios da Hora Rodrigues,
Franco Eusébio Garcia, and Vânia Paula de Almeida Neris

Department of Computing, Federal University of São Carlos, São Carlos, Brazil
paula.souza@ufscar.br, kamila.rios@gmail.com,
{franco.garcia,vania}@dc.ufscar.br

Abstract. Healthcare professionals may employ therapeutic games as playful activities to promote rehabilitation for their patients. However, despite the importance, currently the literature does not provide multidisciplinary approaches to support designing these games. To overcome this scenario, we propose a semiotic-based approach to aid stakeholders with different backgrounds on designing therapeutic digital games. The approach results from a study of the literature and reports of the experience of a multidisciplinary team on the creation of therapeutic games. It explores Participatory Design and Organizational Semiotics methods and artifacts to promote the Problem Clarification, Interaction Modeling, Design Materialization, and Evaluation as fundamental design practices of effective solutions. The approach was evaluated to design new therapeutic games and the results suggest that it helps the team on identifying therapeutic objectives and reaching them.

Keywords: Therapeutic games · Participatory Design
Organizational Semiotics · Evaluation · Games for health · Health

1 Introduction

The market for games is expanding to new areas including education, training and health. For the latter, therapeutic games may promote awareness and provide treatment for patients in efficient and potentially cheaper ways [4]. However, due to their goal – healthcare –, these games require careful development. In special, for their success, it is essential to foster collaborative efforts from multiple stakeholders, including domain specialists (such as healthcare professionals), computer professionals, artists, and, at times, family, government, and patients themselves. Moreover, semantic, pragmatic and social issues should also be considered. The nature of therapeutic systems demands a sociotechnical approach to its design and development [11].

Given the multiple variables involved to ensure success and quality of a therapeutic digital game, we believe a structured process, which recognizes the technical system as part of a whole information system, could assist designing, implementing, evaluating and easing the adoption of these games. However, as far as we know, there is no similar approach in literature. Thus, this paper presents a first step towards this structured process, describing an approach to create therapeutic games, based on Participatory

© IFIP International Federation for Information Processing 2018
Published by Springer International Publishing AG 2018. All Rights Reserved
K. Liu et al. (Eds.): ICISO 2018, IFIP AICT 527, pp. 53–62, 2018.
https://doi.org/10.1007/978-3-319-94541-5_6

Design (PD) [15] and Organizational Semiotics (OS) [8, 17]. OS is a discipline that explores the use of signs and their effects on social practices. In the OS approach, an organization and its information system are considered as a social system in which human behaviors are organized by a system of norms. An organization is understood as an information system in which people use signs for communication towards purposeful and coordinated actions. In this sense, any technological artifact, e.g. a software application, is embedded in a formal system that, by its turn, exists in the context of an informal system [8, 17].

For evaluation, the process was used in a new context and the results suggest it helps the team on identifying therapeutic objectives and supports to reach them.

2 Related Work

Mader et al. [9] affirm that, even though therapeutic games might be very promising, they are still very complex to design and develop. Their reasoning is that therapeutic games present four main design challenges: creating a motivational game, exchanging information, therapeutic gameplay and defining the process. To ease the process, they proposed a model called Player/Game/Therapy (P/G/T). As an analytical tool, the main idea of P/G/T is to analyze each aspect of a therapeutic game independently and the relationships between pairs of them (i.e. player-game, therapy-player and therapy-game). In the model, Player relates to patient, who assumes the role of player in a game. The authors emphasize that it is important to gather general information about the patient, including her/his situation and skills to play, as this data are needed to design a game that is playable and enjoyable for the patient. The Game serves to define game basics (genre, platform and devices), brief description of its story, gameplay and world. Finally, Therapy describes the therapy elements which should be present in the game – including therapeutic goal, protocol and context.

In addition, Mader et al. [9] states that a limitation of their method is that patients are studied but not involved, and health specialists have the role of providing knowledge and validating the design. Thus, we believe that a PD approach could enrich the design and improve the overall effectiveness of the resulting game.

Cheng et al. [3] conducted a survey, through detailed interviews, with 11 game designers. The author's intent was to understand how designers judge and perceive the success of games for health projects, how they think and act on the challenges, how they acquired domain knowledge and rated their games, and what tools they used to support their work. They found that most therapeutic game designers value and practice user-centered design principles (e.g. user focus, user testing from the start), and tended to place emphasis on initial user engagement and user search. Most of the designers mentioned using interviews with target players as being one of the first steps to approach a therapeutic game project. Participants also said they relied on iterative prototyping processes and game tests to refine their understanding of the domain and target users.

Cheng et al. [3] report that incorporating serious content into an engaging gaming experience is an important but difficult aspect. In addition, maintaining successful stakeholder collaboration is also important, but challenging in serious gaming projects for health. They also report that user-centered efforts do not always help with some of the prominent challenges, such as communicating with subject matter experts and conducting enduring experiences for players. These findings indicate that more research is needed to help support designers of therapeutic digital games to overcome the challenges discussed by the respondents.

In this sense, we started working to provide a design approach to aid computer and healthcare professionals in creating therapeutic digital games co-developed by different stakeholders and supported by a sociotechnical view.

3   Methodology to Formalize the Approach

Aiming to acquire relevant requirements, our methodology employed a literature review and an interview with researchers who created a therapeutic game in an ad-hoc way. These requirements supported us to create and formalize an initial approach, which we evaluated and improved by applying it to a new therapeutic context.

In the review of the literature, we searched for papers that reported the design of therapeutic digital games in the Association for Computing Machinery (ACM), Institute of Electrical and Electronics Engineers (IEEE), and Scopus databases. Although several studies described the use or the creation of therapeutic games, most results did not report using any specific methodology for designing therapeutic games. Section 2 summarized the works considered relevant. Among the lessons learned from these works, it is possible to highlight: the importance of involving stakeholders in all stages of therapeutic game design, and the importance of considering relationships between player, game and therapy.

In addition to the literature review, a non-structured interview (carried out as a playful activity using cards, questions and answers) was carried out with researchers from the computing and health domains, who developed the game "Jogar Também Faz Bem!" (Play makes good as well!) to support depression treatment. The game won the best demonstration award at the XV Brazilian Symposium on Human Factors in Computing Systems [12]. We interviewed the project coordinator, three PhD students (two from the healthcare area, one from the computing), a master's student (computing area) and four undergraduate students (three from the computing area, one from healthcare). The aim was to collect lessons learned from their experience on developing a therapeutic game. These results are described in Sect. 4.

From the literature review and the study of the "Jogar Também Faz Bem!" game, it was possible to propose a four stage approach to the design of digital therapeutic games. For evaluation, the approach was instantiated in another therapeutic context.

4   Analyzing the Design of a Therapeutic Game
for the Depression

Our non-structured interview with the "Jogar Também Faz Bem!" researchers started mapping the origin of the game. According to the researchers, an employee of a public hospital which provided treatment to patients with depression contact the research

group from a nearby city university aiming to acquire software to support the rehabilitation of their patients. At the time, a literature search performed by the researchers
indicated a lack of formal methodologies and approaches regarding digital therapeutic
games development, especially aimed for mental health problems.

Therefore, those researchers decided to adopt Baranauskas and Bonacin's view for
a design process [1] and instantiate then to the therapeutic context [11]. Baranauskas
and Bonacin explore a combination of PD [10, 15] and OS [8, 17] practices, considering design as a social process of expressing meaning, communicating intentions and
constructing knowledge, to be carried iteratively and interactively by designers and a
group of stakeholders in a participatory style. A complete discussion on why Baranauskas and Bonacin's view was adopted can be found in [11].

Figure 1 shows the Semiotic Onion, an OS artifact, instantiated by Neris and
Rodrigues [11] to attend the therapeutic information system.

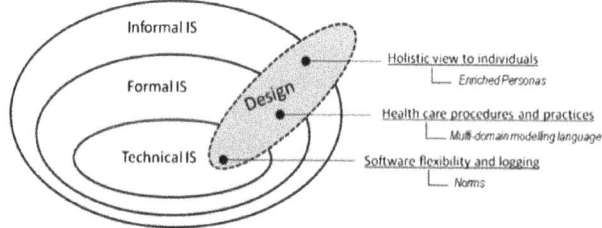

Fig. 1. Semiotic Onion considering signs to therapeutic systems [11].

According Neris and Rodrigues [11], in the therapeutic system scenario, the particularities of each patient should consider a holistic view, including his/her personal
information, family and close people history, healthcare professionals, and academic
and demographic studies. In the formal layer, it is important to identify the health
procedures and protocols which also underline the therapeutic objectives. Finally, in
technical level system flexibility and data logging aspects need to be addressed.
Flexible features can be implemented considering cognitive and physical aspects of the
patients that are important to be respected during the interaction.

Aiming to map patients' medical profiles and needs with design requirements for
the game, the researchers used OS artifacts with the Personas technique proposed by
Cooper [5]. The result of the use of artifacts from OS and Personas was called Personas
Enrichment Process (described in Sect. 5) [14]. The enrichment was carried out in a
participatory way: hospital professionals contributed to propose, improve, and evaluate
the created personas.

In order to identify suitable mechanics and genre for the game, the researchers
employed a participatory practice exploring the PICTIVE technique [10]. In this new
activity, the group of computer professionals provided images for healthcare professionals with illustrations of characters and scenarios of digital games. These professionals analyzed the images and were asked to choose the ones which better matched
their patients' interests and could better suit the therapeutic practice.

Considering the multidisciplinary nature of game creation, the researchers found it could be useful to foster communication and collaboration among stakeholders with different backgrounds. To benefit from domain knowledge of every stakeholder, they defined an Interaction Modeling Language for Therapeutic Applications [6]. The language adopted graphical symbols to promote collaborative design by computer, health, and artists professionals alike, trying to reduce communication and technical barriers required. Moreover, given the therapeutic nature of the game, the researchers considered it was important to allow healthcare professionals to track the progress of patients over several sessions. Thus, they introduced collecting (logging) interaction data of patients' interactions within the game, and evaluation activities to test their cognitive abilities.

Initial functional prototypes of the game to patients and hospital professionals were delivered. Healthcare professionals could generate reports summarizing the collected data to examine if their patients improved over the playing sessions. Besides the built-in game evaluation, playtest with patients also started featuring the Self-Assessment Manikin (SAM) [2] evaluation as a post-section questionnaire for self-assessment of a patient's emotional state. The feedback collected after a playtest session was positive.

Next, a healthcare student of the researchers' group analyzed the game in a new context, using it as an entertainment resource for elderly patients on hemodialysis at a specialized hospital. Despite the difficulties of application, due to the hemodialysis process, the patients appreciated the game. However, for researchers, this was an opportunity to improve the game's accessibility. For this, they incorporated accessibility and usability improvements in the game, including: spoken instructions, transcription in Brazilian Sign Language (LIBRAS), and alternative input schemes (mouse, keyboard, controller).

5   An Approach to the Design of Therapeutic Games

With the results from Sects. 2 and 4, we started defining an approach to support designing therapeutic applications. The approach was divided into four stages (see Fig. 2): (1) Design Problem Clarification, (2) Interaction Modeling, (3) Design Materialization, and (4) Evaluation.

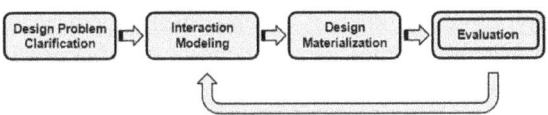

Fig. 2. Stages of the design approach.

Design Problem Clarification aims to understand the use context of the game. Therapeutic games are in a multidisciplinary context; thus, it is useful to explore PD practices to benefit from the knowledge of all stakeholders. In special, healthcare professionals knowledge is essential to discover and understand therapeutic requirements. Stakeholders must work together to determine suitable ways to address these requirements into gameplay. A possible approach to achieve that is exploring the following steps: brainstorming, Personas Enrichment Process, elicitation of therapeutic objectives, elicitation of requirements, and PICTIVE (see Fig. 3).

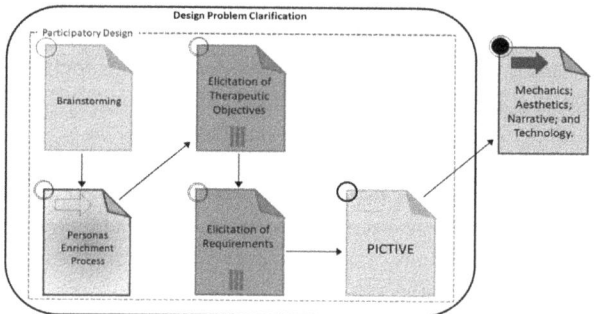

Fig. 3. Design problem clarification.

The application of the brainstorming technique is the event that initiates the flow of this stage, followed by the Personas Enrichment Process (see Fig. 4) [14].

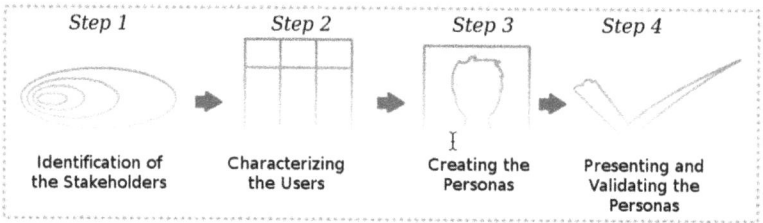

Fig. 4. Personas enrichment process [14].

In Step 1 of the Enrichment Process, a multidisciplinary team uses the Stakeholder Analysis Chart (see Fig. 5a) [14, 16] to identify people and institutions related to the system. Step 2 employs the Evaluation Frame (see Fig. 5b) [14, 16] added to other artifacts, to identify clinical profiles of patients, medical procedures, patients' relationship with other interested parties, and problems involved in creating the application alongside possible solutions.

In Step 3, the fictional characters idealized by healthcare professionals become Personas representing real people. Researchers with computer background should aggregate information from the literature (public health data) to detail the individuals with relevant information. Afterwards, healthcare professionals should evaluate the correctness of the Personas, approving them provided they are suitable (Step 4) [14].

After the validation of the created persons, the therapeutic objectives and the requirements that the game must attend must be raised. It is understood by therapeutic

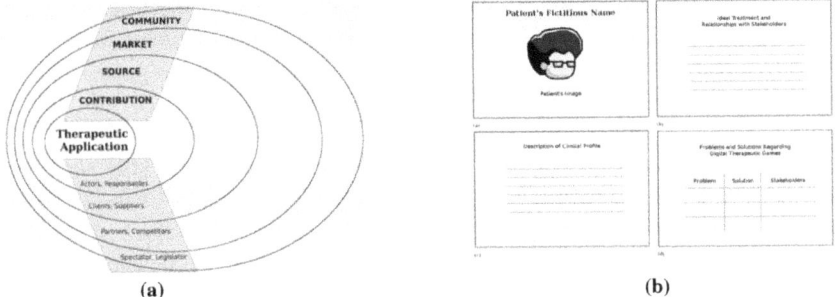

Fig. 5. (a) Stakeholder analysis chart [14, 16]. (b) Evaluation frame and other artifacts [14, 16].

objective, the objective of the game in treating a certain pathology and in how to help in the improvement of this pathology.

For the identification of the dynamics and genre of the game it is advisable to apply the PICTIVE technique [10], this being the last event in the flow of the clarification stage. As a result of this step we have the mechanics, aesthetics, narrative, technology. The techniques, artifacts and processes suggested for this step were described in Sect. 4.

The next stage is **Interaction Modeling**. Considering that therapeutic applications involve a multidisciplinary team, all stakeholders can benefit from an easy-to-understand language – preferably requiring minimal computer-specific knowledge. For this reason, it is advisable to use a Domain Specific Modeling Language (DSML) for the design, such as the Interaction Modeling Language [6].

Next comes the stage **Design Materialization**, consisting of sketching, prototyping and/or defining an initial version of the application based on the chosen DSML. For this stage, exploring PD and prototyping techniques and tools can be useful: screen sketches and prototypes allow drafting the game look and feel before implementing high fidelity prototypes, fostering participation of stakeholders without computer backgrounds and promoting faster design iterations. To enable more people to use the system, it is necessary to consider aspects of universality for the design in a therapeutic context. For instance, health conditions may hinder movement or restrict the use of an arm/hand (as in the case of patients undergoing dialysis).

Finally, due to the critical nature of the therapeutic domain, any proposed solution should be evaluated by healthcare and computer science professionals – this is the goal of the **Evaluation** phase. Evaluation should, thus, happen at all stages of development: from the initial modeling and prototypes to the final product. Evaluation should consider gameplay, accessibility, emotional aspects and therapeutic purposes of the game.

6 Approach Evaluation

To evaluate the approach described in Sect. 5, a group of professionals from another Brazilian public university carried out an extension project in partnership with a public hospital specialized in treatment of childhood cancer. The project aimed to design a digital therapeutic game to support the rehabilitation of children under treatment for cancer [13].

In Stage 1 from this approach, the professionals conducted meetings with a hospital's therapist and used participatory practices to discover the domain and the target audience, to clarify requirements for the game, and to identify the gender and characteristics desirable for the interaction with the game to be developed for children in treatment.

The professionals instantiated the Personas Enrichment Process [14] and used its artifacts to identify stakeholders. By using the Stakeholder Analysis Chart [14, 16] they identified the patients, the family, healthcare professionals and researchers, as well as the hospital and the government, as the main stakeholders in the development of the therapeutic game for the cancer treatment [13]. By applying the Evaluation Frame artifact [14, 16], they identified the clinical profile of the children being treated for cancer in that hospital (from newborns to people with 35 years old, with Leukemia, Osteosarcoma or Central Nervous System (CNS) tumor), medical procedures used in them (e.g. chemotherapy and radiation therapy), the patient's relationship with other interested parties (including healthcare professionals and the very protective caregivers), problems involved in creating and using the game (e.g. side effects in the use of 3D format, etc.), and possible solutions to these problems (e.g. use of 2D format). From these participatory practices, three main Personas were identified [13]. The collected data was enriched with information from the Literature regarding childhood cancer, including INCA (Brazil's National Cancer Institute) registration data about child and adolescent cancer in Brazil [7]. An occupational therapist of the specialized hospital evaluated and validated the resulting Personas [13].

According to the researchers, Stage 1 allowed to identify that each of the three Personas created has different needs, which imply in requirements regarding the flexibility of the game. Some possibilities for the game include features to improve self-esteem (e.g. in pre-teen patients who are in an age of discovering their body) and promote positivism, clarifying the treatment and entertaining children and caregivers. The instantiation of Stage 1 also helped researchers to identify the importance of illustrating in the game, in playful ways, changes that occur in the children's body due to the treatment [13].

In Stage 2, the modeling language was used to model scenarios and interactions for supporting treatment cancer in the therapeutic game. This stage, however, has not yet (at the time of writing) been completed its cycle and, thus, has not yet been evaluated by hospital professionals. Nevertheless, according the researchers [13], part of scenarios foreseen for the game already was modeled. The scenarios illustrate, for instance, the materialization of some peculiar aspects and flexibility pointed out by professionals, among them, the flexibility of parts of the game to meet different user profiles and different therapeutic objectives.

In Stage 3, members of the computer science team created prototypes of the scenarios already modeled. One of these prototypes represent game screen with the hospital room where the healthcare professional (from different areas) explains patient care and caregivers from her/his perspective of her/his area of practice (e.g. Occupational Therapy, Medicine, Nutrition, etc.). The prototypes should validate suitability of modeled interaction and allow hospital professionals to evaluate game creation modeling and flow. However, the researchers point out that, as in Stage 2, the evaluation with the professionals of the artifacts generated in Stage 3 of the approach has not yet occurred, because the modeling of the scenarios is still under development.

About the design approach, the evaluation group emphasize that, following the first steps, it was possible to involve healthcare professionals in the creation of a game that also supports their activities as therapists. According to the researchers, in addition to involving the stakeholders in the process, the artifacts used for collecting requirements provide more reliable information to the domain in study and may allow more adhesion to the proposed therapeutic application.

7 Conclusion and Future Works

To turn digital therapeutic games into tools supporting professional healthcare practices, we need to support the design of effective solutions with methods and techniques. Ideally, a semiotic-based approach to the design of therapeutic games aiming to guide involved stakeholders into game creation could, potentially, help the creation of more effective solutions.

Combining results from the literature with studies carried out by a research group that had developed a therapeutic game to aid depression treatment, this paper presents initial steps towards an approach to support the design of therapeutic games. The approach describes a four stages process to guide the development.

An instantiation of the approach was conducted in a different therapeutic context to evaluate it. Preliminary results pointed by the evaluators suggest positive aspects in the involvement of healthcare professionals as co-producers of the solution in question. Domain-specific features, and therefore, peculiar therapeutic aspects, should not, and cannot, be conceived entirely by computer professionals if aiming for effective therapeutic solutions. Rather, it is important to allow as many stakeholders as possible to contribute their designs. For this, PD may be useful, as it promotes co-creation of the therapeutic solution – which is characterized as serious by the Literature and has the responsibility of helping in therapeutic treatments.

Although the preliminary results of the validation conducted are positive, the design approach must be applied in new contexts in order to further evaluate and improve the process.

Acknowledgements. The authors would like to thank the healthcare professionals and administrators of HEM-Marília and HA-Barretos, and healthcare and computer science researchers from UEMG - Frutal and UFSCar for their effective collaboration. CAPES for financial support.

References

1. Baranauskas, M.C.C., Bonacin, R.: Design—indicating through signs. Des. Issues **24**(3), 30–45 (2008). https://doi.org/10.1162/desi.2008.24.3.30
2. Bradley, M.M., Lang, P.J.: Measuring emotion: the self-assessment manikin and the semantic differential. J. Behav. Ther. Exp. Psychiatry **25**(1), 49–59 (1994). https://doi.org/10.1016/0005-7916(94)90063-9

3. Cheng, J., Putnam, C., Guo, J.: "Always a tall order": values and practices of professional game designers of serious games for health. In: Proceedings of the Annual SIGCHI Annual Symposium on Computer-Human Interaction in Play, (CHI PLAY 2016), Austin, pp. 16–19 (2016)

4. Cheung, M.: Therapeutic Games and Guided Imagery: Tools for Mental Health and School Professionals Working With Children, Adolescents, and Their Families. Lyceum Books, Chicago (2016)

5. Cooper, A.: The Inmates Are Running the Asylum: Why High Tech Products Drive us Crazy and How to Restore the Sanity, 2nd edn. Pearson Higher Education, London (2004)

6. Garcia, F.E., Rodrigues, K.R.H., Neris, V.P.A.: Uma Linguagem de Modelagem de Interação Para Aplicações Terapêuticas. In: Simpósio Brasileiro Sobre Fatores Humanos Em Sistemas Computacionais, São Paulo (2016)

7. INCA - Instituto Nacional de Câncer (Brasil): Coordenação de Prevenção e Vigilância de Câncer. Câncer Na Criança e No Adolescente No Brasil. Instituto Nacional de Câncer, Rio de Janeiro (2008)

8. Liu, K.: Semiotics in Information Systems Engineering. Cambridge University Press, Cambridge, New York (2000)

9. Mader, S., Natkin, S., Levieux, G.: How to analyse therapeutic games: the player/game/therapy model. In: Herrlich, M., Malaka, R., Masuch, M. (eds.) ICEC 2012. LNCS, vol. 7522, pp. 193–206. Springer, Heidelberg (2012). https://doi.org/10.1007/978-3-642-33542-6_17

10. Muller, M.J.: PICTIVE—an exploration in participatory design. In: Proceedings of the SIGCHI Conference on Human Factors in Computing Systems (CHI 1991), pp. 225–231. ACM, New York (1991). http://dx.doi.org/10.1145/108844.108896

11. Neris, V.P.A., Rodrigues, K.R.H.: Design of therapeutic information systems as indicating through signs. In: Baranauskas, M.C.C., Liu, K., Sun, L., Neris, V.P.A., Bonacin, R., Nakata, K. (eds.) ICISO 2016. IAICT, vol. 477, pp. 203–208. Springer, Cham (2016). https://doi.org/10.1007/978-3-319-42102-5_23

12. Nishikawa, D., Novak, L., Azevedo, M., Branco, P.C., Olivi, R., Brandão, R., Garcia, F.E., Neris, V.P.A.: Se Cuidar, Cuidar de Algo, Se Divertir e Aprender Fazem Bem! Demonstração de Um Jogo Para Apoiar o Tratamento Da Depressão. In: Anais Do XV Simpósio Brasileiro Sobre Fatores Humanos Em Sistemas Computacionais, São Paulo (2016)

13. Rodrigues, K.R.H., Conrado, D.B.F., Neris, V.P.A.: Lessons learned in designing a digital therapeutic game to support the treatment and well-being of children with cancer. In: Human-Computer Interaction (HCII 2018). LNCS. Springer, Heidelberg (2018, to be published)

14. Rodrigues, K., Garcia, F.E., Bocanegra, L., Gonçalves, V., Carvalho, V., Neris, V.P.A.: Personas-driven design for mental health therapeutic applications. SBC J. Interact. Syst. **6** (1), 18–34 (2015)

15. Schuler, D., Namioka, A.: Participatory Design: Perspectives on Systems Design. L. Erlbaum Associates, Hillsdale (1993)

16. Stamper, R.K.: Analysing the cultural impact of a system. Int. J. Inf. Manag. **8**, 107–122 (1988)

17. Stamper, R.K.: Language and computer in organized behaviour. In: Riet, R.P., Meersman, R. A. (eds.) Linguistic Instruments in Knowledge Engineering, pp. 143–163. Elsevier Science, Amsterdam (1992)

Intensive Innovation: A Semiotic View

Daniel Galarreta$^{(\boxtimes)}$ (iD)

Centre National d'Etudes Spatiales, 18, Avenue Edouard Belin,
31401 Toulouse Cedex 9, France
daniel.galarreta@cnes.fr

Abstract. We have entered a new innovation regime: that of acceleration and intensification. These situations of intensive innovation and disruption question the identity of the objects. The question of the identity of objects directly refers to epistemological questions. In particular, how objects happen in the world - do they exist before their descriptions? But the question of identity also refers to semiotic questions. In this paper, we will present a semiotic framework in order to analyse the question of how business or IT or Space systems emerge in an interdisciplinary environment. Namely we will present a multi-viewpoints semiotics. In parallel to this approach we will introduce an innovative design theory initiated by Armand Hatchuel and Benoît Weil: The C-K theory. We will then try to better understand what brings the two approaches closer together and what separates them.

Keywords: Intensive innovation · Identity · Organisational semiotics
Viewpoints · Multi-viewpoints semiotics · C-K theory

1 Introduction

According to Le Masson et al. [1] we have entered a new innovation regime: that of acceleration and intensification. Intensive innovation "means that all modes of value formation are nowadays concerned by a logic of innovation and technology is only one of those modes. One of the major evolutions today is the transition from a problem of optimizing enterprise capacity (involving decision theory) to a problem of expanding enterprise capacity (involving design theory).

Traditional, incremental innovation is no longer a sufficient guarantee to accompany the major changes that are disrupting our economy, especially as they occur more and more frequently.

Historically, efforts to rationalize design activity have given rise to theories that have enabled firms to adapt to a certain set design mode, in particular by organizing and structuring design offices. But these structures and associated theories today, however, struggle to account for situations of intensive innovation and disruption, where the identity of objects is constantly questioned [1].

The question of the identity of objects directly refers to epistemological questions, namely how it is possible to account for the existence of world objects on the one hand and their identity on the other. This amounts to questioning the way of thinking how objects happen in the world - do they exist before their descriptions? Are they

K. Liu et al. (Eds.): ICISO 2018, IFIP AICT 527, pp. 63–72, 2018.
https://doi.org/10.1007/978-3-319-94541-5_7

constructions? - and is the identity of an object linked to its morphology, its functional characteristics, its use, its position in a technological phylum? But the question of identity also refers to semiotic questions, namely the way in which a language of any kind - that of advertising, of the industrial designer, as well as of the architect - tries to control the meaning and values of the objects it contributes to bring out in a cultural universe.

In this paper we will compare two answers to this question by placing ourselves within the framework of a reflection on innovation. We will first present a semiotic approach to the question designing multi-viewpoints systems (Sect. 2) and then introduce an innovative design theory that builds its credibility on both the empirical results it achieves and the solidity of conceptual apparatus that it calls for to justify its methodology (Sect. 3). Once the two decors have been set, we go to a conclusion by showing how a semiotic interpretation can be given of the innovation process as modeled by the C-K theory.

2   A Semiotic Approach of Design

In designing business or IT or Space system, a difficult task for the designers who cooperate is to find a common framework where they can efficiently share their knowledge on the same problem. Instead of considering the system they design from a single point of view (e.g. from a functional point of view or from an economical one) we could prefer to consider the system just as a signifying object compatible with all the viewpoints involved in the designing activity [2].

This requirement of interpretability justifies recourse to a particular disciplinary field: namely Semiotics. This requirement is not, of course, a substitute for the requirement of truth, reasonableness, plausibility, or any other kind of requirements that borrows its discourse from a logical theory. It is not a special case either. Thus formulas such as "*the cat is on the carpet*" or "*a boat that can fly*" are open to interpretation without being necessary to rule on their truth value. It is especially up to semiotic theories[1] to account for the conditions under which such formulas manifest their meaning.

According to H Gazendam, the approach that we are to present below is "a knowledge-oriented approach in organisational semiotics by the fact that knowledge is considered as representations or sign structures in the human mind, enabling adequate behaviour of the human actor" [4].

---

[1] There are several semiotic theories. Broadly speaking, those oriented towards the study of signs and their dynamics, whose most important representative is CS Pierce, and those oriented towards the production and interpretation of speeches usually associated with F de Saussure. Greimas and Courtes define semiotics as a theory of signification. Its primary concern will therefore be to explain, in the form of a conceptual construction, the conditions for the grasping and production of meaning [3]. The Hjelmsevian semiotics to which we refer (see below) is clearly on Saussure's side.

2.1   A Multi-viewpoints Semiotics Methodology

Rather than describing the outside world by trying to be as objective as possible, even if it means questioning the description we give of it ex post[2], we will assume that all the descriptions we can produce are always made from particular viewpoints, and the objects that emerge from these descriptions do not pre-exist to these viewpoints and their interactions. This is the epistemological - constructivist - framework we adopt here[3].

In order to give a formal description of viewpoints, our approach refers - at least at start - to the language theory proposed by Danish linguist Louis Hjelmslev (1899–1965), Glossematics. Delving further into the question of Saussurian double distinction between form and substance and content (signified) and expression (significant), [5] proposes an in-depth analysis of the stratified character of the language on which we can build our definitions.

We then define the descriptive concepts, their relations and the operations that can be performed with them. This description constitutes the methodological level of a multi-viewpoints semiotics methodology.

This multi-viewpoints semiotics remains for the moment a methodology, since its epistemological level has not been yet established[4].

2.2   First Definitions

We define a ***viewpoint*** as the correspondence on the content plane, that gives a form, namely a "linguistic value" to a substance[5]:

- Viewpoint: *substance* → linguistic value;
- E.g. Viewpoint of Persian: *sacred animal* → dog (opposed to cat, cow, and so on);
- E.g. Viewpoint of Hindus: *pariah animal* → dog (opposed to cat, cow, and so on).

We need to distinguish between a viewpoint and a view. This is analogous to the distinction between the function f and a value $f(x)$ of this function for the element x.

- e.g. *dog* is a view for *sacred animal* in a Persian's viewpoint;
- e.g. *dog* is a view for *pariah animal* in a Hindu's viewpoint.

A ***view*** is – using the Hjelmslev's terminology – the *manifestation* of the form in the substance: the substance is the *manifestant* and the form is the *manifestatum*. Let us note the relation between *substance* and *form* can also be defined on the *plane of expression*. The opposition between a pronunciation (therefore phonemic *substance*) and a corresponding phonological notation (or a spelling that could be used as such - and therefore a *form*) is an example of such a relation. A viewpoint can therefore be defined also with respect to the plane of expression. Although this could seem odd,

---

[2] Such an attitude will therefore correspond to a realistic scientific approach.

[3] In other words, it is a matter of proposing a theory making it possible to construct semiotic objects.

[4] The main reason is that the notion of "correlation" that is used is based upon the notion of negotiation, which is not yet defined using the notions of this semiotics itself.

[5] For further details, see [5–7]. The examples are due to Hjelmslev himself in [5].

there is no problem with that since the two plane are according to Hjelmslev, equivalent,

We define the ***confrontation of two viewpoints*** by the semiotic function (or semiosis) between the two planes (Fig. 1).

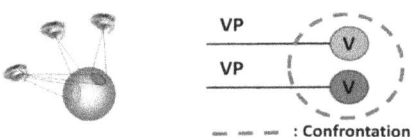

Fig. 1. Confrontation of viewpoints.

Two features of that semiotics need to be underlined. **F1:** A view cannot exist apart from a confrontation of viewpoints (justification is to be found in [5]); **F2:** A viewpoint can only be analyzed within a confrontation of viewpoints. (This results from the definition of a viewpoint and from F1).

What is empirically observed is the interaction of viewpoints corresponding to the different stakeholders of a project involved in the design of an object. Three cases need to be considered:

Confrontation of viewpoints (VPs): the views produced by each VPs make sense to the others, but are not compatible.

Correlation of viewpoints: After a negotiation process, all VP produce mutually acceptable views (Fig. 2).

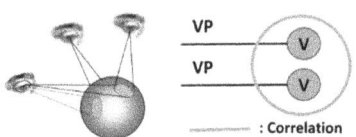

Fig. 2. Confrontation of viewpoints.

Two cases to be considered (empirically observed): (1) All of the considered VPs can evolve during interaction; (2) Only one VP is considered; the interactions with the other VPs are non-evolving processes. These VPs are put between brackets (Fig. 3).

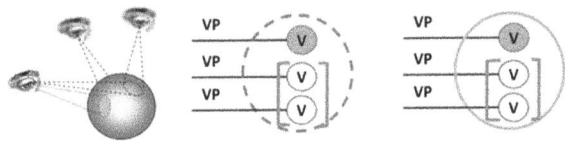

Fig. 3. Viewpoints put between brackets.

The products of these three cases can be used as definitions of *information*, *knowledge* and *data*. Depending on whether there exists a *correlation* or a *confrontation* among all the viewpoints under consideration, we will have either *Modelling Data* or *Schematization Data*. The justifications of these definitions as well as the introduction of this semiotic approach can be found for instance in [7] (Table 1).

Table 1. Types of views according to viewpoints interactions.

	Confrontation of viewpoints	Correlation of viewpoints
All of the considered VPs can evolve during interaction	Information	Knowledge
Only one Vp is considered. These other VPs are put between brackets	Schematization Data	Modelling Data

Let us point out that *scientific data* correspond to *Modelling Data*, whereas *Schematization Data* correspond to the production of a code of **expression** (e.g. a *conceptual graph*) – and not of a content. (See [7]).

The meaning of a view does not have the same practical value according to the context in which it is produced and more precisely according to the question to which it gives an answer. In the following we will try to propose a semiotic interpretation of what is a *question*. In order to do this, we will rely on a typology of ignorance, that is, on what we do not know proposed by Sylvain Bromberger, who defined three types of rational ignorance [8]:

Ignorance of Type 1: 'I know questions whose correct answer I can't tell from incorrect ones: 'What is the distance between London and Paris?', 'How many arithmetic steps are absolutely required in a program for solving a set of linear equa-tions? ', 'What is the Papago word for 'horse'?', 'What is the atomic weight of calcium?". Let us consider the first example. Only the viewpoint of topography which measures the distances between cities is a priori mobilized, independently of any other point of view. Answering a question of this type is tantamount to going from a schematization data with respect to the topographical viewpoint to a modeling data with respect to the same viewpoint (Fig. 4).

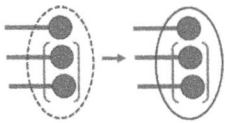

Fig. 4. Ignorance of type 1.

Ignorance of Type 2: 'I know questions to which I know only incorrect answers: e.g. 'What are the heuristics by which a child discovers the grammar of his language?". To know that the answers in the case of S. Bromberger's example are not good, it is necessary that I be able to grasp all the points of view necessary to produce an answer to the question[6]. Answering a question of this kind is tantamount to moving from a confrontation of points of view to a correlation of those same points of view (Fig. 5).

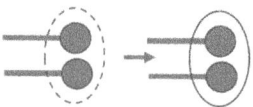

Fig. 5. Answer to an ignorance of type 2.

Ignorance of Type 3: We know problems that we can't solve: e.g. give some people the percentage of a solution of ethylene glycol in water and its density and they will figure out for you the vapor pressure of that solution at 20 °C. We accept here by hypothesis that there are viewpoints that we do not yet know and that must necessarily be mobilized and correlated both between them and possibly with viewpoints already present, in order to produce a satisfactory response. Answering a question of this type is equivalent to moving from confronting a collection of viewpoints to correlating a new collection of viewpoints, the latter being or not able to include all or part of the first collection (Fig. 6).

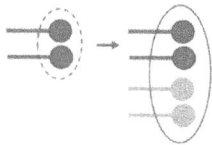

Fig. 6. Answer to an ignorance of type 3.

Let's note that regardless of the type of ignorance, a question corresponds to a confrontation of viewpoints and an answer, to a correlation of theses viewpoints or of a superset of them.

Answering a question can be interpreted as an operation to produce or restore the identity of objects likely to be endowed with different levels of semiotic existences: virtual, actualized, or potential. The restoration of an object identity consisting in restoring or producing a realized semiotic level of existence [9].

It is obvious that it is the third type of ignorance that calls for interdisciplinarity, since it obliges us to mobilize exogenous points of view in relation to the usual multidisciplinary practices[7]. Similarly, breakthrough innovations will correspond to

---

[6] If that **were not** the case, I would have to admit that there are viewpoints that I still do not know and in the absence of which I cannot come up with a satisfactory answer. This situation would then correspond to the third type of ignorance.

[7] If one must be careful not to assimilate a viewpoint and a discipline, one can admit that the exercise of a scientific or technical discipline mobilizes viewpoints when it is analyzed at the semiotic level.

responses to this type of ignorance. It should nevertheless be noted here that innovation has the particularity of involving the creation of financial, economic value in the broadest sense, ethical and so on.

3 C-K Theory, a Theory of Innovative Design

We will now introduce an innovative design theory initiated by Armand Hatchuel and Benoît Weil: The C-K theory. Why do we choose this theory? It is today one of the most cited theories of innovative design. It has had an impact far beyond the scope of innovation management [10].

But what further justifies our interest, however, is the way in which the methodology at work in this theory is interpreted in the semiotic framework we introduced[8]. The difference lies at the level of theoretical foundations or epistemological framework: mathematical in one case[9], semiotic in the other. Besides, the C-K theory shares with the semiotic approach presented the characteristic of questioning the identity of the objects it designs

We have not enough room in this paper to offer a comprehensive presentation of the C-K theory. We will refer the reader to the above reference. We will mention the elements that are useful for our purpose.

3.1 Assumptions and Definition of Design

The four following points are quotation of [10]:

1. "We call K, a "knowledge space", the space of propositions that have a logical status for a designer D. This space is always neglected in the literature, yet it is impossible to define design without such referring space.
2. We call "logical status of a proposition", an attribute that defines the degree of confidence that D assigns to a proposition. In standard logic, propositions are "true or false". In non-standard logic, propositions may be "true, false, or undecidable" or have a fuzzy value. A Designer D may use several logics. What matters in our approach is that we assume that all propositions of K have a logical status whatever it is, and we include here as a logical status all non-standard logical systems. In the following, we will assume for simplicity reasons that in K we have a classic "true or false" logic. But the theory holds independently of the logic retained.
3. We call "concept", a proposition, or a group of propositions that have no logical status in K. This means that when a concept is formulated it is impossible to prove that it is a proposition of K. In Design, a concept usually expresses a group of properties qualifying one or several entities. If there is no "concept" Design is reduced to past knowledge.

---

[8] Since the C-K theory is interdisciplinary in its application, it remains *a priori* compatible with a multi-views points approach.

[9] It is not possible to develop here this mathematical framework. See [11].

4. Definition 1 of Design: assuming a space of concepts C and a space of knowledge K, we define Design as the process by which a concept generates other concepts or is transformed into knowledge, i.e. propositions in K".

3.2   The Dual Dynamics of Design

Let us consider the following design task: design a "new tyres (for ordinary cars) without rubber". We use here an example borrowed from [11]. We define successively the initial *concept* and *knowledge* attached to this case.

Concept: *"there exists a (non empty) class of tyres for ordinary cars without rubber"* is a concept as it can be assumed as undecidable within our present knowledge.

Knowledge: Existing tyres for ordinary cars are all made with rubber and there are no existing, or immediately constructible, tyres without rubber. Moreover, no established and invariant truth forbids the existence of such new objects that we call "no-rubber tyres"

Therefore *"no rubber tyres"* form a class that corresponds to a formula that is undecidable in K and is indeed a concept.

Proving the indecidability of the existence of a class of object such as "no-rubber tyres", with respect to the available knowledge is called a ***disjunction operation from K to C***.

[10] introduce then "expansions" in both K and C:

- "In K, we can attempt to "expand" the available knowledge (intuitively, it means learning and experimenting) if we want to reach a decidable definition of the initial concept
- In C we can attempt to add new properties to the first concept in order to reach decidability. This operation, which we call a partition is also an expansion of the definition of the designed object [...].

Assume that the concept of "non-rubber tyres" is partitioned by the type of material that replaces rubber. This depends of the knowledge we have in K about materials: for instance, plastics, metal alloys and ceramics. Thus we have three possible partitions: "non-rubber tyres with plastics", "non-rubber tyres with metal alloys" and "non-rubber tyres with ceramics". These partitions may create new objects. And testing these partitions may lead to new knowledge in K, for instance new types of plastics, or new materials that are neither plastics, metal alloys or ceramics!"

"In C-K theory, it is crucial to distinguish between two types of partitions in space C: expanding and restricting ones":

- A partition is called an expanding partition if it attempts to expand the definition in our example of tyres by creating new tyres, which are different from existing ones
- A partition is called a restricting partition if it acts act as selectors among existing objects in K, for instance "tyres with white rubber".

"Expanding partitions have two important roles:

- They revise the definition of objects and potentially create new ones; they are a vehicle for intentional novelty and surprise in design;

- They guide the expansion of knowledge in new directions that cannot be deduced from existing Knowledge".

"A design solution is the concept Ck is the first concept to become a true proposition in K". Proving that corresponds to a **conjunction operation from C to K.**

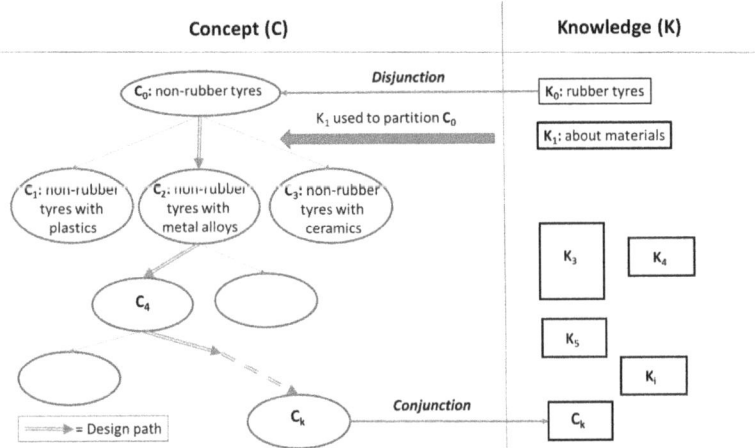

Fig. 7. C-K Diagram (from [11]).

4 Conclusion: Toward a Semiotic Interpretation of the Innovation Process

The semiotic framework we have presented, allows us to propose a semiotic interpretation of the innovation process as modeled by the C-K theory (Fig. 7).

A *concept* in C-K theory will corresponds to a *view* that is produced during the *confrontation of a collection of viewpoints*. If we admit that a part of these viewpoints are put in parenthesis, this view corresponds to a *schematization data*.

The fact that in the example we mentioned, the class of "non rubber tyres for ordinary cars" can be seen as a special kind of set, called C-set, for which the existence of elements is K-undecidable, *is not* an issue in semiotic approach: the signification of a view is independent of its semantic or logical acceptability.

Expanding partition C-K theory generate new objects through chimeras and "crazy" concepts. From a semiotic point of view expanding partition summon (a) knowledge (views) that everyone can have about an object such a tyre and (b) a viewpoint that is usually correlated with other viewpoints that produce views about a tyre. In other words, according to our definitions, a *"tyre without rubber"*, produce a modelling piece of data with respect to the viewpoint of *materials*.

According to C-K theory an ontology of design such as the one proposed by this theory needs a dynamic frontier between **invariant ontologies** (viz. about the physical world) and **designed ontologies**. Since, according to us, the question pertains to semiotics, there is no formal boundary between an invariant ontology and a designed ontology. From a semiotic point of view, the differences between the two types of ontologies depends on the viewpoint that is adopted to analyzed the viewpoints that are correlated on one hand – among them *physical viewpoints* – and the *viewpoints that enter in a confrontation* on the other hand – and that required to be correlated in order to produce objects belonging to a designed ontology.

In C-K theory **voids in knowledge,** should not be confused with the usual "**lack of knowledge**" about something that already exists or is well defined. This distinction corresponds from a semiotic point of view, to two types of ignorance that we have already considered. Two semiotic operations are therefore needed to produce a "piece" of knowledge in each case. As we saw above, the second case corresponds to the mobilization of new viewpoints – as well as already existing ones – in order to produce new semiotic objects and new pieces of knowledge.

These considerations of a sort should be in the future extended to further aspects of the C-K theory.

References

1. Le Masson, P., Weil, B., Hatchuel, A.: Strategic Management of Innovation and Design. Cambridge University Press, Cambridge (2010)
2. Galarreta, D.: Designing space systems in multi-viewpoints semiotics. In: Liu, K. (ed.) Virtual, Distributed and Flexible Organisations. Springer, Dordrecht (2004). https://doi.org/10.1007/1-4020-2162-3_16
3. Greimas, A.J., Courtés, J.: Semiotics and Language: An Analytical Dictionary. Indiana University Press, Bloomington (1983)
4. Gazendam, H.W.M.: Organizational Semiotics: a state of the art report. Semiotix, vol. 1, no. 1, 23 March 2004. http://www.semioticon.com/semiotix
5. Hjelmslev, L.: La stratification du langage. Essais Linguistiques. Editions de Minuit, Paris, pp. 45–77 (1971)
6. Galarreta, D.: A semiotic approach of contexts for pervasive systems. In: 12th International Conference on Informatics and Semiotics in Organisations IFIP WG8.1 Working Conference University of Reading, UK (2010)
7. Galarreta, D.: Are things, objects? A semiotic contribution to the web of things. web of things, people and information systems. In: 14th International Conference on Informatics and Semiotics in Organisations (ICISO 2013). IFIP WG8.1 Working Conference, Stockholm, Sweden (2013)
8. Bromberger, S.: On What We Know We Don't Know. Explanation, Theory, Linguistics and How Questions Shape Them. University of Chicago Press, Chicago (1992). Center for the study of Language and information
9. Galarreta, D.: Approche sémiotique de la multidisciplinarité: contribution à l'analyse de l'interrogation d'un système à base de connaissances multidisciplinaires, Rochebrune (2014). http://www.gemass.fr/dphan/rochebrune14/index.html. Accessed 18 Apr 2018
10. Hatchuel, A., Weil, B.: A new approach of innovative design: an introduction to C-K theory. In: International Conference on Engineering Design ICED 03, Stockholm (2003)
11. Hatchuel, A., Weil, B.: Design as forcing: deepening the foundations of C-K theory. In: International Conference on Engineering Design ICED 07, Paris (2007)

Norm-Based Approach to Incorporate Human Factors into Clinical Pathway: Reducing Human Error and Improving Patient Safety

Jasmine Tehrani[1(✉)], Vaughan Michell[2], and Yu-Chun Pan[3]

[1] University of Bedfordshire, Luton LU1 3JU, UK
Jasmine.hajrezatehrani@beds.ac.uk
[2] University of Reading, Reading RG6 6UR, UK
v.a.michell@henley.ac.uk
[3] University of West London, London W5 5RF, UK
yu-chun.pan@uwl.ac.uk

Abstract. Patient safety and accidental harm or iatrogenic errors are increasingly important healthcare issues resulting in high costs and mortality. The way clinical workflow and actions are communicated can impact patient safety. Although much work has been done to identify the individual human factors and recommendations are made to control and reduce human factor errors, little work has been done to provide a structured methodology to analyse and control human factor influencing patient safety outcomes. In this paper, we build on the previous work on automatic development of clinical pathways, semiotic approach to modelling norm-base clinical pathways and propose a Human Factor Failure Modes and Effects Analysis (HFMA) which offers a systematic approach to define, design and incorporation of human factors into formal design of clinical pathways. Organisational semiotics methods specifically NAM and SAM are applied to identify and analyse controls to reduce the adverse impact of human factors in healthcare settings. This is achieved through modelling and integration of human factors into clinical pathways. This will result in more rigorous control the care process ensuring completeness, consistency and patient safety by enabling the mapping of formal and informal/ safety controls into clinical pathways.

Keywords: Clinical pathways · Process modelling · Organizational semiotics
Norm analysis · Information system · Human factors

1 Introduction

The challenge of achieving significant improvements in patient safety is one of the key tasks facing healthcare at the start of the 21st century. There is broad international agreement on the nature of the task faced and the importance of achieving improvements to quality in this area [1]. Large numbers of people continue to be successfully cared for and treated in the National Health Service, but a significant number of errors and other forms of harm occur. It is calculated that around 10% of patients admitted to NHS hospitals are subject to a patient safety incident and that up to half of these

K. Liu et al. (Eds.): ICISO 2018, IFIP AICT 527, pp. 73–82, 2018.
https://doi.org/10.1007/978-3-319-94541-5_8

incidents could have been prevented [2]. Medical errors are also a serious and challenging issue in the United States. According to the Institute of Medicine 's (IOM's) recent report, To Err Is Human: Building a Safer Health System (1999), between 44,000 and 98,000 people die in hospitals each year as the result of medical errors. Human factors in the provision of health is responsible for a major part of safety problems since the care activity is handled by practitioners and their ability to process multiple pieces of contradictory information is limited. Therefore, safety in medicine is a rapidly developing field and several interdisciplinary research groups have investigated the effect of human and organisational factors on the reliability of healthcare delivery. The latest survey of published work on human factors disclosed that the estimated contribution of human error to accidents in hazardous technologies increased fourfold from the 1969 [4]. The human factors community has developed a variety of methods which are beginning to be adopted in healthcare setting [3]. One of the main tools developed to manage the care quality in healthcare setting are Clinical pathways (CP), also known as care pathways. It is proven that their implementation reduces the variability in clinical practice and improves outcomes. Despite the substantial improvements in modelling and generation of CPs, there is very little account for human factors [14].

This paper builds on previous work on clinical pathway modelling by presenting a normative approach to the analysis and integration of human factors in to clinical pathways in order to accommodate exceptions which have not been dealt with by other conventional methods [23]. The proposed methodology provides a robust mechanism to analyse human factor failure points and to identify and model the controls in to formal process models e.g. CPs. Norm Analysis Method (NAM) is adopted to analyse patterns of behavior and decision-making models of clinicians and the condition under which the behavior will occur. This mechanism is crucial for conceptualizing and developing personalized clinical pathways which describes the conditions and temporality of human factor failure modes.

2 Norm Based Approach for Incorporating Human Factors into Clinical Pathways

In this research, a semiotics method, namely, norm analysis method is chosen to compliment BPMN to enable the modelling of behavior. NAM is used to capture rules, regulations and condition under which every action of an agent is legal, acceptable or prohibited. The norms define a culture or subculture. In a system of agnets, norms reflect regularities in the behaviour of members allowing co-ordination of their actions. Norms are developed through practical involvements of agents in a society and have purposes of directing, coordinating and controlling movements within society [16]. It is proposed that extension of BPMN with norms enables the modelling of modelling a complex business processes. Every activity is made up of one or more norms. Hence it might be difficult to view the relationships between the norms, and how they interact with each other. To improve the practical ability of norms, this research extends the description of process models with norms as a reasonable mechanism to enable the modelling of business dynamics.

Norms define business rules that are imposed on the particular process [22]. For example, in Table 1, Norm N1 reflects rules that must be followed during VTE assessment. Norm N2 includes both the business rules and an exception that will be triggered (caused) when pressure ulcer assessment action has been invoked. Besides handling the business rules and exceptions, the norm provides a degree of flexibility that allows the analysts to model exceptional and alternative situations where decisions are made solely based on human judgment. For example, when performing pressure ulcer risk assessment, if patient develops ulcer during his hospital stay, the nurse is advised to arrange clinical photography. However, the final decision making is solely based on the human agent's judgment. The extension is carried out by incorporating norms into the business process diagram. In the diagram, each control condition is labelled as [N#] where # is the number for identification. The labels are then elaborated in the norm specifications to indicate the condition, the actor and action to be undertaken.

Table 1. Example of norms in a clinical pathway.

Norm No.	Definition
Norm N1	Whenever \<the patient is assessed for venous thromboembolism\> If \<there is bleeding risk \> Then \<doctors\> is \<permitted\> to \<prescribe prophylaxis\>
Norm N2	Whenever \<performing pressure ulcer risk assessment\> If \<Pressure Ulcer is classified as extensive destruction \> Then \<nurse\> is \<obliged\> to \<place patient on a Bi- Wave mattress\>
Norm N3	Whenever \<performing pressure ulcer risk assessment\> If \<patient develops a pressure ulcer during this hospital stay\> Then \<nurse\> is \<permitted\> to \<arrange clinical photography\>

3 Human Failure

Human rather than technical failures now represent the greatest threat to healthcare settings. Managing the human risks will never be 100% effective. Human fallibility can be moderated, but it cannot be eliminated. It is inevitable that errors will occur in healthcare, as they do in other safety critical industries, because they are an intrinsic human trait [18]. An acceptance of this position towards safety, can lead to the achievement of significant improvements in improving safety measures [26]. In recent years, the focus within adverse event analysis, situations in which error and other forms of harm occur, in safety critical industries have moved from a propensity for individual blame to a systems approach. In fact, accepting the fact that people are liable to make errors, system and equipment design, training and other aspects of the work environment are given priority in terms of initiating change to minimise the risk. Furthermore, achieving improvement in patient safety is not possible unless human factors are placed at the heart of improving clinical, managerial and organisational practice leading to improvements in patient safety. Of particular attention is the inner model of clinician's thinking and decision-making models adopted in challenging health provision circumstances, which centres around a complex series of interactions and team-based activities between practitioners and patients as well as numerous technological instruments and information systems that aid decision making and streamline care delivery process. There have been several attempts to include human factors in the analysis of medical errors and patient safety issues. James Reason analysed conditions under which human factors can contribute safety failures and proposed a generic model of accident causation [19]. Chang et al. conducted a series of similar studies and presented an evaluation of existing patient safety terminologies and classifications and grouped the findings into five complementary root nodes: impact, type, domain, cause and prevention [8]. Although various integrated models of error have been produced, few if any focus on the detailed categorisation of the wide range of specific human factors that contribute to error. However, the SHEEP model, was developed from analysis of human factor course participants to identify human factor categories and types that have a bearing on clinical actions [27].

4 Human Factors

Human factors encompass all factors that can influence people and their behavior. One simple definition is design for human use [9]. Chapanis defines human factors as a body of information about human abilities, limitations and characteristics that are relevant to the design process. In a work context, human factors are the environmental, organisational and job factors, and individual characteristics that influence behavior at work. Human factors in the provision of health is responsible for a major part of safety problems since the care activity is handled by practitioners and their ability to process multiple pieces of contradictory information is limited. Therefore, safety in medicine is a rapidly developing field and several interdisciplinary research groups have investigated the effect of human and organisational factors on the reliability of healthcare delivery [9].

5 Failure Mode and Effects Analysis

We have seen how human behaviour and human factors contribute to errors and their risk. Errors come together at the confluence of the organisation, workplace and person in the process. They are typically combatted by identifying the risks of process failure in terms of both the planned process and how the execution may differ in practice. The

Failure Mode and Effects Analysis method of identifying failures in products and processes has been widely used both in industry and in medicine [8]. In summary it involves the identification of the ways in which a process can fail and the apportioning of the risk via the probability a failure of this kind (P), the impact of the failure (I) and the possibility of detection (D). Each of these metrics is typically measured on a scale of 1–10 and then multiplied to provide an overall risk number as high as 1000 as a ranking measure of the risk [27]. Typically, any factor > 7 is considered a high risk factor contributor. FMEA assumes a process model or documentation is available and that events leading to failure can be identified and that remedial risk reduction actions are also identifiable [19].

6 Human Failure Modes and Effects Analysis (HFMEA)

Most FMEA analysis covers human and technology error, but rarely classifies human factors. In this paper, an extension of FMEA is proposed for clinical risks management by identifying a set of human factor potential failure modes hence the proposed methodology is called Human Factors Modes and Effects Analysis (HFMEA). Due to the nature of human error, there are innumerable ways in which human factors can impact a process making it extremely difficult to identify all the potential human factors driven failures and risk protection measures. However, using HFMEA three initial levels of risk are identifiable:

- High: 7+ the patient may die, requiring emergency intervention
- Medium: score 4–6 the patient is impacted resulting in additional significant intervention
- Low 1–3: the patient is inconvenienced resulting in minor changes in intervention to arrive at the original intervention goals to reduce the potential human factors failures to a manageable set to analyse we consider only the high-risk patient related activities.

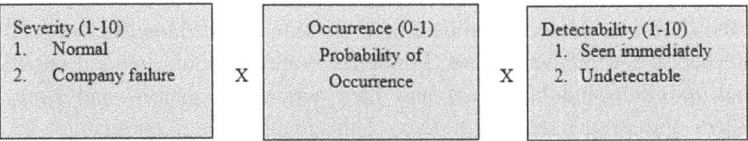

Fig. 1. Failure Mode and Effects Analysis

A high-risk patient activity is considered as an activity where one mistake could lead to a massive adverse impact (I > 7) on the patient if a key action was mistaken. i.e. '1 step to disaster'. For example, miscalculating the quantity of a lethal drug to give an overdose, removing the wrong organ. Patient high risk activities also have low detection rates or few steps in which they are detected as a result of few or poor control norms i.e. D > 7. But how is P > 7 identified. For example, anesthetists and nurses routinely administer lethal drugs with very few failures and hence P ≪ 1 or 2. This is often because the routine nature of the task is just that and there is no significant change in routine leading to unexpected actions or a reduction in perception, evaluative or cognitive capability. As Reason asserts it is often events and unfamiliar or unprepared for situations that give rise to safety errors [19]. The key to how P, the probability of a patient safety risk occurring, might suddenly increase is to identify the conditions under which P will drastically increase due to the removal of 'normal' safety measures as a result of a change in the situation or human behavior. This requires identification of the human factor failure points and the controls employed in the formal process – typically a codified clinical pathway. If we can define these high-risk points for each elective clinical process, we can then define the human factor behaviors that could lead to the catastrophic result and design countermeasures to them. An excellent example is the risk of cabin pressure due to external cabin doors not being correctly locked resulting in the now universal safety control countermeasure of ensuring each cabin crew member that checks a door check their opposite number's doors are safely locked or unlocked.

6.1   Controls

Errors can be reduced via the use of controls at the individual, process and organisational level. Sadiq et al. (2000), suggest the need to ensure a systematic approach to business objectives and control objectives in process design. Although Sadiq's focus was compliance controls, it applies equally well to error controls. Our research suggests there is rarely a systemic approach in clinical pathway design and specifically less to error control design. What is needed is explicit analysis and modelling of the process and defined and reasoned control objectives against a defined clinical risk and set of internal controls to reduce the risk. What often happens is that for clinical processes controls in the form of checklists etc. are often added after errors occur and a root cause analysis occurs as a system of reminders to prevent [31].

6.2   Predictive Controls

The use of FMEA or other methods can produce a set of 'predictive error control points' where predictive controls are defined as controls able to be set up for a known process ahead of time to catch predicted failures. Many procedures are designed around predictive controls with checkpoints. Predictive controls require a good knowledge of the actual activities and behaviors and their variations, actions and states of the stakeholders and known failure modes. This enables the identification of control objectives and needed controls at appropriate risk points. Predictive controls can be modelled as control norms in the human to human interactions and human to information system interactions and hence can only really be applied well to elective surgery in reliable conditions [23].

The use of FMEA or other methods can produce a set of 'predictive error control points' where predictive controls are defined as controls able to be set up for a known process ahead of time to catch predicted failures. Many procedures are designed around predictive controls with checkpoints. Predictive controls require a good knowledge of the actual activities and behaviors and their variations, actions and states of the stakeholders and known failure modes. This enables the identification of control objectives and needed controls at appropriate risk points. Some of the predictive controls are: Process controls: decision points and loops, human monitoring points, Machine monitoring points and memory cues, action sequence rule/knowledge cues. Predictive controls can be modelled as control norms in the human to human inter-actions and human to information system interactions and hence can only really be applied well to elective surgery in reliable conditions.

6.3 Personal Controls

We define a second set of controls as personal controls. We define personal controls as informal control rules or heuristics - i.e. behavioral norms used by the individual to ensure the correct outcome of actions. Personal controls are informal as they are tacit and not formally codified by the organisation. Personal controls depend on the indi-vidual's character and self-discipline for their introduction and are typically the result of experience and concern about the outcome of an activity. They are part of the individual's set of behavioral norms [22]. For example, one interviewee on a patient safety survey always verbally repeated drug volume and strength information and asked for a second check whenever they knew themselves to be tired and hence the possibility of a perception or epistemic error was reduced. However, the enactment of her 'personal patient safety control norm' depends on her discipline and awareness, or 'strength of character', also subject to human factor failings such as stress. Hence the need for personal controls.at stress points or points of high risk needs to be highlighted within clinical pathways.

6.4 Culturally Driven Controls

A third set of controls is culturally driven controls resulting from national, organisa-tional, professional, or team driven learnt and repeated behaviors. These relate to cultural norms. As Reason asserts organisational methods, actions and traditional working practices can create a communal safety culture. The existence of cultural norm beliefs and accepted behaviours creates discomfort and dissonance if the cultural behaviour or belief is violated. However, it can be difficult to measure or define a safety culture and the 'norms' of safety behaviour. Repeated training, examples and practice and consistent control behaviour can develop cultural controls. Cultural controls can be developed through human factors training and repeated application of good practices and reflection.

7 Risk Alleviation Norms to Improve Patient Safety Outcomes

As discussed earlier in this chapter, generally clinical pathways refer to medical guidelines. However, a single pathway may refer to guidelines on several topics in a well specified context. CP is a management tool based on evidence-based practice for a precise group of patients with a foreseeable clinical course, in which the different tasks by the professionals involved in the patient care process are defined and sequenced either by hour (ED), day (acute care) or visit (homecare). Outcomes are tied to specific interventions. Clinical pathways (integrated care pathways) can be seen as an application of process management thinking to the improvement of patient healthcare. An aim is to recentre the focus on the patient's overall journey, rather than the contribution of each specialty or caring function independently. Instead, all are emphasised to be working together, in the same way as a cross-functional team.

In the healthcare domain, the clinical pathways can be seen as the norms developed through the practical medical experiences of healthcare professionals, since they have functions of directing, coordinating and controlling actions in the healthcare process. These norms will provide guidance for medical care staff staffs to determine whether certain medical behaviours at any given time. For clinical pathway design, these norms are analysed, captured and integrated in to the formal organisational process e.g. clinical pathways serving as a basis for designing norm-base clinical pathways that improves patient safety outcomes by addressing formal/informal human factors that influence patient safety outcomes. We use the notion of norms to analyse and formally structure informal/human factors that influence patient safety outcomes. These norms are called risk alleviation norms, which then integrated into clinical pathways design using the normative approach to incorporate human factors in clinical pathways. In the following sections, the methodology for analysing and structuring of human factors affecting patient safety outcome is described in detail. The HFMEA method, described in previous section, is used as an essential part of this mythology to enable the identification of high risk points within the pathway. Subsequently, after identification of high risk points for each elective clinical process, we can then define the human factors behaviours that could lead to the catastrophic result and design countermeasures to them.

8 Extension of Clinical Pathways with Risk Alleviating Norms

Norm analysis method is applied to the analysis and formalisation of human factors. Human factors or factors of human behaviour are a key adverse influence on how clinicians behave, think, make judgements and perceive the world. Although much work has been done to identify the individual human factors and recommendations regarding behaviours to control and reduce human factors errors, little work has been done to provide a structured approach to analyse and develop the human factor behaviour. Hence in this research, a normative approach to regulate and control the effects of human factors on patient safety by modelling and embedding them within clinical pathways as the formal work process models is proposed. The stages involved in this methodology are described in figure below. As it can be seen in Fig. 1, using HFMEA the high-risk points with the formal process map are identified and each high risk point is further organised into high, medium and low risk patient activity. For high risk points within the process map, risk alleviating norms are used to and integrated into the formal process map to reduce the impact of failure on patient. Using risk alleviating norms, controls are introduced and formally integrated into the clinical pathway design.

9 Conclusion

This paper presented a background to the current application of clinical pathways in hospitals and presented a case for the need to consider human factors if significant improvement in patient safety outcomes are intended. It is argued that integration of human factors in clinical pathways design will have a significant role in improving patient safety. In this research, we have built on the previous work on modelling the dynamic behavior of business organisations by presenting a methodology for extending business process modelling notation with norms to enable the modelling the dynamics of business processes and to accommodate exceptions which have not been dealt with by other conventional methods [22, 23]. Norm analysis is adopted as the method for modelling the dynamics of patterns of behaviour which are defined as shared a set of 'norms' which govern how members of the society behave, think, and make judgment [3]. The proposed methodology addresses social and informal/safety factors, which conspire together to influence the outcome of patient safety. To this end, a semiotics-oriented method that adopts organisational semiotics methods, in particular, SAM and NAM are proposed. Semantic analysis method is applied to explicitly represent the semantics of the concepts, their relationships and patterns of behaviour, which offers a basis for analysing human/Informal factors in healthcare setting. Moreover, an extension of FMEA approach is proposed that enables incorporation of human factors failure modes and effects analysis into formal description of clinical pathways (HFMEA). This is the main contribution of this paper which provides a comprehensive platform for analysis and formal strutting of human factors in forms of failure modes and their incorporation into clinical pathways.

References

1. Milligan, F.J.: Establishing a culture for patient safety-the role of education. Nurse Educ. Today **27**(2), 95–102 (2007)
2. Shaw, R., et al.: Adverse events and near miss reporting in the NHS. BMJ Qual. Saf. **14**(4), 279–283 (2005)
3. West, M.A., Guthrie, J.P., Dawson, J.F., Borrill, C.S., Carter, M.: Reducing patient mortality in hospitals: the role of human resource management. J. Organ. Behav. **27**, 983–1002 (2006)
4. Hollnagel, E.: Reliability of Cognition: Foundations of Human Reliability Analysis. Academic, London (1993)
5. Abidi, S.S.R., Chen, H.: Adaptable personalized care planning via a semantic web framework. In: 20th International References (2006)
6. Cabitza, F., Simone, C., Sarini, M.: Knowledge artifacts as bridges between theory and practice: the clinical pathway case. In: Ackerman, M., Dieng-Kuntz, R., Simone, C., Wulf, V. (eds.) Knowledge Management In Action. ITIFIP, vol. 270, pp. 37–50. Springer, Boston, MA (2008). https://doi.org/10.1007/978-0-387-09659-9_3
7. Carthey, J.: Clarke, Julia Field, Campaign; Associate (Safer Care Priority Programme), NHS Institute For Innovation And, Improvement 2010. Leadership for Safety: Implementing Human Factors In Healthcare (2010)

8. Chang, A., Schyve, P.M., Croteau, R.J., O'leary, D.S., Loeb, J.M.: The JCAHO patient safety event taxonomy: a standardized terminology and classification schema for near misses and adverse events. Int. J. Qual. Health Care **17**, 95–105 (2005)
9. Chapanis, A. (ed.): Human Factors in Systems Engineering. Systems Engineering. Wiley, Hoboken (1996)
10. Forster, P.: To err is human. Ann. Hum. Genet. **67**, 2–4 (2003)
11. Helmreich, R.L.: On error management: lessons from aviation. BMJ: Br. Med. J. **320**, 781 (2000)
12. Hurley, K.F., Abidi, S.S.R.: Ontology engineering to model clinical pathways: towards the computerization and execution of clinical pathways, pp. 536–541. IEEE (2007)
13. Liu, K.: Semiotics in Information Systems Engineering. Cambridge University Press, Cambridge, New York (2000)
14. Liu, K., Dix, A.: Norm governed agents in CSCW. Citeseer (1997)
15. Liu, K., Sun, L., Barjis, J., Dietz, J.L.G.: Modelling dynamic behaviour of business organisations—extension of demo from a semiotic perspective. Knowl.-Based Syst. **16**, 101–111 (2003)
16. Milligan, F.J.: Establishing a culture for patient safety-the role of education. Nurse Educ. Today **27**, 95–102 (2007)
17. Plege, M., Ciccarese, P., Kumar, A.: Comparing computer-interpretable guideline models: a case study approach (2012)
18. Osborn, S., Williams, S.: Seven Steps To Patient Safety. An Overview Guide For NHS Staff. Londres: The National Patient Safety Agency 2a Edicion, Abril 2004. Consultado, 08 December 2008. http://www.npsa.nhs.uk/nrls/improvingpatientsafety/patient-safety-tools-and-guidance/7steps/
19. Reason, J.: Understanding adverse events: human factors. Qual. Health Care **4**, 80–89 (1995)
20. Sonnenberg, F., Hagerty, C.: Computer-interpretable clinical practice guidelines. Where are we and where are we going, pp. 145–158 (2006)
21. Stamper, R.: Social Norms in Requirements Analysis: An Outline of MEASUR, pp. 107–139. Academic Press Professional Inc, Cambridge (1994)
22. Stamper, R.: The chemistry of society: organisational semiotics as an empirical social science. In: 11th International Conference in Informatics and Semiotics in Organisations, an IFIP Wg8.1 Working Conference, Beijing, China (2009)
23. Tehrani, J., Liu, K., Michel, V.: Semiotics-oriented method for generation of clinical pathways. In: Zhang, Z., Zhang, R., Zhang, J. (eds.) International Conference on Logistics, Informatics and Service Sciences (LISS). Springer, Heidelberg (2012). https://doi.org/10.1007/978-3-642-32054-5_69
24. Vincent, C., Neale, G., Woloshynowych, M.: Adverse events in british hospitals: preliminary retrospective record review. BMJ **322**, 517–519 (2001)
25. Wright, G.H.: Norm and Action: A Logical Enquiry. Humanities Press, London (1963)
26. Vincent, C., Burnett, S., Carthey, J.: Safety measurement and monitoring in healthcare: a framework to guide clinical teams and healthcare organisations in maintaining safety. BMJ Qual. Saf. **23**(8), 670–677 (2014)
27. Michell, V. (ed.) Handbook of Research on Patient Safety and Quality Care Through Health Informatics. IGI Global (2013)

A Framework to Evaluate Semiotic Interoperability for Information Sharing

Shixiong Liu[(✉)] and Weizi Li

Informatics Research Centre, University of Reading, Reading RG6 6UD, UK
{L.s.liu, Weizi.li}@henley.ac.uk

Abstract. Interoperability is the ability of entities in organisation to work together that covers aspects ranging from the technical to the business level. Over the last decades, the interoperability concept and its context have been changing rapidly. It expands from the largely IT-focused area to business-focused area. The evaluation of interoperability is a rising concern in various research domains. There is increasing number of researchers that have been started concentrating on not just digital aspects, but also business related, human related, and social environment related aspects. Our previous investigation reveals in that interoperability issues from those perspectives are becoming a rising concern. When we study information sharing and business collaboration within organisations, the business activities and operations in organisation, which directly affect business performance, are driven by business processes. Therefore, the interoperability between business processes is the key to information sharing assurance. This paper proposes a framework from a new perspective - semiotics perspective, for enhancing interoperability evaluation. The framework derives from a feasibility study that investigates interoperability barriers in organisation. The framework offers the capabilities of analysing, measuring, and assessing the interoperability between business processes.

Keywords: Interoperability evaluation · Semiotic interoperability
Information sharing · Business process

1 Introduction

In the current industrial and economic context, market demand and technological evolution are changing sharply. Organisations seek to become more agile, responsive and competitive. Enterprises tend to maximise their Information Technology investment in order to support information sharing among not only digital systems, but also business processes (Clabby 2003). Panian (2006) summarises two business drivers: (1) the need to consolidate and globalise, which indicates that many leftover mission-critical systems caused by mergers and acquisitions are requiring a better interoperability between them in order to enhance information utilisation; and (2) the search for increased productivity, indicates that collaboration of business processes can aid organisations to increase productivity and to reduce costs. The successful collaboration provides instant operations for organisations, which lead to optimise decision-making processes (Chen et al. 2008; EN/ISO I9439 2003). Successful information sharing also helps stakeholders to manage in responding to the changes (Kaye 2003), and improve

K. Liu et al. (Eds.): ICISO 2018, IFIP AICT 527, pp. 83–93, 2018.
https://doi.org/10.1007/978-3-319-94541-5_9

organisation's agility by providing the flexibility to quickly adapt information systems in order to accommodate growth and meet arisen business challenges. In order to study the effectiveness of the information sharing between digital systems and between business processes in responding to the changes of market demand and technological innovation, the concept of interoperability, which was originally used for evaluating connection of technical devices and integration of ICT systems, is becoming a widely accepted tool for assessing not just the technical integration, but also collaboration in business in the last decade (Liu et al. 2013).

Interoperability is the ability of entities in organisation to work together that covers aspects ranging from the technical to the business level. Over the last decades, the interoperability concept and its context have been changing rapidly. It expands from the largely IT-focused area to business-focused area. The evaluation of interoperability is a rising concern in various research domains. There is increasing number of researchers that have been started concentrating on not just digital aspects, but also business related, human related, and social environment related aspects. Our previous investigation reveals in that interoperability issues from those perspectives are becoming a rising concern. When we study information sharing and business collaboration within organisations, the business activities and operations in organisation, which directly affect business performance, are driven by business processes. Therefore, the interoperability between business processes is the key to information sharing assurance. This paper proposes a framework from a new perspective - semiotics perspective, for enhancing interoperability evaluation. The framework derives from a feasibility study that investigates interoperability barriers in organisation. The framework offers the capabilities of analysing, measuring, and assessing the interoperability between business processes. The paper starts with a recap of previous study on evaluation of semiotic interoperability, and then conducts a feasibility study that adopts organisational morphology to investigate barriers at three layers (i.e. Informal, Formal, and Technical). The identified barriers and its corresponding solutions are consolidated to form a framework – Semiotic Interoperability Evaluation Framework, which is proposed with discussion in the end of this paper.

2   Background

2.1   Semiotic Interoperability Definition

In our previous work (Liu 2015; Li 2013), the concept of semiotic interoperability is defined based on the semiotic framework from organisational semiotics. As introduced the semiotic framework provides a sound theoretical foundation for understanding of the nature of the sign-based communication, and a holistic view about signs, information, systems and organisations (Stamper 1973; Liu 2000). The semiotic interoperability allows information systems to work together through communication, and also enables collaboration of business processes through understanding of intention and social consequence. Figure 1 describes the concept of semiotic interoperability and its functional context at six constituting levels.

Physical interoperability enables seamless communication between senders and receiver handling the physical tokens transmitted via a route at the destination without loss of physical properties. Interoperability at Empiric level is achieved when the receiver can reconstitute the same sequence of symbols that were sent by the sender, irrespective of any problems at the physical level. Interoperability at Syntactic level is achieved when the expression of information, or language, or formula can be recognised by different information systems. The data structures and format of file and message have to be readable to both ends of communication. Semantic interoperability can be achieved to give the same meaning to exchanged information between information systems, and it requires a conceptual model which describes what information is exchanged in terms of concepts, properties, and relationships between these concepts. More specifically, the semantic interoperability not only entails the data to be universally accessible and reusable, but also address the lack of common understanding caused by the use of different semantic representations, different purposes, different contexts, and different syntax-dependent approaches. Interoperability at the pragmatic level ensures that business processes supported by the information systems in individual contexts can be aggregated to achieve the overall intended purpose. It enables the alignment of business workflows, alignment of processes, and alignment of rules. Besides, the pragmatic interoperability also aligns social aspects such as culture, norms, environment, and actor's behaviour patterns in order to solve conflicts of cohesiveness. Interoperability at Social level ensures the intention or purpose of the sender has led to

	Definition	Functional Context & Relevant Methods
Social level	The resultant interoperable digital systems should be coherent with the social commitment, obligation and norms in the organisation and support organisation's strategy, vision and objectives	Alignment in traditions Alignment in policies Alignment in culture Alignment in ethics Alignment in management style Alignment in environment etc.
Pragmatic level	Business processes supported by the digital systems in their individual contexts can be aggregated to achieve the overall intended purpose	Process reengineering Process alignment Rules modelling Knowledge sharing & knowledge repositories Business strategy alignment etc.
Semantic level	Ability of interpreting and converting information into equivalent meaning to allow information sharing between digital systems	Semantic data representation Data standardisation Schema matching Ontology mapping Semantic matching etc.
Syntactic level	Consistence between data formats, structures and programming languages supporting data transmission	Data warehousing Data integration e.g. ETL (Extract, Transform and Load), EDI (Electronic data interchange)
Empiric level	Compatibility between channels and protocols supporting data transmission	Communication systems Messaging systems
Physical level	Connectivity between networks and hardware and devices	Infrastructure standardisation EA (technology layer) and ITIL (Information Technology Infrastructure Library)

Fig. 1. Semiotic interoperability

a social consequence to the receiver, and the social consequence can be social commitment, obligation, and norms. The social interoperability also ensures that those social consequences support the business strategy, vision, objectives, and the business environment. There are a few sub-areas under the topic of social interoperability such as alignment in traditions, alignment in policies, alignment in culture, alignment in ethics, alignment in management style, and alignment in environment (Barbarito et al. 2012; Boonstra et al. 2011; Gregory et al. 2012; Liu et al. 2014 and Saag et al. 2012), those sub-areas cannot represent all the concerns and issues that social interoperability deals with, because the topic is still under investigation and development.

2.2   Evaluating Interoperability Between Business Processes

The focus of this paper is the upper two levels of the semiotic interoperability: pragmatic and social levels. In our previous studies, a review of all existing interoperability evaluation frameworks points out that most of current works have tackled the interoperability issues at the semantic, syntactic, empiric and physical levels (Liu 2014). But very limited amount of works is concentrating on evaluating interoperability at pragmatic and social levels. According to the definition of semiotic interoperability, the pragmatic interoperability is to ensure that business processes supported by the information systems in individual contexts can be aggregated to achieve the overall intended purpose. To evaluate the interoperability between business processes, this thesis deals with the issue from the organisational morphology perspective. As discussed in the first previous sections in this chapter, organisation can be seen as an information system, because information is created, stored, and processed for communication, coordination and achieving the organisational objectives (Liu et al. 2006). From an organisational perspective, information systems are defined by the cultural and legal norms that regulate people's behaviour (Gazendam and Liu 2005). Thus, the definition of organisation is extended to a wider sense such that, a group of people, a society, a culture, do not only share language, customs, and habits, but also participate in the social construction of their own rules. In summary, the organisation is regarded as an informal information system where meanings are established, intentions are understood, beliefs are formed, commitments are made, and responsibilities are negotiated through the decision of physical actions. The organisation morphology categorises those meanings, intentions, beliefs, commitments, and responsibilities into three layers: the formal, the informal, and the technical. Business processes, at the formal layer, plays dominant role that drives business activity and operation, which directly affects business performance. However, the business process cannot be treated in isolation to aspects at other two layers: the informal and the technical. Because the studies in information system have never treated the information system as a set of separate components but considered it as a whole. Thus, the business process also requires supports from both technical and informal layers. According to the definitions given by Li (2010) and Zutshi et al. (2012), business process is a set of activities that occur in a coordinated manner pursuing one common goal. By looking at the entire information system, the activities are dynamic in nature but consider static aspects as well. The dynamic aspects include culture, norms, different behaviour patterns; and the static aspects include technical system capacity, data structure, data transmission, connection etc. Therefore, to evaluate the interoperability between business processes is to evaluate the interoperability at the formal, the informal, and the technical layers. Table 1 describes the key aspects at each layer.

Table 1. Three layers for evaluating interoperability between business processes.

Layer	Description
Informal	Community, social norm, people, policy, culture, ethics, environment, alliances etc.
Formal	Organisational strategy/vision, business governance, domain analysis, organisational roles, functional profile, rules, procedures, management etc.
Technical	Data semantics, information infrastructure, information model, schema, script, interface, platform, deployment model, resources, products etc.

The informal layer contains aspects such as community, social norm, policy, and culture. Those aspects can be expanded to be different behaviour patterns of both organisations and individuals. The interoperability at this layer is to align the different aspects in order to solve conflicts of cohesiveness. In the formal layer, business process plays dominant role that specifies on how functions should be carried out and how tasks should be performed. The interoperability at this layer is to align procedures and rules in order to achieve higher efficiency. It defines business goals, and models business processes, also brings the collaboration of administrations that aims to exchange information and have different internal structures and processes. The technical layer mostly refers to the technical computer systems and the implementation of their services, integration, and functions. The interoperability at this layer is to align technical functions and interfaces ensuring that the implementation has been done properly in order to achieve higher system productivity.

The organisational morphology theory is applied to evaluate interoperability between business processes from three layers: the formal, the informal, and the technical. The three levels are the foundation for developing the framework - Semiotic Interoperability Evaluation Framework (SIEF). Before proposing the SIEF, it is necessary to investigate the feasibility. To conduct a feasibility study, several industrial cases for interoperability evaluation are investigated. The findings of the feasibility study identify concerns and barriers at the three layers when considering interoperability evaluation between business processes and those concerns and barriers will be later transformed into metrics contributing to the SIEF.

3   Findings of Feasibility Study

The feasibility study is mainly conducted through interviews and surveys in a healthcare software company and one of the hospitals in China where the company provides solutions for. The company currently runs an integration project, which aims to enable information sharing among systems such as Radiology Information Systems (RIS), Electronic Health Record (EHR), and Picture Archiving and Communication Systems (PACS). The Radiology department provides diagnostic and interventional radiology for inpatients, outpatients and general practitioner referrals. Various healthcare services such as Computed Radiography (CR), Computed Tomography (CT), X-ray, and Interventional Radiology produce a huge amount of information regarding patient's healthcare delivery and clinical process. Both relevant employees of the company and clinicians in the hospital are selected for the interview.

To select appropriate case, a method developed by Seawright and Gerring (2008) is adopted. Following the method, firstly the selection method is qualitative research approach. Secondly, the goal of the feasibility study is to support the feasibility of the proposed SIEF by conducting interviews. Thirdly, the size of the case is medium enterprise which has approximately 200 employees working on various projects. The project where this case study conducts involves 28 staff, and from the hospital side, 15 clinicians are involved.

To select appropriate interviewees, several criteria are set up for the screening process. Firstly, by working experiences: should have more than 3-year experiences relating to software and systems development for employee; and should have more than 3-year experiences directly using the above information systems for clinicians. Secondly, by technical relevance: should have been directly involved in the development, other supporting roles are not accepted for employee; because the clinician is the user, this criterion does not apply to them.

Following the two criteria, 31 semi-structured interviews (summarised in Table 2) were conducted with relevant stakeholders. The interviews lasted around 40 min and were on a one-to-one basis. The interviews were tape-recorded and later transcribed and rendered anonymously. The questions asked are derived from the SIEF which is presented in the next Chapter. The results of the interviews are summarised into categories presented in the following sections.

Table 2. Summary of interviews

Sectors	Sample	Years of experience				
		3–5	6–10	11–15	16–20	20+
Industry	22	7	11	2	1	1
Hospitals	9	3	2	1	1	2
Total	31	10	13	3	2	3

22 participants from industry have been interviewed: 6 of them are junior-manager level, 10 of them are senior-manager level e.g. senior system architect, project manager; and 6 of them are executive level e.g. CEO, CTO, director of software design, and director of service delivery.

9 participants from hospitals have been interviewed: 4 of them are physicians, 3 of them are radiology technicians, 1 IT manager with 11 years' experiences, and 1 medical administration manager.

The open interview basically asked what concerns and barriers should not be ignored when assessing interoperability from the three layers: the technical, the formal, and the informal. As the purpose of the interview is to investigate the feasibility of interoperability assessment, thus the questions asked aim to gather wide opinions from those participants, and more specific data analysis techniques such as content analysis are not applied. The key results from the interview are summarised in following paragraphs.

To enable collaboration between business processes, a shared intended purpose plays a key role that supports perceiving of personal beliefs and organisational ground rules, whereas an un-shared purpose may be considerable conflicts between the organisational level and personal level. Issues like restriction to staff behaviour, information collaboration (information channels alignment), and privacy and security concerns are raised attentions. Taking one example from one of the interviewed hospital, the informal level is concerned with the understanding of the healthcare, regulatory, legislative and healthcare environment in which information systems need to be deployed to support healthcare delivery. It requires agreement on key organisational concepts such as policies, processes and roles; it also captures relevant patterns such as compliance, governance, legislative and change management. Table 3 summarises the concerns and barriers at informal layer from the interview.

Table 3. Concerns and barriers at informal layer summarised from interview results

Culture issue	Tacit knowledge has not been explicitly stated and shared
Ethical issue	Appropriateness of taking actions on healthcare service delivery
Behavioural factor	Willingness to be open and to share
Management style	Leadership style influencing the degree of willingness of collaboration
Policy and procedure	Internal control process, work flow, staff relationships, communication patterns, cut-across political boundaries, etc.
Restriction to staff behaviour	Staff's fear on integrated working process as restriction that might control their behaviour
Privacy and security	Sensitive information of patient to be protected by law

At Formal layer, the concerns and barriers are collected from the interview and observation are summarised in Table 4. To assess interoperability, we should not only be concerned with information exchanged between technical systems, but also the knowledge of the context that the information exists within each system or process. As quoted from one IT project managers: "…*It is important to articulate the requirement for context awareness that process representation begins. The context of the target system should also be made available to the origin system. Key questions such as what process will first operate on the information at the target system once it receives it, and what state of preceded processes are should be concerned…*" By understanding this context, the system engineer and integration designer can ensure pragmatic interoperability is addressed for the needs of process integration. To define the context, one manager of the logistics department said that *"Assume that the context is about internal workings of the process, in other words, the initialization state, the end state, the nature of data transformations, and details about the timing of the process are all considered, so that the receiving process can make better use of information it receives. This information is in context, but it also shows the dynamic nature of that context to the receiving system, because it now has specific information about the dynamic context within the originating system."*

Table 4. Concerns and barriers at formal layer summarised from interview results

Organisation structure	Centralised, decentralised, hierarchical, matrix, networked, etc.
Harmonized strategy	Aligned operations to be applicable on the strategic level
Performance constraints	Fewer investment but more effective collaboration
Cost constraints	Unexpected budget
Data source interoperability	Multiple data sources used for supporting process
Context awareness	Knowledge of context of both collaborative parties/processes
Varieties of purchased systems	Purchased systems from various venders with low capability

For example, context is seen as a demand for more information between the Model Manufacturing Demand Service and the Rental Fulfilment Service, so that a specific understanding of the models requested has a deeper meaning. This could be a specific based on the timing of the data, the initialization state of the Rental Fulfilment Service, and the data transformations. This gives a more dynamic picture of the context for the information being produced by one process for another, and allows for a deeper understanding of the meaning of that context.

The purpose at technical level is to make exchanged data available for supporting the processes at upper level. For example, in healthcare environment, it is concerned with the understanding of technical functionality for supporting information systems; from a project management perspective, the manager needs to ensure both data and service integration have been successfully implemented beforehand. It requires agreement on a core set of technical concepts, such as technical components and devices, the interactions between components, interface and technical services; it also captures relevant patterns such as technical architecture styles and styles of component interactions. However, the study at this level is not the focus of the interoperability evaluation in this thesis, although this layer is vital to support the understanding the concerns of pragmatic interoperability. Therefore, during the interview, only few concerns regarding technical level are summarised below (Table 5).

Table 5. Concerns and barriers at technical layer summarised from interview results

Semantic heterogeneity	Refers to the variation of semantic meaning in information resources which will lead to the semantic conflicts and complication for data integration
Ontology structure	Approaches that employ ontologies for information systems
Business semantics	Defining ontology and semantic conversion
Ambiguous terminology	Differences in the use of terms across departments
Implementation of data integration	Defining source and target data format; data transformation and mapping; deploy on execution infrastructure
Implementation of service integration	Services for connecting processes and message exchange

4   Semiotic Interoperability Evaluation Framework

Based on the findings from the feasibility study, key barriers are identified while considering the interoperability assessment. The empirical investigation supports the SIEF to derive its associated metrics. Besides, based on the previous works from Li (2010); Liu et al. (2014) and Meyers et al. (2005), and other widely used interoperability evaluation frameworks, the assessment metrics are developed accordingly. Figure 2 presents the SIEF, and there are no explicit borderlines among the technical metrics, formal metrics, and informal metrics.

Technical metric	Formal metric (Performance measure)	Informal metric (Indicator)
Modelling business document	**Business strategy**	
	Clarity in strategic goals	
High-level model	Formal commitment to prevent termination or premature collaboration	**Tradition and culture**
Components model	Backup strategic plan	
Implementation of data integration	**Management of External relationships**	**Management style**
Source and target data format definition	Partner selection Partner assessment Operation contracts	**Religions**
Data mapping and transformation	Conflict resolution Communication	**Appropriateness of taking actions**
Implementation of service integration	**Collaborative business processes management**	**Employee's motivation**
Deployment on execution infrastructure	Clarity in responsibility Business process modelling	
Services for connecting processes	Clarity in business process Process visibility	**Employee's honesty**
Services for message exchange	**IPR management** IPR protection	**Resistance to change**
Business semantics	Potential IPR IPR Conflicts	**Fear of behaviour control by others**
Ontology definition	**Organisational structures**	
Semantic conversion	Role mapping	

Fig. 2. Semiotic Interoperability Evaluation Framework (SIEF)

This paper tends to not view the interoperability assessment separately by levels, but to think it as a whole. The three levels in the SIEF are all concerned with the pragmatic and social levels in the semiotic framework. If there must be borderline in between, then the group of technical and formal metrics, and informal metrics could match the pragmatic and social levels respectively with overlapping. The relation between the metrics in the SIEF and the levels in the semiotic framework is that the pragmatic levels and social levels comprise but not limited to those levels.

Therefore, the interoperability between the two business processes is the combination of the interoperability at the three levels, which can be presented as the Eq. (1):

$$I(P_a, P_b) = I_{Te}(P_a, P_b) + I_{Fo}(P_a, P_b) + I_{In}(P_a, P_b) \qquad (1)$$

$I(P_a, P_b)$:   Interoperability between two processes A and B;

$I_{Te}(P_a, P_b)$:   Interoperability at technical level;

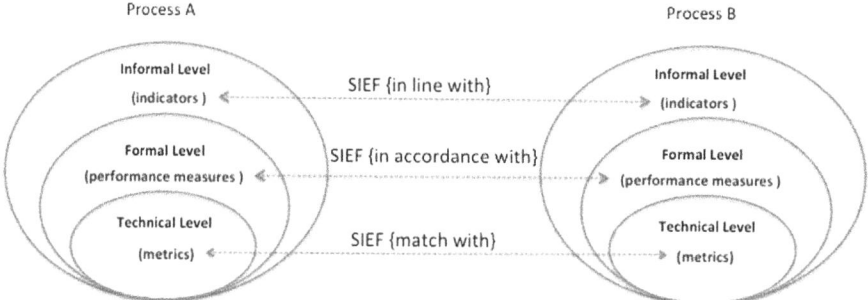

Fig. 3. Interoperability between business process A and B

$I_{Fo}(P_a, P_b)$:   Interoperability at formal level;
$I_{In}(P_a, P_b)$:   Interoperability at informal level.

Figure 3 illustrates how the interoperability evaluation is conveyed between two business processes. In the informal level, the metric is also named indicator, which means the indicators of process A such as the management style, religions, appropriateness of taking actions, employee's motivation, employee's honesty, should be in line with the indicators of process B. in the formal level, the metric is also named performance measure, which means the measures of process A such as clarity in business strategy, backup strategic plan, management of External relationships, clarity in responsibility, should be in accordance with the performance measures of process B. In the technical level, the metrics of process A such as design of services, model of business document, and implementation of data/service integration, should match with the metrics of process B.

5   Conclusion and Future Work

Assessing interoperability is still challenging because those metrics cannot be easily quantified for more specific measurement. As discussed previously, on one hand, the metrics are partly derived from results of the case study, which reflect key concerns and barriers of interoperability; on the other hand, there are also metrics derived from the existing works, which have been explained in the previous section. For each metric/concern/barrier, we have investigated corresponding solutions/methods/tools, which will be used as criteria to evaluate that whether the concern or the barrier has been addressed or not. In this case, to measure each metric, all relevant methods, solutions, and tools will be developed in future work.

References

Barbarito, F., Pinciroli, F., Mason, J., Marceglia, S., Mazzola, L., Bonacina, S.: Implementing standards for the interoperability among healthcare providers in the public regionalized healthcare information system of the Lombardy region. J. Biomed. Inform. **45**(4), 736–745 (2012). https://doi.org/10.1016/j.jbi.2012.01.006

Boonstra, A., Broekhuis, M., Van Offenbeek, M., Wortmann, H.: Strategic alternatives in telecare design: developing a value-configuration-based alignment framework. J. Strateg. Inf. Syst. **20**(2), 198–214 (2011). https://doi.org/10.1016/j.jsis.2010.12.001

Chen, D., Doumeingts, G., Vernadat, F.: Architectures for enterprise integration and interoperability: past, present and future. Comput. Ind. **59**(7), 647–659 (2008). https://doi.org/10.1016/j.compind.2007.12.016

Clabby, J.: Web Services Explained: Solutions and Applications for the Real World. Prentice Hall PTR, Upper Saddle River (2003)

EN/ISO I9439: Enterprise integration—framework for enterprise modelling. Work report (2003)

Gazendam, H., Liu, K.: The evolution of organisational semiotics: a brief review of the contribution of Ronald Stamper. In: Studies in Organisational Semiotics. Kluwer Academic Publishers, Dordrecht (2005)

Gregory, S., Dixon, A., Ham, C.: Health policy under the coalition government: a mid-term assessment Editors. The King's Fund (2012)

Kaye, D.: Loosely Coupled: The Missing Pieces of Web Services. RDS Press, RDS Strategies LLC, Marin County (2003)

Li, W.: The architecture and implementation of digital hospital - information system integration for seamless business process. Ph.D. thesis. Univerity of Reading (2010)

Li, W., Liu, K., Liu, S.: Semiotic interoperability - a critical step towards systems integration. In: International Conference on Knowledge Discovery and Information Retrieval and the International Conference on Knowledge, Management and Information Sharing, 19–22 September 2013, Vilamoura, Algarve, Portugal, pp. 508–513 (2013)

Liu, K.: Semiotics in Information Systems Engineering. Cambridge University Press, Cambridge (2000). https://doi.org/10.1017/CBO9780511543364

Liu, K., Sun, L., Tan, S.: Modelling complex systems for project planning: a semiotics motivated method. Int. J. Gen Syst. **35**(3), 313–327 (2006)

Liu, S., Li, W., Liu, K., Han, J.: Evaluation frameworks for information systems integration: from a semiotic lens. In: Proceedings of 3rd International Conference on Logistics, Informatics and Service Science, Reading, UK, pp. 1333–1340 (2013)

Liu, S., Li, W., Liu, K.: Pragmatic oriented data interoperability for smart healthcare information systems. In: The 14th IEEE/ACM International Symposium on Cluster, Cloud and Grid Computing, Chicago, USA (2014)

Liu, S., Liu, K., Li, W.: Assessing pragmatic interoperability for process alignment in collaborative working environment. In: Proceedings of the 16th IFIP WG 8.1 International Conference on Informatics and Semiotics in Organisations, ICISO 2015, Toulouse, France, 19–20 March, pp. 60–69 (2015)

Meyers, B., Morris, E.: Proceedings of the System of Systems Interoperability Workshop, Software Engineering Institute, Carnegie Mellon University, CMU/SEI-2003-TN-016, pp. 1–37 (2003)

Panian, Z.: Why enterprise system integration is inevitable? WSEAS Trans. Bus. Econ. **2006**, 590–595 (2006)

Saag, K.G., Mohr, P.E., Esmail, L., Mudano, A.S., Wright, N., Beukelman, T., Tunis, S.R.: Improving the efficiency and effectiveness of pragmatic clinical trials in older adults in the United States. Contemp. Clin. Trials **33**(6), 1211–1216 (2012). https://doi.org/10.1016/j.cct.2012.07.002

Seawright, J., Gerring, J.: Case selection techniques in case study research: a menu of qualitative and quantitative options. Polit. Res. Q. **61**(2), 294–308 (2008)

Stamper, R.: Information in Business and Administrative Systems. Batsford, London (1973). http://www.getcited.org/pub/101449585

Zutshi, A., Grilo, A., Jardim-Goncalves, R.: The business interoperability quotient measurement model. Comput. Ind. **63**(5), 389–404 (2012). https://doi.org/10.1016/j.compind.2012.01.002

The Social Layer of Stampers Ladder: A Systematic Approach to the Soft Edge of Organizational Transformations

Auke J. J. van Breemen[1(✉)] and Ralf Nieuwenhuijsen[2]

[1] KiF-advies, Oude Graafseweg 52, 6543PS Nijmegen, The Netherlands
info@KiF-advies.nl
[2] Bibo Trainingen, Van Goorstraat 20, 6512 ED Nijmegen, The Netherlands
ralf@bibotrainingen.nl

Abstract. The social layer of Stampers ladder addresses the problem of responsible agents interacting with each other. It is the layer at which in organizations decisions are made and transformations negotiated. The method we present supports this human interplay. It combines principles of actualism, ontology charts, the knowledge in Formation process model and the Cynefin framework to gather and combine quantitative data with qualitative data, expressing attitudes and perceptions in meaningful diagrammatic representations of business processes. The analytic tool Sensemaker can be used to support decision making.

Keywords: Actualism · Ontology chart · Cynefin
Knowledge in Formation (KiF) · Stakeholder focused modelling
Process · Qualitative and quantitative data · Peircean semiotics

1 Introduction

If *we*, the developers, want to provide *actionable* insight into the human interplay among sign-based world and digital technologies as part of processes of organizational transformation, it is essential that *they*, the users, get insight in what is needed to realize the transformations and can share their experiences with their co-workers. This insight requires that each of the actors is afforded to have an idea of the situation (s)he is acting in and that those ideas are shared where needed. Here we face two alignment issues at once.

The first may be termed vertical alignment. Hoppenbrouwers directs the attention to the human side of information systems building with the distinction between business stakeholders and IT stakeholders. The former being primarily occupied with running the business, the latter with designing, building and maintaining information systems with the risk of misunderstanding and bad performance due to differing goals and conceptual habits in the design stage [1]. Stamper looks at it from a systems side when he proposes his semiotic ladder to distinguish the different levels that must be considered when designing an information system [2].

K. Liu et al. (Eds.): ICISO 2018, IFIP AICT 527, pp. 94–104, 2018.
https://doi.org/10.1007/978-3-319-94541-5_10

The second may be termed horizontal alignment. Its concern is interoperability across (departments of) organizations. Liu et al. following Stampers semiotic framework state that we have semiotic interoperability if signs among systems are successfully communicated in all the six levels Stamper distinguishes. Thus, every sign aspect is covered [3, 4]. Their interest concentrates on five of the six levels: physical world, empirics and syntactics, taken together under the label 'technical', semantic and pragmatic interoperability. This grouping relates their work to the Shannon Weaver distinction in three levels [5] of which the Stamper framework is a refinement from a semiotic perspective. The technical level being formally covered by Shannon's mathematical theory of communication. From there their research climbs the ladder layer by layer, leaving the social layer for the moment unexploited.

Goldkuhl and Ågerfalk remark that it is difficult to distinguish between the pragmatic and social levels on the semiotic ladder because in both signs are produced and such actions are in most cases social actions [6]. It appears that they forget that all levels of the ladder contribute in social actions. Stampers ladder levels are objectifications of sign aspects involved in signs: a word has its qualities (physical), its form and existence (empirics), its combinatory properties (syntactics), its meaning (semantics), its usability (pragmatics) and its habitat (social world). So, all levels of the ladder are involved in the social world, just as Shannon's theory on the technical level is involved in the meaning and effectiveness level. The crux being that it is possible to pay attention to the technical level without taking care of the other levels, but it is not possible, when designing information systems, to pay due attention to the social level without taking account of the involved levels, as the information revolution makes clear.

This leaves us with the question what, if any, the distinguishing characteristics are of the social level of Stampers ladder. Oppl and Hoppenbrouwers provide a good vantage point for an answer with their plea for stakeholder-centric modelling. In [7] they assert that involving business stakeholders in enterprise modelling also helps them to articulate and align their views on their organization. This requires, so they state, that stakeholders must be able to understand and perform conceptual modelling for representing their views on enterprise structure and behavior. I regard this to be part of the vertical view on alignment due to its reliance on the semantical layer and its modelling techniques. At least partly the business stakeholders are drawn into the IT stakeholder's role and must go from their more familiar, informal way of looking at their working situation to a less familiar and more formal approach.

Below we suggest a method that professes to model the social layer. It rests on the assumption that sign processing actors (or stakeholders) are unquestionably to be classified as Information Systems, while IS's are information systems from some perspectives, but also can be viewed as affordances for actors, that are acting in and between organizations, that also can be looked at as actors, for which IS's are affordances.

Since the goal is actionable insight for business stakeholders, we keep our exposition of the method short. In section two we present what we, the developers, could communicate with the (business) project leader who is supposed to be familiar with ontology charts. In section three we describe the KiF-diagram we use with the help of the Cynefin and Sensemaker approach of Snowden. In section four we describe an experimental case study.

2 Actualism, Ontology Charts and Interpretation Processes

Our general model of the social layer for a company starts with the two assumptions of Stampers actualism:

1. No reality without a knowing agent
2. No knowledge of the world without action.

From this we construct the interpretation process [agent or state (a), action or effect (b) >- knowledge or response (c)]. The symbol >- is shorthand for the interpretation process that runs from the event of an effect (b) on an agent in a certain state (a) to its resulting conclusion or response (c). The agent can be relatively simple like a tire responding with a flat when undergoing the effect of a nail, leaving room for a causal explanation. But it can also be complex like a whole company responding to market changes with a reorganization plan. The action likewise can be simple like a nail or itself a manifestation of an agent and complex like another business in B to B transactions. The goal can be concrete like a flat tire, or abstract like business objectives. Abstract goals have their reality in that they tend to co-determine the agent's response on an action in instances of interpretation processes. Abstract goals turn a mechanical process of cause and effect into a triadic relation in which actor, action and goal are the corner stones of a complex process.

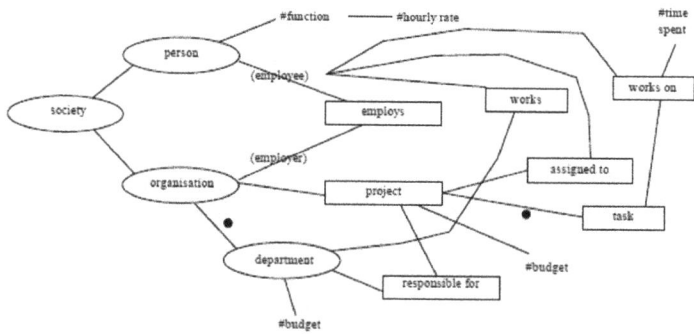

Fig. 1. Ontology chart of project management, cited from Liu [13, p. 79]

For three reasons we will hook our diagrammatic representation of company processes, see below, on the ontology charts of the Semantic Analysis Method (SAM), see Fig. 1:

1. Its definition of an agent as a special kind of affordance, that can be defined as something that performs responsible behavior and can be as diverse as an individual, a (part of) organization, a language group, [...].
2. The dependency relation that is assumed and expressed by taking society as the root node of which all other agents are ontological depended specifications. Both points paraphrased from [8].

3. The correspondence between these notions in our respective approaches enables the connection of the ontology charts of the semantical level with our diagrams on the social level. This suggests the possibility to connect our proposed technical solution with an existing information system.

In the ontology chart of Fig. 1 the ontological dependencies are pictured for *person*, employed by an *organization* for a *department* and assigned to a *project*. In the semantic layer we want to picture the relations between concepts. In the social layer our interest goes to the interactions between the different responsible agents in the execution of their duties. The process definition points the way for a first crude approximation.

Let's say, also as a first introduction of our experimental case below, *organization* is a company that produces complex tools, materials needed in the operation of the tools and some accessories used in the branch they are in. The department in focus is the *sales department* populated with sales representatives, each working a rayon. The project aims at improving the sales. To that end we want insight in the training needs of the sales representatives or in terms of the ontology chart the *person/department* combination. To that end we define the process: Sales Representative (state), Customer (effect) >- Sales (result).

By tracing back to the root node, we find *Organization/Company* as the node on which the sales department ontologically depends. If we take the Management Team as the responsible agents for this node we get the process: MT, business processes >- Performance. Since the goals of the Sales Department are subservient to the overall business goals, the Sales process is an embedded process. Before we show how this can be captured in a meaningful diagram a few words on the node *person* and the reason why it appears on the same level as *organization*.

Suppose that instead of a chart for project management, we want to make an ontology chart for the different organizations a given person contributes to. Besides company, family is an obvious candidate, but also sportive, religious and political organizations are candidates. Each organization has goals the person tries to contribute to in one way or another. And, let's not forget the persons self-interest as a goal pursued. Relevant conflicts of interest may result, and responsibility of agents becomes a subject.

3   The Cynefin Framework, KiF-Diagrams and Sensemaker

The Cynefin Framework, see Fig. 2 left, originates with Kurz and Snowden. The framework offers five contexts in which persons that must make decisions can find themselves to be. It is used primarily "[…] to consider the dynamics of situations, decisions, perspectives, conflicts, and changes in order to come to a consensus for decision-making under uncertainty." It does not aim to categorize a situation but assists in making sense by sharing perceptions [9].

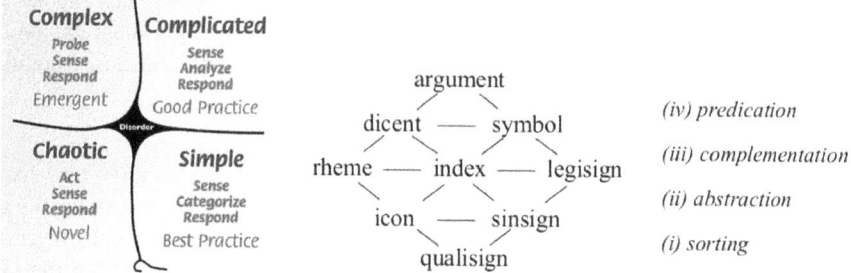

Fig. 2. Left the Cynefin framework with the fifth domain *disorder* in the center. Next to it the KiF-diagram with the Peircean semiotic terms for the sign aspects on the nodes of the dependency structure that analytically describes the moments each realized interpretation process must pass. Right the four stages in that process. The four square Cynefin domains correspond to the four nodes on the corners: Chaotic – qualisign, Simple – legisign or type, Complex – Rheme or term, Complicated – argument. Disorder corresponds to the index position, for KiF the locus of sub-processes needed to reach a given conclusion. KiF describes interpretation processes, Cynefin indicates the domains in which they may fail and facilitates with the help of Sensemaker the search for solutions.

The main division is between ordered (right) and unordered (left) domains. Each domain is characterized according to the cause – effect relationships as they appear to the actors.

- **Simple** or **obvious**: In this domain the relation between cause and effect is known. The cause we sense is familiar.[1] We can categorize the cause and respond according to the habit or well-structured set of habits it activates.
- **Complicated**: In the complicated domain the relation between cause and effect may not be fully known or known only by a small group of people. We must analyze the cause we sense in order to be able to arrange a set of habits for a suitable response.
- **Complex**: In this domain there are cause-effect relations, but we have insufficient *actionable* insight in their relationships. The contingencies of history and unintended consequences of previous actions place us in this domain. We must probe the cause from the different perspectives of the involved stake holders and eventually readjust our habits or device new ones for our responses. Safe to fail strategies are advisable.
- **Chaotic**: Disaster happens. The best course of action is to start acting in order to stabilize the situation, sense the consequences and decide further along the way.
- **Disorder**: This is the domain of conflict between the different stakeholders about what domain we are in with a given cause. Organizational transformations may suffer from neglect for the deep roots of this domain, it is the locus of cognitive dissonance and a source for conflict about the strategy to follow.[2]

---

[1] It is a legisign, alternatively called type or famisign, in Peirce's semiotic terminology.

[2] Paraphrased from [9].

The Cynefin framework facilitates and stimulates dynamical interpretations. A (part of an) organization firmly located in the Simple domain, for instance, may slide into Chaotic if a novelty is recognized not at all, to late or met with a strategy pertaining to a wrong domain. But it does not have a well-defined notion of interpretation processes. The isomorphic KiF-model, first introduced by Farkas and Sarbo [10], contributes one.

In Fig. 2 the KiF-processing scheme is represented with the Peircean semiotic terms that indicate the factors involved in reaching a conclusion (goal) on a sign (effect) that offers itself for interpretation to an interpreting system (state). For details the reader is referred to [11] here we only mention some points relevant for our experimental case.

First, it is important to remark that the KiF-diagram gives an analytical reconstruction of interpretation processes in a dependency structure, it indicates what is involved and does not provide a mechanical bottom up procedure: we suppose the input – output relation to be on a line orthogonal to the index position. Next, we explicate the state and effect below the qualisign position and the goal of the process above the argument position, finally we start to fill in the diagram like a sudoku, see Fig. 3 right for an example of the first approximation.

Explications of Cynefin as a rule start in media res with the domain *obvious* or what is first for us in the order of knowledge. KiF in contradistinction starts with the first in the order of nature from a cosmic, evolutionary perspective, i.e. the primordial soup (Chaos in Cynefin).[3] Semiotically the primordial soup is the confluence of all qualities regarded as aspects of signs present to the mind for a process of interpretation that ends with a response. In actual practice habits take a shortcut to a response, the semiotic analysis explicates what we assume to be involved in those habits of interpretation.

Applying the semiotic notions to Cynefin we get a reconstruction of interpretation processes in the most general terms. At the event of an interaction, the state of the agent and the effect are sorted out of the primordial soup. If both fail to be abstracted we are in a chaotic state in which the only course for action is to *act, sense* and *respond* without any guarantee. If only the state succeeds we are in a complex situation since there is no best practice (legisign, type) that fits the token (sinsign) we are confronted with. We must *probe* and *sense* to familiarize with the effect before an adequate *response* is possible. If the effect can be abstracted into a type, but the novelty does not fit in with the state (Rheme, also term), the state fails in the complementation state and a suitable response is not found. Again, we find ourselves in the complex domain, with the risk of sliding into chaos. Getting an expert might prove this to be a complicated case, enabling: *sense, analyze* and *respond.*

If both succeed and can be complemented, without the emergence of disorder (index), and an adequate response results, we have a best practice and reside in the domain simple. If both can be abstracted but disorder prevents an adequate response we are in the complicated domain. We must *sense* and *analyze* before we *respond.* This is where Sensemaker fits in.

---

[3] Cf Aristotle, *Analytica Posteriora*, 72a. This is what makes Cynefin far superior to the semiotic KiF-framework in explanations for a wider audience of what we do.

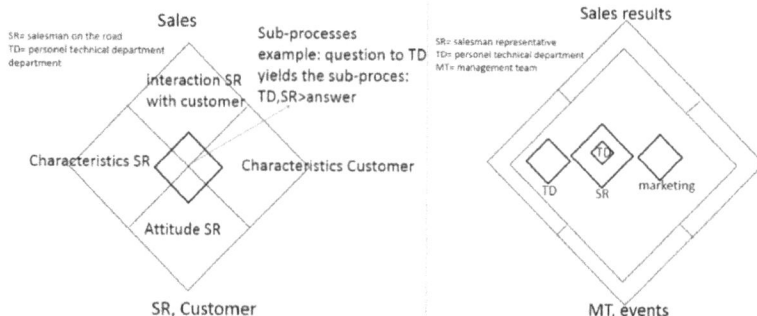

Fig. 3. Left we zoom in on the process [sales representative, customer >- sales]. Right we explicate the sub-processes in the index position from the perspective of sales results.

Quantitative data are excellent means to generalize and categorize, but weak in finding the dynamics in individual cases. Qualitative data, like narratives and suggestions, derived from stakeholders are good probes of individual cases. SenseMaker combines quantitative with qualitative data for analytical purposes. Since the reader will be familiar with quantitative data, we concentrate on Sensemakers dealing with narratives. A typical question for Sensemaker is to pose a subject, ask people to tell their story and have them signify the stories with the help of Triads, see for an example Fig. 4 the left Triad. A Triad is a triangular shape with at each corner a term. The trick is to find three terms that are related and allow for graduation, as in our example. The question posed was: what are your training needs? The score indicates in what amount *product knowledge*, *sales skills* and *market knowledge* are whished for in a training. Of course, in itself the scores on Triads can mean almost anything. But, since the scores are connected to the narratives in the database, by making selections on the scores, the accompanying narratives are retrieved providing the experiences behind the scores, if whished together with gathered qualitative data. Thus, offering handles for interpretation of the scores on the Triads and by that supporting policy making and detecting weak signals.

Use of the Triads in KiF-diagrams differs from their use together with Cynefin. Used together with KiF, the triads must be distributed over the four domains, question and terms on the corners must fit the domain and we ask to provide reasons for the score given. The sign definition, a sign is something (monadic), that presents some object (dyadic relation sign-object), to an interpreting thought (triadic relation of sign, object, interpretant) delivers the format for the terms to choose on the corners, see [12] for the Peircean background. If disorder is an intrinsic feat of the research domain, the Cynefin approach is suited to find weak signals and patterns. If, like in an organization, it is feasible and desirable to resolve disorder, the KiF-diagrams offer a uniform model for all processes and a means to order and distinguish them in dependency structures.

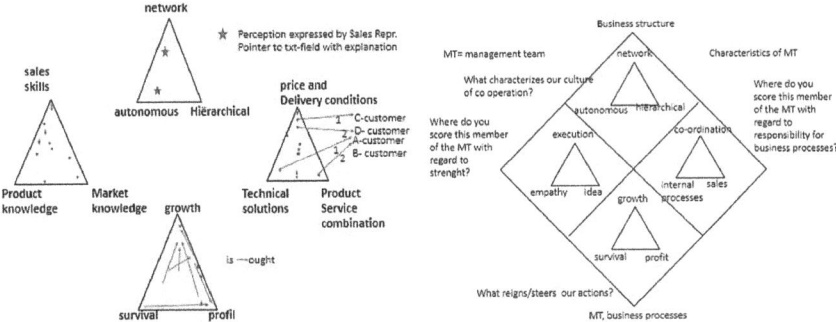

Fig. 4. Left scores of sales representatives for their perceived position on the Trikons. The dots are pointers to texts with explanations for the scores. Right the Trikons we asked the management team members to score themselves on, without the scores.

4   An Experimental Business Case

At some point Nieuwenhuijsen, a trainer in social and commercial skills and interim manager, was asked by a company, vending highly technical tools, to improve the sales of the sales representatives, results deteriorating over time, markets being lost. With Van Breemen he decided that this was a good opportunity to probe the possibilities of the Sensemaking approach for an assessment of the training needs.

The goal of this paper is to propose a diagrammatic method for the social layer, not to analyze a case. For that reason, we will use case data only where it serves the exposition. The actual order of development was: first the left diagram of Fig. 3, next the Trikons[4] left in Fig. 4. The information we got from the sales representatives set us to diagram the remaining two figures for consultation of the MT. Next time we probably will try to follow the order suggested here.

We start with a diagram of the responsible root agent and define the process from the perspective of the goal pursued: MT, events >- sales results, see Fig. 3 right. Ontologically dependent agents are embedded processes that reside in the index position. A sale is an exchange of goods and/or services in exchange for money. The company has a Technical Department (TD) in which the tools sold are prepared for sale and adapted to the house style. Our focus is on the Sales Representatives (SR). We indicate both sub-processes as primordial soups with the agent tag below. Regarding each other the processes are parallel processes. Goal and effect are determined in relation to each other and must fall within the goal of the root process. For feed back to the MT we added marketing, and TD (a second time, as a sub-process of SR).

The left diagram of Fig. 3 presents the sales process after the state, effect and goal are abstracted from the primordial soup. At the semantical level our interest goes to concepts and their relations. That being covered by the ontology charts (and similar techniques of other approaches), the social layer can be reserved for an interest in the

---

[4] Trikons are a special case of Triads because they must adhere to the categorical rules of Peircean semiotics. Space forbids going into details.

social fabric, i.e. the attitudes that co-determine the outcome of interactions, the characteristics of the agents, their set goals and the characteristics of interactions between agents. In the SR, Customer >- Sales process the domain Simple (legisign position) is reserved for the effect, the other domains pertain to the state.[5] In the mirror process Customer, SR >- acquiring production tools, Simple would be reserved for SR. The reason being that the only thing we can do in any concrete interaction is trying to categorize the effect as good as possible, which includes the possibility of a modification of the self-categorization of the effect and adjust our state. In the Chaos domain (Qualisign) we ask for attitudes that steers the interpretation process of the agent in a state, in Complex we ask for the characteristics that determine the relation of the state to the effect, and in Complicated we try to find out characteristics of the interactions.

With this general scheme ready we started to design the Trikons, see Fig. 4 left. Experience with interim management and training did help a lot, besides the SWOT analysis that had been made. The urgency behind the innovation process determined our question in the Chaos (Qualisign) domain. We asked for the individual perceptions of the business attitude. Is it a sense of survival, profit or growth that reigns the atmosphere?

In the Complex (Rheme) domain we probed the desired kind of training as perceived by the SR: product knowledge, market knowledge or sales skills? In Simple (Legisign) we wanted to find out the customers' needs. In what degree do they need technical solutions, product service combinations or best price and delivery conditions? In Complicated (argument) finally our interest went to the social organization of work. Do the SR work on their own, in a hierarchical structure or networked?

In two days we interviewed all SR for an hour each. Van Breemen asked the SR to score on the Trikons after that Nieuwenhuijsen had an unstructured, in debt conversation about the reasons for the scores, while Van Breemen acted as scribe. In Fig. 4 only part of the scores is given. Analyzing the results of the conversation our conclusion is that we have a promising tool for the MT member responsible for guidance of SR personnel. Four types of issues surfaced.

First, we found strict individual issues to be handled on a personal base: one SR, for instance, felt very insecure, but he proved to be very helpful for SR's with technical questions they didn't get answered by the Technical Department out of lack of time and started calling him for advice. Eventually he went to TD.

Second, on group level, we found issues that ask for a meeting to straighten out the diversity of opinion as well on social as on business issues. Look for example at the diversity of opinions at the attitude question. Such issues ought to be policy driven.

Third, the responsible manager of the SR's, can use this method for progress interviews with personnel to check goals, e.g. in a next interview concerning the trainings needs question: What did you learn? What is your current score on the Trikon? Why?

---

[5] If the same process had to be used as a marketing research tool, the domain Complicated would have been devoted to the interaction between SR and customer, but here the focus is on the relations of the SR personnel within the company.

Fourth, we found structural issues. The SR's fell apart in three groups on the question "Who is your responsible manager?" Sometimes SR's had to call their manager during price negotiation. The bottom price differed, giving rise to uneasiness since part of the wages consisted in a percentage of turn over. This instigated us to design Fig. 3 right and Fig. 4 right for discussion with MT about business processes and responsibility.

5 Conclusion

In order to actually facilitate *actionable* insight into the human interplay among sign-based world and digital technologies as part of processes of organizational transformation in and between organizations we have to facilitate horizontal alignment at the social layer level and we have to facilitate vertical alignment between the social and the semantic layer. For the social layer alignment issues, we propose our narrative sense making approach. For the vertical alignment issues in our opinion the most promising way to proceed is to systematically work out the connections between our approach for the social layer and the ontology charts of the semantic layer. The pragmatic layer in between consists in the interactions between all those involved in the transformation process.

References

1. Hoppenbrouwers, S.: Inaugural address (2013). https://www.han.nl/onderzoek/mensen/stijn-hoppenbrouwers/_attachments/intreerede_hoppenbrouwers_2013.pdf. Accessed 13 Apr 2018
2. Gazendam, H., Liu, K.: The evolution of organizational semiotics; a brief review of the contribution of ronald stamper. In: Liu, J.F.K. (ed.) Studies in Organisational Semiotics. Kluwer Academic Publishers, Dordrecht (2005)
3. Liu, S., Li, W., Liu, K.: Assessing pragmatic interoperability of information systems from a semiotic perspective. In: Liu, K., Gulliver, S.R., Li, W., Yu, C. (eds.) ICISO 2014. IAICT, vol. 426, pp. 32–41. Springer, Heidelberg (2014). https://doi.org/10.1007/978-3-642-55355-4_4
4. Liu, S., Li, W., Liu, K.: Assessing pragmatic interoperability for process alignment in collaborative working environment. In: Liu, K., Nakata, K., Li, W., Galarreta, D. (eds.) ICISO 2015. IAICT, vol. 449, pp. 60–69. Springer, Cham (2015). https://doi.org/10.1007/978-3-319-16274-4_7
5. Weaver, W.: The mathematical theory of communication. In: Shannon, C. Some Recent Contributions to the Mathematical Theory of Communication. The University of Illinois Press, Urbana (1949) 1998
6. Goldkuhl, G., Ågerfalk, P.J.: Actability; a way to understand information systems pragmatics. In: Liu, K., Clarke, R.J., Andersen, P.B., Stamper, R.K. (eds.) Coordination and Communication Using Signs: Studies in Organisational Semiotics. INOD, vol. 2, pp. 85–113. Springer, Boston (2002). https://doi.org/10.1007/978-1-4615-0803-8_4
7. Oppl, S., Hoppenbrouwers, S.: Scaffolding stakeholder-centric enterprise model articulation. In: Horkoff, J., Jeusfeld, Manfred A., Persson, A. (eds.) PoEM 2016. LNBIP, vol. 267, pp. 133–147. Springer, Cham (2016). https://doi.org/10.1007/978-3-319-48393-1_10

8. Bonacin, R., Baranauskas, M.C.C., Liu, K.: From ontology charts to class diagrams: semantic analysis aiding systems design. In: ICEIS, no. 3, pp. 389–395 (2004)

9. Kurtz, C.F., Snowden, D.J.: The new dynamics of strategy: sense-making in a complex and complicated world. IBM Syst. J. **42**(3), 462–483 (2003)

10. Farkas, J.I., Sarbo, J.J.: A logical ontology. In: Stumme, G. (ed.) Working with Conceptual Structures: Contributions to ICCS 2000, pp. 138-151. Shaker Verlag, Darmstadt, Germany (2000). **2**(5), 99–110 (2016)

11. Sarbo, J.J., Farkas, J.I., van Breemen, A.J.J.: Knowledge in Formation: A Computational Theory of Interpretation. Springer, Heidelberg (2011). https://doi.org/10.1007/978-3-642-17089-8

12. van Breemen, A.J.J.: Quality of service in the long tail: narratives and the exploitation of soft metadata. In: Liu, K., Gulliver, S.R., Li, W., Yu, C. (eds.) ICISO 2014. IAICT, vol. 426, pp. 22–31. Springer, Heidelberg (2014). https://doi.org/10.1007/978-3-642-55355-4_3

13. Liu, K.: Semiotics in Information Systems Engineering. Cambridge University Press (2000)

A Hidden Power of Ontology Charts from Affordances to Environmental States

José Cordeiro(⌂)

Setúbal School of Technology, Polytechnic Institute of Setúbal, Campus do IPS,
Estefanilha, 2914-508 Setúbal, Portugal
jose.cordeiro@estsetubal.ips.pt

Abstract. Ontology Charts are a powerful model element in Organisational Semiotics used to depict a stable and precise view of a business system. They show affordances and ontological dependencies as, respectively, nodes and links between them. Spite their apparent simplicity, they are many times hard to create. In this paper we refer to some common issues regarding the creation of Ontology Charts. Nevertheless, they have a hidden power of defining anchors for a stable information system supported by the affordance concept. In NOMIS – a **NO**rmative **M**odelling of **I**nformation **S**ystems – affordances are transformed to states and environmental states and used as stable state paths within an information system. This paper shows how this transformation takes place and some advantages and possibilities of using it.

Keywords: Information systems · Information systems modelling
Human-centred information systems · Organisational Semiotics
Ontology Charts · NOMIS · NOMIS views · States · Environmental States
Business processes · Goal and context modelling

1 Introduction

Organisational Semiotics (OS), as proposed by Stamper [1, 2] uses Ontology Charts as a diagrammatic language in which an organisation or business is modelled. In these diagrams, two types of elements are represented: affordances and ontological dependencies. These are key concepts in OS. A main use of Ontology Charts (OC) is in the elicitation of information system requirements. OCs offer a stable and precise view of organisational requirements. Spite their simple appearance, they are hard to produce with required accuracy. On the other hand, NOMIS, a modelling approach to information systems proposed in [3], uses other diagrams, similar to OCs, where a new modelling element known as Environmental State (ES) is used. This is an adaptation of the affordance concept. Also ontological dependencies are adapted to existential dependencies in NOMIS. This adaptation reveals the power of Ontology Charts.

In this paper, we make a brief description and analysis of Ontology Charts and we show how OS *affordances* and *ontological dependencies* became *environmental states* and *existential dependencies,* respectively, in NOMIS. Moreover, we emphasise the advantages and power of using ES and its associated diagrams and we point some research directions to explore these concepts.

© IFIP International Federation for Information Processing 2018
Published by Springer International Publishing AG 2018. All Rights Reserved
K. Liu et al. (Eds.): ICISO 2018, IFIP AICT 527, pp. 105–114, 2018.
https://doi.org/10.1007/978-3-319-94541-5_11

This paper is organised as follows: Sect. 2 gives a brief overview and analysis of Ontology Charts, Sect. 3 presents NOMIS and its State View, referring to Environmental States, Existential dependencies and its correspondence to affordances and ontological dependencies, Sect. 4 emphasises the power of Environmental States, providing some ideas for further research, Sect. 5 describes some related work and Sect. 6 concludes, pointing future work.

2   Ontology Charts

Ontology Charts (OC) are used in Organisational Semiotics to represent graphically a business map of an organisation, its ontological schema. In these charts, we find affordances and ontological dependencies as, respectively, nodes and lines connecting them. Affordances, are the most important element in OCs representing the organisation key business terms. By using these charts, meaning of any business term is made clear and precise. OCs are the most stable representation of an organisation. In Organisational Semiotics, OCs are an artefact, created by the MEASURE methods [4] for requirements elicitation. In particular, OCs are the outcome of applying the Semantic Analysis Method (SAM) to an organisational problem. In the next sections, we detail some simple aspects of OCs relevant to this work, the way they are produced and we make an overall analysis.

2.1   Agents and Affordances

According to Gibson's theory of perception [5], adapted by OS, affordances are the invariants which the agent recognises from the flux of information he/she perceives from the environment. In OS, each affordance represents a state of affairs affording or making possible for the agent some repertoire of behaviour. An affordance can be simply described by "what the environment can do for an agent" or "what it affords an agent to do". As an example from [6], an agent with a pen (an invariant) affords him/her the capability of writing. Also, an agent with a pen and a piece of paper will be able to write a letter. A pen affordance for a certain human agent will assign him the ability to perform a set of actions such as writing. Affordances, shown as nodes, are represented as words in OCs that are selected from the business domain description as the supporting elements of its organisational behaviour. In Fig. 1, there is an example of an OC of a conference organisation. In this OC we observe, as nodes, key terms from this activity, such as participant, work, program committee, conference, etc.

2.2   Ontological Dependency

Ontological dependencies (OD) are relationships between affordances where one affordance – the dependent - cannot exist without the co-existence of another one – its antecedent. Behaviour afforded by a dependent affordance can only be realised when the behaviour of its antecedent is being realised [1]. While affordances are represented as words in OCs, ODs are represented as solid lines (arcs) connecting these words. Also, in OCs antecedent affordances are shown on left side and dependent affordances

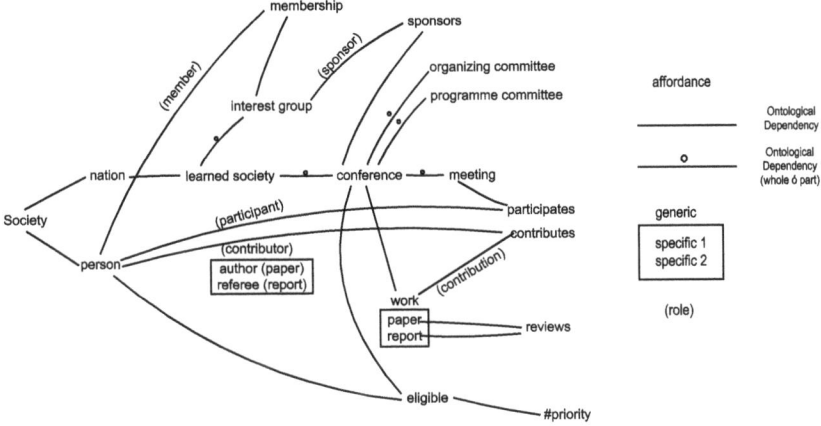

Fig. 1. Ontology chart of a conference [1].

on the right side making OC a directed chart. As an example of an OD, there is no conference sponsor without the coexistence of an interest group as sponsor and a conference, this is shown in Fig. 1 using two arcs connecting these affordances. An important effect of ODs is that, if an antecedent affordance ceases to exist, then all dependent affordances ends their existence as well. For example, without a conference, the meeting, the person as a participant and his/her work as a contribution stop all their existence in this context. There are also two rules to follow when creating OCs related to ODs. First, the most left affordance is always the society, a root node from where all other affordances depend directly or indirectly. Without society, any organisation or business, would not have any meaning. The remaining rule is that an affordance cannot have an OD from more than two other affordances. In this case, a simple justification is that it is not needed.

2.3 Semantic Analysis Method

As mentioned before, the Semantic Analysis Method of MEASURE has, as its outcome, an Ontology Chart. This method starts from a problem specification and produces a conceptual schema or 'business map' of an organisation (an OC). According to [2], conducting a Semantic Analysis involves four steps:

1. **Problem definition** – To understand the problem domain and collect the terms to be used in the semantic analysis.
2. **Candidate affordance generation** – Each identified term or semantic unit will be selected as a candidate affordance for the next step.
3. **Candidate grouping** – Selected affordances will be categorised as affordances or agents. Next, prior to the complete OC, identified elements will be used to create small chunks of interconnected affordances related by ontological dependencies.

4. **Ontology charting** – Connects all chunks of affordances and pieces in a unique Ontology Chart that represent the final ontological schema of the business system.

The business terms or affordances in OCs are usually identified and established by business stakeholders contributing also to their preciseness.

2.4   Analysis of Ontology Charts

In the creation process of OCs, is relatively easy to identify affordances because anything in the problem description can be an affordance. In fact, an affordance is something in the environment seen as "an invariant within the flux of information" that affords an agent some action. It can be a reference for a physical object, an agent, an organisation term, etc. Usually affordances are enablers of actions but do not represent themselves actions, therefore verbs are rarely used as affordances. In OS theory, Stamper added the notion of a social affordance where some social concepts can also act as affordances, for example, contracts, organisations, society, nation, etc. Additionally, there is a distinction between regular affordances and agent affordances, where agents are human actors or organisations. Therefore, although easy to find they may be difficult to select. There are no precise rules or guidelines for this selection. A second difficulty in the recognition of affordances is that some of them are not included in the problem description, usually are tacit knowledge, such as learned society or nation in Fig. 1. This leads to another consequence: getting affordances from a general domain may lead us to add other affordances that are essential but not important for the problem description resulting, possibly, in an over specification problem. Another difficulty is to link the different affordances using ODs in chunks of connected affordances. In general, an OD is a dependency of a kind of state on another state where these states are represented as affordances. The first state is a permanent state that must exist whenever the second state exists. If this first states ends, the second state and all connected states end their existence as well. This means that a transient state should not be taken as an affordance and, particularly, that mutually exclusive states should not depend on one another. As an example, consider an open and closed door situation. We may say that an open door is an affordance allowing a close action. Also, we only have a closed door affordance if the door is previously open (we cannot close a closed door). We may be tempted to create an OD between the open and the closed door but this is wrong as they behave as transient states. A last problem, related to ODs is the dependency nature, which varies according to a specific view. Looking to Fig. 1, is possible to identify different hidden types of ODs. The existential dependency between participant and person is, clearly, a physical dependency. On the other hand, the OD between sponsor and conference should be understood as a legal dependency. Other views can be identified confusing an inexperienced OC creator.

Nevertheless, an OC is in fact rather unique among the different Information Systems methodologies. None of them take into account important 'existential' dependencies between their elements. Also, a "correct" OC may lead to a very stable representation of a business organisation, making it to survive to requirement changes.

3 NOMIS State View Representation

NOMIS, described in [3], is a human centred information systems modelling approach based on human observable actions. It proposes a vision of information systems composed by a set of views addressing human interaction, action processes and context for actions inspired and based on, respectively, Enterprise Ontology (EO) [7], the Theory of Organized Activity (TOA) [8], and Organisational Semiotics (OS) [2]. In this section we describe the NOMIS state view, based on OS, and we will describe its relation to Ontology Charts.

3.1 NOMIS Brief Overview

NOMIS is a social-technical approach that understands information systems "as human activity (social) systems which may or may not involve the use of computer systems" [9]. It is based on human observable actions, those perceived by the human sensory system. This focus is originated by its foundational philosophical stance – Human Relativism [10] – that sees observable reality as "more consensual, precise and, therefore more appropriate to be used by scientific methods".

NOMIS proposes a vision of an information system composed by four complementary views – **Interaction View**, **Physical View**, **State View** and **Information View** – addressing, respectively, human interactions, action processes, context for actions, and information. For modelling purposes, it provides a set of diagrams a tables utilized by each of these views. The *elements* represented in NOMIS views correspond to key concepts in NOMIS, namely:

- Human *observable* actions
- Actors – human performers
- Bodies – physical things
- Information Items – *information* without any physical support
- Language Actions (or Coordination-acts)
- States and Environmental States

In this paper we focus on the *State View*, inspired by OS, in particular its Ontology Charts, which is described in next section.

3.2 NOMIS State View

NOMIS state view looks into environmental conditions or states that enable a human agent to act. This is an adaptation of the OS affordance concept. In this case, it distinguishes two types of states:

1. A simple **state** – only applied to physical things (bodies). If applied to an agent takes the form of a *role*.
2. An **environmental state** – a composite of NOMIS elements, namely, bodies and actors, possibly in a specific **state**, and actions. It is used to represent essential business states.

States, in these view, may be related to other states by existential dependencies. This is also an adaptation of Ontological Dependencies. Furthermore, there are three different types of diagrams used to represent this view (Fig. 2):

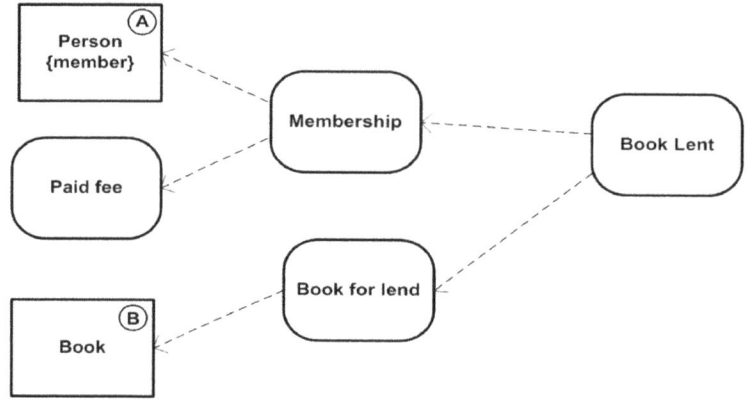

Fig. 2. An existential dependency diagram of a library system [3]

1. **Body State Diagram** (BSD) – shows the different states of a single *body*.
2. **Existential Dependencies Diagram** (EDD) – shows Environmental States and their existential dependencies. This is similar to Ontology Charts.
3. **Environmental State Diagram** (ESD) - details each Environmental State by showing its composing elements.

In Fig. 2, there is an example of an EDD of a library system. It results from modelling a simple use case of a library system described in [7]. In this figure, we can see Environmental States (ES) represented by round corner rectangles. A Book Lent ES depends on the existence of an ES of Book in a for lend state and a valid membership state.

3.3   Environmental States and Affordances

Environmental States and their existential dependencies, in NOMIS, are inspired by OS affordances and their ontological dependencies but they differ in many aspects. An ES is a collection of one or more elements precisely defined. In this case, an ES is reached if each of its composing elements is present. Because NOMIS models Information Systems and intends, mainly, to support development and implementation of computerised information systems, each NOMIS element is, in fact, information inside a computer. So, physical things (bodies), persons, actions, and everything else is just stored data. Looking at Fig. 2, a membership ES depends on a person, registered in the system, as a library member, and his/her paid fee information. If the contact information of this person is lost or if she/he did not pay her/his membership fee, the ES state is not valid. Also, the existential relationship between ES applies: a book is not in a lent state if there is no member lending it. In NOMIS, ES are always related to the data where they are based and must be though as it.

Existential Dependencies, are also different from Ontological Dependencies. Existential Dependencies relates Environmental States and are always data dependency states, contrary to ontological dependencies that can exhibit dependencies according to some specific view, for example, physical or legal views.

For representation purposes, EDD can be used to reproduce Ontology Charts but they do not have to follow its rules. There is no society or any other root node, neither is necessary to have a limitation of a maximum of two dependents in each dependency.

4   The Environmental State Advantage

Environmental states, inspired by OS affordances, are expected to exhibit a similar power in modelling an organisation in a precise and stable way. Besides their representational benefits, they are intending to have a practical application in information systems development. In this section, we address some possible advantages of using Environmental States and trace a research path to explore this new way of looking and representing information and business systems.

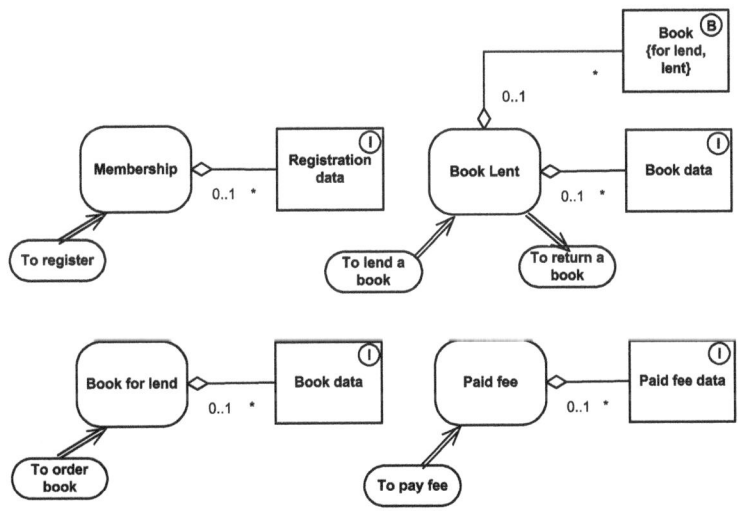

Fig. 3. An ESD of a library system [3].

4.1   Environmental State Modelling

As mentioned before, EDD diagrams, such as the one shown in Fig. 2, shows Environmental States, its composing elements, and its existential dependencies. A more detailed diagram is the ESD diagram that adds to EDDs a representation of actions or activities entering or leaving a state. In ESDs, entering actions or activities are represented in a round corner rectangle with leaving arrows pointing to an ES. This action correspond to a necessary process to reach that state. For example, in Fig. 3 representing an ESD of a library system, there is a lend book activity before reaching the lent book ES. This activity could be implemented as a typical business process of the library system. On the other hand, leaving actions or activities, are in fact actions enabled by that state. Similar to affordances, allowing for certain actions, these actions are also allowed by the correspondent ES. It is the case of return a book action that is available from a book lent ES. What is impressive in the ESD shown in Fig. 3 is that it shows a complete overview of the library system, including the different business process identified in this case study. Additionally, the ES states represented should be considered stable. It is possible to change, for example, the register, order book, lend book business processes and the ESD is still valid. Moreover, these states can be seen as information system anchors for a specific system, supporting different action or activities. A research question is: can we model other systems with ES diagrams, such as they represent an overall stable and usable view of that system?

4.2   Environmental States and Business Processes

NOMIS is based on human observable actions. Therefore, any action or activity is always related to a human performer. A business process represented as a sequence of actions, in NOMIS, involves exclusively human actions. As a consequence, a particular sequence of actions may not be followed by a human performer, these actions are not hard coded in a system. Anyway, ESs represent a composite of elements that may have their related data stored in a system. We may use this data to support any (human) business process. In this case, ESs are the support for business processes. Also, they are the system stable parts, allowing business processes to change and adapt to the context. This could be a major advantage, as business processes are usually dynamic, changing and making information system to change often. Also, another research question, is to assess the system adaptability and responsiveness for business processes changes.

4.3   Environmental States and Context/Goal Modelling

Environmental States exhibit another interesting properties. They can act as context or as goals. Regarding context, an ES is a state (or a kind of affordance) that allows for some actions or activities. This can be seen and modelled as context. Effectively, it is possible to represent context as an ES. In the library system case study, the lend a book action is possible during library open hours, in a specific library desk. The desk and the timetable may be modelled as ESs elements required for that action.

Concerning goals, ESs can also be understood as goals. Taking as example the same case study, in this library system a goal is to have books for lend and registered members to lend those books. Both goals relates to system states: books in a for lend state and registered members in a membership. This is a perfect match with the ESs identified before. So, a last research question is: can we map goals and context modelling to ESs models, and provide a precise and applicable base for them?

5   Related Research

Ontology Charts are analysed in [11] where they are compared to a few other modelling techniques. There are a few attempts to use OCs in formal ways within information system development. Firstly, in [12], some heuristic rules for UML class diagram derivation from OCs are proposed. In this work are just given some simple hints on how to obtain (and translate) the OC elements into UML elements. These UML elements are limited to classes and associations, compositions and generalizations relationships among then. In [13], Ontology Charts are modelled with UML profiles. In this work, UML adaptation issues related to Ontology Charts, are reported. [14], proposes the generation of a prototype system from Ontology Charts. The solution uses a database structure to store information from the elements in the OC. [15] suggested later the generation of UML 2 use cases from Ontology Charts. They map agents to actors and communication acts to use cases. This transformation is not suitable as well for NOMIS as it does not cover the required detailing. Also, in NOMIS there is a current proposal in [16] to use a Model-Driven System Development approach to derive application code from NOMIS Models. In this case, EDD are supposed to be implemented as state machines, inside a specific business middleware.

6   Conclusions and Future Work

In this paper, Ontology Charts are presented together with its key concepts of affordances and ontological dependencies. This artefact, used in Organisational Semiotics to represent key business terms, is analysed and some difficulties in creating OCs are reported. On the other hand, an equivalent diagrammatic representation, the Environmental Dependency Diagram, used by NOMIS is introduced. This EDD is used by NOMIS State View to represent environmental states and its existential dependencies. EDDs were inspired by OC, and also, its elements are versions of affordances and ontological dependencies. The relation between both diagrams is explained and the EDD power, inherited by OCs is revealed. Some advantages an research directions are pointed for EDDs.

As future work, EDDs and other modelling diagrams used in NOMIS, are planned to be used by a Model-Driven System Development approach. In this case, a new domain specific language is to be created for expressing NOMIS, and some model transformations will be created and applied to derive part of an information system application code as reported in [16].

References

1. Stamper, R.: Signs, information, norms and systems. In: Holmqvist, B., et al. (eds.) Signs of Work. Walter de Gruyter, Berlin (1996)
2. Liu, K.: Semiotics in Information Systems Engineering. Cambridge University Press, Cambridge (2000)

3. Cordeiro, J.: Normative approach to information systems modelling. Ph.D. thesis. The University of Reading, UK (2011)
4. Stamper, R., Althans, K., Backhouse, J.: MEASUR: method for eliciting, analysing and specifying user requirements. In: Olle, T.W., Verrijn-Stuart, A.A., Bhabuta, L. (eds.) Computer Assistance During the System Life Cycle, Proceedings of the IFIP WG 8.1 Working Conference on Computerized Assistance During the Information Systems Life Cycle, CRIS 1988, Egham, England, 19–22 September 1988, North Holland, pp. 67–115 (1988)
5. Gibson, J.: The Ecological Approach to Visual Perception. Houghton Mifflin, Boston (1979)
6. Stamper, R.: New directions for systems analysis and design. In: Filipe, J. (ed.) Enterprise Information Systems. Springer, Dordrecht (2000). https://doi.org/10.1007/978-94-015-9518-6_2
7. Dietz, J.: Enterprise Ontology: Theory and Methodology. Springer, Berlin (2006). https://link.springer.com/book/10.1007%2F3-540-33149-2
8. Holt, A.: Organized Activity and Its Support by Computer. Kluwer Academic Publishers, Dordrecht (1997)
9. Buckingham, R.A., Hirschheim, R.A., Land, F.F., Tully, C.J.: Information systems curriculum: a basis for course design. In: Information Systems Education: Recommendations and Implementation. Cambridge University Press, Cambridge (1987)
10. Cordeiro, J., Filipe, J., Liu, K.: Towards a human oriented approach to information systems development. In: Proceedings of the 3rd International Workshop on Enterprise Systems and Technology, Sofia, Bulgaria (2009)
11. Cordeiro, J., Filipe, J.: Comparative analysis of ontology charting with other modelling techniques. In: Proceedings of the 8th International Workshop on Organisational Semiotics, Toulouse (2005)
12. Bonacin, R., Baranauskas, M.C.C., Liu, K.: From ontology charts to class diagrams - semantic analysis aiding systems design. In: Proceedings of the 6th International Conference on Enterprise Information Systems, ICEIS 2004, Porto, Portugal. vol. 1, pp. 389–395 (2004)
13. Cordeiro, J., Liu, K.: UML 2 profiles for ontology charts and diplans - issues on meta-modelling. In: Proceedings of the 2nd International Workshop on Enterprise Modelling and Information Systems Architectures, St. Goar, Germany (2007)
14. Tsaramirsis, G., Poernomo, I.: Prototype generation from ontology charts. In: Fifth International Conference on Information Technology. New Generations, Las Vegas, NV, pp. 1177–1178 (2008)
15. Tsaramirsis, G., Yamin, M.: Generation of UML2 use cases from MEASUR's ontology charts: a MDA approach. In: Lano, K., Zandu, R., Maroukian, K. (eds.) Model-Driven Business Process Engineering, pp. 67–76, Shariqah, United Arab Emirates, Bentham Science Publishers Ltd. (2014). ISBN 978-1-60805-893-8
16. Cordeiro, J.: Developing information systems with NOMIS – a model-driven system development approach. In: Proceedings of the Seventh International Symposium on Business Modeling and Software Design, Barcelona, Spain (2017)

Digital Business Ecosystems and Value Networks

Exploring the Cloud Computing Loop
in the Strategic Alignment Model

Belitski Maksim[1](✉), Fernandez Valerie[2], Khalil Sabine[3], Weizi Li[1],
and Kecheng Liu[1]

[1] Henley Business School, University of Reading, Whiteknights Campus,
Reading RG6 6UD, UK
m.belitski@reading.ac.uk,
{weizi.li,k.liu}@henley.ac.uk
[2] Department of Economic and Social Sciences, Telecom ParisTech,
46 Rue Barrault, 75013 Paris, France
valerie.fernandez@telecom-paristech.fr
[3] ICD – International Business School,
12 rue Alexandre Parodi, 75010 Paris, France
skhalil@groupe-igs.fr

Abstract. Since its emergence, Cloud Computing (CC) has revolutionized
organization through offering them a large range of easily accessible, scalable,
and non-expensive services. As CC has been gaining popularity, it has an impact
on the strategic and operational level of every organization. Thus, wondering
about its impact on the organizational strategic alignment is a must. This study
develops the Cloud Computing framework of Strategic Alignment Model,
where strategic fit between operational and strategic levels in organization is
achieved through cloud-enabled multiple iterative processes. The study aims to
understand whether cloud computing increases operational and strategic efficiencies of organization and if yes then how. After presenting the theoretical
background, the hypotheses, and the built cloud framework, we discuss the way
strategic alignment theory helps us to better understand how information flows
within the strategic fit of business and IT and what is the role of CC in it. This
study addresses the strategic alignment as well as the cloud computing literature.

Keywords: Cloud Computing · Strategic Alignment
Operational management · Validation

1 Introduction

Although an intense research has been done about the strategic value of information
technology adoption using resource-centered view [1] the contingency-based view [2–
4], semiotic framework [5] and leadership and management view [6–8], there is a
paucity of research assessing a value created by cloud computing technology (CC) [9]
and the mechanism of CC adoption in organization [5]. Cloud computing, referring to
information technologies enabling convenient, on-demand network access to a shared
pool of configurable computing resources and has fundamentally changed the way
companies operate and co-create value [10–13]. As a transformative technology, CC has

K. Liu et al. (Eds.): ICISO 2018, IFIP AICT 527, pp. 117–124, 2018.
https://doi.org/10.1007/978-3-319-94541-5_12

changed various aspects of business and social interactions in the way businesses operate, exchange data and engage with customers [9]. To better understand a value creation process enabled by CC, more theoretical underpinning and practical evidence is required regarding the role that CC plays in improvement of the organization's operations, innovation, efficiencies as well as used to design a robust IT and business strategy. It is important to operationalize previous findings and results that are focused on issues associated with information technology adoption and a framework to analyze it [4, 14].

CC continues revolutionizing the ways business collect, process, analyze, review and manage information [15, 16] with a special attention on consistent measurements [17] of returns associated with CC by organization [18]. We use the term organization in this study to further emphasize the vast and far-reaching impact of cloud technology investments which goes beyond a separate business unit such as organization or business.

Although interest of IS scholars and practitioners on the cloud's impact on organizational operations and performance has been growing, the prior research related to CC and efficiencies has primarily focused on adoption or operations, cost reduction, exploiting the IT resource mobility offered by the CC as well as other supplementary technologies. There has been little attention paid to CC as an asset but also a strategic tool, creating more agile and flexible IT infrastructure, business operations, skills, administrative infrastructure and IT architecture. CC is likely to result in changes in administering and operations; higher rate of new product development, higher engagement of executives in IT investment and management decision-making, business growth, meticulous design of IT and business strategy within budget, time and scope. These and other important issues related to CC have not been explicitly discussed within the Strategic Alignment (SA) framework [14, 19, 20] with a lack of evidence on how information flows to achieve strategic fit and integration [21]. Neither has been investigated the interplay between CC, strategic operations and strategic performance of organization with the published work being fragmented and incomplete [20].

CC can play a major role in SA in organization described in [14] as the difficulties of achieving alignment for professional organizations; the limitations, organizations have in being agile; the rationale for acquiring technology and determining IT skills; the imperative meaning that CIOs attribute to IS alignment. To demonstrate the role that CC plays ion IS in organization we build on Information Systems (IS) [4, 22], Strategic Alignment [23–27] and organizational performance literature [28, 29].

This study makes the following contribution. We develop and test the "cloud-enabled mechanism of validated learning" embedded into IS alignment model. More specifically we develop the Cloud Computing framework of SA, where strategic fit between operational and strategic levels in organization is achieved through cloud-enabled multiple iterative process.

This study offers practical implications for managers to better understand the complementary nature of new technologies and CC's embeddedness in Strategic Alignment Model. Understanding how information is collected, assessed, distributed and analyzed should enable decision-makers to design more effective and robust business and IT strategy. We argue for the need to study the continuous organizational adaptation of evolving CC because of the challenges such technologies pose for users, as well as the operational capabilities and strategic skills they demand.

2 Theoretical Background and Hypotheses

2.1 Strategic Alignment Lens in Cloud Computing Framework

Cloud computing is as a strategic asset and tool rather than a service [9]. In order to assess the impact of CC, managers need to be aware that it has become another strategic asset embedded in strategic alignment of IT and business [5, 9, 19, 20, 23]. Being attributed to an improvement in data sharing, technology standardization and infrastructure, administering and operations, CC is further associated with the ability in delivering new projects and applications within budget, time and scope, changing strategy and engaging different stakeholders [9]. It changed the paradigm of IT investment moving from operational expenditure (OPEX) to capital expenditure (CAPEX) and decreased usage of hardware [12, 16, 31–33].

Furthermore, CC is related to greater scalability, flexibility and operation ability. This enables organizations to improve organizational infrastructure and business services [31, 32]. The ubiquitous nature of CC [31, 32, 34, 35] enables greater alignment of business and IT strategies, where different business units can integrate and use cloud solutions anywhere and anytime. On the one hand, CC is thought to be a reliable source when organizations acquire standardized solutions from trusted providers, therefore once adopted by organisational and IT infrastructure it affects strategic choices made by executives and related to investment in IT and business [31, 34].

To build our theoretical framework on the role of cloud technology adoption in organization we use Strategic Alignment lens [30, 36]. First, we conducted a detailed literature review to identify relevant theories of alignment and validated learning. Our extensive literature search failed to unearth theories addressing strategic alignment between strategy and technology with the important stage of validated learning. This is important when investigating the fit and integration between strategy and operations [21, 23, 30].

2.2 Stages of Theoretical Framework

Our theoretical framework consists of three stages associated with Apprehension of Information, Unitization of Information, and Validated Learning. All three stages rely on 'continuous adaptation and change' within SA model [23]. Our theoretical framework illustrates various steps in information gathering, conceptualization, optimization, implementation and validated learning.

At the first stage, apprehension of Information is done through generating insights, gathering information and a process of conceptualization. It is associated with people gaining knowledge and experience through using CC for operations and as a part of IT infrastructure development. Employees who access CC may not immediately understand CC solutions until they have experienced them. Apprehension of information stage is about 'finding the answer' where 'finding' is something more than mere retrieval of information. It is about adoption and use of CC in daily processes. This changes the cognition of users, focused on pure knowledge acquisition by experiencing and absorbing it [28, 37]. In addition, it requires generating and conceptualizing. Generating involves getting CC in place for operational and IT infrastructure. Generative thinking involves imagining possibilities where CC could be applied to automate processes and increase efficiencies. It further requires, questioning, sensing new opportunities and viewing IT and business processes from different perspectives and gathering information through experience and validated learning from previous iterations. The process of decision-making at this stage starts with exploring options (divergence), selecting and continues with exploiting and applying solutions with conceptualizing (convergence). The ambiguity of CC on alignment-operational should be pinned down. Conceptualizing results in putting new ideas together on how to use CC more efficiently.

At the second stage, Utilization of Information features the outcomes of cloud adoption and performance. At this stage, IT and business strategy can be designed reflecting on information received at stage one through optimizing and implementing strategy. It demands decision makers to apply knowledge obtained at the first stage to design strategy. They may either design a brand-new strategy, or update the existing strategy in light of changes in business processes and IT infrastructure triggered by CC. At this stage optimisation and implementation are required. Optimisation gains understanding of CC for organizational and IT strategy. This results in developing practical solutions and plans from abstract ideas, trends and insights. Given a well-defined solution, decision makers should be able to sort through large amounts of information to pinpoint the critical factors and processes where cloud is required. They should be confident in their ability to make a sound, logical evaluation of transformative impact of CC and integrate those processes. Finally, implementation is execution of designed strategy. Implementation of strategy requires complete understanding of how business operations and IT infrastructure are going to be affected by the CC. In case of strategy complete or partial failure or as a result of changes in external environment (e.g. technology, institutions, market competition, etc.), decision makers need to be agile and respond quickly. This requires transition from the second to the third stage of "Validated Learning".

At the third stage, Validated Learning measures the strategic efficiencies on both sides of IT and business. At this stage the performance is assessed and the application of CC is redesigned adjusting to environmental changes or addressing gaps in performance outcomes. Validated learning offers two choices: first, either retaining IT and business strategy or revising the way CC is implemented. At this stage the use of CC will be reshaped and redesigned to feedback to management in order to improve the efficiency of the next round of iteration of the cloud-enabled loop.

3 The Model

When an organization learns through development, implementation, measurement and feedback, the impact of CC could become more pronounced and ubiquitous [9]. This permits us to measure its value more distinctively. In particular, we can measure the

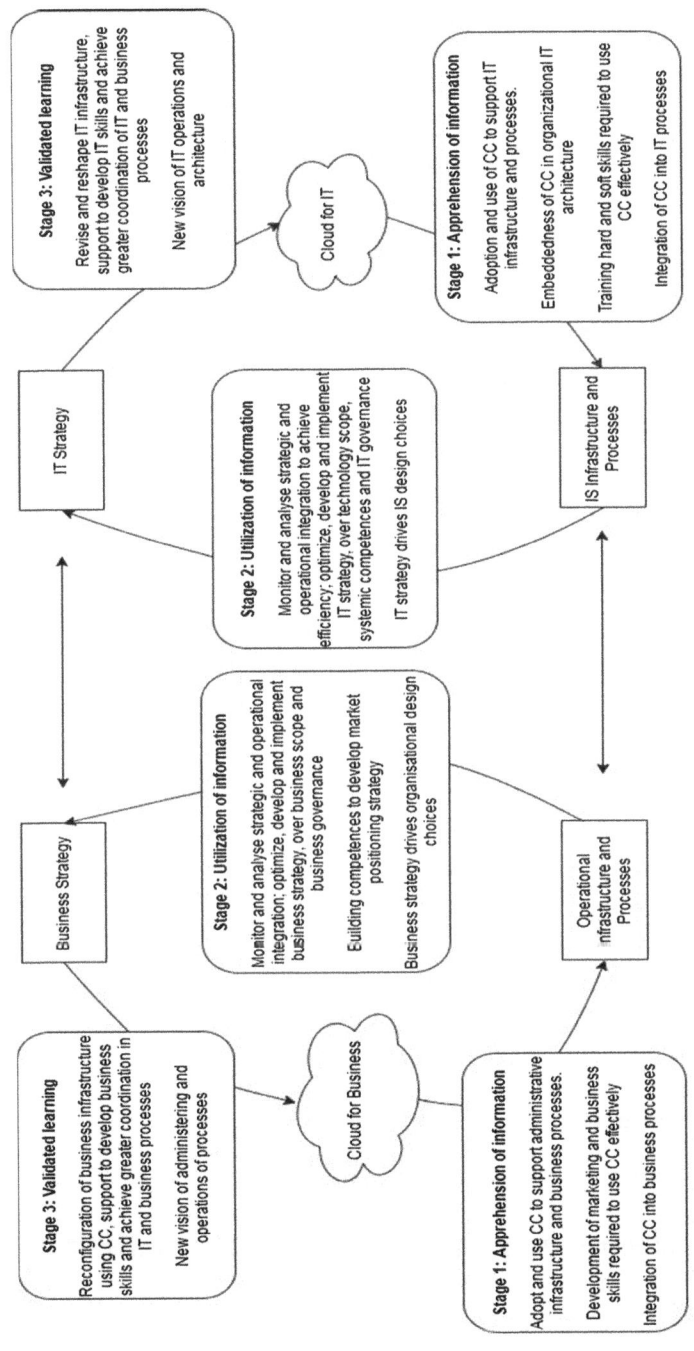

Fig. 1. Theoretical framework of cloud enabled validated learning in strategic

transformative impact of CC by analysing its relation to innovation, strategy, development of new products and services, standardizing and sharing data, management operations, changes in processes.

Figure 1 illustrates the place of CC within SA model which can be considered in terms of three interdependent dimensions of cloud-enabled validated learning loop. The first stage in a loop represents the Apprehension of Information through cloud adoption to improve organisational and IT infrastructure and processes. The second stage represents the Utilization of Information received from operations. Both stages are preconditioners to the third stage of Validated Learning which enables the assessment of CC efficiencies and advises action.

The theoretical framework supports the interplay between operations, strategic efficiencies and use of CC. The mechanism is iterative and can be described in stages as adopt – measure – learn – rebuild. The loop changes the way SA works, Strategic alignment is seen a process of continuous adaptation and change which could be achieved both through iterations and technology-enabled experimental learning [14, 23].

4 Discussion and Conclusion

Cloud computing marks a paradigm shift in the way business is done and is greatly associated with delivering high quality and timely service to customers.

The major benefits of CC found in this study are as follows. First, investing in CC enables rapidly easing the administering and operating processes within the organization and with external partners; second, it reduces cost of network maintenance, information exchange; third, CC decreases time solution and new products are developed; fourth, it improves security and compliance; and finally, it enables global deployments of solutions and faster decision making.

Building on the extent literature [4, 13, 23, 27] this study develops the Cloud Computing Framework of Strategic Alignment Theory by theoretically discussing and empirically validating the cloud-enabled mechanism embedded into business and IT alignment within SA model of organization [23]. More specifically, we established and described three distinctive stages of cloud's transformative impact on organizations: first, Apprehension of Information through cloud adoption to improve organisational and IT infrastructure and processes; second, Utilization of Information received from operations and deciding on business and IT strategy; third, Validated Learning which enables to assess the role that CC plays in operations and strategic fit and advise changes. When an organization learns through generalization, development, optimisation implementation and validated learning, the impact of CC could become more pronounced and ubiquitous facilitating both operational and strategic levels of organization.

Our contribution in the scholarship of IS and SA is as follows. First, we applied Strategic Alignment lens to demonstrate how each of three stages of cloud-enabled validated learning process contribute to business operations and IT infrastructure, business and IT strategy. Each of three stages forms a cloud-enabled loop of validated learning used by organizations as part of their "adopt – measure – learn – rebuild" strategy. Second, our methodological contribution is in applying a multi-level mixed method and used various sources of data to test our theoretical framework.

The future research will need to focus on evaluating to what extent CC changes strategic integration between IT infrastructure and business operations as well as between IT and business governance. Scholars would also like to know how investment in CC will to affect strategic fit between IT and business of economic agents when their performance and operations are interconnected, such as digital ecosystems. It may appear that strategic alignment of organization is not any more dominant unit of analysis, and strategic alignment of an ecosystem could be viewed as an alternative unit of analysis. In a new digitized economy, when operations and efficiencies of ecosystem players are complementary, CC is likely to benefit the entire ecosystem of inter-connected organizations, rather than a focal organization. This is because CC makes access, processing, sharing and transforming data faster, easier and more secure. Future research needs to offer theory and implications on how CC will support operations and efficiencies of inter-connected organizations.

References

1. Barney, J.: Frim resources and sustained competitive advantage. J. Manag. **17**, 99–120 (1991)
2. Fry, L.W., Smith, D.A.: Congruence, contingency, and theory building. Acad. Manag. Rev. **12**(1), 117–132 (1987)
3. Tosi, H.L., Slocum, J.W.: Contingency theory: some suggested directions. J. Manag. **10**(1), 9–26 (1984)
4. Oh, W., Pinsonneault, A.: On the assessment of the strategic value of information technologies: conceptual and analytical approaches. MIS Q. **31**(2), 239–265 (2007)
5. Mingers, J., Willcocks, L.: An integrative semiotic methodology for IS research. Inf. Org. **27**(1), 17–36 (2017)
6. Wang, P., Ramiller, N.C.: Community learning in information technology innovation. MIS Q. **33**(4), 709–734 (2009)
7. LEAD: E-Leadership skills for small and medium sized enterprises project. European Commission, Directorate-General for Enterprise and Industry Online Publication, 15 July 2014
8. Li, W., Liu, K., Belitski, M., Ghobadian, A., O'Regan, N.: e-Leadership through strategic alignment: an empirical study of small and medium sized enterprises in the digital age. J. Inf. Syst. **31**, 185–206 (2016)
9. Willcocks, L., Venters, W., Whitley, E.: Moving to the Cloud Corporation. Palgrave, London (2014)
10. Gold, J.: Protection in the cloud: risk management and insurance for cloud computing. J. Internet Law **15**(12), 24–28 (2012)
11. Juels, A., Oprea, A.: New approaches to security and availability for cloud data. Commun. ACM **56**(2), 64–73 (2013)
12. Yeboah-Boateng, E.O., Essandoh, K.A.: Factors influencing the adoption of cloud computing by small and medium enterprises in developing economies. Int. J. Emerg. Sci. Eng. **2**(4), 13–20 (2014)
13. Winkler, T.J., Benlian, A., Piper, M., Hirsch, H.: Bayer healthcare delivers a dose of reality for cloud payoff mantras in multinationals. MIS Q. Exec. **13**(4) (2014)

14. Silva, L., Figueroa, E., González-Reinhart, J.: Interpreting IS alignment: a multiple case study in professional organizations. Inf. Org. **17**(4), 232–265 (2007)
15. Noor, T.H., Sheng, Q.Z., Zeadally, S., Yu, J.: Trust management of services in cloud environments: obstacles and solutions. ACM Comput. Surv. (CSUR) **46**(1), 12 (2013)
16. Garrison, G., Kim, S., Wakefield, R.L.: Success factors for deploying cloud computing. Commun. ACM **55**(9), 62–68 (2012)
17. Brynjolfsson, E.: The productivity paradox of information technology. Commun. ACM **36** (12), 66–77 (1993)
18. Barua, A., Konana, P., Whinston, A.B., Yin, F.: An empirical investigation of net-enabled business value. MIS Q. **28**(4), 585–620 (2004)
19. Preston, D.S., Karahanna, E.: Antecedents of IS strategic alignment: a nomological network. Inf. Syst. Res. **20**(2), 159–179 (2009)
20. Gerow, J.E., Grover, V., Thatcher, J.B., Roth, P.L.: Looking toward the future of IT-business strategic alignment through the past: a meta-analysis. MIS Q. **38**(4), 1059–1085 (2014)
21. Coltman, T.R., Tallon, P.P., Sharma, R., Queiroz, M.: Strategic IT alignment: twenty-five years on. J. Inf. Technol. **30**(2), 91–100 (2015)
22. Sabherwal, R., Chan, Y.E.: Alignment between business and IS strategies: a study of prospectors, analyzers, and defenders. Inf. Syst. Res. **12**(1), 11–33 (2001)
23. Henderson, J.C., Venkatraman, N.: Strategic alignment: leveraging information technology for transforming organizations. IBM Syst. J. **32**(1), 4–16 (1993)
24. Hirschheim, R., Sabherwal, R.: Detours in the path toward strategic information systems alignment. Calif. Manag. Rev. **44**(1), 87–108 (2001)
25. Peppard, J., Campbell, B.: The co-evolution of business/information systems strategic alignment: an exploratory study. J. Inf. Technol. (2014)
26. Avison, D., Jones, J., Powell, P., Wilson, D.: Using and validating the strategic alignment model. J. Strateg. Inf. Syst. **13**(3), 223–246 (2004)
27. Aanestad, M., Jensen, T.: Collective mindfulness in post-implementation IS adaptation processes. Inf. Org. **26**(1), 13–27 (2016)
28. Dehning, B., Richardson, V.J., Zmud, R.W.: The value relevance of announcements of transformational information technology investments. MIS Q. 637–656 (2003)
29. Devaraj, S., Kohli, R.: Performance impacts of information technology: is actual usage the missing link? Manag. Sci. **49**(3), 273–289 (2003)
30. Henderson, J.C., Venkatraman, N.: Strategic alignment: a framework for strategic information technology management. Working Paper No. 190. Center for Information Systems Research, MIT, Cambridge (1989)
31. Dutta, A., Peng, G.C.A., Choudhary, A.: Risks in enterprise cloud computing: the perspective of IT experts. J. Comput. Inf. Syst. **53**(4), 39–48 (2013)
32. Armbrust, M., Fox, A., Griffith, R., Joseph, A.D., Katz, R., Konwinski, A., Lee, G., Patterson, D., Rabkin, A., Stoica, I., Zaharia, M.: A view of cloud computing. Commun. ACM **53**(4), 50–58 (2010)
33. Buyya, R., Yeo, C.S., Venugopal, S., Broberg, J., Brandic, I.: Cloud computing and emerging IT platforms: vision, hype, and reality for delivering computing as the 5th utility. Future Gener. Comput. Syst. **25**(6), 599–616 (2009)
34. Tiers, G., Mourmant, G., Leclercq-Vandelannoitte, A.: L'envol vers le Cloud: un phénomène de maturations multiples. Syst. d'Inf. Manag. **18**(4), 7–42 (2014)
35. Leavitt, N.: Is cloud computing really ready for prime time. Growth **27**(5), 15–20 (2009)
36. Ciborra, C.U.: De profundis? Deconstructing the concept of strategic alignment. Scand. J. Inf. Syst. **9**(1), 67–82 (1997)
37. Harvey, O.J., Hunt, D., Schroeder, H.: Conceptual Systems and Personality Organization. John Wiley, New York (1961)

A Framework for Assessing the Social Impact of Interdependencies in Digital Business Ecosystems

Prince Kwame Senyo[1,2(✉)] (iD), Kecheng Liu[2], and John Effah[1]

[1] Department of Operations and Management Information Systems,
University of Ghana Business School, Accra, Ghana
{pksenyo,jeffah}@ug.edu.gh
[2] Informatics Research Centre, Henley Business School,
University of Reading, Reading, UK
k.liu@henley.ac.uk

Abstract. As digital technology continues to pervade many organisations, new collaborative models such as digital business ecosystems (DBEs) emerge. DBE is a socio-technical network of digital platforms, processes, individuals and organisations from different industries that collectively create value. In DBEs, participants interdepend on each other and technology platforms to develop individual capabilities required to deliver value to end-users. Notwithstanding the benefits of DBE, a key challenge for focal partners is how to assess the social impact of the various interdependencies. Social impact refers to the social effect of interdependencies on DBE participants. More often, the focus has been on assessing the operational impact of interdependencies while limited attention has been paid to the social perspective. However, we argue that the social impact of interdependencies is equally important since it can significantly affect value co-creation. In this study, we develop a framework to help focal partners assess the social impact of interdependencies in DBEs. An empirical case study of a port DBE is used to illustrate our framework.

Keywords: Digital business ecosystem (DBE) · Interdependence assessment Social impact assessment · Organisational semiotics · Framework

1 Introduction

Organisations are forming strategic alliances beyond their traditional industry boundaries to collectively create greater value. As such, new collaborative value creation webs such as digital business ecosystems (DBEs) have emerged. DBE is a socio-technical network of digital platforms, processes, individuals and organisations from different industries that collectively create value [7]. DBE platforms offer participants opportunities to develop individual innovations that serve as inputs in value co-creation. At the core of DBE are complex interdependencies between entities such as technology platforms, processes, individuals and organisations.

Interdependence refers to an interaction between entities such as processes [2], organisations [14] and technologies [1]. These interactions create a network of

K. Liu et al. (Eds.): ICISO 2018, IFIP AICT 527, pp. 125–135, 2018.
https://doi.org/10.1007/978-3-319-94541-5_13

interdependencies that influence value co-creation, effectiveness and resilience of DBEs. As a result, for focal DBE partners, it is extremely important to understand the impact of the various interdependencies. However, due to multiple DBE interdependencies, this ideal understanding is difficult to obtain [8]. Thus, there is a need for systematic approaches to assess the impact of DBE interdependencies, especially from the social perspective.

There have been some approaches to assess interdependencies such as interdependence pattern measurement [8], interdependence process assessment [2], technology interdependence measurement [1] and interdependence profitability assessment [5]. However, per our knowledge, no study has accounted for the social impact of interdependencies in DBEs. We define social impact as the social effect of interdependencies on DBE participants [3, 11]. For instance, the effect of a new interdependence on someone's job security could be referred to as a social impact of the interdependence. In recent times, calls have been made for expansion in the scope of assessment approaches to consider social factors [6, 13]. In addressing some of these calls, this study develops a framework to assess the social impact of interdependencies in DBEs.

The rest of this paper is structured as follows. Section 2 presents the background and related works on DBE, interdependence impact assessment approaches and social impact effects. Next, Sect. 3 presents the proposed framework while Sect. 4 illustrates its application in a vehicle clearing domain of Ghana's main port, Tema Harbour hereafter referred to as Ghana's port DBE. Section 5 concludes the paper with implications for research and practice.

2 Background and Related Works

2.1 Digital Business Ecosystem

DBE is an internet driven socio-technical environment that focuses on collective value creation between diverse entities [12]. Typically, DBEs are characterised by complex interdependencies between organisations and individuals, technology platforms and processes that cut across industry boundaries. With these interdependencies come conflict of norms, values, beliefs and strategies due to diversity of participants. In some cases, the perception of stakeholders about an interdependence may affect their productivity [6]. Indeed, there may be resistance and sometimes sabotage from stakeholders if they feel unease about the impact of some interdependencies. Thus, it is important to constantly assess the impact of interdependencies to address conflicts that may affect productivity.

Though there have been some studies on DBE, a key aspect such as interdependence assessment is still under-researched. In the extant information systems literature, some studies have focused on providing a foundational understanding of DBE by explicating definitions, origin and characteristics [7, 12]. Alternatively, some DBE studies also focus on platforms [15], capability development [9], system integration [4], and norm evolution [10]. Notwithstanding the contributions from these studies, a critical area like social impact assessment of DBE interdependence is still open and less researched. Hence, the need for further studies to consolidate understanding and support development of DBE.

2.2   Interdependence Impact Assessment Approaches

Although there is a paucity of approaches for interdependence assessment in general, a few exceptions exist [e.g., 1, 5, 8]. For instance, Pentland et al. [8] present an approach conceptualised as "interdependence thermometer" that transforms digital trace data into networks to visualize and measure patterns of routine interdependencies. The findings reveal that using artefacts to evaluate interdependence enables better understanding and visualising of relationships that are intuitively difficult to comprehend. In another strand, Bailey et al. [1] proposed the "technology gap" approach to understand how two groups of engineers traverse interdependencies between technologies during their course of work. The findings reveal that the first group of engineers built automated data transfer process to address technology interdependencies gaps while the others allowed the gaps to exist, resulting in delays.

While these insights from the existing approaches are important, some limitations still exist. First, the extant approaches focus on measuring patterns of interdependence while understanding of the social impact of these interdependencies remains limited. Second, the existing approaches have largely assessed interdependencies at the organisational level [5] while limited understanding exists at the DBE level. Given the current pace at which DBEs are emerging across organisational boundaries, it is only prudent to develop approaches that align with this new collaborative network.

2.3   Social Effects of Interdependencies in DBEs

From organisational semiotics, social effect refers to conditions that influence people's perception of a situation [11]. For instance, social effects may have an impact on people's well-being, values and norms. In the extant information systems literature, social effects have not been largely accounted for in prior interdependence assessment approaches, calls have been made [6, 13] for this consideration as these effects may influence people's productivity. In some cases, the perception of individuals about an effect may create fear and resistance to undertake certain activities. As a result, this may negatively affect how they undertake their work. In this study, we draw on Hall's [3] 10 social dimensions as the foundation for our proposed social impact assessment framework. Table 1 presents the 10 social dimensions and their description.

Table 1. Ten social dimensions [3, 13]

Aspects	Description
Association	Grouping, alliances e.g., the formation of teams to evoke competitiveness and sense of belonging of participants
Subsistence	Physical and economic matters related to existences e.g., impact of an interdependence on income or job security
Classification	Differentiation of people by gender, age, level of education e.g. whether an interdependence improves equal opportunity for all
Territoriality	Accessibility e.g., the impact of an interdependence may lead to an erosion of control, influence, or loss of authority
Temporality	Time division, synchronous, asynchronous e.g. issues of time zone differences caused by an interdependence
Learning	Sharing knowledge, gaining awareness e.g., de-skill or more opportunity for learning new skills within an interdependence
Recreation	Fulfilment, joy e.g., whether the job becomes more interesting or boring within an interdependence
Protection	Fairness, rights e.g., granting file rights access to the appropriate groups of people and maintain the confidentiality of information
Exploitation	Individual's vs organisation's interests e.g., cutbacks on operating costs with salary-cut, retrenchment or longer working hours
Interaction	Interrelations and communications, e.g., fostering collaborative attitudes in the workplace

3 Framework for Assessing the Social Impact of DBE Interdependencies

This section presents our proposed framework to assess the social impact of DBE interdependencies. The framework as presented in Fig. 1 has three main components, namely: (1) DBE context articulation, (2) interdependence profiling and (3) interdependence social impact assessment. These components as discussed below iteratively depict inherent steps to assess the social impact of DBE interdependencies.

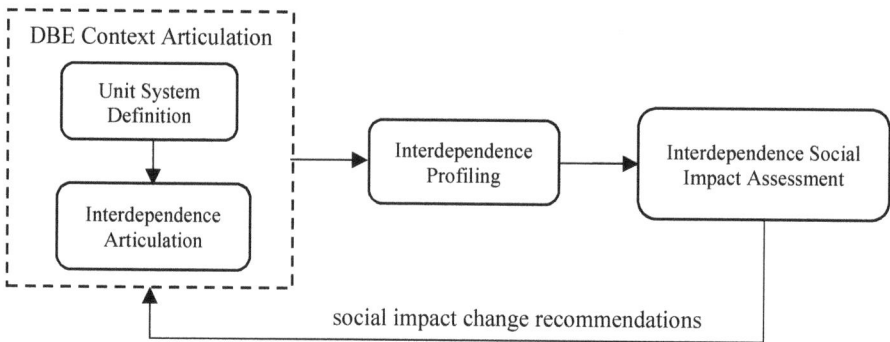

Fig. 1. DBE framework for assessing the social impact of interdependencies

DBE Context Articulation. This component establishes the setting for the interdependence social impact assessment. Typically, a DBE involves several relationships. As a result, it is important to clearly delineate the scope to evaluate. This component consists of two approaches – unit system definition and interdependence articulation. The unit system definition enables articulation of subsystems in a domain. The unit system definition as presented in Fig. 2 involves identification and examination of the various subsystems in a domain through observation, review of standard operating procedures and interactions with participants. The main elements of the unit systems definition are date, unit system ID, version of analysis, unit system name, description as well as sub-unit systems involved.

Date:	Unit system ID:	Version No:
Unit System Name		
Unit System Description		
Sub-Unit Systems		

Fig. 2. Unit system definition approach

After defining the unit systems in a DBE, the various interdependencies are articulated. We propose an interdependence articulation approach (See Fig. 3) to aid this process. The independence articulation approach supports the identification of the various interdependencies in a unit system. The main elements of the approach are unit system, interdependence ID and name as well as DBE entities involved in an interdependence. Interdependence articulation can be undertaken by observation, review of standard operating procedures and interaction with relevant stakeholders.

Unit System	Interdependence ID	Interdependence Name	Entities Involved

Fig. 3. Interdependence articulation approach

Interdependence Profiling. This component derives relevant information on interdependencies needed to conduct the social impact assessment. Figure 4 shows the interdependence profiling approach and details its elements, namely interdependence ID, date, version number, name, description, outcome, business processes, as well as entities involved. The ID is a unique identifier for interdependencies while date and version details the period and number of analysis iterations undertaken respectively. The interdependence description details what an interdependence entails while the outcome presents the goal of an interdependence. The business processes depict series of actions to accomplish an interdependence. Lastly, the entities involved in an interdependence are listed with their respective responsibilities.

Interdependence ID:		Date:		Version No:
Interdependence Name:				
Interdependence Description:				
Interdependence Outcome:				
Business Processes:				
Entities Involved	Entity	Responsibility		

Fig. 4. Interdependence profiling approach

Interdependence Social Impact Assessment. This last component measures and provides results on the social impact of interdependencies in a DBE. The social impact assessment determines the perception of partners in relation to interdependencies they participate in and how these interdependencies affect their ultimate productivity. We draw on Hall's [3] 10 social dimensions as criteria for the social impact assessment. Figure 5 shows the social impact assessment approach that articulates how stakeholders perceive interdependencies in a DBE.

Interdependencies	INT1	INT2	INT3	INT...n	
Partners / Dimensions	Partner 1	Partner 2	Partner 3	Partner...n	$C_j = \sum_{i=1}^{10} Vij$
Subsistence					
Classification					
Territoriality					
Temporality					
Learning					
Recreation					
Protection					
Exploitation					
Association					
Interaction					
$S_i = \sum_{j=1}^{n} Vij$					

Fig. 5. Social impact assessment approach

Each partners' perception is assessed with a positive and negative scale where +3 and −3 represent the most positive and negative impacts respectively with respect to their interdependencies. At the end, the total scores are aggregated based on the two equations below to determine the overall perception of partners on the social impact of interdependencies.

$$C_j = \sum_{i=1}^{10} Vij \qquad (1)$$

where Cj is the total score of all partners on an interdependence (e.g. INT1) by aspect i

$$S_i = \sum_{j=1}^{n} Vij \qquad (2)$$

where S_i is the total score of the impact of the 10-social dimensions assessed by partner j; n is the total number of partners

4 Case Study: Ghana's Port Digital Business Ecosystem

To illustrate the applicability of our framework, we used Ghana's port DBE as a case study. We selected this case because it provides an empirical instantiation of a DBE, featuring characteristics of complex interdependencies between diverse participants from different industries, technology platforms and processes. Ghana is an African country bordered by the Gulf of Guinea and the Atlantic Ocean to the South. As such, some landlocked countries heavily utilise Ghana's ports as a transit point. The key partners in the port are the Ghana Ports and Harbours Authority (GPHA), the Customs Division of the Ghana Revenue Authority (hereafter referred to as Customs), shipping lines, scanner operators, freight forwarders, terminal operators, Government Ministries, Departments and Agencies as well as importers and exporters.

To illustrate our framework, we present a high-level generic vehicle clearing process as follows: (1) Importer relies on the electronic ministries, departments and agencies (e-MDA) platform to obtain unique consignment reference (UCR), (2) Importer relies on the e-MDA platform to submit import declaration form (IDF), (3) Importer depends on the Pre-Arrival Assessment Reporting System (PAARS) to apply for Customs Classification and Valuation Report (CCVR), (4) Customs valuation officers use the PAARS to process application for CCVR, (5) Importer uses the Ghana Customs Management Systems (GCMS) to submits Customs declaration, (6) Customs compliance officers process declaration using the GCMS, (7) Importer relies on the bank to make duty and other charges payment, (8) Importer uses the Ghana Integrated Cargo Clearance System (GICCS) to make request for shipping release, (9) Customs examination officers use GCMS to release vehicle after physical examination and (10) Importer relies on the Driver and Vehicle Licensing Authority (DVLA) for temporary number plate. For this study, four separate set of questionnaires were designed in conjunction with Hall's 10 social dimensions for data collection. Data were collected from each group of partners in the interdependencies. This is because different groups of partners are involved in each interdependence in the vehicle clearing process.

Using our framework (see Fig. 1), the result of the unit system definition in Ghana's port DBE is presented in Fig. 6. From the case, Ghana's port DBE can be decomposed into many unit systems. As established earlier, our focus is the vehicle clearing domain, so we identified this as the unit system (U_1) of concern. From the analysis, U_1 is composed of four sub-unit systems represented as $U_{1.1}$ to $U_{1.4}$ which can also be further decomposed to lower granularity if necessary.

Date: 17/1/2018	Unit system ID: U_1		Version: 1.0
Unit System Name	<<Vehicle Clearing Unit System>>		
Unit System Description	This unit system covers activities involved in clearing vehicles at Ghana's port.		
Sub-Unit Systems	$U_{1.1}$ Import declaration processing, $U_{1.2}$ Duty and taxes payment, $U_{1.3}$ Physical examination and $U_{1.4}$ Vehicle release processing		

Fig. 6. Unit system definition in Ghana's port DBE

Next, we articulate interdependencies in the unit system defined (U_1). Using the interdependence articulation approach, we identified 10 interdependencies in the unit system. Figure 7 shows the unit system, interdependencies articulated as well as entities involved.

Unit System	ID	Interdependence Name	Entities Involved
U_1 <<vehicle clearing domain>>	INT1	Importer relies on the e-MDA platform to obtain UCR online	• Importer • E-MDA
	INT2	Importer relies on the e-MDA platform to submit IDF	• Importer • E-MDA
	INT3	Importer depends on the PAARS to apply for CCVR	• Importer • PAARS
	INT4	Customs valuation officers use the PAARS platform to process CCVR online	• Customs • PAARS
	INT5	Importer uses the GCMS to submits Customs declaration	• GCMS • Importer
	INT6	Customs compliance officers process declaration using the GCMS	• Customs • GCMS
	INT7	Importer relies on the bank to make duty and other charges payment	• Importer • Bank
	INT8	Importer uses the GICCS to make shipping release request	• GICCS • Importer
	INT9	Customs examination officers use GCMS to release a vehicle after a physical examination	• Customs • GCMS
	INT10	Importer relies on DVLA for temporary number plate	• Importer • DVLA

Fig. 7. Interdependence articulation from U_1 of Ghana's port DBE

Based on the second component of our framework, we perform interdependence profiling on our case study. The aim of interdependence profiling is to analyse the interdependencies articulated in the unit system (U_1) so that more information can be derived to enable the social impact assessment. Figure 8 shows a sample interdependence profile detailing information on the description, outcome, business processes, entities involved as well as their responsibilities.

Interdependence ID: INT3	Date: 5/07/2017	Version No:1
Interdependence Name: Importer depends on the PAARS to apply for CCVR		
Interdependence Description: This interdependence supports the importer to apply for CCVR using PAARS		
Interdependence Outcome: Enables successful, timely and cost-efficient CCVR processing		
Business Processes:		
• Importer submits vehicle clearing application to Customs through PAARS		
• Customs performs classification and valuation and generates CCVR		
• Customs issues an electronic copy of CCVR to the importer and sends a copy to GCMS		

Entities Involved	**Entity**	**Responsibility**
	Importer	Submits CCVR application through PAARS
	PAARS	PAARS allows the importer to submit an application if all necessary requirements are met

Fig. 8. Independence profiling

Lastly, we perform the social impact assessment on the interdependencies identified in the vehicle clearing unit system. For all the interdependencies identified, we first compute the average score for each interdependence based on the ten social dimensions. Second, we aggregate the score for each social dimension in respect of each interdependence horizontally and vertically using Eqs. (1) and (2) above. Figure 9 shows the social impact scores of the various interdependencies on the ten social dimensions.

Dimensions	INT 1	INT 2	INT 3	INT 4	INT 5	INT 6	INT 7	INT 8	INT 9	INT 10	$c_j = \sum_{i=1}^{10} v_{ij}$
Subsistence	1	3	2	1	2	2	3	-1	1	-1	13
Classification	2	2	1	0	2	2	1	0	3	0	13
Territoriality	3	2	2	0	3	-1	-1	-1	1	-3	5
Temporality	-1	0	2	-2	0	2	-1	1	0	-1	0
Learning	0	1	2	1	1	2	-1	-1	-1	-2	2
Recreation	0	2	2	0	2	1	1	-1	2	-2	7
Protection	2	2	2	1	2	2	0	0	2	-1	12
Exploitation	-2	-1	0	-2	0	2	0	-1	0	-1	-5
Association	1	1	1	-1	1	1	0	-1	0	-1	2
Interaction	0	2	1	0	2	2	0	0	-2	-1	4
$S_i = \sum_{j=1}^{n} v_{ij}$	6	14	15	-2	15	15	2	-5	6	-13	

Fig. 9. Interdependence impact scores of the vehicle clearing unit system

From the results, interdependencies INT 3, 5 and 6 have the most positive impact scores (15) in the vehicle clearing domain U_1. Conversely, interdependencies INT 10, 8 and 4 have the most negative impact scores (-13, -5 and 2) respectively. For instance, the importers in interdependence INT 10 perceived it to have the lowest negative impact. This negative impact score can be explained by the face-to-face interactions involved in the interdependence. Importers require fast processes as delays may result in more operational cost. However, this interdependence requires importers to queue at DVLA's office to purchase a temporary number plate to move vehicles from the port. This manual process results in delays, favouritism and corruption. As such, importers view this interdependence as a hindrance to effective and efficient processes in vehicle clearing.

On the ten social dimensions, the results show that subsistence and classification aspects had the highest impact on interdependencies in U_1. This can be explained by the perception of partners on the limited threat of job security of these interdependencies. Currently, the laws in Ghana's port DBE protects jobs of most key participants, hence the positive attitude regarding the social impact of interdependencies in U_1. The limited discrimination in the port can be attributed to high process automation, thereby reducing face-to-face interaction in most interdependencies. Conversely, the exploitation, temporality, learning and association aspects recorded the lowest impact scores respectively. This result can be attributed to the presence of some loopholes in some interdependencies where importers are exploited. Also, in the current clearing processes, most activities are undertaken during the day, hence the low temporality impact score. At present, the clearing procedure offers limited avenues to learn new skills due to the routine nature of processes, hence the low impact score. Lastly, the low association score can be explained by digitalisation of many processes, leading to limited collaboration among partner groups.

In sum, we argue that critical attention is needed on interdependencies INT 10, 8, 4 and 7 since their social impact scores might negatively affect ultimate productivity of the unit system. Similarly, more attention should be paid to exploitation, temporality, learning, interaction and association aspects of interdependencies in the unit system as these have all recorded awful social impact scores. However, attempts should be made to improve on other interdependencies and social dimensions that recorded reasonable social impact scores.

5 Discussion and Conclusion

This study developed a framework to assess the social impact of interdependencies in DBEs since limited attention has been paid to the effect of social factors in prior approaches [e.g., 1, 5, 8]. The case illustration above demonstrates how our framework offers mechanisms to assess the social impact of interdependencies taking into consideration multiple perceptions of partners in a DBE. Using our framework, we successfully articulate a DBE's context, interdependencies and their social impacts. From our results, it is evident that interdependencies that involve face-to-face interactions recorded low social impact scores as they are largely characterised by corruption, extortion and delays. Conversely, interdependencies that occur via technology platforms recorded high social impact scores.

By providing a framework and demonstrating how to assess the social impact of interdependencies of a DBE, our study makes contributions to research and practice. From research perspective, this study brings new theoretical inspiration to DBE research through our framework and application of organisational semiotics principles. In addition, we contribute to research by applying Hall's social dimensions in two new domains – DBE and interdependence domains since it has mostly been used for information technology systems analysis, planning and development. Practically, our framework presents a tool for practitioners in DBEs to assess and respond to social impact of interdependencies. With this tool, practitioners can make decision on which interdependencies to revise or maintain to improve value co-creation in a DBE. Our study is limited by the sole focus on social impact assessment. Thus, future studies may add other assessment dimensions such as operational and strategic aspects to present a complete evaluation method. Also, our study is limited to one-to-one interdependencies. Future studies can investigate one-to-many or many to many interdependencies.

References

1. Bailey, D.E., et al.: Minding the gaps: understanding technology interdependence and coordination in knowledge work. Organ. Sci. **21**(3), 714–730 (2010)
2. Crowston, K.: Process as theory in information systems research. In: Baskerville, R., Stage, J., DeGross, J.I. (eds.) Organizational and Social Perspectives on Information Technology. ITIFIP, vol. 41, pp. 149–164. Springer, Boston, MA (2000). https://doi.org/10.1007/978-0-387-35505-4_10
3. Hall, E.: The Silent Language. Doubleday And Company, New York (1959)
4. Korpela, K., et al.: Digital supply chain transformation toward blockchain integration. In: Hawaii International Conference on System Sciences, pp. 4182–4191 (2017)
5. Lenox, M.J., et al.: Does interdependency affect firm and industry profitability? An empirical test. Strateg. Manag. J. **31**(2), 121–139 (2010)
6. Liu, K., et al.: Modelling complex systems for project planning: a semiotics motivated method. Int. J. Gen Syst **35**(3), 313–327 (2006)
7. Nachira, F., et al.: A network of digital business ecosystems for Europe: roots, processes and perspectives. In: Digital Business Ecosystem. European Commission Information Society and Media (2007)
8. Pentland, B.T., et al.: A thermometer for interdependence: exploring patterns of interdependence using networks of affordances. In: International Conference on Information Systems, Fort Worth (2015)
9. Selander, L., et al.: Capability search and redeem across digital ecosystems. J. Inf. Technol. **28**(3), 183–197 (2013)
10. Senyo, P.K., Liu, K., Sun, L., Effah, J.: Evolution of norms in the emergence of digital business ecosystems. In: Baranauskas, M.C.C., Liu, K., Sun, L., Neris, V., Bonacin, R., Nakata, K. (eds.) ICISO 2016. IAICT, vol. 477, pp. 79–84. Springer, Cham (2016). https://doi.org/10.1007/978-3-319-42102-5_9
11. Stamper, R.: Information in Business and Administrative Systems. Batsford, London (1973)
12. Stanley, J., Briscoe, G.: The ABC of digital business ecosystems. Commun. Law - J. Comput. Media Telecommun. Law **15**(1), 1–24 (2010)
13. Sun, L., et al.: Evaluating business value of IT towards optimisation of the application portfolio. Enterp. Inf. Syst. **10**(4), 378–399 (2016)
14. Tan, F., et al.: Towards a self-organizing digital business ecosystem: examining IT-enabled boundary spanning practice of China's LeEco. In: International Conference on Information Systems, pp. 1–12, Dublin, Ireland (2016)
15. Tiwana, A.: Evolutionary competition in platform ecosystems. Inf. Syst. Res. **26**(2), 266–281 (2015)

Introducing the Strategy Lifecycle: Using Ontology and Semiotics to Interlink Strategy Design to Strategy Execution

Jamie Caine[1,2]([⊠]) [iD] and Mark von Rosing[2] [iD]

[1] Department of Computing, Sheffield Hallam University, Sheffield, UK
J.Caine@shu.ac.uk
[2] The Global University Alliance, Birmingham, UK
MvR@globaluniversityalliance.org,
http://www.globaluniversityalliance.org

Abstract. The ability of existing strategy concepts to analyse strategy, design strategy and execute strategy within organisations has an alarmingly poor historical track record. Based on the long-standing semiotics and ontology research work of the Global University Alliance (GUA) and its members, a *Strategy Lifecycle* is introduced. The *Strategy Lifecycle*, underpinned by ontology and semiotics incorporates all the constructs that can be found in the most popular strategy concepts and frameworks. It explains the value of the underlying strategy ontology and the relationship between the strategy meta model, the *Strategy Lifecycle* and various artefacts used around strategy work. The paper concludes with future scope and application that lies ahead for the *Strategy Lifecycle*.

Keywords: Strategy Lifecycle · Strategy artefacts · Strategy meta model
Strategy semiotics · Strategy ontology · Strategy architecture

1 Introduction

The challenge of taking your strategy design through to execution has been well documented [2–4, 7, 12]. In fact, there has been an overwhelming rate of failure reported within the last two decades [2, 3]. Scholars of strategy have been critical of strategy implementation and its success rate [29]. Bridges, an organisation that has been surveying strategy implementations since 2002 reported in their 2016 survey a failure rate of 67% [2]. Their recent survey revealed that the main three reasons for implementation failure are: poor communication, lack of leadership and using the wrong measures. Only one in five organisations review their implementation on a monthly basis [2]. Lessons learned from some of the epic failures highlight (in Kodak's case) the inability to map strategy against the market forces [8]. Another significant learning curve highlights the failure in organisations' abilities to architect their strategy into daily operations that are monitored in accordance to meeting the strategy objectives [14].

This paper positions itself around addressing these challenges and more through introducing the Strategy Lifecycle. This consists of six distinct stages: Analyse and Understand, Strategy Options & Design, Strategy Development, Strategy Execution, Strategy Governance and Continuous Strategy Improvement. We start with providing a summary in the traditional ways of strategy thinking indicating where the gaps are and alluding to areas where the Strategy Lifecycle addresses these gaps. This is followed by introducing the Strategy Lifecycle, its purpose, relevance to strategy and its compatibility with enterprise strategy regardless of industry. The strategy way of working follows with examples of how each stage can be applied to an enterprise. The extent of the model is then presented with its embedded ontology and semiotics followed by the conclusion which summarises the validity and highlights the future work surrounding this area.

2   Strategy and Traditional Ways of Thinking

The notion of strategy by its most simple definition; "A plan of action designed to achieve a long-term or overall aim" [9] goes thousands of years beyond business strategic management science that has existed since the 1960's [6] However, it is from the work of academia and industry practice since the 1960's where we can examine how strategy has developed within the context of organisation. Decades leading up to the year 2000 have witnessed significant developments in organisation strategy. Godfrey describes these shifts as; "interests, priorities and concerns in response to the wider social, political and economic concerns of the day" [6]. A collection of influential publications in the 60's established the foundation of strategic management. Two academics and one practitioner paved the way for further development within the strategic management discipline. Chandler's Strategy and Structure [5], Slone's My Years with General Motors [11], and Ansoff's Corporate Strategy [1] are regarded as the break through literature in this field [6, 10]. It is from their works that a more structural approach towards strategy was formed. Concepts such as separating implementation from formulation, return on investment and policy from tactics were some of the formalised schools of thought [13]. Three stages within the Strategy Lifecycle (Develop, Execute, and Govern) build upon these thoughts and in the later chapters we discuss the significance of these stages.

The 70's witnessed the rise of the consulting firms imprinting their influence on the development of strategy. GE-McKinsey matrix and the Boston Consulting Group Matrix focussed on diversification and growth strategies (Design stage in the lifecycle) [10]. Academia continued to further develop the science behind strategy which by the end of 1970's, strategy management was firmly established as a discipline [6]. The 1980's witnessed the intervention of Michael Porter's strategy paradigm. Renown for the Five Forces [15] (Analyse & Understand stage in the Strategy Lifecycle), Value Chain [16] (Execution stage in the Strategy Lifecycle) and Generic Strategies [17] (Design stage within the lifecycle) his works is still part of academic and industry practice today [18, 19]. Resource Based View (RBV) made its imprint in the 90's, adopting a more focussed lens on internal resources, capabilities and competencies. Innovation and value dominated strategic thought from 1990 onwards [6, 10]. Each model and theory had its industrial demands, social and economic setting during its time [6]. In spite of this, many of these developments still have use and relevance today. However this does not discard the fact that there is somewhat a disjointed landscape when we try to holistically understand the theory and models that represent strategic management today.

Whilst this is a very brief summary of the development in strategy concepts, it is important to understand the gaps in the existing theoretical strategy landscape. For example Porter's Five Forces does not integrate with strategy options and strategy design, the BCG Matrix does not integrate with strategy execution. The Value Chain which has the highest level of organisational view, does not integrate with the developed strategies or even strategy governance. Newer concepts such as the strategy map, are neglecting the needed links to internal or external forces and trends, the organisational competencies, roles involved in terms of owners, as well as an absent relationship to mission and vision. The gap between the relationship of strategy and its context i.e. forces, mission, vision, organisational components, owners, etc. in existing theory is what separates the ability to work with strategy in the course of its lifecycle. In the later chapters we will delineate gaps filled by the Strategy Lifecycle and through doing so establish its position.

3   A Strategy Lifecycle Way of Thinking

We have just elaborated on the various gaps in the existing theoretical strategy land-scape and how there is a need to work with strategy in the course of its lifecycle. What we need is to manage the entire Strategy Lifecycle, from strategy understanding and analysis, strategy options and design, strategy development to strategy execution as well as strategy governance and continuous strategy improvement. A lifecycle approach is needed, as it is an instrument to represent the course of developmental changes through which the strategy evolves during its lifetime. Both in terms of evolution but also changes as it passes through different phases during its lifetime ex-instance. As illustrated in Fig. 1, from strategy understanding and analysis, strategy options and design, strategy development, strategy execution as well as strategy governance and continuous strategy improvement, the lifecycle helps guide the strategy practitioners to work with the strategy during its development phases and lifespan. It enables the mapping of relevant components such as forces and trends, risk, organisational competencies, owners as well as the specification of activities needed for strategy execution and governance. What is also worth commenting is the necessity of continuous strategy improvement that facilitates the feedback loop in a systematic approach, where depending on the degree of change it can help an organisation opti-mise its underlying strategy and activities to achieve more efficient results.

The Strategy Lifecycle thereby consists of a set of phases in which each phase is inter-linked with the previous one. It provides a highly useful sequence of phases and steps that any strategy practitioner, executive, business analyst or even business architect can follow, regardless of industry and size of organisation. The proposed Strategy Lifecycle concepts are as discussed interlinked between each other, but it also can be combined with any kind of other lifecycle thinking, such as the product life-cycle, value lifecycle, service lifecycle, process lifecycle, application lifecycle or an enterprise architecture lifecycle [27]. The previously mentioned possibility to integrate lifecycle thinking, helps various practitioners place focus on all relevant strategy aspects from business, information and technology aspects. Which on the one hand is a part of strategy execution, but can also help with the Strategy Lifecycle phases of strategy analysis, strategy design input as well strategy development.

4 Strategy Way of Working

When a practitioner or organisation decides to use the Strategy Lifecycle to lay the foundation of what we call 'the strategy way of working'; all employees across all organisational boundaries of the enterprise, now have a conjoint way of working with strategy in the course of its lifecycle. This means that a common understanding and consensus has been reached within the organisation, which immediately increases the level of strategy maturity. In Fig. 2 is an illustration of the most common steps in the Strategy Lifecycle phases. You will notice that the steps are not linear and interlinked, this is due to the fact that this is not a waterfall approach. This should be viewed as an agile on demand concept, that depending on your specific situation, different compo-nents and thereby steps matter. Therefore, all these different steps should be seen as building blocks of the Strategy Lifecycle. Due to space limitation of this paper, we will only illustrate the most relevant building blocks involved.

Typical artefacts that are used in these phases are specified in Fig. 2 as letters e.g. A: Forces Model. Obviously other artefacts could be used in the various phases, such as a Vision & Mission Map, Stakeholder Map, Change Model, Innovation & Transfor-mation Canvas. However some organisations will not develop any artefacts for the defined steps but rather, work through them in a workshop fashion. Therefore we have included the most common examples.

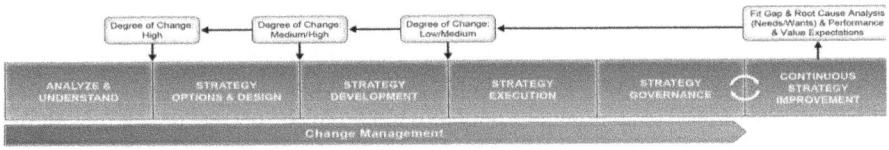

Fig. 1. Six phases within the Strategy Lifecycle

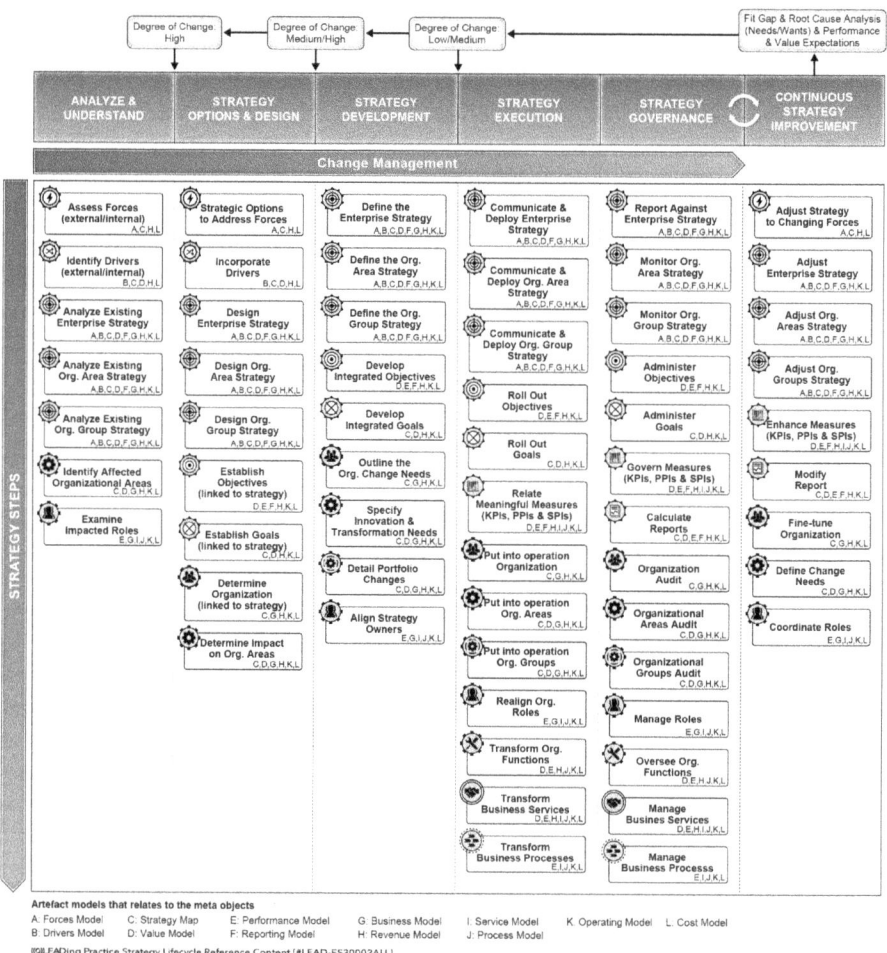

Fig. 2. The Strategy Lifecycle building blocks and relevant artefacts

5 The Value of an Underlying Strategy Ontology

An ontology is an intentional semantic structure that encodes the set of objects and terms that are presumed to exist in some area of interest (i.e. the universe of discourse or semantic domain). Furthermore this includes the relationships that hold among them and the implicit rules constraining the structure of this (piece of) reality [21, 22]. In this definition, intentional refers to a structure describing various possible states of affairs, as opposed to extensional, which would refer to a structure describing a particular state of affairs. The word semantic indicates that the structure has meaning, which is defined as the relationship between (a structure of) symbols and a mental model of the intentional structure in the mind of the observer. In the context of the strategy ontology, we have used semantics which are an aspect of semiotics, like syntax, to distinguish valid from invalid symbol structures, and like pragmatics, it relates symbols to their meaning within a context e.g., the community in which they are shared [20]. Ontologies can be categorised and classified according to several criteria (e.g., context, semantic relations) [25]. When ontologies are classified according to their universe of discourse, we distinguish foundational, domain, task and application ontologies [23]. The strategy ontology would be considered to be an application ontology, as it relates to a very specific universe of discourse. Figure 3 displays the GUA Ontology Meta Model in which the strategy meta model is derived.

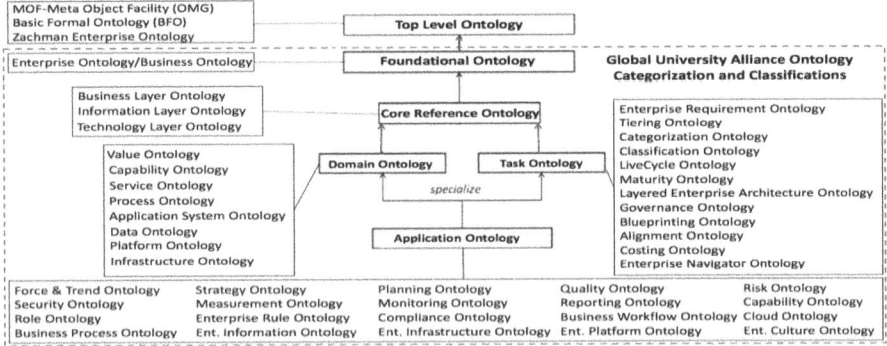

Fig. 3. GUA Ontology Meta Model

The strategy vocabulary is built based on the existing applications/uses and as specialisations of the enterprise ontology terms [24]. As illustrated in Fig. 4, the strategy ontology provides an overview of the most common strategy related meta-objects, but it also provides the relationships between the objects and how they are used across the Strategy Lifecycle phases and within various strategy relevant artefacts. The Strategy Ontology Meta Model has the purpose of portraying the strategy relevant meta objects and the relationship between the objects. Furthermore, it documents the semantic relations as well as describing which artefact has that specific object. Unlike other strategy meta models the Strategy Ontology Meta Model aims to encapsulate all the relevant aspects that semantically related to strategy. Giannoulis's et al. [28] development of 'A meta-model of strategy maps and balanced scorecard' intentionally focuses on Kaplan and Norton's work on strategy maps and the balance scorecard. Although these are two well utilised approaches in strategy they do not, nor does the meta model enable a practitioner to navigate their way through design to execution. Building integrated and standardised strategy relevant artefacts which are relevant for strategy practitioners does require an underlying fully integrated meta model with semantic richness that enables interoperability between the artefacts and the lifecycle phases. Meta models that incorporate multiple artefacts/views use the semantic relations and their rules associated with the meta objects connectivity. For example, the link between the meta-object 'force' and the meta-object 'stratgey' enables the practitioners to understand the forces that impact the organisation and which forces that need to be addressed by the strategy. There are also objects that have multiple semantic relations. For example the measure meta-objects intersect with objectives, organisational functions, roles, process, functions and reports. Each one of the other meta objects has multiple artefacts to model that subject. As it has the same object, consequently, the content of one artefact can through the same object also be reused in a different artefact [14]. During the different phases of the Strategy Lifecycle various objects i.e. subjects and thereby artefacts are used. Appreciating the full semiotic depth of the strategy ontology is therefore considered an essential part for any practitioners work with and around various relevant strategy concepts [26]. As illustrated in Fig. 4, the Strategy Lifecycle is therefore built upon ontological and semiotic concepts, which have been studied and observed to apply to almost any strategy modelling, engineering and architecture concept. The Strategy Lifecycle approach is therefore expected to provide a powerful tool to assist in the identification and capture of relevant strategy aspects.

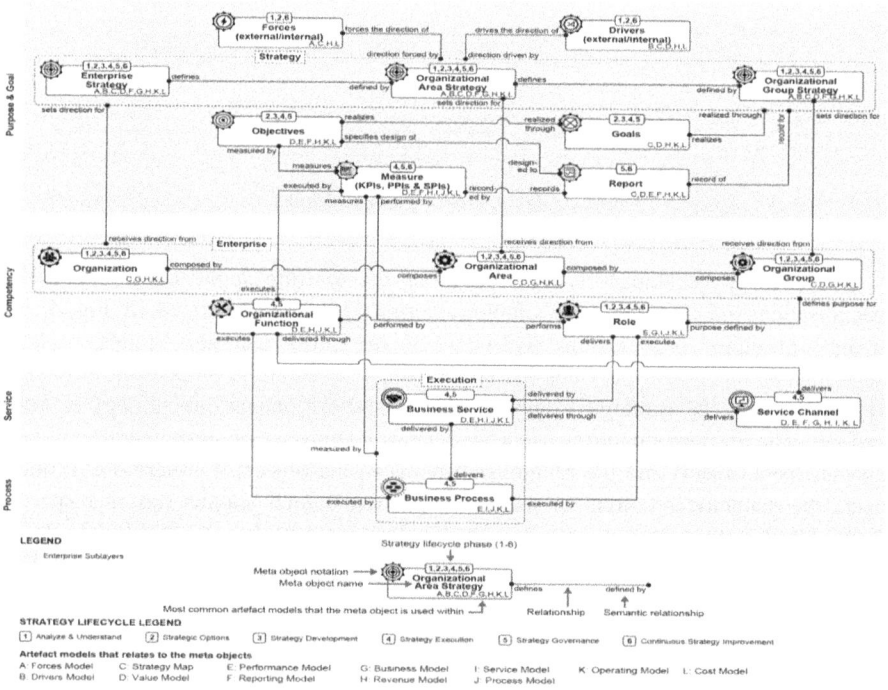

Fig. 4. Strategy Ontology Meta Model

6   Conclusion

The Strategy Lifecycle provides a truly interlinked approach from strategy design to strategy execution. The underlying ontology and semiotics allows us to take any organisational strategy and integrate it into the way of thinking, working and modelling regardless of industry type. The Strategy Lifecycle is based upon an empiric ontology, meaning that its roots lie in both practice and research. Consequently, it covers all aspects of the strategy phases. Some of the gaps discussed in the strategic theory and models can therefore be fulfilled with the Strategy Lifecyle approach. It is designed to be vendor neutral/agnostic and it can therefore be used with most existing frameworks, methods and (or) approaches that have any of the mentioned relevant strategy meta-objects. Due to the limitations placed on this paper we were only able to demonstrate a brief overview of its usefulness.

While it can be used as described, in order to attain the desired level of completeness, it is complemented with elicitation support such as guiding principles for creating, interpreting, analysing and using strategy engineering, modeling or architecture concepts within the Strategy Lifecycle. In future publications this will be extended to evidence deeper in-sights into aspects such as enterprise ontology and semantics, strategy architecture, business architecture and multiple modelling disciplines including value modelling, revenue modelling, performance modeling and service modelling.

References

1. Ansoff, H.I.: Corporate Strategy: An Analytic Approach to Business Policy for Growth and Expansion. McGraw-Hill, New York City (1965)
2. Bridges Business Consultancy: Strategy implementation Survey Results (2016). http://www.implementation-hub.com/resources/implementation-surveys
3. Cândido, C., Santos, S.: Strategy implementation: what is the failure rate? J. Manag. Organ. **21**, 237–262 (2015)
4. Carucci, R.: Executives fail to execute strategy because They're too internally focused (2017). https://hbr.org/2017/11/executives-fail-to-execute-strategy-because-theyre-too-internally-focused
5. Chandler, A.D.: Strategy and structure: chapters in the history of the American industrial enterprise. Massachusetts Institute of Technology (1962)
6. Godfrey, R.D.: Strategic management: a critical introduction. Routledge, Abingdon/London/New York (2016)
7. Mellat-Parast, M., Golmohammadi, D., Mcfadden, K.L., Miller, J.W.: Linking business strategy to service failures and financial performance: empirical evidence from the U.S. domestic airline industry. J. Oper. Manag. **38**, 14–24 (2015)
8. Mui, C.: How Kodak failed (2012). https://www.forbes.com/sites/chunkamui/2012/01/18/how-kodak-failed/3/#4ba895d74a97
9. Oxford University Press: Strategy—definition of strategy in English by oxford dictionaries. https://en.oxforddictionaries.com/definition/strategy (2018)
10. Pettigrew, A.M., Thomas, H., Whittington, R., Pettigrew, A.M.: Handbook of Strategy and Management. SAGE, London (2002)
11. Sloan, A.P.: My Years with General Motors. Sidgwick and Jackson - Pan, London (1965)
12. Smith, R.R.: The Reality Test: Still Relying on Strategy?. Profile Books, London (2013)
13. Whittington, R.: What is Strategy - And Does it Matter. Thompson Learning, London (2001)
14. von Rosing, M., Urquhart, B., Zachman, J.: Using a business ontology for structuring artefacts: example - northern health. Int. J. Conceptual Struct. Smart Appl. **3**, 42–85 (2015)
15. Porter, M.E.: How competitive forces shape strategy. Harv. Bus. Rev. **57**, 137–145 (1979)

16. Porter, M.E.: The value chain and competitive advantage, pp. 50–66 (2001)
17. Porter, M.E.: What is Strategy? Harv. Bus. Rev. **74**, 61 (1996)
18. Prasad, A.: Strategy as "inferior" choice: a re-interpretation of porter's "what is strategy?". J. Manag. Res. **10**, 15 (2010)
19. Valos, M.J., Bednall, D.H.B., Callaghan, B.: The impact of Porter's strategy types on the role of market research and customer relationship management. Mark. Intell. Plan. **25**, 147–156 (2007)
20. Cordeiro, J., Filipe, J.: The semiotic pentagram framework–a perspective on the use of semiotics within organisational semiotics (2004)
21. Genesereth, M.R., Nilsson, N.J.: Logical Foundations of Artificial Intelligence, vol. 58. Morgan Kaufmann, Burlington (1987)
22. Giaretta, P., Guarino, N.: Ontologies and knowledge bases towards a terminological clarification. Towards Very Large knowl. Bases: Knowl. Build. Knowl. Shar. **25**, 307–317 (1995)
23. Guarino, N.: Semantic matching: formal ontological distinctions for information organization, extraction, and integration. In: Pazienza, M.T. (ed.) SCIE 1997. LNCS, vol. 1299, pp. 139–170. Springer, Heidelberg (1997). https://doi.org/10.1007/3-540-63438-X_8
24. von Rosing, M., Laurier, W.: An introduction to the business ontology. Int. J. Conceptual Struct. Smart Appl. **3**, 20–41 (2015)
25. von Rosing, M., Laurier, W., Polovina, S.M.: (2015)
26. von Rosing, M., Arzumanyan, M., Zachman Sr., J.A.: The relationship between ontology and modelling concepts: example role oriented modelling. Int. J. Conceptual Struct. Smart Appl. **5**, 25–47 (2017)
27. von Rosing, M.: The Complete Business Process Handbook Body of Knowledge from Process Modeling to BPM, vol. I. Elsevier, Amsterdam (2014)
28. Giannoulis, C., Petit, M., Zdravkovic, J.: Modeling business strategy: a meta-model of strategy maps and balanced scorecards, pp. 1–6 (2011)
29. Klag, M., Langley, A.: Critical junctures in strategic planning: understanding failure to enable success. Organ. Dyn. **43**, 274–283 (2014)

Role of Digitisation in Enabling Co-creation of Value in KIBS Firms

Mona Ashok$^{(\boxtimes)}$

Henley Business School, University of Reading,
Whiteknights, Reading RG6 6UD, UK
m.ashok@henley.ac.uk

Abstract. The affordability, reliability, access and mass adoption of information and communication technological advances is a key trigger to digitisation. Digitisation significantly influences the global economy, as it impacts interpersonal and organisational relationships, disrupts organisational practices, and enables innovation. Digitization is transforming a firm's interaction with its external partners (including users), through the use of digitally-enabled business processes, online chats, digital services, online tools/applications and automated systems. This paper focuses on the role of digitisation in innovation in services, because services account for a significant proportion of GDP and employment in developed economies. In specific, the paper explores the topic in the context of Knowledge-Intensive Business Service (KIBS) firms (that exhibit high levels of innovations as users, producers and diffusers of innovation). This conceptual paper explores how KIBS firms can maximise the value extracted from external knowledge/collaboration through digitisation (since KIBS firms demonstrate the highest degree of adoption of digital technologies) to enhance process innovation outcomes. Process innovation is chosen because it plays a fundamental role in delivering efficiency and market share. This paper proposes that digitisation will moderate the relationship between collaboration (breadth of external partners and depth of user engagement) and internal resource commitment to enhance the benefits derived from process innovation.

Keywords: Absorptive capacity · Co creation of value · Digitisation
Innovation · Internal resource commitment
Knowledge-intensive business services (KIBS)

1 Introduction

The affordability, reliability, access and mass adoption of information and communication technological (ICT) advances have played a fundamental role in triggering digitization at five levels [22]. At economy level, ICT has improved connectivity, enabled market creation and digital-service introduction. At an individual level, ICT has lead to an explosion in the number of internet users, online/web activities and mobile application usage. At an industry and organization level, ICT has transformed the business processes and the interactions between firms and their external partners; substantial ICT investments have led to enhanced digital capabilities. Finally, at a client/buyer level, ICT has significantly increased online solution usage, self-service usage and evaluation of online experience.

In this paper, *digitisation is defined* as the transformation of the operations through digital communications and applications. Thus, digitisation "encapsulates the social transformation triggered by the mass adoption of digital technologies that generate, process and transfer information" [21, p. 314]. Widespread digitisation of organisational operations and business models is reshaping the global economy; digitisation plays a key role in delivering operational efficiency and competitive advantage [6, 23]. The World Economic Forum's (WEF) [40] white paper on digital transformation emphasises that digitisation has created unparalleled value propositions and changed the way we do business, however, it has introduced a major source of risk. The impact of digitisation is so substantial that 90% of organisations have acknowledged they have adjusted their operations considerably [39]. OECD's Digital Economy Outlook [29] highlights that digital advances hugely impact the society and enable transformation; OECD indictors show that ICT investment in 2015 in the OECD area was 2.3% of GDP and 11% of total fixed investment. We now discuss the research context.

Services are a key source of growth in advanced economies, thus there is a growing academic and practitioner focus on services. OECD [30] indicators show that Services contributed, as percent of value added by activity, 73.72% in the European Union (2016), 78.61% (estimated) in the UK (2017), and 78.92% in the US (2015). Although, scholars argue there is a great deal to learn from innovation in services [15], innovation theories and measures have historically focused on the manufacturing industry, thus creating a research gap. In this paper, *services are defined* as the application of specialised skills and knowledge for the benefit of another entity or the entity itself [39]. *Innovation is defined* as "the implementation of a new or significantly improved product (good or service), or process, a new marketing method, or a new organisational method in business practices, workplace organisation or external relations" [31, p. 46]. However, services are heterogeneous, and the extent of innovativeness and the nature of innovations undertaken differ within the service sector [37]. This paper, thus, focuses on one service sector: Knowledge-Intensive Business Service (KIBS), because KIBS firms are noted for their vital role in the knowledge-based economy, and are a key enabler, source, and user of innovation [12, 18]. *KIBS are defined* as, "economic activities which are intended to result in the creation, accumulation or dissemination of knowledge" [27, p. 18].

Similarly, innovations are heterogeneous. This paper focuses on process innovation, a source of competitive advantage. *Process innovation is defined* as the implementation of a new or significantly improved production or delivery method that is of value to the user; process innovation includes significant changes in techniques, equipment and/or software [31]. The implementation of process innovation is important, because it supports other innovations and provides several firm-level benefits: such as generating efficiency gains through cost controls and improved capability, and delivering value-add to the users through productivity gains and enhanced quality [15]. Further, process innovation is fundamental in the KIBS context, because process-oriented and intangible knowledge flows are a defining characteristic of the KIBS provider and consumer relationship [9, 18]. Research shows that this relationship creates a self-sustaining cycle of innovation for both the KIBS provider and its users. Next, we introduce the key constructs used in the paper.

The need for both internal and external knowledge sources for innovation is emphasised in the literature. While internal knowledge flows are essential to learning and benefiting from new knowledge, the interaction between a firm and its environment is recognised to be significant for innovation as it enables the exploitation of external knowledge [11, 19]. Collaboration with external partners is valuable because external feedback helps firms to effectively understand problems, develop solutions and make informed decisions. The continual exchange of knowledge with external partners also helps firms to develop the ability to collaborate in the long-term; in fact, the lack of this ability creates severe competitive disadvantages for firms.

This paper explores both the breadth of external collaboration and the depth of user collaboration, because KIBS firms show a higher propensity in engaging with external partners, especially customers to co-create value [18]. In this paper, *collaboration is defined* as the joint creation of value by a firm and its partners, and involves exchange, sharing and co-development [39]. Therefore, *co-creation of value implies that,* "both the offeror and the beneficiary of service collaboratively create value" [39, p. 8]. *User is defined* as the individual who is the consumer and co-producer of value and who expects benefits from using a product or service [19, 39].

Extensive literature shows that firms need to invest resources in developing absorptive capacity to maximise the benefits extracted from internal and external knowledge [11]. *Absorptive capacity is defined* as the ability of a firm to integrate, internalise and exploit knowledge for financial gains [11]. Whilst the concepts of absorptive capacity and learning from external knowledge sources are extensively researched, few studies have explored internal resources commitment (to develop absorptive capacity) [41] and its interplay with collaboration [2–4] in the context of innovation.

1.1   Research Gaps and Business Needs

Several business problems underlie the lack of attractiveness of process innovation projects for KIBS firms [2–4]. Firstly, under tough economic conditions service firms find it easier to adopt cost-cutting strategies that seem to produce immediate results. Secondly, these firms seem to have limited competence in defining a supportive environment for process innovation. Thirdly, KIBS firms enjoy close working relationships with users; however, they seem to struggle to translate this engagement into value. Lastly, research on the impact of ICT on the absorption of digitised or non-digitised knowledge is lacking [34].

Further, investments in innovation (including process innovation) are always confronted by uncertainty [19]. Research shows that a significant proportion (between 50 and 90%) of process innovation projects fail, or are abandoned after huge investments, or are implemented but fail to achieve the projected gains [1]. Thus, this paper provides a conceptual model (Fig. 1) and propositions to maximise process innovation output: by exploiting the gains extracted from collaboration, understanding the role of digitisation, and studying the interplay of collaboration with commitment of internal resources (for the development of absorptive capacity).

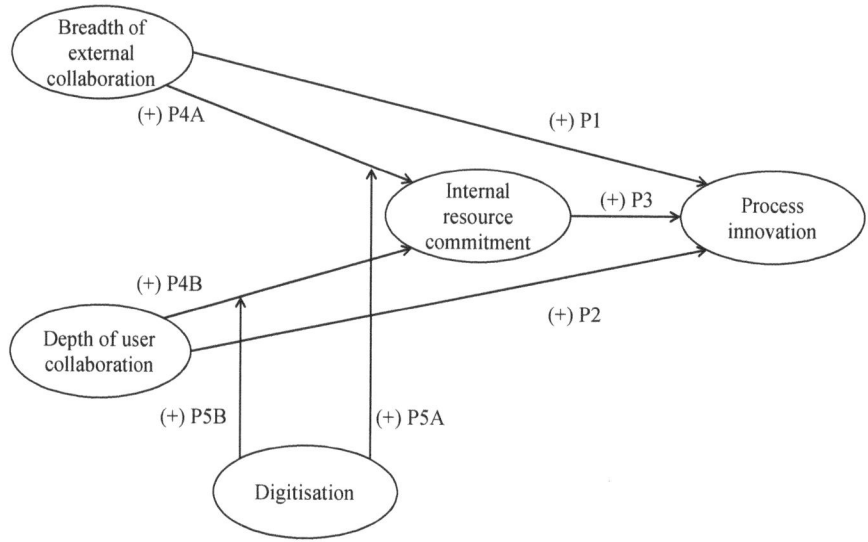

Fig. 1. Conceptual model, based on [3]

2 Theoretical Background and Propositions

2.1 Impact of ICT Advances and Digitisation in the Global Economy

ICT remain crucial for organisational change [10]. This is because ICT advances have significantly reduced the cost of "generating, storing and reproducing information" [12, p. 217], and ICT plays a fundamental role in triggering digitization [22]. Despite the advances in ICT, firms find it difficult to reap benefits from ICT investments. For example, in a survey of 1,200 CEOs, KPMG [24] report that 72% of CEOs recognised that their organisations were struggling to keep up with new technology; 14% of the CEOs agreed that becoming more data driven was a critical challenge they expect to face in the next three years. Similarly, PwC's [32] Digital IQ Survey (based on 1,988 respondents from 51 countries) concluded that: although, 90% of the business leaders expected technological breakthroughs to influence their organisations, they acknowledged that their organisations lacked the competencies to transform successfully. Firms are further challenged because there is a need to leverage the ICT potential in order to foster innovation, economic growth, digital inclusion/acceptance and capabilities: as highlighted in the European Commission's Digital Agenda [23, 40].

  Scholars and practitioners agree that digitisation has transformed the global economy and society. Digitally enabled applications, solutions, services, innovation and business models are influencing business operations and markets (eCommerce) [6, 29, 40]. However, these transformations are challenging as they lead to a tension between existing and new ways of working. For example, OECD [29] report indicates that while 90% of businesses are connected to the internet, only 20% use digital technologies to sell products online. It is important to note that KIBS firms demonstrate the highest degree of adoption of digital technologies; evidence from the 2016 Community Innovation Survey (CIS) in Germany [7].

2.2   Innovation in Services

The study of innovation in services is of great academic and practical interest. For several decades, the service sector has been a major source of growth in the developed economies. By the mid-1980s, this sector was contributing towards 50% of employment and output in such economies [5]. Its influence has increased progressively, as shown in recent studies and OECD indicators [30].

Despite the sector's pivotal role in economic development, the understanding of innovation in services has lagged. Until the 1980s, it was presumed that this sector adopted supplier-driven innovations and was not very innovative; hence, the lack of focus on the study of innovation in services [36]. Historically, innovation measures have largely ignored the characteristics of services, which include intangibility of output, the involvement of the user in service provision, the concurrence of production and consumption, and the difficulty in detecting the service quality changes [15].

2.3   Need for Innovation in KIBS in the Context of a Knowledge Economy

KIBS firms are not only innovative, but also motivate knowledge transfer and innovation in their client firms; they employ highly qualified personnel and are distinguished by the use of professional knowledge [12, 18]. KIBS firms are key hubs in the knowledge-based society, and are key contributors of economic value [9, 12, 13]. KIBS firms are estimated to represent 10% of the total value added in OECD countries, and 15% of the volume of market service businesses in Europe [13]. In 2015, KIBS firms accounted for 16% of total innovation expenditure in Germany.

KIBS firms play a central role in the economy: they work very closely with their users, often in multi-disciplinary teams, they enable learning in their customers, and they facilitate their client firms to translate new information and extract tacit knowledge from the partners [13]. This industry is rapidly growing and amongst the most innovative. Despite this importance, [18] reports that the industry is seldom the focus of research and policy guidelines – a research gap that underpins this paper.

2.4   The Strategic Role of Process Innovation, Especially in the Context of KIBS

A leading emphasis of the innovation literature is the study of product innovation and new product development, however process innovation, the other source of competitive gains, has received far lesser attention [17]. This is problematic because research shows that process innovation is intrinsic to organisational change and product (or service) innovation [35]. Process change delivers hard-to-imitate competitive advantage, however few empirical studies have investigated the factors impacting process innovation at the firm-level [22]. However, limited research on process innovation in services shows encouraging signs that when balanced with a portfolio of service types, process innovation increases KIBS firms' efficiency and market share [9].

2.5   The Need to Collaborate and Exploit External Knowledge

Firms are unlikely to possess all the skills or capabilities to innovate in-house, and the sources of novel ideas are not restricted to the boundaries of a firm [20, 28]. This is supported by extensive research; for example, the 2011 UK Innovation survey shows that on average firms allocate only 35% of the innovation expenditure for internal R&D, and the remainder is spent on other innovation activities [38]. Innovation processes are becoming more open, with a stress on collaborative arrangements to access capabilities, to recombine knowledge and to share resources across organisational boundaries. Service providers are unlikely to rely solely on internal knowledge for innovation and they often depend on external knowledge and experience.

Breadth of External Collaboration. Wide-ranging innovation surveys provide empirical evidence of the importance of broad knowledge sources for innovation [38]. In specific, openness to external knowledge sources is more likely to be prevalent in process innovation than product innovation [35], however, empirical investigation of the impact of the breadth of external collaboration on process innovation is under-explored [20]. Some studies, however, have shown a positive association between the breadth of external collaboration and a firm's ability to undertake process innovation [16], especially in the KIBS context [3, 4]. This is because knowledge plays a central role in KIBS firms; they are known to recombine tacit and codified knowledge to develop value propositions and solve customer problems [12, 35]. In doing so KIBS firms depend on both internal and external knowledge (sourced from external partners). Advancing on the discussion above:

Proposition 1 (P1): The breadth of external collaboration will positively influence process innovation results in KIBS firms.

Depth of User Collaboration. [39's] seminal paper highlighted the service-dominant view of economic development. The service-dominant view is that firms offer a value proposition, but the consumer evaluates the value-in-use, thus the customer is always a co-producer of value. The collaboration between the consumer and a firm is a defining characteristic of service provision [36], in which users are not passive consumers of services: in fact, they work jointly with the firms to innovate [19, 20]. This co-operation is extremely beneficial for a service provider as users often pioneer new services, and because user-developed services diffuse faster than producer-developed services [8].

The provision of KIBS brings together the knowledge capital of the provider, and the needs, experiences and knowledge of the users to create unique solutions for the consumers' distinctive requirements [36]. Thus, it is no surprise that KIBS firms are characterised by a highly interactive relationship with their users to solve problems; these firms rely on user knowledge much more than other service providers and manufacturing firms [13].

Proposition 2 (P2): User collaboration will positively influence process innovation results in KIBS firms.

2.6   The Commitment of Internal Resources in Extracting Value from Collaboration

The source of innovative ideas is not confined within the boundaries of a firm, but lie at the intersection of a firm and its environment [31]. Thus, firms collaborate with external partners with a view to accessing new capabilities (ideas, knowledge, or practices). The process of accessing external knowledge sources enhances a firm's knowledge base and widens its future learning, technological and organisational innovation trajectories [26]. Diverse knowledge develops a firm's learning capability, and broadens the opportunities available in the future [13].

However, the benefits of new knowledge acquired because of collaboration are not automatic, but subject to a firm's actions [14]. This is because firms face the problem of translating knowledge (both possessed internally and acquired from external partners) into organisational advantages. This translation is dependent on a firm's commitment of internal resources in developing absorptive capacity. Research shows that the investment of resources in developing the capability to learn from diverse sources is especially important for KIBS firms [3, 4]. Thus, this paper proposes:

Proposition 3 (P3): Internal resources commitment will positively influence process innovation results in KIBS firms.

2.7   Internal Resources Mediate the Impact of Collaboration on Process Innovation

[20, 28] has argued that in the current economy – which is global, open, networked and technologically advanced – a firm's ability to reap profits from innovation is subject to the effective translation of consumer needs into value-propositions. Thus, gains from collaborative innovation are dependent on a firm's underlying processes, and are subject to its ability to appropriate value from external knowledge [28]. Specifically, the gains from user collaboration are contingent on the translation of knowledge into organisational and individual learning [20, 28, 35]. This premise is supported by a study that reported that the effect of customer collaboration on product innovation performance was indirect and fully mediated by organisational practices [14]. Another wide-ranging survey of open innovation activities across UK firms found that collaboration was positively correlated with investment intensity [28]. It can therefore be concluded that a firm's strategy towards the commitment of resources is important for the extraction of value from external knowledge.

The importance of the study of the interplay of internal resources and collaboration for innovation is evident in the absorptive capacity literature. Several literature review articles propose that absorptive capacity will mediate the impact of knowledge source (and collaboration processes) on a firm's performance (and competitive advantage) [41]. Although there is extensive interest in the study of firms' investments and collaborative practices for innovation, several research gaps exist. There is limited understanding of the interrelationship between a firm's collaborative (open) innovation practices and its capability to generate financial gains [25].

Some recent research, however, demonstrates the significance of internal resource commitment in extracting value from collaboration for process innovation in the KIBS context [2–4]. Building on the arguments above, this paper proposes:

Proposition 4A (P4A): The positive effect of breadth of external collaboration on process innovation will be mediated by the firm's commitment of internal resources in KIBS firms.

Proposition 4B (P4B): The positive effect of user collaboration on process innovation will be mediated by the firm's commitment of internal resources in KIBS firms.

2.8   Role of Digitisation in Enabling Co-creation of Value in KIBS Firms

Digitisation has created new opportunities for KIBS firms, who are able to maximise the benefits extracted from collaboration with external partners by codifying knowledge [12]. Existing indicators show that digitisation enables the interaction of the firm with its external partners, for example firms are reporting the benefits of using social technologies in interfacing with the network of external partners [23, 40]. Telecommunications, digitally-enabled platforms, digitised back- and front-office business processes makes it easier for organisations to engage in open innovations. In the context of process innovation in services, there is growing evidence of end-to-end digitally-enabled business processes that integrate the service providers with their external partners [33].

In reference to a service firm's relationship with its users, digitised interactions like: online chats (customer service), contact centre calls routed through automated systems, automated speech recognition have transformed the service provider-customer engagement [23, 40]. Large-scale innovation studies have shown that the top three digital technologies diffused in German firms in 2016 are digital networks and linkages with customers, suppliers and digital networks in production and service provisioning [7]; this strengthens the importance of digitisation for collaboration.

However, current evidence [29] indicates that ICT investments are unlikely to (independently) enable transformation or innovation. This is because a key building block of successfully implementing change is to reinforce new structures, processes and systems, while acknowledging the push-pull stress of new versus old knowledge. Thus, digitisation is expected to moderate the benefits derived from collaboration with external partners, including the value created with users, in order to maximise process innovation outcomes. Thus, this paper proposes that,

Proposition 5A (P5A): Digitisation will moderate the effect of breadth of external collaboration on internal resources in KIBS firms.

Proposition 5B (P5B): Digitisation will moderate the effect of user collaboration on internal resources in KIBS firms.

3   Next Steps and Future Research Opportunities

This paper builds on current research and presents an enhanced conceptual model, based on research in [2–4]. This paper extends theory by incorporating the important concept of digitisation and it proposes the role of digitisation in enabling co-creation of value in KIBS firms. The author plans to empirically investigate the propositions by testing the model and drawing comparisons across two different KIBS sectors. The next steps thereby build on existing literature and provide an opportunity to develop academic and practitioner implications on the use of digitisation in the KIBS context.

References

1. Abdolvand, N., et al.: Assessing readiness for business process reengineering. Bus. Process Manag. J. **14**(4), 497–511 (2008)
2. Ashok, M., et al.: Buyer (dis)satisfaction and process innovation: the case of information technology services provision. Ind. Mark. Manag. **68**, 132–144 (2018)
3. Ashok, M., et al.: End-user collaboration for process innovation in services: the role of internal resources (2014)
4. Ashok, M., et al.: How do collaboration and investments in knowledge management affect process innovation in services? J. Knowl. Manag. **20**(5), 1004–1024 (2016)
5. Barras, R.: Towards a theory of innovation in services. Res. Policy **15**(4), 161–173 (1986)
6. Barrett, M., et al.: Service innovation in the digital age: key contributions and future directions. MIS Q. **39**(1), 135–154 (2015)
7. Behrens, V., et al.: Innovation activities of firms in Germany-Results of the German CIS 2012 and 2014: background report on the surveys of the Mannheim Innovation Panel Conducted in the years 2013 to 2016 (No. 17-04) (2017)
8. Van Der Boor, P., et al.: Users as innovators in developing countries: the global sources of innovation and diffusion in mobile banking services. Res. Policy **43**(9), 1594–1607 (2014)
9. Campagnolo, D., Cabigiosu, A.: Innovation, service types, and performance in knowledge intensive business services. In: Agarwal, R., Selen, W., Roos, G., Green, R. (eds.) The Handbook of Service Innovation, pp. 109–121. Springer, London (2015). https://doi.org/10.1007/978-1-4471-6590-3_6
10. CIPD: Landing transformational change: closing the gap between theory and practice (2015)
11. Cohen, W.M., Levinthal, D.: Absorptive capacity: a new perspective on learning and innovation. Adm. Sci. Q. **35**, 128–152 (1990)
12. Consoli, D., Elche, D., Rullani, F.: Employment and skill configurations in KIBS sectors: a longitudinal analysis. In: Agarwal, R., Selen, W., Roos, G., Green, R. (eds.) The Handbook of Service Innovation, pp. 213–235. Springer, London (2015). https://doi.org/10.1007/978-1-4471-6590-3_11
13. Doroshenko, M., et al.: Knowledge Intensive Business Services as Generators of Innovations (2013)
14. Foss, N.J., et al.: Linking customer interaction and innovation: the mediating role of new organizational practices. Organ. Sci. **22**(4), 980–999 (2011)
15. Frishammar, J., et al.: Antecedents and consequences of firms' process innovation capability: a literature review and a conceptual framework. IEEE Trans. Eng. Manag. **59**(4), 519–529 (2012)
16. Gadrey, J., et al.: New modes of innovation: how services benefit industry. Int. J. Serv. Ind. Manag. **6**(3), 4–16 (1995)
17. Gallouj, F., Savona, M.: Innovation in services: a review of the debate and a research agenda. J. Evol. Econ. **19**(2), 149–172 (2009)
18. Den Hertog, P.: Knowledge intensive business services as co-producers of innovation. Int. J. Innov. Manag. **4**(4), 491–528 (2000)

19. Von Hippel, E.: Democratizing innovation: the evolving phenomenon of user innovation. The MIT Press, Cambridge (2005)
20. Huang, F., Rice, J.: Openness in product and process innovation. Int. J. Innov. Manag. **16**(4), 1250020 (2012)
21. Katz, R.L., Koutroumpis, P.: Measuring digitization: a growth and welfare multiplier. Technovation **33**(10–11), 314–319 (2013)
22. Keupp, M.M., et al.: The strategic management of innovation: a systematic review and paths for future research. Int. J. Manag. Rev. **14**(4), 367–390 (2012)
23. Kotarba, M.: Measuring digitalization – key metrics. Found. Manag. **9**, 1 (2017)
24. KPMG: Global CEO Outlook 2015: The growth imperative in a more competitive environment (2015)
25. Lane, P.J., et al.: The reification of absorptive capacity: a critical review and rejuvenation of the construct. Acad. Manag. Rev. **31**(4), 833–863 (2006)
26. Leonard-Barton, D.: Core capabilities and core rigidities: a paradox in managing new product development. Strateg. Manag. J. **13**, 111–125 (1992)
27. Miles, I., et al.: Knowledge-intensive business services: users, carriers and sources of innovation (1995)
28. Mina, A., et al.: Open service innovation and the firm's search for external knowledge. Res. Policy **43**(5), 853–866 (2014)
29. OECD: OECD Digital Economy Outlook 2017 (2017)
30. OECD: Value added by activity (indicator). https://doi.org/10.1787/a8b2bd2b-en
31. OECD, Eurostat: Oslo Manual Guidelines for Collecting and Interpreting Innovation Data (2005)
32. PwC: 2015 Global digital IQ survey. https://www.pwc.com/gx/en/advisory-services/digital-iq-survey-2015/campaign-site/digital-iq-survey-2015.pdf
33. Rai, A., Sambamurthy, V.: Editorial notes-the growth of interest in services management: opportunities for information systems scholars. Inf. Syst. Res. **17**(4), 327–331 (2006)
34. Roberts, N., et al.: Absorptive capacity and information systems research: review, synthesis, and directions for future research. MIS Q. Manag. Inf. Syst. **36**(2), 625–648 (2012)
35. Robertson, P.L., et al.: Managing open incremental process innovation: absorptive capacity and distributed learning. Res. Policy **41**(5), 822–832 (2012)
36. Salter, A., Tether, B.S.: Innovation in services: an overview. In: Haynes, K., Grugulis, I. (eds.) Managing Services: Challenges and Innovation. Oxford University Press, Oxford (2014)
37. Trigo, A.: The nature of innovation in R&D and Non-R&D-intensive service firms: evidence from firm-level latent class analysis. Ind. Innov. **20**(1), 48–68 (2013)
38. UKIS: First Findings from the UK Innovation Survey 2011: Science and Innovation Analysis (2012)
39. Vargo, S.L., Lusch, R.F.: Service-dominant logic: continuing the evolution. J. Acad. Mark. Sci. **36**(1), 1–10 (2008)
40. WEF: Digital Transformation of Industries: In collaboration with Accenture (2016)
41. Zahra, S.A., George, G.: Absorptive capacity: a review, reconceptualization, and extension. Acad. Manag. Rev. **27**, 185–203 (2002)

Cluster Nodes as a Unit for Value Co-creation: The Role of Information Technologies in Competitiveness of the Oil and Gas Industry

Vitaly Ambalov[1] and Irina Heim[2([⊠])] [iD]

[1] National Agency for Development of Local Content, Astana, Kazakhstan
vimsgm@gmail.com
[2] Henley Business School, University of Reading, Reading, UK
i.heim@pgr.reading.ac.uk

Abstract. Both the national competitiveness paradigm and cluster theory have prompted decision-makers in emerging countries to take a closer look at the cluster approach, and to consider the possibility of using this approach to boost economic growth. However, this has not led to wider use of cluster analysis as a major instrument for studying complex economic processes in these countries. The reason for this is that the majority of the reviewed concepts of cluster development implemented in emerging countries, such as Kazakhstan and Russia, use of the cluster approach based on foreign experience disregarding the importance of initial local conditions. Thus a more formal study of clusters in emerging countries, taking into account the impact of institutional factors and the individual structural uncertainty of economic systems, recurrent crises and market shocks, is required This research fills the gap by proposing a cluster node as a unit of analysis that allows subdivision of any big industrial and commercial groups, of economic sectors, and of multinational enterprises (MNE) and other structures, into interconnected nodes of a smaller scale, and applying this up to the smallest nodes that are of interest to researchers. This concept will create theoretical foundations for the transformation of national economic clusters, which is strategically important for national governments seeking to attract foreign investments (FDI) and increase local content, thus attracting MNEs to invest in national economies. This research demonstrates how the concept of cluster nodes can be applied to the analysis of linkages between oil and gas industry (O&G) and industries responsible for the development of information and communication technology (ICT) in Kazakhstan.

Keywords: Eclectic paradigm · Value co-creation · Clusters · MNEs
ICT · Oil and gas industry · Local content policy

1 Introduction

The national competitiveness paradigm and cluster theory were introduced by Porter in 1990s [14, 15]. They are the result of a large-scale research project that led to global changes in the perception of international trade and the manufacturing industry. These

K. Liu et al. (Eds.): ICISO 2018, IFIP AICT 527, pp. 155–163, 2018.
https://doi.org/10.1007/978-3-319-94541-5_16

transformations evolved in the increasing role of specialized firms, and accelerated development of science and technology, in particular in the ICT sector. Simultaneously, the share of R&D services in the added value had been steadily increasing [2], while the competitiveness of goods and services had come to rely on harmonized cooperation and simultaneous competition of firms as part of an economic cluster. The role of multi-national enterprises has changed dramatically. Going beyond national borders MNEs have introduced new products and services into the global market, offering tremendous opportunities to small and medium-sized enterprises that could never before have claimed a share in foreign markets. Such transformations prompted decision-makers in emerging countries to take a closer look at the cluster approach and to consider the possibility of using this approach to boost economic growth.

However, the extensive interest in the cluster approach has not led to wider use of cluster analysis as a major instrument for studying complex economic processes. In emerging countries, a cluster is viewed as a geographically limited association of small and medium-sized enterprises providing services to homogeneous market segments. This has led to mistakes on the side of government decision-makers who seek to create a vertical regulation structure and to implement an industrial policy that views the cluster approach as a concept which has nothing to do with the major economic sectors. In the majority of the reviewed concepts of cluster development implemented in emerging countries, such as Kazakhstan and Russia, the cluster approach is based on copying foreign experience that disregards "the importance of initial conditions and the danger of arguing that one cluster structure is necessarily always more effective than another one" [19]. These circumstances prompt a more formal study of clusters, taking into account the impact of institutional factors and the individual structural uncertainty of economic systems, recurrent crises and market shocks. For the purposes of formalization of cluster systems, we make use of the results of many years of work of international business researchers, and, first and foremost, an eclectic paradigm, which we strongly believe most accurately defines the nature of a company that often acts using apparently incompatible strategies (eclectically), achieving incredible results in an eclectic environment.

2 Theories and Literature

2.1 Theory of Clusters and Competitiveness

Spatial clustering or agglomeration of firms with similar interests might yield agglomerative economies and an industrial atmosphere, external to the individual firms, but internal to the cluster [8]. The era of alliance capitalism demonstrated the impact of "trans-border elements" on cluster functioning [8, 19]. Therefore, it is critical to identify a cluster in which MNE will utilize its own advantages. This identification seems deceptively simple, but in reality, it is a complex task, because there is no definitive and unambiguous understanding of the term "economic cluster". The need for cluster analysis arises when a researcher studying a large system needs to select elements of a certain class from its entire assembly. A classic example is using cluster analysis in order to study country competitiveness. In accordance with the task, Porter

[14, 15] confined the selection of objects for analysis to a specific geographical zone and defined a cluster as a geographically close group of interrelated companies and associated agencies united by common external factors and areas of activity. This definition of competitiveness underpins the concept of the Global Competitiveness Index, reflecting the growing demand to take into account a larger and more complex set of factors that have an impact on a country's prosperity. At present, global organizations work with the definition offered by Porter: "Competitiveness is defined as the set of institutions, policies, and factors that determine the level of productivity. The level of productivity, in turn, sets the sustainable level of prosperity that can be earned by an economy (and) a more competitive economy is one that is likely to grow at larger rates over the medium to long run" [20]. However, many researchers criticize this definition of competitiveness at the macro-level [e.g. 1, 12, 16] arguing that this gives a distorted picture of competitiveness due to the protectionists regulations used by the countries to protect their markets. For example, Atkinson [1], defines competitiveness as the ability of a nation's non-mineral-based traded sectors to effectively compete in global markets in the absence of subsidies and government protections, while receiving a strong price premium that enables strong terms of trade. The approach suggested by this definition will be used to interpret the increasing competitiveness as a result of value co-creation in clusters.

2.2   Value Co-creation in Clusters

Value co-creation is a concept that "encompasses all the specific theoretical and empirical occurrences in which companies and customers generate value through interaction" [11, 21]. Co-creation in MNE settings can be defined as the interaction between headquarters, subsidiaries, employees, subcontractors, and customers with each other for the development of new business opportunities [10]. The major actors in the process of value co-creation in MNE settings – Headquarters, Subsidiaries, Employees, Customers and Subcontractors – interact with each other in trying to meet customer expectations. To this end, each of the actors adds value. However, it should be taken into consideration that knowledge of customers' needs is also an important value that plays a crucial role in resource transfer managed by the MNE's subsidiary. The responsibility to do this is delegated to the subsidiary by the headquarters. Each cycle of adding value is preceded by a transaction of resource exchange. We would like to emphasize that the process itself does not create any value for the participants of the value co-creation process. The value is generated once a transaction is complete. Thus, in different periods each of the actors specified by the model can be either a supplier or a recipient of resources.

2.3   Eclectic Paradigm

The modern MNE has to be a 'meta-integrator', able to leverage knowledge within and between the different constituent affiliates of its international network, which requires efficient internal markets and well-structured cross-border hierarchies [13]. These empirical findings confirm that the major factors of competitiveness of domestic companies is not protection of the market against MNEs, but rather local content development through technological upgrade and growth, based on value co-creation in clusters comprising foreign and indigenous companies.

The study of related literature [2, 9, 13] and other literature brings us to the conclusion that the eclectic paradigm [3–7], coupled with internalization theory [17, 18] is a representative analytical basis for describing structure, and the genesis of economic systems of any tier, not excluding economic clusters of various typologies. The eclectic paradigm is based on three easily definable factors (OLI factors or OLI): the first is the ownership advantage – O, which allows distribution between firms of advantages associated with owning various types of assets. The second is locational advantages – L, which is the advantage of location, such as natural and man-made resources and assets, institutional system of restricting actions of economic actors, as well as factors related to human capital. The third factor is internalization advantages – I, which can be viewed as advantage in terms of systemic links. Inter- and intra-cluster links (I) is one of the important indicators of cluster formation and will be studied in this research.

3 Theoretical Frameworks

The abovementioned properties and principles of the eclectic paradigm that bring together numerous heterogeneous elements and arrange them into three uniform groups, create a foundation for introducing a new unit to analyze interrelated industrial and commercial structures; such as industrial agglomerations, economic clusters, and MNEs. The new unit of analysis should encompass company capacities in conjunction with locational and internalization advantages. We use the term cluster node (CN) as such a unit of analysis, where CN is a set of interdependent factors.

In this research we define cluster node as a dynamic scale-invariant economic OLI system with institutional regulation of internalization of locational advantages (L), in which internalization (I) serves as a link between L and O advantages in this location, and a link with other cluster nodes outside this location. The use of a cluster node as a unit of analysis allows division of any large industrial and commercial groups, economic sectors, MNE and other structures into interconnected nodes of a smaller scale and applying this up to the smallest nodes that are of interest to researchers. The typology of the cluster nodes is discussed in the next section (see Table 1 below for definitions).

Investments in national economic cluster are always accompanied either by the internalization of existing cluster nodes, or the appearance of new cluster nodes. Moreover, independent if the investor is local or foreign, they need to exactly identify the type of the cluster node they invest as well as develop the strategy for value co-creation within the national cluster node. This is especially important for MNEs as OLI should best be seen as a way of looking at the phenomenon of multinational enterprises and their activities, resulting in answers on the important questions of MNE activities: why, where and how. Each of these questions can be addressed at a different level: macro, meso or micro [9].

Table 1. Classification of cluster nodes. Source: Authors.

Type of a cluster node	Acronym	Definition
National economic cluster	Cn	Advantages and their owners as well as institutions regulating internalization in certain countries
Territorial cluster	Ct	Advantages and their owners as well as institutions regulating internalization in certain territory
Industry cluster	Ci	Actors taking part in value creation of certain types of products
Clusters alliance	Ca	Actors with weak links, interacting and competing with each other
Clusters group	Cg	Actors with strong links and low competition (hierarchical corporations, including state-owned holdings)
Company	Cc	Company where processes are determined
Node process	Cp	Process performed in a company
Clusters skill	Cs	Person, owner of the technical knowledge and skills required for successful career in the industry

Figure 1 below shows the three-level architecture of a national economic cluster, in which a territorial cluster and an industry cluster, complying with restrictions imposed by national and supranational institutions, may have a common coordination body, while the remaining nodes should necessarily conform with the restrictions imposed by regulatory bodies (top officials), or coordinating bodies (the so-called cluster organizations).

The inclusion of people in the typology of clusters (clusters skill/Cs), has a number of significant reasons. The information that is created, accumulated and transferred in the network, the movement of knowledge holders within the created network, as well as internetwork links, all have an impact on the efficiency of the subsidiary and the very MNE that equals, or is even greater, than that of the processes determined by the system. This is the impact of a human being both as an owner and carrier of intellectual property. Therefore, each employee should be viewed as a self-similar and invariant

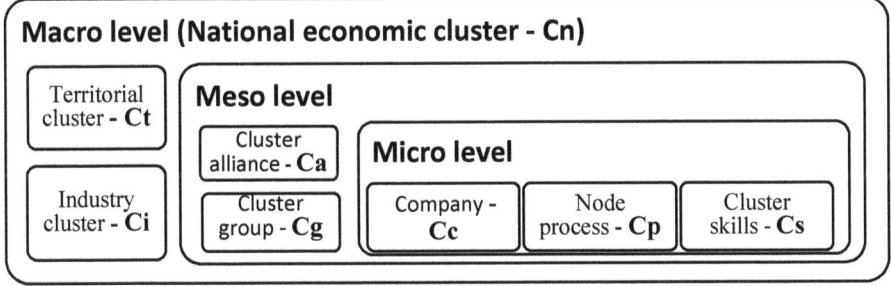

Fig. 1. Architecture of the national economic cluster. Source: Authors.

actor of the network communication because the cluster analysis will be incomplete without the intellectual component. Indeed, in any cluster and in any firm, tangible assets and internalization do not make sense without inclusion of the owners/ professionals who act as knowledge holders.

The eclectic paradigm does allow one to go a step further by relating the OLI configuration facing MNEs to a number of structural or contextual variables [4]. This research will adopt the theory of value co-creation [21] as a theoretical lens through which IT-enabled local capabilities (or OLI contextual variables) development in clusters is explained.

4   Case Study: Linking Kazakhstan's Oil and Gas and ICT Clusters

This concept is a promising instrument for optimizing the existing cluster nodes and synthesizing new cluster nodes, including in the complementary O&G and ICT sectors. The complementarity is based on three factors: (i) digitalization of business and broader use of sensing systems and other high-tech devices, which lead to the accumulation of big data, to be selectively used by managers and technical specialists; (ii) accumulation of big data prompts drastic transformation of the system itself – data as such will be viewed as a valuable source of knowledge about an object and its current status and behavior. This will help to improve the system of quality management, as well as to synthesize innovative tasks and run projects. In other words, there will be integration of all components of two sectors; (iii) a capability to analyze the current status of the system and total automatization of processes, which will gradually erase borders between ICT and business, and emphasize the importance of specialists being able to work with big data.

We study the possibility of increasing the local content and accelerating the growth of the ICT cluster node of Kazakhstan by linking it with the O&G cluster node, integrating this pool with national clusters of other countries, thus making use of the mutually beneficial cooperation with the unified international cluster system. The cluster nodes concept allows cluster analysis to be conducted across selected indices describing competitiveness. In this case we have used one index, namely the index showing the change of the share of products assembled by Kazakhstan's ICT, and consumed by the O&G industry. Figure 2 below shows the matrix of the current status of the explored system.

The matrix is based on official statistical data and information provided by international institutions. These data confirm the country's progress in high-technology sectors. In particular, in line with The Networked Readiness Index 2016, Kazakhstan is ranked 39th out of 139 countries. Thus, Kazakhstan is ahead of Turkey, Poland and Italy and is close to the Czech Republic in this index [22]. The analysis of the OL matrix reveals that Kazakhstan's cluster nodes responsible for telecommunications and provision of computer equipment and communication facilities are well balanced in terms of supply and demand. Institutions that are necessary for regulation of value co-creation processes in cluster nodes are created (National ICT Holding "Zerde", National Agency for Development of Local Content "NADLoC" and other). However,

O Advantages L Advantages	O&G Business processes, international transactions, equipment, ICT	Education Training of ICT specialists	Education and R&D in ICT and O&G
O&G cluster	Capital investment: $26.83 billion Production volume: oil – 86 million tones (80% MNE) gas – 61.6 billion m^3	13,558 graduates with degree in electronics and ICT	21,269 peopled employed in R&D (all sectors)
Internalization advantages	Laws and regulations aiming to attract FDI Local content regulations Regional legislation, including Eurasian Economic Commission World Trade Organization membership		
ICT cluster	Market size: $2.68 billion, including: O&G cluster is < 10% Services and software: $644 million, or < 25%	Low demand for software and R&D specialists, a low number of software programmers	
O&G cluster demand for ICT products and services	Added value of products and services related to ICT is estimated to exceed $1.0 billion	Insufficient financing of projects to develop high-technology solutions	
Number of specialists in ICT cluster	Communication: 34,500 people Information services: 7,600 people Computer programming, consulting and services: 3,000 people		
Demand for human resources in ICT cluster	High demand for highly qualified specialists		

Fig. 2. Matrix of the links between two nodes: ICT and O&G, current status (2017). Source: Authors based on data provided by the Committee on Statistics, the Ministry of National Economy of the Republic of Kazakhstan, RAEX rating agency, Kazakhstan and authors calculations based on media reports.

certain disproportions in the linked nodes have come to the surface. Indeed, the potential demand of Kazakhstan's O&G industry for computing equipment and services (over $1 billion annually) is not yet saturated. This fact allows high-tech companies, including subsoil users, not to consider the ICT cluster node as a partner able to address these needs. At the same time, information and communication technologies for the O&G industry are developed and purchased outside Kazakhstan's CN.

Apart from this, the Ownership-Location matrix demonstrates: (i) weakness of the ICT cluster node responsible for software development, which is a serious challenge for the ongoing local content policy because information technologies are and will be a key instrument for enhancing the performance of the domestic O&G industry. (ii) another weak point is unavailability of hands-on experience for graduates of new university departments/new universities because of an inadequate number of projects related to development of original IT solutions. At the same time, the launch of new IT projects is prevented by inadequate competencies of programmers. (iii) the country's education system in the ICT field has made considerable progress and domestic universities turn out more graduates for this field than the national economic cluster currently can employ.

Nevertheless, the capacities of the linked nodes of ICT and O&G can be augmented, if the IT business, supported by government institutions, uses FDI instruments to team up with a developed IT cluster of a country that is similar in culture and other parameters determining distance. In line with the cluster nodes concept, if Kazakhstan's leading IT firms set up subsidiary companies in the countries that have developed IT clusters, the available significant advantages will meet to enable large-scale projects and to provide university graduates with an opportunity to get hands-on experience.

5   Conclusions

The traditional approach to studying and defining economic clusters focuses on geographically close groups of companies, and is based on using companies as a unit of analysis. In this work, we suggest the consideration of a cluster as a dynamic OLI system defined as a node, a unit of analysis in a cluster node model. The study of economic clusters in Kazakhstan suggests that competitiveness of clusters is determined by a number of firm specific advantages, available to all cluster participants. The analysis of ICT and O&G clusters of Kazakhstan reveals that the concept is a promising instrument for optimizing the existing cluster systems and synthesizing new systems.

References

1. Atkinson, R.D.: The Competitive Edge: A Policymaker's Guide to Developing a National Strategy. ITIF. http://www.itif.org. Accessed 15 Apr 2018
2. Castellani, D., Piva, M., Schubert, T., Vivarelli, M.: R&D and Productivity in the US and the EU: Sectoral Specificities and Differences in the Crisis. Henley Business School. http://www.henley.ac.uk. Accessed 15 Apr 2018
3. Dunning, J.H.: Toward an eclectic theory of international production: some empirical tests. J. Int. Bus. Stud. 11(1), 9–31 (1980)
4. Dunning, J.H.: The eclectic paradigm of international production: a restatement and some possible extensions. J. Int. Bus. Stud. 19(1), 1–31 (1988)
5. Dunning, J.H.: Reappraising the eclectic paradigm in an age of alliance capitalism. In: The Eclectic Paradigm. Palgrave Macmillan, London (1995)
6. Dunning, J.H.: The eclectic paradigm as an envelope for economic and business theories of MNE activity. Int. Bus. Rev. 9(2), 163–190 (2000)
7. Dunning, J.H.: Location and the multinational enterprise: a neglected factor? J. Int. Bus. Stud. 40(1), 5–19 (2000)

8. Dunning, J.H.: Regions, Globalization, and the Knowledge-Based Economy. Oxford University Press, Oxford (2002)
9. Eden, L.: A critical reflection and some conclusions on OLI. In: Cantwell, J., Narula, R. (eds.) International Business and the Eclectic Paradigm: Developing the OLI Framework. Routledge, London (2003)
10. Heim, I., Tian, T., Ghobadian, A.: Value co-creation in ICT services company: a case study of a cross-border acquisition (2018, in press). https://doi.org/10.1080/10669868.2018.1467841
11. Jaakkola, E., Hakanen, T.: Value co-creation in solution networks. Ind. Mark. Manag. **42**(1), 47–58 (2013)
12. Krugman, P.: Competitiveness: a dangerous obsession. Foreign Aff. **73**(2), 28–44 (1994)
13. Narula, R.: The modern MNE as an efficient meta-integrator: emerging market MNEs need to foster internal embeddedness to succeed. Henley Business School Discussion Paper. Henley Business School (2014). http://www.henley.ac.uk. Accessed 15 Apr 2018
14. Porter, M.: The competitive advantage of nations. Harvard Bus. Rev. **68**(2), 73–93 (1990)
15. Porter, M.: On Competition. Harvard Business School, Cambridge, Boston (1998)
16. Psofogiorgos, N.-A., Metaxas, T.: Porter vs Krugman: history, analysis and critique of regional competitiveness, MPRA Paper 68151. University Library of Munich, Germany (2015)
17. Rugman, A.M.: Regional strategy and the demise of globalization. J. Int. Manag. **9**(4), 409–417 (2003)
18. Rugman, A.M.: Reconciling internalization theory and the eclectic paradigm. Multinatl. Bus. Rev. **18**(2), 1–12 (2010)
19. Rugman, A.M., Verbeke, A.: Multinational enterprises and clusters: an organizing framework. Manag. Int. Rev. **43**(3), 151–169 (2003)
20. Snowdon, B.: The enduring elixir of economic growth. World Econ. **7**(1), 73–130 (2006)
21. Vargo, S.L., Lusch, R.F.: Service-dominant logic: continuing the evolution. J. Acad. Mark. Sci. **36**(1), 1–10 (2008)
22. WEF: The Global Information Technology Report 2016. World Economic Forum, Geneva. WEF. https://www.weforum.org/. Accessed 15 Apr 2018

Socially Aware Knowledge Engineering

Unifying Speech and Computation

Martin John Wheatman[(⊠)]

Yagadi Ltd., Preston, Lancashire PR3 2ND, UK
martin@wheatman.net

Abstract. A novel approach to programming computing machinery is demonstrated by the Enguage[TM] language engine: programming by utterance. The running of a command is modeled as a deductive process; the mechanism by which meaning is ascribed to utterance—induction—is described. A full example of the factorial function is given. The paper then develops utterance not only as a form of issuing commands to hardware, but also of storing, retrieving, and manipulating spoken information—a programmable UI. Because such utterances can be generated by speech-to-text software, such interactive computation does not require a program as a written artifact.

Keywords: Programmable UI · Interactive computation
Speech understanding

1   Introduction

The science of computing introduced by the Church Turing model [1, 2] is a layered approach: source code, as a written representation of algorithm, is compiled into a machine readable code. Programming languages use keywords and tokens to define syntax: an ostensibly unambiguous structure with which to specify that translation. A user interface layer is also required: we may code *int n = 1;* but to be visible n must transcend the process address space. Typically, this means printing in some form. Text-to-speech and speech-to-text technology can fulfill this function. However, there is a need—and the ability—to turn speech directly into action, not merely to augment the control panel metaphor. The context-free approach is not conducive to understanding speech, however, because of its dependence on structure: speech simply does not use reserved words and tokens; often it is repeated, clichéd and unrefined [3]. This paper shows how understanding can be created, not merely supplying values, but constructing behavior—functions—vocally.

The bias of language towards writing is not new; at the turn of the C20th, Saussure claimed the primacy of writing as a rigorous, academic endeavor, over the common, unrefined activity of speech [4]. However, this primacy is misplaced: speech is a human cognitive activity—an innate ability; whereas, writing is a technology—a learnt skill. Further, writing is predated by speech, and can only ever be an approximation to it. Furthermore, there are many cognitive issues which prevents writing from being a universal medium. Any visual medium (think of keyboards on touch-screens!) disentitles those already excluded by physical or mental limitation—a digital society must be for all. Therefore, a truly universal machine must be implemented vocally, through

Published by Springer International Publishing AG 2018. All Rights Reserved
K. Liu et al. (Eds.): ICISO 2018, IFIP AICT 527, pp. 167–176, 2018.
https://doi.org/10.1007/978-3-319-94541-5_17

speech understanding. The obvious caveat, perhaps, are the profoundly deaf or mute, who may prefer screens or, as with the deaf-blind, may have other methods of accessing utterance [5]; however, access to computing should be for all. A way forward, here, is provided by Speech Act Theory (SAT) which defines a pragmatic explanation of language where understanding is judged by outcome [6]. Rather than attributing meaning to words and word types, e.g. nouns and noun-phrases, SAT models understanding not on the words used, nor on what is meant meta-physically, but what the reaction is to the utterance in context.

Such understanding, not speech-to-text but utterance-to-action, is achieved by the lang*uage eng*ine, Enguage™. Examples can be found on [7] The specification of arbitrary text transformation as pattern and its associated list of intentions was originally devised for a software engineering project [8]. These translations are a deductive (i.e. rule-following) process [9]; their creation—the inductive process—has been found also to be deductive: a self-constructing, or *autopoietic*, process [10], much in the same way as a C compiler is written in C. Such interaction affords the ability to program by voice [11]; which, as will be shown in this paper, removes the need for a program as a written artifact.

This paper describes the mechanisms supporting understanding in Sect. 2, including written and vocal repertoires. In Sect. 3, a simple function definition is described, and the test results of how the factorial function is constructed are presented. Section 4 develops the argument that, despite the limitations of the specialize solution, this research represents a novel computing system in itself. The significance is summarized Sect. 5.

2   Understanding

Information Systems, such as SQL [12] or the HTTP protocol [13], place less emphasis on the translation to an underlying representation; and, more on the translation between an input request and an output response. Typically in textual form, this can be viewed abstractly as *name = "value"*, where the name is the URL and the value is the web page content. However, the value during mapping may be processed, such as in HTTP with PHP or JavaScript, or transmitted over TCP/IP, rather than it being an atomic mapping. This complexity-in-reference, or *interpretant* [14], can be seen in Enguage [9]; however, both the request and response are arbitrary arrays of strings, allowing a bi-directional conversation to be constructed [15]. Further, meaning is modeled within internal arbitrary arrays, or intentions, specifying action.

2.1   Unequivocal Response

Enguage models utterances, arbitrary lists of strings, and their context. From SAT, intentionality should provide perlocution, an unequivocal reply reassuring the user of the interpretation that has been made [16]. A meaning is achieved by transforming an utterance into a reply, e.g. ["what", "does", "2", "+", "2", "equal"] is replaced by ["2", "+", "2", "equals", "4"]. Each reply should be unequivocal like this: because it uses pattern matching; one utterance may match several patterns, so there may be many replies. The user is seeking the most appropriate reply and may be presented with each candidate in turn, in order of pattern complexity. The presentation of the next candidate is controlled by the user: no..., is the pattern to re-present the last utterance [17]. In practice, it has been found that this often involves simply selecting an alternative utterance. Thus, Enguage is a mediator of appropriate reply, rather than an interpreter, per se.

The structure for the meaning of an utterance, or *sign*, is composed of a pattern, and a *monad*, a list of internal utterances, serving as intentions with which to elicit action. The intentions are invoked until the action is a reply. If interpretation is positive, or felicitous, it is presented to the user. If there is anything infelicitous to interrupt this, intentions prefixed with *if not*, are followed. The interpretation of intentions continues until the end of the monad, or a *reply...* (or *if not, reply...*) is encountered.

2.2   From Written to Vocal Autopoietic Repertoire

A concept is supported by a repertoire of utterances. Written repertoires have been used to describe the action performed on matching an utterance [9]. An example sign description, taken from the Enguage need repertoire, is:

```
On "SUBJECT needs PHRASE-OBJECTS":
    set output format to "QUANTITY,UNIT of,,LOCATOR LOCATION";
    OBJECTS exists in SUBJECT needs list;
    reply "I know";
    if not, add OBJECTS to SUBJECT needs list;
    if not, append OBJECTS onto SUBJECT needs list;
    then, reply "ok, SUBJECT needs ...".
```

A simple mapping, of the colon/semi-colon list, turns this pattern and monad into a list of standalone utterances in a self-creating, or autopoietic, repertoire [16], which constructs the machine representation of a sign. Uppercase words here represent contextual variables, set on matching the pattern and read from the environment by each intention. Lowercase pattern give a context sensitive framework for each pattern. A reply is a formatted answer. The answer is obtained by an underlying call to a traditional program, a database query or TCP/IP connection, and replaces the ellipsis in the reply. Intentions may voice change to the context within which an utterance is interpreted; so in the above example, *Martin needs a coffee* may elicit *ok, Martin needs a coffee*; but, its next utterance will elicit *I know*.

The written repertoire, outlined above, is now succeeded by a vocal autopoiesis [10]. The main issue was the ability to represent variables and values without resorting to the unspoken distinction between case; plus, the ability to note when rules are being constructed rather than interpreted. The first was simply solved by noting variables with the word variable, and a descriptor if required, e.g. numeric variable quantity. The ellipsis is replaced by the (configurable) word whatever. Induction is noted by a variable which is set, then unset on the subsequent utterance of ok.

2.3   Structured Language

Some natural language does follow simple structure—*seven fifteen* is almost certainly a time—and this is incorporated into Enguage. One example of this is Number, which is implied in natural language, as in *I need a cup of coffee*, meaning *I need [quantity = "1", unit = "cup", object = "coffee"]*; which can be extracted from the pattern `i need NUMERIC-QUANTITY UNIT of PHRASE-OBJECT`. These valeus help contextualize subsequent utterances, *and another* meaning *[quantity = "+1", unit = "cup", object = "coffee"]*. A numerical pattern variable is signified by the prefix NUMERIC-, which requires the evaluation of numeric expressions, such as *2 times 3 all squared*. Being in natural language, numeric expressions do not use parenthesis tokens, but even with this limit in complexity they remain very useful.

Floating qualifiers [18] can be extracted as temporal and spatial modifiers, e.g. *I am meeting my brother at the pub at 7 pm*, meaning: *I am meeting my brother [time = "7 pm", location = "the pub", locator = "at"]*. Recent developments include late-binding floating qualifiers, allowing location, for example, to be identified by pattern, not *a priori* knowledge.

Further—and pertinent to this paper—expressions can be used to determine the meaning of utterances. In particular *the height of Martin is 194 cm* implies that *height* is an attribute of whatever class from which *Martin* is instantiated. However, because *the square of n is n times n* contains *n times n*, an expression, it is implied that *square* is a function and that *n* is a parameter.

The next section details the example of these solutions in use in a spoken description of the mathematical function factorial.

3   A Working Description of Factorial

This section presents an example of how the complete description of a function—factorial—can be presented as a working *programme* of utterances. The British spelling is used here to distinguish a textual monad from the traditional representation of algorithm, of functions assignments and control structures. These examples form part of the Enguage text suite available at [19].

3.1   A Specialized Function Definition

An algorithm description as structured language (see Sect. 2.3 above), has been incorporated into an Expression mechanism, and is demonstrated in the Enguage test suite. At the time of writing, this only implements simple—non-recursive—functions. An example of a recursive function is given in Sect. 3.2 below.

Functions can either be created or evaluated. The creation sign description is:

```
On "the FUNCTION of AND-LIST-PARAMS is EXPR-BODY":
    #set the PARAMS of FUNCTION to BODY;
    perform "function create FUNCTION PARAMS / BODY";
    then, reply "ok, the FUNCTION of PARAMS is BODY".
```

The *and-list*, created for this sign, represents a list of parameters, such as *a and b and c*. The defines the induction of a function, such as *the sum of a and b is a plus b*. The EXPR- prefix matches an expression-as-value, confirming this as a function definition, as opposed to an entity-attribute operation, such as *the height of martin is 195*.

```
On "what is the FUNCTION of PHRASE-PARAMS":
    perform "function evaluate FUNCTION PARAMS";
    if not, reply "I do not know";
    then, reply "the FUNCTION of PARAMS is ...".
```

The evaluation sign works by substituting the actual parameters for the formal parameters within the body. This, then, describes a number, much in the manner of substitution in Lambda Calculus [1]. So, *what is the sum of 3 and 4*, is evaluated by substituting *3* and *4* into the function body *a plus b*. The resultant *3 plus 4* can be interpreted by the Number mechanism of Enguage giving *7*. This also supports *the factorial of 1 is 1*; however, whether this is interpreted as a value (by matching *the ATTR of ENTITY is VALUE*), or an expression, is immaterial—they both act in the same way.

Numerical expressions have been supported by Enguage for sometime, allowing verbal arithmetic to be performed. This is unlike written numerical expressions, as written expressions use parenthesis, whereas Enguage offers some control of the order of evaluation by the use of the word all: for example, *1 plus 2 times 3* would give *7*; whereas, *1 plus 2 **all** times 3* would give *9*. At the moment the numerical abilities are hard-coded with English terms.

Recursive function descriptions such as *the factorial of n is n times the factorial of n minus one* have not yet been implemented due to time constraints, and the an alternative implementation which is described next.

3.2   A General Function Definition

An extensible method of programming vocally is described here. Vocal interpretation descriptions, inductive utterances, consist mainly of the patterns: *to X reply Y/this implies Z*; and, *interpret X thus/first Y/then Z/ok*. *Go on* is the unequivocal reply for induction until it is concluded by uttering *ok*. The *perform* intention introduces an internal command, so this might not reflect natural speech. Otherwise, this listing is self-documenting. This example forms part of the current Enguage unit test, from which these results below have been cut and pasted.

```
Factorial Description
=====================
user> what is the factorial of 4
enguage> I don't understand.

user> to the phrase what is the factorial of 1 reply 1
enguage> Go on.

user> ok
enguage> Ok.

user> what is the factorial of 1
enguage> 1.

user> interpret multiply numeric variable a by numeric variable b thus
enguage> Go on.

user> first perform numeric evaluate variable a times variable b
enguage> Go on.

user> ok
enguage> Ok.

user> multiply 2 by 3
enguage> 6.

user> interpret subtract numeric variable c from numeric variable d thus
enguage> Go on.

user> first perform numeric evaluate variable d - variable c
enguage> Go on.

user> ok
enguage> Ok.

user> subtract 2 from 3
enguage> 1.

user> interpret what is the factorial of numeric variable n thus
enguage> Go on.
```

```
user> first subtract 1 from variable n
enguage> Go on.

user> then what is the factorial of whatever
enguage> Go on.

user> then multiply whatever by variable n
enguage> Go on.

user> then reply whatever the factorial of variable n is whatever
enguage> Go on.

user> ok
enguage> Ok.

user> what is the factorial of 4
enguage> 24 the factorial of 4 is 24.
```

4   Discussion

This section argues Enguage's position as a novel approach to creating software. It starts by distancing itself from three existing approaches to language understanding. Then it explains how the results, given in Sect. 3 above, equate to software engineering —creating programs.

4.1   Technology Review

This project is primarily an interface. It contains the ability to receive and present information, much in the same way as a windowing system, but in vocal rather than visual form.

Enguage is not a chatbot, the intention is not to maintain a conversation. Despite being concerned with an interface to natural language, this research has nothing to do with the Turing Test. The simple argument for this is that typical examples of such entrants [20, 21] use a keyword search to determine a theme and to reply with something convincingly intelligent. Where pattern matching is used, they resort to traditional methods of interpreting those patterns: that one of many preset values is used in reply to an utterance [21, 22]. These responses are defined by some meta-language, typically represented in XML. In contrast, this research must consume the entire utterance, which is achieved solely by pattern matching, and must provide an unequivocal reply: no deception is intended.

Further, Enguage is not an evolution of existing voice based systems. While many personal assistants can be generalized as front ends to internet search, Amazon's Alexa [23] does present an interesting case. It allows devices to act upon commands such as, "Alexa, tell the garage door to open." However, because Alexa, and the development of

Alexa skills, are rooted in traditional techniques—using web-based tools—it does not contain the ability to self-create which is central to Enguage. Thus, it falls short of a range of speech modes available (i.e. inductive as well as deductive) In short, we need to be able to say things like, "Tell Alexa how to open the garage door."

Furthermore, there is reluctance within the Computational Linguistics community to believe such an approach can work because of the reliance on syntax to define language. It takes a quantifiable coverage of natural language understanding, often quoting success at language understanding as a percentage rate. However, this is based on the analysis of language as it stood in the 1930's. Enguage achieves an appropriate interpretation, from which the user decides whether this is as intended; mediation of understanding, including the disambiguation of utterances, is part and parcel of the process of language, rather than being an exceptional, or failure, case. This more natural approach is that of speech act theory [16]. Further, this disambiguation can also be automated to some extent, such as in lines 5 and 6 of the written repertoire in 2.1. If the first attempt to add an item to the needs list fails (such as in *martin needs to go to town*: the intention, *add to go to town to martin needs list* makes no sense), the second one, using a different phrase, *append to go to town onto martin need list* probably will. Enguage demonstrates interpretation being ordered by pattern complexity, presenting —but not guaranteeing—the most appropriate interpretation first.

4.2   Utterance as an Information Processing System

Enguage simply models an utterance as an arbitrary string, and maps one onto a reply: $u_{utterance} \rightarrow r_{reply}$. Rather than '$\rightarrow$' being an atomic mapping, the rules for that mapping are constructed, also by voice, to capture the cultural reasoning behind the words. But how does this equate to being a computing system?

The instructions can be encoded in one language, say English, and the patterns can represent Chinese symbols; therefore, the mechanism behind Searle's Chinese Room thought experiment, can be implemented [24]. This is not to confuse Enguage with Artificial Intelligence: Enguage, ostensibly, is nothing more than a user interface to underlying state-holding software (databases, internet services and the like). But it holds the utterance-to-action behavior, and because it can now construct these as functions, it can be seen as an information processing system in the traditional sense.

While the presented description of factorial resorts to calls to an internal command to perform arithmetic, this is conceptually no different to a CPU deferring processing to an arithmetic logic unit. The recursive nature of factorials is encapsulated entirely within what is effectively spoken word, thus the spoken word is computable. This demonstrates that loops can be implied even though looping is not generally seen as a reliable cognitive function.

5   Conclusion

Viewing computing as a process of mapping utterances to replies imposes few limitations: vocabulary is only limited by the abilities of the speech-to-text software. Enguage argues for utterances to not need a syntax—interpretation is all done by pattern matching. Perhaps patterns represent a custom, context sensitive, syntax; a flat structure constructed of constants and variables. Certainly, it seems, understanding works at two levels: the words which form a context sensitive framework which we share to engage in understanding, such as *i need...*; secondly, there are the words which we use which are in fact personal to the speaker, such as *coffee*. What is my preference for coffee: its not found online [25].

The vocal abilities of Enguage will not make programming any easier. Indeed, it may result in programs being written down to be read. Arithmetic functions, such as factorials, will not be encoded within a natural language system, as they already are available in compiled libraries; however, this paper shows not only that the feat is possible, and that Enguage has the ability to support new functions orally, on-the-fly. It should also lead to other inductive language which is not available on deductive-only systems, such as—already implemented in Enguage—*X implies Y*. Further inductive examples are being developed, and an implementation of *why*.

Despite the progress that has been made, such an approach may take sometime to gain acceptance, since it breaks down the barrier between applications. Rather than running separate programs (word-processors, spreadsheets) to achieve different effects, one interpreter can handle many repertoires. This might not stop it being used for bespoke software, and this is where funding is being sought; but it may form a barrier to the adoption by, say, the mobile app community.

Ultimately, computing is not simply the running of programs, it includes the creation of programs, a significant component of which are functions. Turing argued for the use of finite-sized values which can be read, processed and written to/from positions on an endless tape [2]. Modern information systems combine these alphabetic characters to compose the large, unwieldy, values which he shunned. With an arbitrary textually mapping between utterance and reply [8] any function, including function constructing functions, can be represented. Turing highlighted one of many issues with writing; while it is sparse enough for words to be guessed as a glance, multiple-repeated digits are incomprehensible. But, speech-to-text/text-to-speech software can adequately generate and consume Turing's otherwise un-memorable numbers. Thus, these large values can be spoken, and what they represent—programs—need no longer be a written artifact.

References

1. Church, A.: An unsolvable problem of elementary number theory. Am. J. Math. **58**(2), 345–363 (1936)
2. Turing, A.M.: On computable numbers with application to the Entscheidungsproblem. Proc. Lond. Math. Soc. **2**(42), 230–265 (1936)
3. Andersen, P.B.: A Theory of Computer Semiotics: Human Computer Interaction, vol. 3. Cambridge University Press, UK (1997)
4. de Saussure, F., Bally, C., Sechehaye, A., Riedlinger, A., Harris, R.: Course in General Linguistics, 3rd edn. Duckworth, London (1915)
5. Sense. https://www.sense.org.uk/content/computing-aids. Accessed 01 Dec 2017

6. Austin, J.L.: How to do Things With Words, 2nd edn. Oxford University Press, Oxford (1962)
7. Wheatman, M.J.: https://www.youtube.com/channel/UCjTXFBHVNhC4dd_ZBxgx0ww
8. Liu, K., Wheatman, M.J.: Automating software design pattern transformation. In: 7th IEEE International Conference on Industrial Informatics CF-000825 (2009)
9. Wheatman, M.J.: A semiotic analysis of if we are holding hands, whose hand am I holding. Comput. Inf. Technol. **22**(LISS 2013), 41–52 (2014)
10. Wheatman, M.J.: An autopoietic repertoire. In: Bramer, M., Petridis, M. (eds.) Research and Development in Intelligent Systems XXXI, pp. 165–170. Springer, Cham (2014). https://doi.org/10.1007/978-3-319-12069-0_11
11. Wheatman, M.J.: Programming without program or how to program in natural language utterances. In: Bramer, M., Petridis, M. (eds.) SGAI 2017. LNCS (LNAI), vol. 10630, pp. 61–71. Springer, Cham (2017). https://doi.org/10.1007/978-3-319-71078-5_5
12. Chamberlin, D., Boyce, R.F.: SEQUEL: a structured english query language. In: ACM SIGFIDET Workshop on Data Description, Access and Control Proceedings, pp. 249–264. Association for Computing Machinery (1974)
13. HTTP RFC. https://tools.ietf.org/html/rfc7230. Accessed 09 Apr 2018
14. Peirce, C.S.: Logic as semiotic. In: Buchler, J. (ed.) The Philosophical Writings of Peirce, Selected Writings, pp. 98–119. Dover Publications (1955)
15. Wheatman, M.J.: A semiotic model of information system. In: Jorna, R., Liu, K., Faber, N.R. (eds.) 13th International Conference on Informatics and Semiotics in Organizations Proceedings (2011)
16. Searle, J.R.: Speech Acts: An Essay in the Philosophy of Language. Cambridge University Press, Cambridge (1969)
17. Wheatman, M.: A pragmatic approach to disambiguation in text understanding. In: Baranauskas, M.C.C., Liu, K., Sun, L., Neris, V., Bonacin, R., Nakata, K. (eds.) ICISO 2016. IAICT, vol. 477, pp. 143–148. Springer, Cham (2016). https://doi.org/10.1007/978-3-319-42102-5_16
18. Wheatman, M.J.: Context-dependent pattern simplification by extracting context-free floating qualifiers. In: Bramer, M., Petridis, M. (eds.) Research and Development in Intelligent Systems XXXIII, pp. 209–217. Springer, Cham (2016). https://doi.org/10.1007/978-3-319-47175-4_14
19. Wheatman, M.J.: Enguage source code. https://github.com/martinwheatman/enguage.and
20. Weizenbaum, J.: ELIZA—A computer program for the study of natural language communication between man and machine. Commun. ACM **9**, 36–45 (1966)
21. ALICE AI Foundation (2017). www.alicebot.org/about.html. Accessed 1 Dec 2017
22. Wilcox, B.: ChatScript. https://en.wikipedia.org/wiki/ChatScript. Accessed 1 Dec 2017
23. Amazon Alexa. https://developer.amazon.com/alexa. Accessed 1 Dec 2017
24. Searle, J.: Minds, brains, and programs. Behav. Brain Sci. **3**, 417–424 (1980)
25. Wheatman, M.J.: What Google doesn't know. In: IT Now Spring 2017. British Computer Society, pp. 48–49 (2017)

A Framework to Support the Design of Digital Initiatives in Social Science Based Research

Stuart Moran(✉), Sophie Berckhan, and Alison Clarke

Digital Research Team, University of Nottingham, Nottingham, UK
{stuart.moran, sophie.berckhan,
alison.clarke}@nottingham.ac.uk

Abstract. The rapid development of new digital technologies has increased the expectations of academic research outputs. To meet these pressures, researchers have greater expectations of their digital work environments. In this paper we outline the drivers for digital transformation at our institution and how this manifested itself in a series of exploratory projects called digital initiatives. Based on our findings we propose a Digital Research Initiative framework to support research institutions in assessing and implementing digital transformation.

Keywords: Academic support · Digital research · Digital transformation

1 Introduction

For the past decades, academic institutions have undergone rapid change driven by globalisation, greater social mobility, new funding patterns and the introduction of new technologies [1]. This has led to a change in the way institutions operate, moving away from a self-centred to a self-determined model and environment [2]. More recently, several new trends have emerged relating to the scale at which research is undertaken, the need to evidence the public benefit of research and a changing set of government and funder regulatory requirements. This has placed new pressures on researchers to deliver high quality results, at a fast pace, with real-world relevance and in compliance with regulations. Consequently, researchers have ever increasing expectations of their institution to offer the appropriate tools and environment that enable them to respond to these pressures. This is perhaps most prominent in terms of the Information Technology (IT) provision, with researchers expecting timely access to the very latest and ever changing digital tools and services. This has created new opportunities for institutional IT services to make a shift from being a purely operational function, toward a strategic enabler and leader. This role change will result in digital services that not only continue to support research but also actively inspire new research possibilities.

In this paper we seek to outline the formation of our institution's digital research vision and explore how this manifested itself through a series of small-scale digital transformation projects specific to Social Sciences. Based on our findings we then propose a framework that can support institutions in assessing their readiness for digital transformation and broadly inform decision making on the types of solution to implement.

K. Liu et al. (Eds.): ICISO 2018, IFIP AICT 527, pp. 177–186, 2018.
https://doi.org/10.1007/978-3-319-94541-5_18

2   The Need for Digital Transformation

Prior to exploring our institution's digital transformation vision, we must first understand more clearly the broader research context and drivers of change:

Transparency and Compliance. Research councils and funders are placing greater emphasis on the need for research transparency and open access to research findings. This will also include in the requirement that research data be suitably archived and preserved for the long term [3]. In terms of the management of data, the General Data Protection Regulation (GDPR) also places new constraints on the way personally identifiable research data is acquired and managed [4]. Cybersecurity is also a major consideration particularly in light of sensitive research data topics, commercial partners and patentable research outputs.

Collaboration and Skills. A stronger emphasis is now placed on large scale critical mass research driven, amongst others, by the Global Challenges Research Fund [5]. These are often addressed by multi-disciplinary and multi-institutional consortia driving the need to work collaboratively on larger projects. To be competitive research groups must continually refine their areas of expertise and promote their ability to add value in interdisciplinary projects more clearly. Interestingly, this behaviour means that while researchers are actively exposed to new techniques and knowledge from other disciplines, they do not necessarily need to apply and acquire those skills for themselves. This puts groups with specialist skills in high-demand [6], creating bottlenecks in interdisciplinary research.

Digital Equipment and Data. Recent developments in precision manufacturing and technology development have made numerous highly specialised instruments available to researchers [7]. The high cost of these equipment and services means effective resource sharing is required. This has led to the consolidation of research equipment into large centres and shared regional and national facilities. The Wakeham Review [8] concluded that shared resources and services will provide opportunities for better science. However, as instruments can generate significant volumes of data, their centralisation has created new challenges about the speed and safety of moving this data between institutions. Furthermore, the amalgamation of equipment has also further consolidated the availability of expertise [9].

Impact and Metrics. With public funds used to support research, there is a growing need to demonstrate the public benefit of research outputs. These developments have led to a greater emphasis on research metrics with a focus on the production of outputs with the highest possible influence. The presentation of research outcomes to the public has created opportunities for recognition outside of academic disciplines through a range of media channels [10].

Underpinning Digital Capabilities. Institutions are in an intriguing situation where digital technologies and services both serve as the cause of the changing environment but also as the route to a viable solution. Research funders have an expectation that institutions will provide researchers with a "well-founded laboratory" that includes IT infrastructure and services. Many institutions are in a position where the digital demand

and expectations of researchers currently outweighs their ability to offer the capabilities. Without a step-change in the digital provision, institutions risk not being able to serve what is becoming a basic research need and will fail to support researchers in fulfilling their research ambitions. This would in turn reduce an institutions research income, power and reputation.

3 Informing the Digital Research Strategy

In response to the changing work environment of researchers, our institution took steps toward creating a research environment that not only supports researchers' current needs, but also actively encourages them to increase the scope of their ambitions. A digital research vision was formed that recognized that the existing digital service provision was no longer viable, and that there was an opportunity for the IT function to not only enable, but to actively create innovative research. The vision outlined a research environment that would not only facilitate high quality research, but ultimately change the culture and working practices of researchers. While at a high level, the areas that needed investment were broadly known, they were ill-defined and poorly understood. This is in part due to communication and knowledge barriers between IT services and the highly specific and complex research areas across the institution.

Without a means of bridging this gap, the institution was not in a position to deliver an appropriate research environment. In response, a small innovative and strategic Digital Research Team was established within IS, made up of specialist post-doctoral researchers each with a portfolio of ambitious digital research projects. The collective research experience of the team covered all five faculties of the institution. It was anticipated that this unique combination of research knowledge and experience would allow researchers' needs to be more effectively captured and articulated to the IT delivery teams. Furthermore, these roles would provide the expertise to challenge and inspire researchers with new digital research opportunities. A survey of Russel Group universities revealed a focus on digital humanities centres, academic-led digital innovation centres, or specific roles such as research software engineers, data managers and data scientists. There were no indications that a similar institution-wide strategic digital research team is currently in place at these institutions. In order to establish the specific research needs of the institution, researchers across each faculty were approached by the Digital Research Team. The remainder of this papers focuses on the findings of the Faculty of Social Sciences as due to the broad range of disciplines it suitably represents the challenges faced across the institution.

3.1 Digital Research Environment in Social Science

At our institution Social Science is an exceptionally broad field, with a range of research methods applied across different disciplines in different contexts. In order to better understand the 'digital-readiness' of the faculty, approximately 100 researchers were met with over a 6-month period. This was on a one-to-one basis and intended to establish (1) the types of research methods adopted (2) the digital barriers faced by researchers and (3) an outline of the long-term research ambitions. Following these discussions, three key themes emerged around *digital skills*, *digital systems* and *digital support*.

Digital Skills in Research. As research technologies have advanced over the last 15-20 years, a digital divide has emerged, with those who make use of technologies to their fullest, and those who miss opportunities. Particularly in the qualitative space, there appears to be either a misunderstanding as to the broad capabilities of current technologies, or a perception that technology cannot support their work. For those who engage in quantitative work, there are many challenges around selecting the most computationally efficient technique or hardware platforms to use for a given dataset. Where programming is required, researchers are generally self-taught and often viewed their code and statistical modules as inefficient. This was often cited as the reason for not sharing these research outputs more widely. Without a complete understanding of the research possibilities with the latest digital tools, techniques and technologies, researchers are missing opportunities to do more with their research with fewer resources. However, it is the barriers to entry, not the ambition, that frequently out-weigh the digital opportunities available.

Digital Systems in Research. There is a large variety of data being created and captured by researchers, both in terms of their file formats and the degree of sensitivity of their content. Researchers are offered many different storage solutions by our institution considering their data requirements. However, a consequence of being able to satisfy this range of needs is that identifying the appropriate solution is difficult, creating barriers for researchers. Furthermore, in order to practically and safely share research data with the community, researchers are required to adhere to a cumbersome controlled access process, which acts as a barrier to sharing data. In some extreme instances, researchers have chosen not to pursue lines of enquiry due to the inefficient and uncertain storage mechanisms. Computationally intensive research is often completed using 'always-on' local desktop machines, running for days at a time. This is because the high performance computer at our institution not only requires a set level of expertise to access and utilize, but is also limited exclusively to the use of the Linux operating system. There are also a range of digital devices that can support the capture of research data that are underutilized.

Research findings and opportunities are missed as a consequence of data not being stored or data being unusable due to poor management. Similarly, without the appropriate compute facilities, key insights into large data sources continue to be difficult to elicit or simply unachievable.

Digital Support in Research. Researchers are broadly unaware of the types of professional support that is already available to them, in areas such as social media, digital research, data management and intellectual property. Some support services are run by researchers for researchers but gaining timely access to these can be difficult due to limited resources. There are also no current services available to help develop small scale code pilots or advise on specific statistical technologies. While the institution does provide state-of-the-art computational facilities and guidance on its use, there is a perception that this is tailored toward expert users. Without support and awareness of the use of new research technologies and techniques, researchers are unlikely to adopt them, resulting in missed opportunities and less competitive grant applications.

4 Digital Research Initiatives

Following the elicitation of researcher needs across the institution, three key strategic areas for investment were identified: Research Data Management, Compute and Analytics and Communication and Collaboration. The aim was to introduce new digital technologies and services that support researchers in each of these key areas which support and challenge the working practices and culture of research. In order to explore what digital technologies and services are likely to be most successful for researchers, a small scale rapid-delivery approach was adopted. These projects, or digital research initiatives (DRIs), seek to introduce and explore innovative research methods, off-the-shelf and custom technologies, and specialist knowledge. The DRI's are essentially meta-research projects with the goal of exposing researchers to new ways of working and technologies, and directly demonstrating their value. In order to secure buy-in from researchers, the DRI's were designed to align with existing practices where possible, and produce research outputs such as publications and grant applications. The outcomes of the projects were then used as case studies to inspire the wider research community to engage in new ways of working. In the next section we discuss some of the most successful DRI's implemented in Social Science in terms of Skills, Systems and Support based initiatives. As these projects are currently unpublished research they have been consciously obfuscated and described at a high level.

4.1 Skills-Based Initiatives

The following interventions were focused on demonstrating the value of how advanced digital skills can lead to new research opportunities. In both instances, new skills were made available to researchers through targeted collaborations with digital experts.

Agent Based Modelling. A group of Geographers had built a large longitudinal dataset over a 30-year period and carried out typical statistical analysis on the data. Given the size and content of the dataset the researchers were not realizing the full potential of their data. An opportunity was identified to apply a new research method and analytical technique, which was outside the skillset of the researchers. A specialist research software engineer was injected into the team and developed a prototype agent-based model that was grounded in the data. This model was then run using our institution's high-performance computer, creating new data and insights for the researchers to work with. This exposure to new digital possibilities led to an increase in their research ambition.

Virtual Reality. Digital technologies can be extremely effective at engaging people in ideas, particularly in immersive experiences. A specialist virtual reality (VR) expert was sought to collaborate with Politics and Law researchers on developing an engaging experience. A portable VR game was developed from the ground-up with the intent of exposing players to the sensitive topics in an interactive and playful way. The system was designed to present players with different introductory instructions (independent variable) and capture in-game behaviours and decisions (dependent variable). Based on the players actions, a set of tailored outcomes are automatically generated and used to stimulate post-experience discussions. By using an immersive game, players will be able to better reflect on their experiences and perceptions, creating higher quality interview data.

4.2   System-Based Initiatives

The following interventions were designed to introduce new technologies for capturing, analysing and showcasing research data. Primarily these off-the-shelf and custom systems enhance the management of text, audio and image-based research data.

Optical Character Recognition. Many researchers work with paper-based research data, including historical records, newspapers and legislation. The challenge for researchers is the speed at which this data can be searched through, and the ability to hold an accurate mental model of the entire contents. Furthermore, the data is not easily shareable, and is at risk of accidental loss. Optical character recognition (OCR) essentially makes any text machine readable and the researchers were not aware of this possibility. By using a scanner and a text analytics tool, researchers were able to not only accurately search through the data, but also create statistical information a linguistic analysis. This transformed the nature of the research, with the ability to query the data in new and unprecedented ways.

Handwriting Technologies. The most widely used form of paper-based research data is in the form of hand written notes. These are made by field-based researchers making observations or notes around interviews. Sharing, searching and securing these notes can be a challenge, particularly given the amount that can be generated through ethnography. In recognition of this, a range of off the shelf 'smart pen' devices were trialled with researchers. These devices create digital copies of hand written notes using real paper and ink. Unique codes are printed onto each page, which allows the user to retroactively change the content of pages physically and digitally. Other than charging the device, there is no change to the practice of taking notes, meaning all the digital benefits are achieved with no barriers. The integrity of the data is protected and becomes easily searchable and shareable. The technology can even record audio, pairing digital notes with the audio files.

Automated Transcription. Researchers typically spend time transcribing their audio interviews themselves or pay for a transcription service to transcribe the data. The consequence of these resource (time/cost) heavy tasks is that the transcription of audio files is done on a priority basis. This means significant amounts of research data are not being fully utilized or shared; essentially the information is lost. Using Azure cognitive services and working with a software developer, a customized solution was developed that allows researchers to save audio files to their computer and automatically return a transcript. This can be done in bulk, meaning all existing audio files can be transcribed and even translated automatically. This then creates the opportunity for researchers to effectively search through their audio data and even conduct quantitative analysis.

4.3   Support-Based Initiatives

The following interventions were intended to explore the role of new specialized support services. Their main aim is to offer consultancy to researchers on the effective use of digital tools and technologies for their research.

Research Software Engineering. Researchers in Geography who conduct computationally intensive research were not aware of nor able to realise the full potential of their work due to the perceived technical barriers. An expert software engineer was introduced into the research team, and worked with the researchers on restructuring their code and data, which in turn allowed them to fully utilise the high performance computing facility at our institution. During the project, the researchers were also exposed to the potential of cloud computing. The initiative meant that the researchers could not only complete what they originally planned faster, but could run more simulations with the same resources. Optimisation of their code meant that they are now able to run larger models, increasing the accuracy and scale of their outputs i.e. they can model entire countries rather than a few islands.

Research Data Management. In May 2018 the GDPR [11] becomes enforceable, and will strengthen the rights of users over their data. Social Science is one of the research areas to be strongly affected by this change, as much of the work involves the digital capture and management of personal data. However, researchers were generally unaware of the new regulations. In response to this, a technology-legal expert was consulted to review the current governance processes around personal data how data is shared. Working with researchers, the legal expert amended and reinforced the institutions existing data access and user agreements in full recognition of the legislation and digital technologies used by researchers. This intervention will allow researchers to continue to digitally capture personally identifiable data in an ethical and legal way.

5   Digital Research Initiatives Framework

Following the implementation of the DRI's in the faculty, we began to reflect on the areas of success. While the initial focus of the DRI's was on skills, systems and support, it became clear through the implementation that there were attributes that were more impactful than others. This led to the formation of the DRI Framework (Fig. 1) which is based on the relationship between three specific types of intervention in an academic setting. The first are Digital Technologies which are broadly defined as systems (hardware and/or software) that create or manipulate digital data. The second are Research Methods which are defined as systematic processes for creating data or concepts with the intent of answering a scientific research question. The third is Expert Knowledge, which refers to specific expertise in an area of specialism. We now consider the areas of intersection between these characteristics and relate back to the initiatives above.

Digital Research Data. Digital technologies are often know to create or capture digital data. However, is only when they are used as a part of a specific research method that digital *research* data is generated. Consider both OCR and handwriting technologies, these produced digital research data only when used as a part of the research process.

Specialised Digital Solutions. Digital technologies are ubiquitous in academic institutions and industry. However, simply having access to a technology does not make it effective or useful. Experts with specialist knowledge can help to customise, build and advise on the best use of the tools for a given purpose. Even without designing a specific technology from the ground up in a research context, these specialized solutions can be of use to researchers. The automated transcription is a clear example of this, where the digital tools were available and expert knowledge helped to construct a service around the technology – all of which was driven without a specific research method in mind.

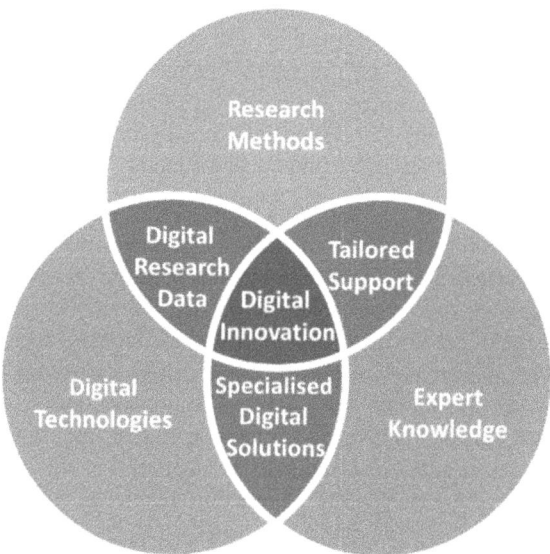

Fig. 1. The digital research initiatives framework (DRIF) allows institutions to assess current digital research capabilities and assist in the design of digital initiatives.

Tailored Support. While researchers are experts in their specific area of interests, there are techniques and principles from other fields, particularly in Computer Science, that can advance their research. This was demonstrated by the introduction of the research software engineer in use of parallelization and the lawyer in managing research data.

Digital Innovation. Digital Innovation is where digital technologies, research methods and expert advice come together. This is the goal of our institution's digital research strategy, to maximize the interplay of these three areas. The immersive VR environments and agent based modelling projects were the most revolutionary for the researchers involved, as it opened new avenues and increased the ambitions of their research.

5.1 Using the Digital Research Initiative Framework

The framework can be used to assess the readiness of an institution for digital research transformation, but also to help guide the types of areas that might be implemented. The aim is to position a project or opportunity in the framework based on the three attributes, and to then determine the type of intervention required to 'pull' the project toward the centre. The first step is to assess an institution's capabilities in terms of three areas, research methods, digital technologies and expert knowledge. The second is to consider how these areas currently, or could, overlap to create new opportunities, these can often be the low hanging fruit. The final step is to consider how areas of overlap might be further enhanced, and 'pulled' toward the centre of the framework by introducing the appropriate third attribute. For example, our institution has used the framework to design three new exploratory and transformational projects

- Internet of Things devices (*digital technologies*) are built by non-researchers (*expert knowledge*). By considering the role of *research methods*, a new initiative was identified to explore the ethical considerations for use of this technology in research.
- A Sociology researcher is using a linguistic analytical tool (*digital technologies*) to apply a specialist technique (*research method*) to digital text. By considering the role of *expert knowledge*, a new initiative was identified to introduce a machine learning expert to help further develop the technique.
- Specialist economics researchers are developing code (*expert knowledge*) and exploring game theory (*research method*). By considering *digital technologies*, a new initiative was identified to introduce an eye-tracking device to capture new data.

To the best of our knowledge there are no other examples in the literature of conceptual frameworks for assessing the digital readiness of an academic institution. Although notably Arribas and José [12] have proposed such a readiness framework in the context of the fashion industry. However their framework is exclusively grounded in digital technologies and drivers, and unlike the DRIF, fails to consider the role of expert knowledge. In a broader context, the DRIF directly informs Matt et al. [13] Digital Transformation Framework by proposing a series of new elements to be included in each of their "four cornerstones" of digital transformation; thereby grounding it in the context of an academic research institution.

6 Conclusion

Universities are complex organisations that operate in a challenging climate. It can therefore be arduous for institutions to define areas for transformation and successfully implement meaningful change. The strategic framework presented here enables institutions to introduce digital transformation in research via a three-pronged approach. By assessing the state of research methods, digital technologies and expert support available to researchers, this framework was used to successfully deploy practical methods for achieving our institution's digital research strategy.

References

1. Altbach, P.G., Reisberg, L., Rumbley, L.E.: Trends in Global Higher Education : Tracking an Academic Revolution. In: UNESCO 2009 World Conference on Higher Education, vol. 278 (2009). https://doi.org/10.1016/j.bse.2004.04.006
2. Gewirtz, S., Cribb, A.: Representing 30 years of higher education change: UK universities and the times higher. J. Educ. Adm. Hist. **45**, 58–83 (2013). https://doi.org/10.1080/00220620.2013.730505
3. Research Councils UK, Hefce, Universities UK, Wellcome: Concordat on Open Research Data (2016)
4. Chassang, G.: The impact of the EU general data protection regulation on scientific research. E-Cancer Med. Sci. **11**, 1–12 (2017). https://doi.org/10.3332/ecancer.2017.709
5. UK RC Global Challenges Research Fund. https://www.ukri.org/research/global-challenges-research-fund/. Accessed 17 Apr 2018
6. Davé, A., Hopkins, M., Hutton, J., Krčál, A., Kolarz, P., Martin, B., Nielsen, K., Rafols, I., Rotolo, D., et al.: Landscape review of interdisciplinary research in the UK (2016)
7. Brynjolfsson, E., McAfee, E.: The Second Machine Age: Work, Progress, and Prosperity in a Time of Brilliant Technologies, 1st edn. W.W. Norton & Company Ltd., New York (2014)
8. Wakeham, W.: Wakeham Review of STEM degree provision and graduate employability, 90 (2016). https://www.sheffield.ac.uk/polopoly_fs/1.576073!/file/wakeham-review_2016.pdf
9. Van Der Wende, M.: International academic mobility: towards a concentration of the minds in Europe. Eur. Rev. **23**(S1), S70–S88 (2015)
10. Stilgoe, J., Lock, S.J., Wilsdon, J.: Why should we promote public engagement with science? Pub. Underst. Sci. **23**, 4–15 (2014). https://doi.org/10.1177/0963662513518154
11. European Parliament: General data protection regulation 2016/679. EUR Lex **11**, 1–341 (2016). http://eur-lex.europa.eu/pri/en/oj/dat/2003/l_285/l_28520031101en00330037.pdf
12. Arribas, V., José, A.: Digital transformation of a small fashion house: a PLM implementation. In: Global Fashion Conference 2016, Stockholm (2016)
13. Matt, C., Hess, T., Belian, A.: Digital transformation strategies. Bus. Inf. Syst. Eng. **57**(5), 339–343 (2015)

A Metamodel for Supporting Interoperability in Heterogeneous Ontology Networks

Rodrigo Bonacin[1,2]($\boxtimes$), Ivo Calado[3], and Julio Cesar dos Reis[4]

[1] UNIFACCAMP, Rua Guatemala, 167, Campo Limpo Paulista,
SP 13231-230, Brazil
[2] CTI, Rodovia Dom Pedro I, km 143,6, Campinas, SP 13069-901, Brazil
rodrigo.bonacin@cti.gov.br
[3] Federal Institute of Alagoas, Rio Largo, AL 57100-000, Brazil
ivo.calado@ifal.edu.br
[4] Institute of Computing, UNICAMP, Campinas, SP, Brazil
jreis@ic.unicamp.br

Abstract. Ontologies are central artifacts in modern information systems. Ontology networks consider the coexistence of different ontology models in the same conceptual space. It is relevant that computational systems specified with distinct models based on different methods, as well as divergent metaphysical assumptions, exchange data to interoperate one with the other. However, there is a lack of techniques to enable the adequate conciliation among models. In this paper, we propose and formalize a metamodel to enable the construction of data models aiming to support the interoperability at the technical level. We present the use of our metamodel to conciliate, without explicit transformations, Ontology Charts from Organizational Semiotics with Semantic Web OWL ontologies and less structured models such as soft ontologies. Our results indicate the possibility of identifying an entity from one model into another, enabling data exchange and interpretation in heterogeneous ontology network.

Keywords: Ontology Chart · OWL ontologies · Soft ontologies
Metamodeling

1 Introduction

The adopted solutions for expressing and representing meanings in information systems differ according to various contexts, needs, and design approaches. The term ontology in Computer Science is often used to refer to the semantic understanding (a conceptual framework of knowledge) shared by individuals participating in a given knowledge domain. More specifically, an ontology is used to formally specify the concepts and relationships that characterize a certain body of knowledge (domain) [9]. The Semantic Web ontologies provide means for data semantic interpretation and enable inference features in intelligent systems.

In this context, we can point out different ontology models to represent knowledge domain. For instance, Web ontologies are used for distinct purposes and in several phases of Information Systems specification, design, and use. Soft ontology is another

K. Liu et al. (Eds.): ICISO 2018, IFIP AICT 527, pp. 187–196, 2018.
https://doi.org/10.1007/978-3-319-94541-5_19

conceptual approach, in which, in contrast to Web ontologies, with fixed hierarchies described in Web Ontology Language (OWL), refers to flexible set of meta-data [8]. This is useful to represent dynamically evolving information domains. These ontologies have individual elements associated with values in a non-structured *a priori* hierarchy.

Ontology Charts (OCs) in Organization Semiotics (OS) [10] play a central role in understanding the affordances, capture the behaviour of the involved agents, and the ontological dependencies at design time. OCs are the results from the Semantic Analysis Method (SAM), which aims to produce a clear ontological commitment concerning the nature of reality. In this sense, in SAM, ontology is understood in a metaphysical position [15]. This makes possible, with others OS' methods, a rigorous treatment of the Information Technology (IT) system at the non-technical semiotic levels [15].

Several types of ontological representations may coexist in computational systems. Thus, it is necessary to find related entities from one model into another to allow data exchange and cross-model interpretation. However, a key challenge is to enable the conciliation of data from computational systems (or part of the same system) that adopt these ontologies, because each system can interact with several knowledge domains in a variety of ways. We propose the concept of a network of ontologies to enable the coexistence of different models. The use of a network of ontologies opens up the possibility of mixing up various types of ontologies.

Although the literature has proposed several approaches to obtain interoperability among models and transformation rules (*e.g.*, [4]), we still need proposals suited to enable ontologies of distinct nature to coexist in the same conceptual space, *i.e.*, without thoroughly transforming one model into another. We assume that OCs and soft ontologies might coexist with Web ontologies that model more rigid hierarchies to represent domain concepts. Nevertheless, it is still an open research problem how to support the coexistence of these different models.

In this article, we propose a meta-model that allows the specification of models to support the connection of concepts of the distinct ontologies. Our proposal enables the use of a network of ontologies obtaining interoperability among the models. Given an entity in one model, our solution provides a way to identify connected entities into other models. The proposed meta-model defines the types of entities, their connections, and the beliefs associated to the connections (of any type). We describe the reached meta-model and formalize the main aspects involved.

Our approach is exemplified by assuming two computational systems (or subsystems) that must interoperate, systems *A* and *B*. In system *A*, the "*House*" class is described in an OWL model, and in system *B*, there is the affordance "*Home*" specified in an OC. The goal is not to assign that the "*House*" class is equivalent to the affordance "*Home*". They are not equivalent (or same as) concepts, once "*House*" is defined as a class (from the OWL conceptual perspective) and "*Home*" is defined as an affordance (from OC perspective), as well as the terms are not semantically equivalent. Thus, our goal is to provide a meta-model that allows us to model how they are connected at the technical level allowing data exchange. The obtained results indicate the possibility of reconciling ontology models of different nature via our proposal.

The remainder of this article is organized as follows: Sect. 2 presents the foundations and related work. Afterwards, we thoroughly describe the proposed metamodel (Sect. 3). Section 4 reports on an application scenario to exemplify our proposal. Section 5 discusses the findings and Sect. 6 wraps up the article.

2   Foundations and Related Work

In the Computer Science context, ontologies aim to represent semantics in computational systems [7] and have been designed to provide rich machine-decidable semantic representations. They refer to a formal specification of some domain, representing a conceptualization of a domain in terms of classes, properties and relationships between classes. Usually, a syntactic structure models the concepts of a knowledge domain and serves as schemes that organize data expressing instances of concepts according to logical properties. The classes are the focus of ontologies because they describe the domain concepts representing groups of individuals that share properties. Data properties characterize individual attributes, whereas object properties specify the relationships between individuals of the same or different classes.

Another relevant methodology to model a knowledge domain is the Semantic Analysis Method (SAM). SAM uses a subjective philosophical stance and an agent-in-action ontology to determine the underlying semantics of a social context and the relationship between the human agents and their patterns of behavior [13]. The SAM supports the analysis and representation of a social system. The method assists problem-owners in representing meanings in a formal and precise semantic model, the Ontology Chart (OC). This refers to a conceptual model that describes a view of responsible agents in the focal domain including their affordances, and the ontological dependencies between them [10].

Gibson [6] introduced the concept of Affordance to express the invariant repertories of behaviour of an organism made available by some combined structure of the organism and its environment. In SAM, the concept introduced by Gibson was extended to include behaviour invariants in the social world [10]. Agent is a special kind of affordance, which takes responsibility both for their own actions and the others' actions, *e.g.*, an individual person, a cultural group, a society, *etc.*

Kaipainen *et al.* [8] proposed the concept of soft ontology to conceptualize dynamic domains. A soft ontology declares a set of meta-data to describe a domain by means of spatially conceptualized properties. According to the authors, soft ontologies can be used to represent evolving information domains, such as those of collaborative tagging. They explore the concept of *ontodimension*, as a finite set of items (terms), to define a domain. For each item, a degree (weight) is used to prioritize each ontological dimension. In a technical perspective, we propose to represent soft ontologies via RDF model. To accommodate the prioritization of terms, we use an adapted RDF fuzzy model [11].

Our proposal relies on the concept of metamodel as an alternative to define a "language" to design models. The aim is promoting the interoperability among computational systems, which are based on heterogeneous ontological models. Considering a model as an artifact that provides abstraction of the reality via a description of concepts, a metamodel represents a model to describe what are these concepts, and how they are linked. Elements of the models refer to instances of the metamodel. By defining a metamodel, we address the challenge of identifying the elements of each model investigated in this study.

Regarding to previous studies on this matter, OS literature presents investigations aiming to promote the use of OCs with other models. Bonacin et al. [2] inquired the use of OC for system design at the technical level modelling with UML. The authors proposed a sequence of steps and a group of heuristic rules to construct UML class diagrams from OCs. In [1], the authors focused on the mapping of OCs to UMLs class diagrams preserving the semantic normal form. Other studies presented alternatives for the transformation from OCs into class diagrams [14].

Previous work also suggested a semiotic approach to design Web ontologies. Dos Reis et al. [3] proposed to enrich the representation aspects of OWL ontologies based on the use of Agents, Affordances and Ontological Dependencies to describe OWL classes. For this purpose, existing study defined heuristics for semi-automatic generation of Web ontologies from OCs [5]. The heuristics created explicit relations between the elements of the models to construct Web ontologies from OCs. A computer assisted process was defined to build the Web ontologies [4] and implement such heuristics. The authors defined transformation rules for deriving an initial Web Ontology described in OWL from OCs.

In the context of Web ontology integration, Umer and Mundy [17] investigated an ontology integration process relying on three different scenarios: ontology reuse, ontology mapping and ontology merging. These authors proposed a framework for ontology integration composed of three layers (Syntax Analyzer, Semantic Analyzer and Taxonomy Analyzer). Their approach compared ontology's concepts based on their syntax, semantics and relationship between concepts. Similarly, Nguyen and Truong [12] investigated the integration of fuzzy ontologies addressing critical issues related to different fuzzy structures of concepts and relations. The authors proposed a two-step approach relying on a distance calculation of the involved datasets and applied a consensus algorithm to obtain the integration.

In the context of authoring tools, Timm and Gannod [16] analyzed the usefulness of model-driven development to speed up the process of building semantic web services. Their work associated OWL-S specifications via the development of standard UML models. The authors argued that by using transformations from equivalent UML constructs, difficulties caused by a steep learning curve for OWL-S can be mitigated with a language that has a wide user base.

Literature has presented key aspects to be considered in ontology integration and transformation between distinct models. However, mostly of the existing studies focus on the integration of ontologies described in an equal language, or they have emphasized those models that share similar philosophical stances. In this investigation, unlike the others, we define a metamodel to facilitate the development of ontology networks, which accommodate models with different conceptions (including various language) for promoting data exchange and cross-ontology interpretation.

3   Constructing the Metamodel

The first step was the definition of the goals of the metamodel, which can be summarized as follows: (1) it should allow to represent connections between entities of various models, aiming to promote data exchange and cross interpretation in networks of ontologies; (2) it should assume a neutral position, as much as possible, with few assumptions and premises; and (3) it should be restricted to modeling the connection between models, *i.e.*, it should not emphasize the support of the modelling of internal aspects of ontologies. In the second step, we identified the building blocks that compose the target models we aim to conciliate. These elements enabled us to understand the connected entities along the models. The final step was the definition and formalization of the metamodel based on the detected correspondences.

We analyzed a set of modelling approaches, including OWL, OC, fuzzy soft ontology, Simple Knowledge Organization Systems (SKOS) and RDF(S). The first three were selected for the development of a proof of concept. These models represent different approaches for semantic modelling, whose key characteristics can be briefly summarized as follows: (1) OWL is a description logic-oriented language, with formal and rigid descriptions allowing logical inferences and computer interpretation; (2) OC focuses on the agents, their patterns of behaviors, and ontological dependencies, where ontology is understood in a metaphysical position; and, (3) Fuzzy soft ontologies emphasize less rigid representations enabling dynamic relationships and represent aspects related to uncertainty.

Based on the above assumptions, we defined M_2 as our interoperability metamodel that represents concepts to interrelate the different models. We developed an instance of the metamodel defined as the M_1, which aims to interrelate the three targets model. The M_0 stands for the instances of the M_1 models. Section 4 presents an application scenario with examples of M_0 instances.

Figure 1 illustrates our metamodel (M_2) in a graphical representation based on conceptual maps. The concept "*Language*" is used to describe Entities from a model. For instance, the OWL language describes Classes and Object properties, whereas the OCs language describes Affordances and Agents. The concept "*Connection*" is central in the proposal. This concept enables creating relationships from an entity in a model A to a model B. The "*Connection*" has a description via the element "*Connection_Description*".

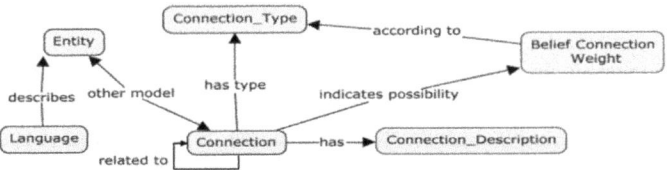

Fig. 1. Representation of the proposed metamodel M_2

We represent the nature (*e.g.*, conjunctive, disjunctive or assertive) of the "*Connection*" via the element "*Connection_Type*". The metamodel expresses that a "*Connection*" has a "*Connection_Type*" with a degree of belief. To describe it, the element "*Belief Connection Weight*" associates a value ranging *[0,1]* according to the "*Connection_Type*"; alternatively, a discrete scale can be used to represent degrees of belief. The *M_2* enables the "*Connection*" with various instances of entities and self-connections. This allows representing that a "*Connection*" c_1 can be related to another different "*Connection*" c_2.

Figure 2 presents the *M_1* as an instance of the *M_2*. We assume, in a simplified view, that the OWL language describes the following set of Entities: {*Classe, Object Property, Data Property, Instances*}. Considering the OC as instance of "*Language*", it describes the following Entities: {*Affordance, Agent, Role, Ontological Dependence, Determiner*}. Similarly, we assume the entities for the soft ontology based on a Fuzzy RDF language as follows: {*Subject, Predicate, Object, Type, Val Deg*}.

Figure 2 shows the instances of Languages that describe the Entities standing for all possible elements that the languages express. We consider that a "*Connection*" is expressed by a unique identifier *URI*. The concept "*Connection_Type*" can assume three values as *conjunction, disjunction*, and *assertion*. This enables to relate one connection with another. As a *disjunction*, the model expresses that if a connection is of one entity instance, it cannot be of another entity. The "*Belief Connection Weight*" describes a degree of confidence between the "*Connection*" and its type. It expresses a fuzzy value or even a qualitative value. The "*Connection_Description*" enables us to describe the relationship that a "*Connection*" determines. This describes, for instance, that an entity in one model is an "*instance*" of another model, or it is "*part_of*".

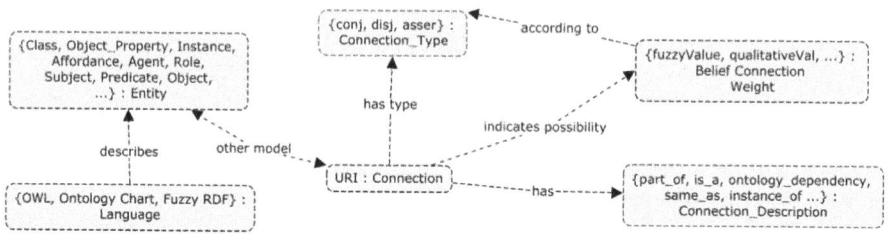

Fig. 2. Example of Instance of the Metamodel (*M_1*)

Figure 3 presents an excerpt of formalization of our metamodel using an extended *Backus-Naur* form (eBNF) based notation, as used in the OWL specification. Simplicity was a premise in this specification, which can be extended to support complex logical descriptions, such as data transformation and axioms.

```
OIDM ::= 'Oidm (' [ oidmID ] { language } ')'
language ::= 'Language (' languageID langName { axiom } ')'
axiom ::= entity | connection
entity ::= 'Entity (' entityID entityName ')'
connection ::= 'Connection (' connectionID [connectionName] connectionRestriction
connectionDescription ')'
connectionRestriction   ::=   connectionType  '('  connectionRestrictionID  entityID
{entityID} beliefConnectionWeight ')'
connectionType ::= 'DisjointConnection' | 'ConjuntiveConnection' | 'AssertConnec-
tion'
connectionDescription ::= 'is a' | 'part of' | 'same as' | 'instance of' | plainLiteral
beliefConnectionWeight ::= floatingPointNumber | valueScale
floatingPointNumber :: = bindigit ['.' digit {digit} ]
digit ::= 0 | 1 | 2 | 3 | 4 | 5 | 6 | 7 | 8 | 9
bindigit :: = 0 | 1
valueScale = '[' {plainLiteral ','} plainLiteral ']'
langName ::= plainLiteral
entityName :: = plainLiteral
connectionName :: plainLiteral
connectionTypeName :: plainLiteral
oidmID ::= URIreference
languageID ::= URIreference
entityID ::= URIreference
connectionID ::= URIreference
connectionTypeID ::= URIreference
connectionRestrictionID ::= URIreference
/* reused from OWL */
plainLiteral ::= lexicalForm — lexicalForm@languageTag
lexicalForm ::= as in RDF, a unicode string in normal form C
languageTag ::= as in RDF, an XML language tag
```

Fig. 3. Excerpt of the metamodel eBNF code

4   Application Scenario

We present three examples of *M_0* related to the same application scenario to illustrate the use of our metamodel to integrate OWL ontologies, Ontology Chart and soft ontologies. Figure 4 includes an example of disjunction using our metamodel. This scenario connects "*John*" (in *M_0*), as instance of Subject in Fuzzy RDF (*M_1*). The subject "*John*" can be connected to two disjoint possibilities. The model expresses that there is a belief "*John*" is instance of a *Dog* Class in an OWL ontology, or "*John*" is connected to a *Person* Affordance in an OC. The "*Belief Connection Weight*" is associated with the pair "*Connection_Type*" (disjunction) and the respective connection (*0.9* for *Person* and *0.1* for *Dog*).

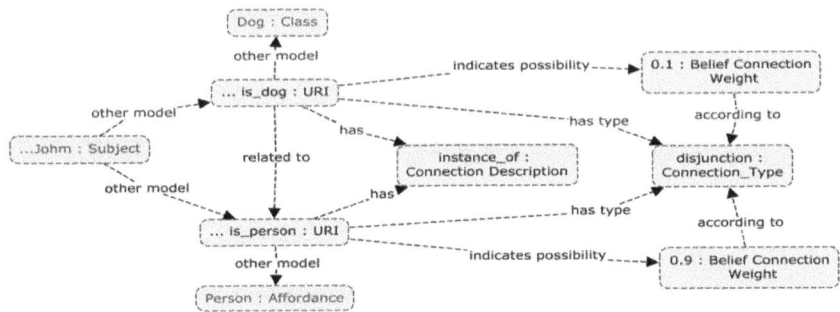

Fig. 4. Example: connection type *DisjointConnection*

Figure 5 presents an example of conjunction. In this scenario, as defined by the conjunction *Connection_Type*, "*John*" can be either employed in *CTI* and *FACCAMP*. In this case, the "*Belief Connection Weight*" determines the degree to which we believe this type of connection holds for them (*0.9* for *CTI* and *0.7* for *FACCAMP*). Note that both connections are related to each other.

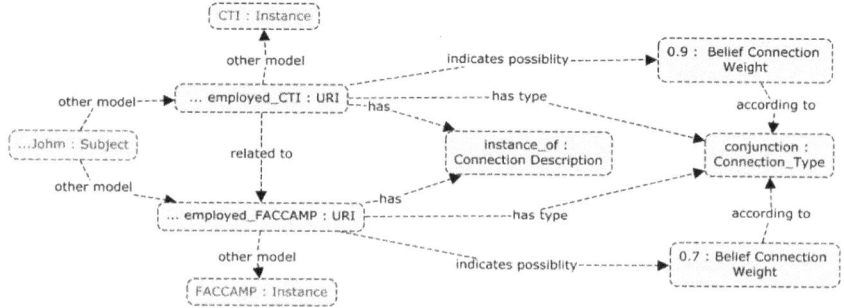

Fig. 5. Example: connection type *ConjuntiveConnection*

Figure 6 presents an example to express a statement regarding the *sameAs* assertion. In this case, a RDF fuzzy model defines the degree to which "*John*" is *Anger* and *Sadness* (this is an internal representation of the RDF fuzzy model). Our metamodel enables to relate that the *Anger* object is equivalent to an OWL Class in another model with *95%* of belief. Similarly, we relate the object *Sadness* to an Affordance *Sadness* in an OC.

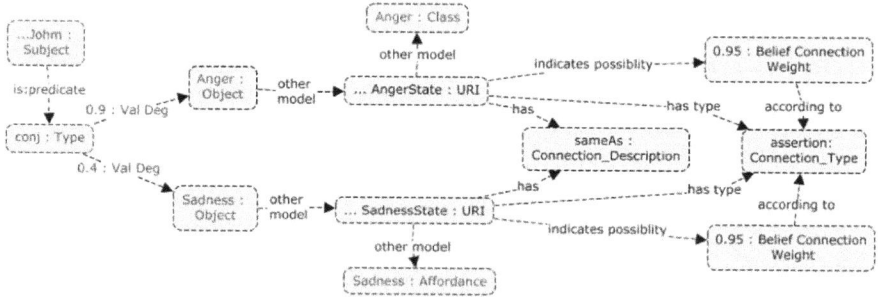

Fig. 6. Example: connection type *AssertConnection*

5 Discussion

The formal nature of ontologies makes them amenable to machine readability and provides a well-defined semantics for defined terms. Nevertheless, the use of different formalism to represent a knowledge domain prevents the properly interoperability between different systems. This is not even mitigated when considering the use of adopted formalisms such as Web ontologies, ontology charts and soft ontologies.

This work dealt with the conciliating of different ontology formalisms by proposing a metamodel that allows the construction of a network of ontologies. Our formal metamodel defined elementary building blocks that are instantiated to correspondent elements in the target formalisms.

We found that is possible to accommodate conceptual entities in the metamodel to create data connections from one model to another, *i.e.*, without transformation operations. We explored the concept of Belief Weight, inspired by RDF Fuzzy models, to determine the degree of confidence between elements from different model formalisms. This aspect refers to the key originality in this research. The presented application scenario showed the benefits and limitations of our findings. The practical examples illustrated how a concept in a Web ontology was connected to an Affordance in OCs with a given degree of confidence based on our model. The examples explored the different types of connections to illustrate the effectiveness of the proposal.

Our metamodel is still unable to represent formal axioms from Web ontologies as well as OS' norms, however our model focuses on supporting data interoperability. Future work will involve a refinement of the metamodel in addition to implement and test the provided formalization. We plan to study how our proposal can be employed in scenarios where ontologies evolve over time, since new concepts are created, modified, and removed along the system execution.

Another challenge to be undertaken is how to make inferences in "cross models" representations. This is a known difficulty in distributed ontology networks and models. This difficulty is furthermore aggravated by the fact of dealing with heterogeneous networks. Practical issues, such as the performance using real-world ontologies and systems should also be analyzed.

6 Conclusion

Ontologies are central artifacts to represent meanings in information systems. However, different conceptual models are hardly conciliated in the same conceptual space. In this paper, we proposed a metamodel to enable different ontology models to coexist in a network of ontologies. Findings revealed that the metamodel is suited to represent distinct connection types considering a belief connection weight. The presented examples illustrated the findings in an application scenario. Further aspects such as inference strategies, deepening in theoretical issues, and the use of the metamodel in real-world situations shall be investigated. Our future work mostly involves addressing the dynamic aspect of the ontology network, the study of the inference issues, and the application of the metamodel in the specification of a network for an enactive system.

Acknowledgements. This work is supported by the São Paulo Research Foundation (FAPESP) (Grants #2015/16528-0 and #2017/02325-5).

References

1. Ades, Y., Umar, F.B., Poernomo, I., Tsaramirsis, G.: Mapping ontology charts to UML: an SNF preserving transformation. In: Proceedings of the 10th International Conference on Organisational Semiotics (2007)
2. Bonacin, R., Baranauskas, M.C.C., Liu, K.: From ontology charts to class diagrams: semantic analysis aiding systems design. In: 6th International Conference on Enterprise Information Systems (ICEIS 2004), pp. 389–395 (2004)
3. Dos Reis, J.C., Bonacin, R., Baranauskas, M.C.C.: A semiotic-based approach to the design of web ontologies. In: 12th International Conference on Informatics and Semiotics in Organisations (ICISO 2010), pp. 60–67 (2010)
4. Dos Reis, J.C., Bonacin, R., Baranauskas, M.C.C.: An assisted process for building semiotic web ontology. In: 13th International Conference on Informatics and Semiotics in Organisations (ICISO 2011), pp. 167–174 (2011)
5. Dos Reis, J.C., Bonacin, R., Baranauskas, M.C.C.: Constructing web ontologies informed by semantic analysis method. In: 13th International Conference on Enterprise Information Systems (ICEIS 2011), pp. 203–206 (2011)
6. Gibson, J.J.: The theory of affordances. In: Perceiving, Acting, and Knowing: Towards an Ecological Psychology. Wiley, Hoboken (1977)
7. Gruber, T.R.: Toward principles for the design of ontologies used for knowledge sharing. Int. J. Hum. Comput. Stud. **43**(5–6), 907–928 (1995)
8. Kaipainen, M., Normak, P., Niglas, K., Kippar, J., Laanpere, M.: Soft ontologies, spatial representations and multi-perspective explorability. Expert Syst. **25**(5), 474–483 (2008)
9. Kalyanpur, A., Golbeck, J., Banerjee, J., Hendler, J.: Owl: capturing semantic information using a standardized web ontology language. Multiling. Comput. Technol. Mag. **15**(7) (2004)
10. Liu, K., Li, W.: Organisational Semiotics for Business Informatics. Routledge, Abingdon (2014)
11. Lv, Y., Ma, Z.M., Yan, L.: Fuzzy RDF: a data model to represent fuzzy metadata. In: IEEE International Conference on Fuzzy Systems. IEEE World Congress on Computational Intelligence, pp. 1439–1445 (2008)
12. Nguyen, N.T., Truong, H.B.: A consensus-based method for fuzzy ontology integration. In: Pan, J.-S., Chen, S.-M., Nguyen, N.T. (eds.) ICCCI 2010. LNCS (LNAI), vol. 6422, pp. 480–489. Springer, Heidelberg (2010). https://doi.org/10.1007/978-3-642-16732-4_51
13. Salter, A; Liu, K.: Using semantic analysis and norm analysis to model organisations. In: Proceedings of the 4th ICEIS, pp. 847–850 (2002)
14. Santos, T.M.D., Bonacin, R., Baranauskas, M.C.C., Rodrigues, M.A.: A model driven architecture tool based on semantic analysis method. In: Proceedings of the ICEIS, pp. 305–310 (2008)
15. Stamper, R., Liu, K., Sun, L., Tan, S., Shah, H., Sharp, B., Dong, D.: Semiotic methods for enterprise design and it applications. In: Proceedings of the 7th International Workshop on Organisational Semiotics (OS) (2004)
16. Timm, J.T.E., Gannod, G.C.: A model-driven approach for specifying semantic web services. In: International Conference on Web Services, pp. 313–320 (2005)
17. Umer, Q., Mundy, D.: Semantically intelligent semi-automated ontology integration. In: Proceedings of the World Congress on Engineering (2012)

Enactive Systems and Children at Hospitals: For More Socially Aware Solutions with Improved Affectibility

Elaine C. S. Hayashi[1]([⊠]), Roberto Pereira[2], José Valderlei da Silva[1], and M. Cecília C. Baranauskas[1]

[1] University of Campinas (UNICAMP), Campinas, SP, Brazil
{hayashi,vander.silva,cecilia}@ic.unicamp.br
[2] Federal University of Paraná (UFPR), Curitiba, PR, Brazil
rpereira@inf.ufpr.br

Abstract. One of the challenges faced by designers when creating technology is to be aware of social responsibilities when proposing a new digital artefact. With the popularization of computational technology among children, the challenge gains new proportions. Varied digital solutions have been presented for children at hospitals to lessen anxiety, stress and loneliness caused by hospitalization. If designers do not consider the broader view of the context, the social consequences of the use of their solutions might worsen users' initial situation. In order to better understand the context and obtain a more comprehensive view from the state of the art in this subject, we used a Semiotic Framework and the Principles for Affectibility to analyze artefact solutions proposed for hospitalized children. As a result, we identified gaps that represent new opportunities for research. The results are discussed towards more social awareness towards new, contemporary interfaces that defy traditional interaction forms.

Keywords: Organizational semiotics · Enactive systems · Children care

1 Introduction

Enactive systems have been defined as computer systems consisting of human and technological processes dynamically linked, i.e., forming feedback loops using sensors and data analysis, enabling a seamless interaction between human and computer [4, 22]. The presence of new technologies and new forms of interaction (tangible, wearable and natural interfaces), coupled with the ubiquity of computing and social networks, present challenges that require the consideration of new factors (emotional, physical and cultural) in the design of systems we are naming socio-enactive. Such systems represent a complex scenario for which there is still no theoretical and methodological basis and no practical experiences suitable for its design. The ways people will interact in socio-enactive environments is not easy to explain and to predict at design time. Consequently, the essence of how to develop systems of this nature requires the treatment of technological aspects in which the consideration of the social

© IFIP International Federation for Information Processing 2018
Published by Springer International Publishing AG 2018. All Rights Reserved
K. Liu et al. (Eds.): ICISO 2018, IFIP AICT 527, pp. 197–207, 2018.
https://doi.org/10.1007/978-3-319-94541-5_20

dynamics is enhanced by concepts such as Universal and Participatory Access, Affective Computing, Ubiquitous, Values and Pragmatics.

In this paper, we present preliminary results from Project Socio-enactive systems [6] in which the concept of a socio-enactive system is being constructed. Adopting a socially-aware view [5] for the design of systems, we applied a Semiotic Framework inspired structure and the Principles for Affectibility to analyze artefact solutions proposed for hospitalized children. The results provided better understanding of the context, more comprehensive view of the state of the art, pointing out to gaps that represent new opportunities for research. More than contributing to problem understanding in the context of our study, the paper shows how a Semiotic Framework can be used as a thinking tool for organizing related works and guiding discussions on the subject. This article is organized as follows: Sect. 2 informs the theoretical background; Sect. 3 shows related works on digital solutions for hospitalized children; Sect. 4 analyses the related works based on a Semiotic Framework inspired structure and the Design Principles for Affectibility; Sect. 5 concludes this article.

2 Background

In earlier days, computer use was limited to performing tasks that were well defined and most often spatially confined to individual offices. Current ubiquitous and immersive scenario demands new forms of interaction. More in line with contemporary needs is the concept of "enactive systems". According to Kaipainen et al. [12], an enactive system does not assume traditional interfaces (i.e., one that uses graphical interface manipulated by traditional input devices such as mouse, keyboard and touchscreen), and do not follow patterns of goal-oriented interaction models and conscious human actions.

Enactive Systems come from the concept of enaction discussed by Varela et al. [22]. The premise is that interactions occur in an "embodied" way – that is, it is guided by the body's involvement and the human agent's spatial presence. Moreover, in these interactions, a conscious control of the system is not assumed to exist [12]. In an enactive system, the system can pick up information (e.g., collect user data) during interaction and respond accordingly. The user then reacts to the system's response, generating new inputs to the system. This cycle goes on in a dynamic and nondeterministic way. Other concepts that characterize the enactive approach are: autonomy ('autopoiesis'), sense-making, embodiment, and experience [21].

Usually, enactive systems rely on findings from Artificial Intelligence and Affective Computing. In Affective Computing [14], users' emotional responses are recognized in an automated way by computer systems and they are used to promote interaction improvements. This type of approach, based on objective information, can be considered as an "informational approach". In contrast to informational approaches, there are the "interactional approaches" [7]. Such approaches seek to preserve the subjective nature of emotions. Boehner et al. [7] argue that affective interactions are dynamic, culturally mediated and socially constructed experiences. That is, affection is a product of society. The values and culture of society are important in building meaning for affective states, affective behaviors, and words that denote such states and behaviors.

On the one hand, purely informational approaches lose the richness of meanings and accuracy of actual emotions. On the other hand, purely interactive approaches can produce results that are considered too subjective or too specific for a certain group. We argue in favor of both approaches in enactive systems that are meant to be enacted within social groups. One possible way to get closer to this balance in enactive systems is to consider the Affectibility of the systems, while still counting on advances from Affective Computing and Artificial Intelligence.

The term Affectibility [9] is similar to the terms usability, learnability or playability in the sense that it is concerned with aspects that provide improved affective quality to interaction with computational systems or devices. While the principles for Affectibility might not be enough to guarantee users' satisfaction, they indicate elements that can be directed when aiming at enhanced quality in 'interactional' interfaces. The principles are summarized in Table 1. Examples can be found in [9].

Table 1. Design principles for affectibility.

Principle for affectibility (PAf.)	Definition
PAf. 1	Free interpretation and communication of affect: the system should provide ways for users to freely express and interpret feelings and emotions, avoiding sole automatic identification
PAf. 2	Pride in social values and local culture: the system should reflect users' social context, including what users value and what are part of their culture
PAf. 3	Feeling of identification and appropriation with personal adjustments: the system should allow users to tailor the interface according to their preferences
PAf. 4	Connectedness in collaborative construction: the system should support collaborative construction
PAf. 5	Virtual closeness and social awareness: the system should make the presence and affective responses of other users noted
PAf. 6	Setting the mood with varied media and modes of interaction: the system should explore the use of different media (e.g. image, sound, and video) and modes (e.g. tangible, natural) of interaction

Sensors and automatic recognition of emotions provide for enactive systems in terms of inputs for a system to be capable of responding to one user. A new generation of enactive systems should go beyond that; and the principles for Affectibility could address this need. This is one of the facets that shall compose the socio-enactive [6] concept. Socio-enactive systems shall not only transcend individual use by accommodating entire communities, but also it shall encompass dynamic, social and cultural aspects of interaction. The principles can be used both to evaluate an existing solution and guide the creation of new ones. In this article the principles are used to analyze and compare solutions from the literature review.

3 Entertaining Hospitalized Children

When exploring the literature we searched for investigations on computational technology for hospitalized children. Only articles that present a specific artefact were included. It was not in our scope: studies or evaluations of existing commercial applications; solutions directed to specific diseases (e.g., children with asthma) or the treatment or monitoring of health; and solutions in which children were not the patients (e.g., technology for children visiting the hospital). We searched for combinations of terms like "children", "hospital"/"hospitalized" and "interaction", "design" at the IEEE and ACM digital bases. Citations that appear in the resulting articles were also included.

The simplest solution is the robot CareRabbit [8]. The authors argue it is quick, easy and secure to implement. It is a device in the form of a white rabbit that receives and plays mp3 files. Family and friends can send messages, stories and music to children in hospitals via the CareRabbit. Orb [24] is another object that, like the CareRabbit, allows one-way communication and was designed to have minimal functionality. Orb is a large light globe placed in a classroom in order to represent the child who is away at the hospital. From the hospital and using a laptop a child can control the color displayed by Orb, thereby suggesting the child's presence in the classroom. The child is free to choose the color, which may represent an affective response. Children at school are free to interpret the meaning of the color displayed. This communication served as a simple phatic connection between the classroom and the child [23]. The authors of Orb further developed the idea and after conducting co-design workshops, they proposed an application for tablets. The Presence App [23, 24] shows colors as Orb does, but now in a two direction communication, as both classmates and the hospitalized child are able to send and receive colors. The colors are shown as "blobs" that move around the app's interface. The speed in which the "blobs" move indicate the amount of activity going on in the classroom (the higher the sound level in the classroom, the faster the "blobs" move). Moreover, the app allows photo exchange and it displays the schedule of the class.

In the category of tangible interactions, most of the solutions presented a mix of manipulation of an object and the visualization of video that are displayed in separate monitors. Zootopia is a system composed by a board game (map made of cardboard) with action figures and a monitor. The action figures are in the form of animals, and an avatar to represent the child. The child can freely move the avatar around the map and the avatar is embedded with RFID reader. The map has RFID tags and whenever the avatar is placed in one of them, a video starts playing at the monitor. The video is related to the corresponding animal placed in the map. The same authors of Zootopia also proposed Push Planet [2]. The last one keeps the idea of displaying videos of different animals; however, they make use of many props without the need of a cardboard base. These props include a stuffed planet (a soft ball covered with an atlas made of fabric), a wooden airplane to simulate flights around the planet, among other toys. They also rely on the RFID technology for interaction. The fabrics that cover the toys are removable and washable. Billow [16] is an older tangible proposal (from 1997) that is still relevant for today's settings. The child handles an object in the shape of an egg in order to control the images of clouds that are displayed on a monitor. The egg can command the clouds to play music. The egg has buttons, a microphone and it connects via radio to a local computer, placed under the child's bed. The egg can also be used to command the establishment of voice connection with a child from another room in the hospital.

For children who are not confined to a room and can walk around hospital's common areas, Huerga et al. [10] have conducted two design play workshops, one for each game: Doctor Giggles and X-Safari. With Doctor Giggles, the image of an interactive operating room is displayed on a monitor and children can interact with its elements, like X-ray machine, scissors, and syringe. These objects, however, have different uses in the game (e.g., syringe is a magic wand) and the objective is to make the character (a doctor) laugh. The authors asked children to create their own play characters using X-ray sheets. It is not clear how the characters were incorporated into the game. With the second game, X-Safari, children wear a glove device to hold the characters they create – as in Dr. Giggles they create their play characters out of hospital supplies. With the glove device children control a character that is displayed in the monitor. One solution for playful communication system between child and parent is The Huggy Pajama [20]. This system is intended to allow parents to send hugs to their children. At one side, the parent hugs a doll. The doll, equipped with 12 sensors, senses the hug and transmits it to a wearable device. The wearable device consists of a pajama that changes color and that has 12 air actuating devices. The air actuating devices correspond to the 12 sensors in the doll. Air is pumped into the devices in a way that the pressure it exerts simulates the feeling of being hugged. The pajama has a flower pattern made of thermodynamic ink that is activated by conductive yarn. The changes in color indicate the distance the parent is from the child and the warmth contributes to the sensation of being hugged. Another proposal involving the idea of hugging is Huggable [11, 19]. Huggable is a robot developed at the MIT[1]. It is a teddy bear that can be operated remotely; it moves its joints (elbow, shoulder, etc.) and nods and tilts its head. Given a specific coordinate, which is transmitted via wireless communication, Huggable can look at specific directions. The joints of Huggable are flexible enough to allow not only its movements by command, but also to allow children to manually move the robot's arms and legs, as they would in a regular teddy bear. Moreover, Huggable has eyelids that can move and pupils that can vary in size. All these movements together provide Huggable with emotional expression and non-verbal communication skills. Capacitive touch and pressure sensors are spread throughout the body of the robot. The pressure sensors located in its paws are meant to let children express intensity of pain by pressing the paws in a harder or softer way. These sensors located at the bear's arms can be replaced by other sensors or parts. For example, in order to let children pretend that they are applying an injection to the bear a place for injection can be attached to the arm. Also, like in Push Planet [2] the fur is removable and washable. This was intended as an infection control mechanism at hospitals. Even though Huggable was designed based on medical staffs' suggestions, it stills needs further testing. Very similar to Huggable, there is Probo [17]. Probo is also

---

[1] http://web.mit.edu/.

intended to be huggable. It looks like an elephant and it can also express emotions via its eyes, which can move and tilt. Probo's trunk, ears and mouth move to aid to the expression of emotions. The remote communication with family and friends takes place from Probo's belly, which has a touch screen interface. Probo is expected to make sounds, as a non-existing, affective language.

4   Literature Results Through the Lens of a Semiotic Framework

Previous works have used the structure of the Semiotic Ladder with the purposes of organizing systems requirements [3], and even of showing different focusses of a literature review [14]. Similarly, we organized the discussion on the main issues related to the artefacts proposed for 'hospitalized children' in a Semiotic Framework [13, 18] inspired structure, with six layers: physical world, empirics, syntactics, semantics, pragmatics and social world. The physical world includes physical devices – mainly hardware or other objects – that are used to build structures that represent something else (an animal, the sensation of being hugged, presence, etc.). Most of these devices are in the form of sensors that are set inside an object. Be it a toy, board game or wearable device, usually the interaction happens via a tangible object. Also relevant for the physical layer – however not considered in the works retrieved – are power supply issues: How the object of interaction will be powered? Are they adequate to the hospital environment in terms of not interfering on the functioning of other equipment, for instance? The concerns related to the empiric layer can also be related to the object of interaction: how many users can handle the object? Does the internet server or connection support this amount of information? How long does it take since the recognition from a given sensor takes place until a feedback is displayed? The information captured by sensors or other devices must be treated in a defined structure so that the system can use it. This structure is represented in the syntactic layer and it serves as basis for the semantic layer, informing possible ways to support meaning. The sense people make and the effective use of the solution (pragmatic layer) is the base for the social world: the changes in the daily life of stakeholders and the impacts in society. Based on this appropriation of the Semiotic Framework, we organized related works on digital technology for hospitalized children (Table 2).

We used the Principles for Affectibility (PAff) as a method for comparing the technological solutions for children at hospitals regarding their way of implicit or explicitly addressing or evoking affective responses. For this analysis we observed whether the solutions complied with each principle or not. A higher amount of principles observed in a solution should be an indicator of good Affectibility. Table 3 shows this analysis. While most of them were preoccupied in adding varied media and modes of interaction, they did not explicitly involve collaborative construction (i.e., a group of children constructing/learning with each other) nor explicitly displayed instances of child's particular social contexts/values. Enactive systems are based on pure "informational" data. A possible way to mingle "interactional" is by using PAff. Having a system that complies with all principles is a challenging goal and the development of the socio-enactive concept is a possible path towards that goal.

Table 2. Main characteristics of related work organized in the layers of a semiotic framework structure.

	Related work grouped by type of interaction device				
	Robot [17, 19]	Toy or object [8, 23]	Wearable [20]	Tangible [1, 2, 10, 16]	Tablet [24]
Social world	Design is aware of possible safety hazards in hospital environments				Design is aware of privacy issues and social presence
Pragmatics	Interactive robot that allows (emotional) communication	Object transmits and plays mp3 files [8] or display colors [23] for commun.	Connects parent and child by simulating hugs from distance	Tangible props that are related to a movie play on separate monitor	Communication between hospitalized child and classroom via mobile app
Semantics	Representation of emotions by movements of robots' facial elements	Meaning depend mostly on the content of audio file	Connotation of pressure from pajama	Play involving toy animals [1, 2] or hospital elements [10]	Free expression and interpretation using colors and photos
Syntactics	Speed and direction of movements of facial elements; toy's affordance; softness of material	Personalized audio files played by object [8] or colors displayed [23]	Air inflation that makes pressure in the child who is wearing the pajama	Movement of objects activates video	Display of varied colors for two way communication
Empirics	Internet connection rate; computational capacity	Internet connection rate	Internet connection rate; computational capacity	Response times	Internet connection rate
Physical world	Animal-like robot covered in washable soft fabric; sensors, capacitors and actuators; wireless connection	Plastic object, lamp; mp3 player, speakers, Wi-Fi [8]; object in the format of a lamp/person [23], lamp	Pajama with thermodynamic ink, air pumps, conductive yarn; doll with touch/pressure sensing circuit	RFID tags and readers [1, 2]; 3D figures and objects; monitor; gloves with sensors [10]; radio comm. [16]	Tablet, Wi-Fi

Table 3. Design principles for affectibility in related work.

Design principle for affectibility	Related work grouped by type of interaction device				
	Robot	Toy or object	Wearable	Tangible	Tablet
PAf. 1 Free comm. of affect	[17]	[23]			[24]
PAf. 2 Values and culture					
PAf. 3 Tailoring	[17]	[8]		[10]	
PAf. 4 Collaborative construction					
PAf. 5 Social Awareness		[23]	[20]		[24]
PAf. 6 Media and modes	[17, 19]	[8, 23]	[20]	[1, 2, 10, 16]	[24]

4.1   Discussion

One aspect that all articles shown in previous sections have in common is their concern about soothing children's stay at hospitals. The goal is to provide relief, reduce stress and allow communication. However, this concern is rather isolated, aimed at a child, without considering its surroundings. For example, the communication supported by some of the solutions is usually one to one. At most, games are provided for group play. The concept of Socially Aware Design goes beyond considering more than one child. It is about being responsible in a broader sense, considering the society as a whole; worrying about how the technology can affect the community of users.

To focus on the development of the technology alone is a rather common practice, as the result of the analysis using Semiotic Framework indicated (Table 2). Notice that the row for 'Social World' has few items. In this row were considered only works that explicitly discussed social implications of the digital artefact. Most often, it is not due to lack of responsibility of developers, who do care about the wellbeing of users, that this happens. Usually, it is due to lack of resources or lack of awareness of the implications, or lack of an adequate design method. While the robots Huggable and Probo seem to represent the state of the art in terms of technology, Presence App [23] presents relevant concerns regarding the community of users and their values. The analysis using the design principles for Affectibility corroborates this result, as PAf 4 (collaborative construction) is missing in all works. While X-Safari and Doctor Giggles allow more than one player, they do not actually promote collaborative construction as children simply happen to be together in the same room. Not only children interacting together at a given moment, but also children who have been at the hospital before could add to a global socio-enactive experience. None of the works presents characteristics that would make them enactive systems. They all act in deterministic ways. Solutions for children interaction in hospital settings could not only benefit from more natural activities from enactive systems, but also they could be improved if designed for social awareness (PAf. 5) and group constructions (PAf. 4). The product of interactions from groups of users, physically present or not, could allow collective creations, which in turn could be used as new inputs for the system. The continuation of this cycle has the potential of promoting more natural, meaningful and engaging interactions. Moreover, it is important to use methods that could elicit other possible problems of the Social World. Solutions based mainly on informational approaches are usually focused on the three base layers of the Semiotic Framework (physical world, empirics, and syntactic). Interactional ones are often more concerned with the top three layers, for which meanings, intentions and social impacts are main issues. Solutions for embodied interactions for children in hospitals can benefit from both the informational and interactional approaches to design for Affectibility. The informational methods can provide for systems that use automatic recognition via sensors and other devices; the interactional approaches can inform the design that is socially aware and aims for collective creations. The development of such artefacts, keeping in mind possible social impacts and principles for affectibility, is our current work.

5 Conclusion

The design of contemporary technology based in sensors and actuators needs a methodological approach that could value the ubiquitous nature of the technology on the one side and the capacity of the artefacts to evoking affective responses in people on the other side. This article presented how the Semiotic Framework and the Principles for Affectibility were used to organize and analyze related works on technology for hospitalized children. Results point to the potential of that theoretical referential in informing about the lacks in literature making clear the challenges towards research in socio-enactive systems [6]. It is important that the design process be based on the awareness of possible social consequences that the technology might bring to the relation of users and their surrounding environment. We argue that the pervasiveness and ubiquity of systems should be further explored in systems towards the development of the concept of 'socio-enactive' systems. These systems should contribute to improved wellbeing for the children and communities in hospitalization contexts.

Acknowledgments. We would like to thank the financial support of CNPq (306272/2017-2); CAPES (1644511); and process grant # 2015/165280 and #2015/24300-9 from São Paulo Research Foundation (FAPESP).

References

1. Akabane, S., Leu, J., Araki, R., Chang, E., Nakayama, S., Shibahara, H., Terasaki, M., Furukawa, S., Inakage, M.: ZOOTOPIA: a tangible and accessible zoo for hospitalized children. In: ACM SIGGRAPH ASIA 2010 Posters, p. 31 (2010)
2. Akabane, S., Leu, J., Iwadate, H., Choi, J.W., Chang, C.C., Nakayama, S., Terasaki, M., Eldemellawy, H., Inakage, M., Furukawa, S.: Push planet: a tangible interface design for hospitalized children. In: CHI 2011 Extended Abstracts on Human Factors in Computing Systems, pp. 1345–1350 (2011)
3. Almeida, L.D.A., Baranauskas, M.C.C.: Um prospecto de sistemas colaborativos: modelos e frameworks. In: Proceedings of the VIII Brazilian Symposium on Human Factors in Computing Systems (IHC 2008), pp. 204–213 (2008)

4. Arpetti, A., Baranauskas, M.C.C.: Enactive systems & computing: mapping the terrain for human-computer interaction research. In: 43° SEMISH – Seminário Integrado de Software e Hardware, CSBC 2016 (2016)
5. Baranauskas, M.C.C.: Social awareness in HCI. Interactions **21**(4), 66–69 (2014)
6. Baranauskas, M.C.C.: Sistemas Sócio-Enativos: Investigando Novas Dimensões no Design da Interação Mediada por Tecnologias de Informação e Comunicação. FAPESP Thematic Project (2015/165280) (2015)
7. Boehner, K., de Paula, R., Dourish, P., Sengers, P.: How emotion is made and measured. Int. J. Hum. Comput. Stud. **65**(4), 275–291 (2007)
8. Blom, S.R., Boere-Boonekamp, M.M., Stegwee, R.A.: Social connectedness through ICT and the influence on wellbeing: the case of the CareRabbit (2012)
9. Hayashi, E.C.S., Baranauskas, M.C.C.: Designing for affectibility: principles and guidelines. In: Stephanidis, C. (ed.) HCI 2015. CCIS, vol. 528, pp. 25–31. Springer, Cham (2015). https://doi.org/10.1007/978-3-319-21380-4_5
10. Huerga, R.S., Lade, J., Mueller, F.: Designing play to support hospitalized children. In: Proceedings of the Symposium on Computer-Human Interaction in Play, pp. 401–412 (2016)
11. Jeong, S., Logan, D.E., Goodwin, M.S., Graca, S., O'Connell, B., Goodenough, H., Anderson, L., Stenquist, N., Fitzpatrick, K., Zisook, M., Plummer, L.: A social robot to mitigate stress, anxiety, and pain in hospital pediatric care. In: Proceedings of the International Conference on Human-Robot Interaction Extended Abstracts, pp. 103–104 (2015)
12. Kaipainen, M., Ravaja, N., Tikka, P., Vuori, R., Pugliese, R., Rapino, M., Takala, T.: Enactive systems and enactive media: embodied human-machine coupling beyond interfaces. Leonardo **44**(5), 433–438 (2011)
13. Liu, K.: Semiotics in Information Systems and Engineering. Cambridge University, Cambridge (2000)
14. Maike, V.R.M.L., Buchdid, S.B., Baranauskas, M.C.C.: Designing natural user interfaces scenarios for all and for some: an analysis informed by organizational semiotics artifacts. In: Liu, K., Nakata, K., Li, W., Galarreta, D. (eds.) ICISO 2015. IAICT, vol. 449, pp. 92–101. Springer, Cham (2015). https://doi.org/10.1007/978-3-319-16274-4_10
15. Picard, R.: Affective Computing. MIT Press, Cambridge (1997)
16. Rueb, T., Wardzala, J., Millstone, J.: Billow: networked hospital playspace for children. In: CHI 1997 Extended Abstracts on Human Factors in Computing Systems, pp. 357–358 (1997)
17. Saldien, J., Goris, K., Yilmazyildiz, S., Verhelst, W., Lefeber, D.: On the design of the huggable robot Probo (2008)
18. Stamper, R.: A semiotic theory of information and information systems. In: Invited papers for the ICL/University of Newcastle Seminar on Information (1993)
19. Stiehl, W.D., Lee, J.K., Breazeal, C., Nalin, M., Morandi, A., Sanna, A.: The huggable: a platform for research in robotic companions for pediatric care. In: International Conference on Interaction Design and Children (IDC 2009), pp. 317–320. ACM (2009)
20. Teh, J.K.S, Cheok, A.D., Choi, Y., Fernando, C.L., Peiris, R.L., Fernando, O.N.N.: Huggy pajama: a parent and child hugging communication system. In: Proceedings of the 8th International Conference on Interaction Design and Children (IDC 2009). ACM (2009)
21. Thompson, E., Stapleton, M.: Making sense of sense-making: reflections on enactive and extended mind theories. Topoi **28**(1), 23–30 (2009)
22. Varela, F.J., Thompson, E., Rosch, E.: The Embodied Mind: Cognitive Science and Human Experience. MIT Press, Cambridge (2017)

23. Vetere, F., Green, J., Nisselle, A., Dang, X.T., Zazryn, T., Deng, P.P.: Inclusion during school absence: using ambient technology to create a classroom presence for hospitalised children. Telecommun. J. Aust. **62**, 5 (2012)
24. Wadley, G., Vetere, F., Hopkins, L., Green, J., Kulik, L.: Exploring ambient technology for connecting hospitalised children with school and home. Int. J. Hum.-Comput. Stud. **72**(8), 640–653 (2014)

Design Practices and the SAwD Tool: Towards the Opendesign Concept

José Valderlei da Silva[1], Roberto Pereira[2], Elaine C. S. Hayashi[1(✉)], and M. Cecília C. Baranauskas[1]

[1] Institute of Computing, University of Campinas (UNICAMP), Campinas, SP, Brazil
{vander.silva,hayashi,cecilia}@ic.unicamp.br
[2] Federal University of Paraná (UFPR), Curitiba, PR, Brazil
rpereira@inf.ufpr.br

Abstract. The main idea behind the Open Source model of software development is to promote open collaboration in a decentralized process of coding. Varied endeavors have taken place in order to encourage, support and maintain the Open Source initiative, always focusing on the programming part of software development. Little to none has been said regarding decentralized, open collaboration in the system design process as a whole. Aiming at understanding what an OpenDesign initiative for information systems design would be, this article further explores the SAwD tool in a case study that considers the context of designing IoT solutions for airports. Organisational Semiotics and the Socially Aware Design constitute the theoretical basis of this work.

Keywords: Organisational Semiotics · Socially Aware Design
Human-computer interaction · IoT

1 Introduction

The development of information systems pushed by its technological aspects is unfortunately a rather common practice. As the demand for computational systems grows, it becomes clearer that hardware and software may cause varied problems if developers skip phases. Early design phases as problem clarification and identification of interested parties can be vital for the success of a system. The lack of awareness in such phases of system development may imply profound social consequences, affecting society in many levels (economic, ethical, political, etc.). These problems can be avoided by not neglecting the social context of design.

The creation of systems that make sense to the target community of stakeholders demands the systemic view of socio technical approaches. These are approaches that recognize that the technical solution is an embedded part of a much more complex social system, from which behavior patterns, beliefs and values may rise.

Usually, software and hardware developers focus their work only on the technical aspects of development, often because they are not aware of design techniques that support this required broader view. Other developers do know about design techniques, but they lack specific knowledge or they cannot get hold of informants that can

K. Liu et al. (Eds.): ICISO 2018, IFIP AICT 527, pp. 208–217, 2018.
https://doi.org/10.1007/978-3-319-94541-5_21

contribute by adding to the creation of a bigger picture. When it comes to the variety of participants exploring and discussing the social context of a technical solution, the more the merrier. This process, however, must be well organized and documented following methods that can support collaborative work.

Open collaboration is supported in the software development context of the Open Source communities. In this process, developers create their products by developing, using and/or modifying freely shared source codes. This decentralized process of software development offers benefits as optimized and enhanced quality, since many different improvements can be added to the original code, suggested by many different points of view.

While open source is a common practice in the development of system's code, it is much less common to find such practices in the system design process. This concept is being developed by the OpenDesign Project [2]. As part of the OpenDesign Project, this article explores earlier phases of design process as a preliminary work towards the characterization of the 'Open Design' concept. As part of this investigation, we have conducted two workshops in order to idealize IoT solutions for airports. The first workshop took place during the ICISO'16 [1] conference, which was held in University of Campinas, in the city of Campinas, in São Paulo, Brazil, in 2016. The second workshop was conducted as a masterclass during the IHC'17 symposium [6], in Joinville - Santa Catarina, Brazil, in 2017. Both workshops had the Socially Aware Design [3] (more on Sect. 2) as theoretical and methodological basis. Both workshops had the same goal: identify problems faced by people at airports with the objective of proposing conceptual solutions for an IoT system. The first workshop was focused mainly on problem clarification and we observed how artefacts could be used to promote discussions. The second workshop started with the same discussion on problem understanding and it went further, resulting in concepts for technological solutions.

Both workshops were conducted with participants working together in person; only afterwards were the ideas transcribed to the online tool SAwD[1] (the Socially Aware Design [13]). SAwD is a CASE tool[2] that supports cooperative work in early design activities. More specifically, SAwD supports the problem clarification and the proposal of computational solutions based on activities from Organisational Semiotics and Participatory Design.

These workshops and SAwD served as basis for a preliminary discussion that, along and throughout the 2 years of the OpenDesign Project, shall inform and direct the following questions: What characteristics compose the OpenDesign concept? and How can platforms support the OpenDesign to be developed?

The airport setting presents an interesting case context, especially when considering socio-technical approaches for design processes. An airport gathers people from different cultures who often do not share a common language for communication, but share interests (e.g. traveling) and difficulties (e.g. lost items).

---

[1] www.nied.unicamp.br/dsc.

[2] Computer-aided software engineering (CASE) tool is a tool used in the design and/or development of applications.

This article is organized as follows: Sect. 2 presents our theoretical, methodological and technical references; Sect. 3 describes the workshops; Sect. 4 informs the results from the workshops; Sect. 5 discusses the findings and Sect. 6 concludes.

2 Organisational Semiotics, Socially Aware Computing and the SAwD Tool

The preliminary practices to explore methodologies and tools that support OpenDesign consider that Organizational Semiotics [14] and the Socially Aware Design [3] should be the basis for the evolution of the Open Design concept. Some of the artifacts already produced based on these theories are collaborative and participatory, involving stakeholders as co-designers. This section describes the theoretical and methodological background that guided our practices. They are the same ones that will be used as fundamental material for OpenDesing concepts and practices.

Organisational Semiotics is a branch of semiotics that "is based on the fundamental observation that all organised behavior is affected by people's communication and interpretation of signs, both individually and in groups" p. 24 [9]. Organisational Semiotics is positioned under the philosophical stance of the radical subjectivism [9, 14]. In this paradigm reality is understood as a subjective and social product, constructed by agents' behaviors, which implies that "there is no knowledge without a knower" and "there is no knowing without action". Subjectivity and responsibility play important roles in this stance [8].

Designers are responsible for the impacts that a technological artefact brings to the community of users even when they are not aware of the reach of the consequences derived from its use. For that reason, it is vital to consider wider, holistic views in the design process. The Socially Aware Computing [3] calls for methods and artefacts to support the design that is aware of the social reaches of a technological solution. Not only technical aspects should be considered in the design process, but also informal and formal ones. Informal, formal and technical are the layers of the Semiotic Onion [15], one of the artefacts from Organisational Semiotics used in the Socially Aware Computing. A computational system (technical information system) is part of the formal part of an organisation, which in turn, is part of the whole organisation, including the informal part of it. The Semiotic Onion offers a structure that helps making explicit the system of beliefs, intentions, values and culture of the organisation, which are often neglected.

Other artefacts and techniques that can be used in initial stages of a design process are described in PAM – Problem Articulation Method [8, 15]. PAM is part of MEA-SURE – Method for Eliciting Analysing and Specifying Users Requirements [8, 15]. Among the techniques that compose PAM are the 'Stakeholder identification Diagram' and the 'Valuation framing'. As the name indicates, Stakeholders Identification Diagram (SID) helps in the process of identifying interested and relevant parties. The Valuation framing helps to reveal stakeholders' perspectives on ten different aspects of culture [9]. Similarly, to the Valuation framing, the Evaluation Framing [4] (EF) also puts into evidence stakeholders' perspectives, but in this technique problems are anticipated and ideas for solutions are generated. Another artifact is the Semiotic framework or the Semiotic Ladder (SL). SL provides a tool to help seeing information (signs) from different perspectives.

SID, EF and SL have been applied within Semio-participatory practices [3] in varied contexts in order to clarify the problem amongst stakeholders. SAwD was developed [13] in the endeavor of allowing remote participation of interested parties in an open and collaborative environment. For that, the artefacts were transferred and adapted to a digital format in an online usage. With SAwD participants are able to contribute in their own time and schedule, without the need to travel distances for physical encounters.

3 The Evolution of the Airport Scenario: A Case Study

As mentioned before, two workshops were held and in both of them, the scenario of an airport was used as the motif for the creation of an IoT system. Airports host an entire world in itself. They are equipped with many signals, installations and facilities to support arrivals and departures of people and objects from domestic and international flights. Airports must offer the entire infrastructure to accommodate passengers and their families and belongings, aircrafts, air companies' staff and other employees from the airport, etc. In order to provide a comfortable experience for passengers, airports offer terminals with a wide range of services and facilities as restrooms, stores, playgrounds, VIP lounges, emergency services, places for worship, museums, restaurants, coffee places, etc. International airports have to control, in addition, immigration, customs and passport control. People from all over the world can be found in airports. This means that, in a same physical environment, there are people from different cultures, who follow varied values and social rules. The differences go on: varied languages (spoken and signed), age, gender, sexual orientation, height and body size, travel experience, disabilities, abilities, etc. These people may interact among each other, with airport staff, and also they may interact with objects, as conveyor belts or baggage carousels, information panels and displays, gates, escalators, elevators, etc. These interactions allow passengers to reach common goals, for example, they may claim their luggage, find boarding gates, restrooms, etc. In the same way as people interact with 'things' in the airport, also airport things could interact with passengers and staff. Things could also interact with other things, being proactive in helping themselves, other people and employees, automatizing services like transportation of people and luggage, cleaning, security, etc.

The first workshop, proposed as a half-day activity, explored the use of SID and EF. Both artefacts were used with the objective of promoting discussions for problem understanding. In regards to EF, participants were asked to converge the discussions to rather specific problems and their corresponding solutions and ideas. Problems and solutions should concern each stakeholder previously identified with SID.

The second workshop was a whole-day activity and had different participants. Moreover, in addition to SID and EF, other artifacts were used: SL and other participatory design techniques. The result was the proposal of concepts for IoT solutions for the airport scenario. For both workshops, the artifacts were printed as posters into which participants could place post-it's filled with their ideas and contributions. The two workshops are described as follows: Sect. 3.1 presents the first workshop, and Sect. 3.2, the second. The results are presented in Sect. 4.

3.1 Problem Clarification

Twenty participants took part in the first workshop. Participants were from different cultures and countries (Brazil, China, Chile and others). The activity started with a discussion about the Socially Aware Design followed by an explanation on the design problem: the airport scenario. First participants brainstormed about the feelings (both positive and negative ones) related to trips, considering airports as the setting. This first moment helped directing the group towards a common problem. Once the scope was clear, participants were asked to consider the 'things' around an airport and the 'things' people carry on their trips. This should lead the discussions towards the definition of solutions for internet of things that could help passengers and other people related to the airport scenario.

Participants were invited to explore the IoT concept as a network in which objects exchange messages. It was highlighted that the things related to the airport scenario should provide support for people involved or affected during the actions of travelling. Therefore, the IoT should be thought in a more analytical manner: as the Internet of Human Things (IoHT). Most things are objects created by people to satisfy human needs. Some of these things are composed by other systems, from which people want information (e.g., information about the weather). When designing an IoT system, the concern is to embed technology in objects in order to exchange information and investigate events that occur in that environment. For this reason, the Human should be the center of attention when creating an IoT environment. In this sense, Internet of Things (IoT) becomes an Internet of Human Things (IoHT).

3.2 From Problem Clarification to Concept Proposal

In the second workshop twenty-four participants joined the discussions. They were all from Brazil, but from different regions. Like in the first workshop, the group was organized in two subgroups. Each group had their own set of posters. The difference from the first workshop is that this time discussions did not end at problem clarification, as the second workshop lasted all day. The groups went further, brainstorming concept ideas and preliminary interface elements for the envisioned system. At the end, each group presented their solutions regarding the IoT systems for the airport scenario.

After filling SID and EF, participatory design techniques were used to elicit ideas for the solution to be proposed. The techniques were: BrainWriting [5] and BrainDraw [10]. In the BrainWriting technique, a group sits in a circle and each member of the group starts writing their idea. A few seconds later, an alarm rings to inform that they should stop writing and pass the paper to the person next to them. This person will then read the content of the paper and either agree or disagree with it and then continue the idea by adding their own contribution until the alarm rings again. This goes on around the circle until the person receives back the paper he had started. The BrainDraw works in a similar way, but this time instead of writing, participants are supposed to draw user interface elements of the prospective system. The results from BrainWriting (main concepts) provide ideas for Brain Draw. Each group also had a flipchart in which they wrote notes on their ideas or used it to explain their thoughts. At the end of the activities, each group presented their results to the other.

4   Results

The first workshop provided important basis for the conduction of the second one. Having the same objective and scenario, the two workshops explored the use of varied artifacts from OS and participatory design practices. The first workshop explored SID and EF; while the second, besides SID and EF, also explored SL as well as concept ideas for applications. SID, EF and SL from both workshops were latter transcribed into the SAwD tool. The complete transcriptions are available in [7].

The first workshop resulted in the identification of stakeholders and related problems and solutions. One of the SIDs shows a general concern with safety: smoke detectors, earthquake alarms and security cameras were some of the ideas for the source information layer of SID. The other SID layers from the first workshop had many contributions directed to pets: pet's cage and accessories (contribution layer), health insurance for pets (source layer) and animal welfare department (community) are some of the results. Figure 1 illustrates a moment from the first workshop.

The second workshop also resulted in the identification of stakeholders and possible problems and solutions. Moreover, it went further and continued with the discussion and proposition of concept ideas for IoT solutions. One of the solutions was based on the situation of a person traveling for the first time. The other, explored the problem of finding a connection at an unknown airport. For the first situation, participants considered how insecure and apprehensive passengers would be and idealized that this person would benefit from help for completing varied activities in the airport, like confirming flight schedule, checking in, dropping luggage and other boarding procedures. The proposal included a mobile application that would identify the person as he or she arrives at the airport. The group did not clearly define how the identification process would technically occur; options like retina scan, mobile phone and

Fig. 1. Group discussion during the first workshop: SID (left) and EF (right).

cards were discussed. He or she would then be guided to the places needed, which would be previously marked around the place. The application would use resources already available at airports and it should promote a stress-free travel experience for first-time passengers.

For the second situation, the proposal consisted in a personal assistant that should guide passengers during flight connections. Other orientations would also be provided: disaster procedures, indoor map, gate finding, time schedules, time organization, transfer to nearby airports, food services, etc. Such assistant would be composed of: mobile application, RFID tags, billboards, avatars and sensors (e.g. placed in plane's chairs). Interactions could take place via audio, text, images, sensors, signals, animations and/or vibrations. The application could be tailored for each user with multiple language resources.

5 Discussion Towards Open Design

Designers should be aware of the impacts that the insertion of a technological solution might bring about to a community of users [3]. With that in mind, when considering the expansion of the Open Source concept to Design processes, we argue that it is necessary that tools and platforms be developed in order to support the entire cycle, including early phases of the design process.

In order to start the investigation on the Open Design concept, we have used the SAwD tool to simulate the workshop activities in an online manner, including online versions of artifacts from Organizational Semiotics. For this exercise, the scenario of an airport was chosen. As mentioned before, airports present many interesting opportunities. It houses people with varied languages, cultures and values in a same place, bringing them close as they share similar objectives. Designing for such varied audience can be challenging, especially when accounting for a Socially Aware Design.

By observing the conduction of the two workshops that took place without digital technology, we were able to better understand the main characteristics that a platform or tool should have in order to make an online and collaborative Open Design Project a feasible experience. The transcription of the results from the artifacts from the workshops (EF, SID and Semiotic Framing) into the SAwD tool served as basis for a preliminary investigation and evaluation of SAwD as a potential platform for this purpose.

Concerning SID, the comparison between the poster filled during in-person activity and the SAwD tool filled afterwards (Fig. 2) indicates that the activity could be conducted online with the support of the tool. The SAwD supported the same input type in a collaborative way. During the workshop, each participant wrote their contribution in a post-it and stuck it on the SID poster. Some of them discussed the ideas before writing the post-it. In a similar way, participants would be able to fill SID with their contributions in SAwD. The online tool also supports discussions via the chat feature with one important advantage: the online chat can be retrieved later if needed. Even if one records the discussions in in-person activities, retrieving specific information would be easier in SAwD.

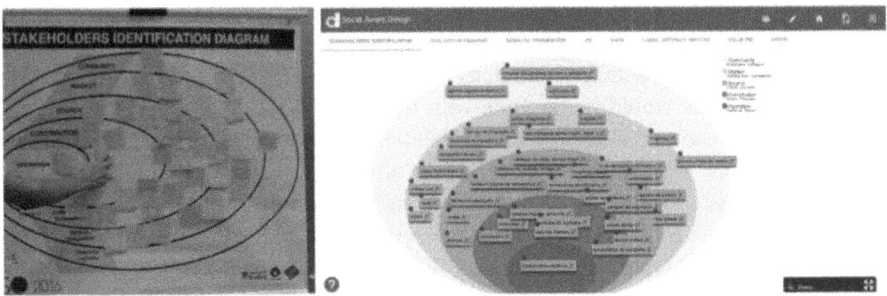

Fig. 2. From left to right: poster of stakeholders identification diagram being filled during the first workshop; the same artifact on the SAwD tool.

Differences were only found when handling the EF. The main difference observed was that the SAwD tool supports the interaction exactly as the artifact was intended for: it directly relates stakeholders to possible problems and ideas for solutions. When using the EF in person with post-it's, participants were able to insert problems at random without relating them to stakeholders. This is not possible in the present version of the SAwD tool. This difference between the original physical artefact and its online adaptation has positive and negative consequences. While SAwD does not reflect the interaction that happens in person, it forces the specified use of the artifact, making the activity more productive in terms of both effectiveness and efficiency.

Another important advantage of the SAwD tool is that it is easier to manipulate for recording and later analysis. When the workshops were over, the posters had to be rolled up and carried with care so that the post-it's would not be lost during transportation. Moreover, in order to read the results, one would need to open the entire poster and find a place to hang it. When dealing with an increased number of workshops, storing all the resulting posters becomes a troublesome task. Also the costs are higher in the in-person activity as it is necessary to have the posters with the artifacts printed; buy post-it's and pens; plus the additional costs of a physical installation (rent, facilities like restrooms and cleaning, etc.). This characteristic results in the main contribution of the SAwD tool in its value for an OpenDesign project. Since the artifacts in SAwD are easy to store and use, they are therefore easy to share. Other projects that are intended for similar scenarios can use the same results from a previous activity. The filled artifacts may serve as a starting point for different design projects. They may be used as they are or they may inspire other creations. Just like in Open Source projects, the SAwD tool will make it possible to leave the contributions for the Open Design community to use them as pleased or needed.

By analyzing the results from both workshops, which had the same central theme (airports), we can observe that some results were the same in both workshops. For example, as SID results both had passenger, attendant, etc.; and as EF results, time for check in and for landing, concerns with luggage, etc. In this sense, we can hypothesize that, if participants from the second workshop had had the chance to access the artifacts that resulted from the first workshop, they could have benefited from that knowledge and could have started with a preliminary understanding from the point of view of a different group. This would be possible with the SAwD tool.

From all of these advantages that were mentioned, in summary, one may affirm that the adaptations that were made so far to use the artifacts from Organizational Semiotics and Socially Aware Design as online tools were successful. The SAwD tool, as it is today, already provides support for all of the activities that usually takes place in face-to-face encounters. Moreover, it supports the concept of Open Design, as it allows sharing, coping, and editing the already existent design processes. However, more investigation is needed in order to enhance the SAwD tool even further. Tracking the decisions and changes that are made during the discussions could be a differential for the tool, as any contribution or change could be recovered. In addition, one of the challenges that is part of our future work is to include the role of a mediator. As it occurs in the face-to-face workshops, participants can profit from a mediator to inform and guide the discussions.

Only SF and EF were mentioned in this article; however, SAwD also supports dynamic online collaborative work with the Semiotic Onion [8, 9, 14] and Semiotic Ladder [8, 9, 14]; VIF [12]; CARF [12], Value Pie [11] and others.

6 Conclusion

The OpenDesing philosophy presupposes an open production in which what is produced belongs to everyone and not only to the creators of it. This means that a design solution can be extended or reapplied by others, whenever proponents agree to create an OpenDesign. The shared solution assumes that anyone can join or leave the team at any time. Each person can instantiate a design solution or part of it for a reuse of what has already been produced.

This article described two workshops that took place as in-person activities at a conference in 2016 and a symposium in 2017, to investigate the use of Organizational Semiotics and the Socially Aware Design artifacts to support ideas of Open Design. The analysis of the results and the comparison of the same activities using the online and collaborative tool SAwD indicate that SAwD has the potential of supporting the OpenDesign concept. This preliminary investigation has also indicated possibilities for the enhancement of the SAwD tool. Next steps include further development and evaluation of SAwD, as well as deeper investigation on the OpenDesign concept.

Acknowledgments. We would like to thank our colleagues from InterHad for insightful discussions. We also thank the financial support of CNPq (306272/2017-2); CAPES (1644511); and process grants # (#2015/24300-9) and (#2015/16528-0) from São Paulo Research Foundation (FAPESP).

References

1. Baranauskas, M.C.C., Liu, K., Sun, L., Neris, V.P.A., Bonacin, R., Nakata, K. (eds.): Socially Aware Organisations and Technologies. Impact and Challenges. Springer, Cham (2016). https://doi.org/10.1007/978-3-319-42102-5
2. Baranauskas, M.C.C.: OpenDesign: técnicas e artefatos para o design socialmente consciente de sistemas computacionais. Propostas FAPESP/MCTI/MC – 2015 Pesquisa Estratégica sobre a Internet 2015, #2015/24300-9 (2015)
3. Baranauskas, M.C.C.: Social awareness in HCI. Interactions **21**(4), 66–69 (2014)
4. Bonacin, R., Baranauskas, M.C.C., Santos, T.M.: A semiotic approach for flexible e-government service oriented systems. In: 9th ICEIS 2007. v. ISAS, pp. 381–386 (2007)
5. Boy, G.A.: The group elicitation method for participatory design and usability testing. Interactions **4**, 27–33 (1997)
6. Gasparini, I., Piccolo, L.S.G.: IHC 2017 Emoção e Movimento - Proceedings of the 16th Brazilian Symposium on Human Factors in Computing Systems (2017, to be published)
7. Hayashi, E.C.S., Silva, J.V., Pereira, R., Baranauskas, M.C.C.: Socially aware design in action - practices and results. Technical report, IC (2018, to be published)
8. Liu, K.: Semiotics in Information Systems and Engineering. Cambridge University Press, Cambridge (2000)
9. Liu, K., Li, W.: Organisational Semiotics for Business Informatics. Routledge, London (2015)
10. Muller, M.: Participatory Practices in the Software Lifecycle. In: Handbook of Human-Computer Interaction, pp. 255–297. Elsevier Science (1997)
11. Pereira, R., Baranauskas, M.C.C.: Value pie: a culturally informed conceptual scheme for understanding values in design. In: Kurosu, M. (ed.) HCI 2014. LNCS, vol. 8510, pp. 122–133. Springer, Cham (2014). https://doi.org/10.1007/978-3-319-07233-3_12
12. Pereira, R., Buchdid, S.B., Baranauskas, M.C.C.: Values and cultural aspects in design: artifacts for making them explicit in design activities. In: Cordeiro, J., Maciaszek, L.A., Filipe, J. (eds.) ICEIS 2012. LNBIP, vol. 141, pp. 358–375. Springer, Heidelberg (2013). https://doi.org/10.1007/978-3-642-40654-6_22
13. da Silva, J.V., Pereira, R., Buchdid, S.B., Duarte, E.F., Baranauskas, M.C.C.: SAwD - socially aware design: an organizational semiotics-based case tool to support early design activities. In: Baranauskas, M.C.C., Liu, K., Sun, L., Neris, VPdA, Bonacin, R., Nakata, K. (eds.) ICISO 2016. IAICT, vol. 477, pp. 59–69. Springer, Cham (2016). https://doi.org/10.1007/978-3-319-42102-5_7
14. Stamper, R.: A semiotic theory of information and information systems. Invited papers for the ICL/University of Newcastle Seminar on Information (1993)
15. Stamper, R., Liu, K., Hafkamp, M., Ades, Y.: Understanding the roles of signs and norms in organisations: a semiotic approach to information systems design. J. Behav. Inf. Technol. **19**(1), 15–27 (2000)

Reformulating Requirements Modelling for Digitalisation: A Structuration and Semiotic Informed Approach

Adrian Benfell[(✉)] and Zoe Hoy

University of Portsmouth, Richmond Building, Portland Street,
Portsmouth PO1 3DE, UK
{adrian.benfell,zoe.hoy}@port.ac.uk

Abstract. Articulated within this paper is a qualitative investigation into using structuration and semiotic theories that suggests improvements to communication when developing new software. Forming the analysis, an Information System (IS) designed using the Unified Modelling Language (UML) allied with the Agile software development process exposed a key factor: the need for effective communication. This factor caused a negative outcome when developing a new IS necessary to support the digitalisation of a business. Analysing the conditions and adjusting requirements modelling with structuration and semiotic theories, team members expressed with clarity requirements for their new IS as real-world effects and causes. Such cause and effect statements align to Peircean interpretant signs that facilitated effective communication.

Keywords: Structuration · Semiotics · Requirements modelling
Digitalisation

1 Introduction

Digitalisation, the digital transformation of business, requires businesses to be more agile, people-orientated, pioneering, and customer-centric. Some articles point to digital technologies and their transforming properties, for example [4, 19, 22, 41]. Extracting key themes from [4, 19, 22, 41] suggests that effective communication is a requisite in any digitalisation process that needs new software. To realise digitalisation however, some persistent challenges must be answered. For instance, [15, 34, 36] draw attention to the limitations of requirements modelling for software development. They highlight that communication inconsistencies between people when embarking upon requirements modelling can cause negative project outcomes. Hence, in this paper we focus upon improving communication in relation to software development.

Based upon our experience with an Information Systems Development (ISD) project, we argue that when using the Unified Modelling Language (UML) [42] combined with Agile [1], as contemporary requirements modelling tools, do not promote effective communication during software development. Our view follows [5, 10] who emphasise that communication underpins requirements modelling. Many researchers place an emphasis upon effective communication when requirements modelling, however few

K. Liu et al. (Eds.): ICISO 2018, IFIP AICT 527, pp. 218–227, 2018.
https://doi.org/10.1007/978-3-319-94541-5_22

provide empirical evidence to resolve this challenge. In this paper we take a similar position to [5, 10] and judge communication to be a permanent and relevant issue when requirements modelling.

Using UML as an up-to-date example, challenges to effective communication during requirements modelling start with UML Use cases. Modelling them further with UML Activity diagrams and narrative to describe functional properties changes the dynamics of communication between project stakeholders. Hence, communication focuses upon Use cases to depict state changes between the functional elements of IS and end-users. Extracting functionality from Use cases with Activity diagrams, the three stereotype classes, entity, boundary and controller, as they comply with the model-view-controller architectural design pattern [23], stabilise requirements when UML Communication modelling early in the requirements modelling process. Also, at the start of UML Communication modelling to show how stereotype classes communicate with each other, complexity increases when detailing requirements with full Object-Orientated (OO) class notation.

We assert, that during requirements modelling, intricacies that materialise when using UML modelling techniques to specify IS functionality impedes effective communication. In this paper we use [3, 12, 26, 30, 33] who define modelling techniques as abstract representations of the problem domain using narrative combined with diagrams. Modelling techniques format communication during ISD, hence recognising how communication works in organisations should become a primary mechanism to facilitate improvements in requirements modelling. This view takes us to structuration and semiotic theories and frames the research questions (RQ) in this paper as:

RQ1: What can structuration and semiotics inform about communication when requirements modelling?
RQ2: How can structuration and semiotics reformulate requirements modelling to improve communication?

To answer the RQs, the structure of this paper is as follows. The next section, theoretical background, presents structuration and semiotic theories as they relate to requirements modelling and acts as preparation to answer the RQs. Following the theoretical background, the research method section includes a case study as supporting empirical evidence derived from an ISD project. The theoretical background provides the scope to assess the case study. Also, to fit digitalisation, the research method section includes recommendations to resolve communication issues when requirements modelling. This paper finishes with a conclusion that discusses outcomes and further research.

2 Theoretical Background

Giddens [16–18] defines the relationship between structure (the rules and resources that reproduce social systems) and agency (the conduct of an individual and of others) as structuration theory. A broad range of viewpoints exists regarding structure and agency. First, Durkheim [13] who emphasised stability and durability of structure, and second, Marx [28] who defined structures as protecting the few and doing little to meet the needs of many. Giddens [17] however places structure at different levels within society. At the top-level, society comprises socioeconomic stratifications, for example social class. On a mid-level scale, institutions and social networks, and at a lower-level, a community or a grouping of social norms that outlines agency. By developing structuration theory, Giddens defines the 'duality of structure', whereby social structure is both the medium and the outcome of social action and people (as agents) share an 'equal ontological status'.

Giddens's framework offers three parts to structuration theory. First, signification, where signs used in communication convey meaning specific to organisations. Communication reference points [11], for example police uniforms, acronyms in professional languages and so on, are organisation specific signs. Charlton and Andras [11] also suggest that specialised communication reference points demarcate organisations from others. Second, legitimation includes normative perceptions rooted as social norms that govern people in their actions and understanding in organisations. Third, domination, links to how individuals in influential roles apply power to control resources also in organisations. Hence, the mix of signification, legitimation, and domination links to semiotic theory which are discussed next.

2.1   Signification

Giddens [17], whilst taking a semiotic view of signs and their interpretation, provides little guidance about semiotics. However, semiotics includes two strands, one by de Saussure [35] and the other by Peirce [32]. Both strands have a subjective element to understanding signs present in communication, as signs can have different meanings in different organisations. However, Saussurean semiotics focuses upon communicative acts and text only [14] but Peirce's view of semiotics helps to comprehend signs used in communication and requirements models. For example, to understand a sign Peirce and Saussure defined the term semiosis, the process of interpreting signs based upon different elements. In Peircean semiotics, the interaction between three combined parts: a sign, an object and an interpretant forms semiosis. A sign may align to three types: symbolic, iconic, and indexical. Regarding Fig. 1, symbolic signs identify their objects through cultural conventions such as words; iconic signs represent their objects by similarities, such as images; and indexical signs have causal links to their objects, for example smoke identifying fire.

Regarding the process of semiosis in Fig. 1, a sign refers to an object, and the object verifies its sign. Therefore, the object is the semantic meaning of a sign due to the ontological association. Interpretant signs add to the sign – object association, as an interpretant is a more developed sign in someone's mind. Hence, the interpretant gives the contextual meaning given to a sign and may comprise social norms. Giddens view of legitimation and domination identifies how social norms provide the rules by which meanings emerge as interpretant signs. Also, according to Liu [24], semiosis is a sign-mediated process in which people give meanings to signs.

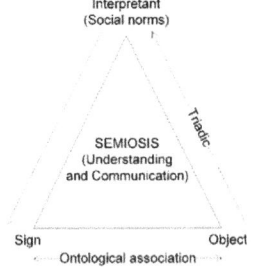

Fig. 1. Semiotic triangle, the sign – object association and interpretant signs

2.2   Legitimation

The interaction of agent and structure, as a system of normative behaviour supports structuration. Legitimation is applicable when attempting to understand communication issues when requirements modelling. For example, Giddens [17, 18] uses the term reflexivity to describe normative behaviour as cause and effect cycles that occur when people revise their social world and alter their place in structures. In this setting, the interaction of people with structures induces normative behaviour. The interaction depicts how people understand their environment through an array of influences, marking out behavioural patterns that when followed define social normative behaviour [40]. Hence, social norms evolve through the interaction of people when following expected conventions within organisations [7]. Social norms emerge as legalised constraints in a contract, or surface resulting from reflexive social interaction [17].

2.3   Domination

Charlton and Andras [11] and Luhmann [27] suggest that previous dialogue forms communication reference points that sustain contact whilst shaping ongoing discourse. People when they belong to an organisation have conversations using specific communication reference points. Thus, organisation specific communication reference points help to distinguish social norms owned by one organisation from another. An influence on social norms includes domination. Identified within structuration theory, domination identifies how people exert control over the rules and resources that influence social norms. However, through reflexivity, people may accept and change social norms shaped in power relationships. Domination thus influences understanding of social normative behaviour as interpretant signs.

3   Case Study

To answer the RQs, we present empirical evidence in a case study format split into four sections: (3.1) overviews the context of the study; (3.2) outlines the ISD challenge based upon UML and Agile; (3.3) details an observation and analysis from the viewpoint of the theoretical background and answers RQ1; (3.4) includes proposals to reformulate requirements modelling to improve communication answering RQ2.

3.1   Project Context

Based upon a digitalisation project that started in 2013, its remit was to develop and deploy an IS to manage accommodation. The team comprised seven support managers, a senior support manager and a head of residential services. The team was self-managed and where possible involved team members in many stages of the Agile approach. Related to Information Technology (IT), all team members showed competence when using known computer-based office products. Team members provided feedback comments only and did not take part in software coding.

Provision for the project came from a service department offering computing support, of which two further staff members helped to scope initial project requirements. One author of this paper involved with the ISD project took the title requirements engineer, whilst the other provided expertise associated with Agile. Working with the accommodation management team, the requirements engineer carried out requirements modelling and software development, organised and attended review meetings, and catalogued feedback. Access granted to historical hard copies of documentation associated with core business processes identified the ISD project context.

The project included one year for ISD, one year for a post implementation review, and a third year (and a fourth if required) for any modifications. The project took three-and-a-half years to complete. Additional supporting data collection methods included documentation associated with the ISD project as versioned requirements models, meeting agendas, and recorded minutes. Interviews were unnecessary as ample information, assembled by the requirements engineer, describes the situation.

3.2   An Outline of the ISD Challenge

The approach taken to develop the new IS, at the request of the computing department, asked that the project to undergo a full systems analysis and design strategy to suit the needs imposed by ITIL and its Service Design guidelines [21]. UML selected as a standardised set of modelling techniques suited ITIL, and UML Use case modelling shaped requirements modelling prior to systems design in an iterative ISD process cycle following Agile principles. In addition, to drive requirements modelling, UML Activity and Communication modelling techniques aligned to Use cases and Agile User stories, baselined requirements. The Agile approach followed the most popular Scrum VersionOne [43] that helped create an iterative and incremental approach to ISD. Meetings, iterations, and iteration planning according to VersionOne [43] formed the generalised ISD process. Iteration planning had a longer-term outlook and determined the high-level requirements as features needed for the new IS. User stories identified the Use cases which helped capture initial requirements, following the concept introduced by [6].

For the plan-driven approach taken, a Computer Aided Software Engineering (CASE) tool facilitated requirements modelling. User stories included a small amount of narrative, one paragraph only, to help create a shared understanding between all team members [31]. At the end of each iteration, team members provided feedback informing any changes needed [20]. With all team members in different locations presented challenges. This included working different shift patterns, and distances travelled. As a result, this reduced the number of opportunities to have consistent communication with all team members.

The versioned requirements models produced from UML modelling techniques informed initial and detailed class design as development iterations. For implementation, a completed class model coupled with relational database design advised software coding specifications. Also, it was compulsory that the class and relational database models complied with the model-view-controller design pattern to suit a client-server architectural setting for multi-user access. The database installed on the server (as the model), controller classes programmed to handle data transactions in Structured Query Language (SQL) commands across a network, and the views constructed to conform to the underlying data structure, followed the needs of all team members.

The planned Agile software development process linked to the UML Use case driven approach had a supporting project lifecycle and agreed milestones. Sanctioned by all team members, a project initiation document detailed the overall scope of the ISD project and included a short and precise narrative explaining the outcomes. Accomplished in team meetings and by visiting each team member, Agile User stories and linked UML Use cases formed the initial baselined requirements. UML Use cases underwent further development using UML Activity and/or Communication diagrams. UML Communication models aligned to Use cases helped to generate a final Communication model in the CASE tool. Applying UML stereotype classes in the final UML Communication model assisted in designing classes to fulfil the model-view-controller architecture. This approach intended to formalise requirements before moving to software coding.

3.3   Observation and Analysis

After achieving an initial agreement for Agile User stories and associated UML Use case model, complications surfaced. Information encapsulating reflexivity as social norms against communication reference points in an interpretive scheme (signification), proved difficult to capture using UML modelling techniques. To ensure that the new IS met with success, we deemed this information essential to realise the needs of each team member and match it over to the information required to create class diagrams to remove complications. The attempt to capture and represent this information resulted in numerous modifications to the UML Use case model, Agile User stories, and UML Activity and Communication diagrams but without success. Hence, the project ran into severe time difficulties.

To capture requirements for the new IS implied that previous dialogue formed communication reference points, which we did not expect, for the basis of contact between team members whilst shaping on-going discourse based upon social norms, aligning to [11]. In addition, the requirements engineer intervened attempting to keep the project on target as many of the Agile User stories became invalidated as the project advanced through requirements modelling towards software coding. However, team members identified and agreed upon real-word effects. For example, with the existing IS one team member stated, "we produced more accurate case reports when updating case details with correct time allocations". Team members detailed effects that occurred in the real-world and agreed to them, and in doing so, identified what we described as social norms linked to communication reference points.

When discussing functionality with Agile User stories and UML Use cases, team members lost the link between the functional description and what they wished to achieve. However, a prototype relational database designed from an existing, but incomplete, requirements model helped meet the initial one-year deadline. This plan eased time pressure, but the prototype required further development. A review into how requirements modelling could meet the fast-changing demands placed by team members allowed us to consider how communication reference points, linking to social norms, could reformulate requirements. The idea was to generate requirements for the project as short and precise statements. First signifying communication reference points in a process of semiosis. Second, aligning reflexive cause and effect cycles to Peirce's view of sign and object. Third, using legitimisation and domination to identify social norms as Peirce's interpretant signs.

3.4   Reformulating Requirements Modelling

To represent communication reference points, we identified a suitable scheme that provided a means to categorise information harvested during requirements modelling. Peircean semiotics, further explained by [2, 9, 37, 38] provided a way to adjust requirements modelling using symbolic, iconic and indexical signs. First, symbolic signs as particular words structured what we called Normative Statements based upon Fig. 2. Symbolic signs included the rules that governed how words formed phrases and sentences within each information element (such as Project, Project Scope and so forth in Fig. 2). Second, icons as oval shapes with names identifying UML Use Cases and linked Normative Statements. Third, indexical signs depicted the association between communication reference points and social norms, and between causes and effects structured as narrative declarations. Hence, Normative Statements modelled reflexivity as cause and effect cycles understood and communicated by team members. To ensure consistency when deciding cause and effect statements, we followed necessary and sufficient conditions [8]. Also, each cause statement that supported an effect became a candidate function within a candidate class. Normative Statements as we designed them, codified interpretant signs.

Normative Statements for each UML Use case emerged by collective agreement across connected team members as Roles (shown in Fig. 2). For revision to requirements modelling, each Normative Statement promoted effective communication. For example, Normative Statements allowed an autonomy of expression with short natural language blocks of text [34] that allowed team members to detail supporting necessary conditions to real-world effects. They also captured a balance between agency and structure through the principle of legitimation and domination. Based upon Fig. 2, Normative Statements forming a complete requirements model emerged within two months, four months shorter than when using UML, and reflected the demands placed by team members.

Using Normative Statements helped us to meet the original ISD project timeframe. This approach also removed the need for further modelling with UML Activity and Communication diagrams. We claim Normative Statements simplified requirements modelling, improved communication, and validated the use of structuration and semiotic theories to understand communication issues.

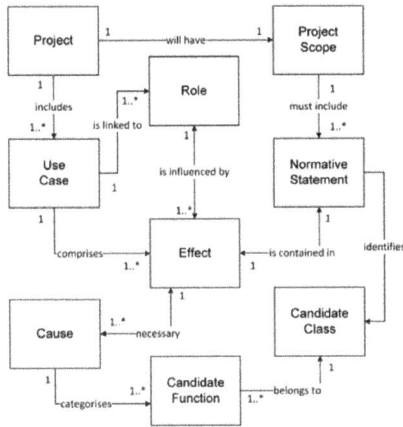

Fig. 2. The structure of normative statements and codification of interpretant signs

4   Discussion and Conclusion

Structuration and semiotic theories provided a method to understand and modify communication when requirements modelling. For example, signification identified the use of communication reference points in communication that link to social norms based upon legitimation and domination. Combined, these items demarcate organisations and semiotic theory helped to represent this phenomenon. Thus, communication reference points in the form of Normative Statements acted as a prime mechanism by which team members understood and communicated requirements for the ISD project.

Underpinned by necessary and sufficient conditions [8], supporting real-world effects structured by Fig. 2 are our view of Peircean interpretant signs. This approach considered how words and phrases, structured inside Normative Statements, combined to represent meaning attached to them by team members for requirements [34]. The necessary and sufficient conditions allowed team members to understand and communicate reference points and social norms.

Using structuration and semiotic theories as the focal point for research, generalisations are possible with similar situations in organisations. For further research, testing the propositions in this paper needs to advance by considering design artefacts and attaching their composition to Fig. 2. Although UML and Agile are useful to develop software artefacts that support IS, our recommendations suggest that an alternative way of requirements modelling incorporating Giddens structuration theory and Peircean semiotics is plausible to meet communication challenges, and therefore digitalisation. However, semiotics needs more research in a digitalisation context.

Stamper [39]; Liu [24] and Liu and Li [25] place an emphasis on studying the effect of signs in organisation contexts. Their view of semiotics forms an inquiry system approach to analysing organisations from the viewpoint of sign creation, utilisation and meaning that govern the behavioural aspects of interaction. Stamper devised a 'Semiotic Ladder' as an Organisational Semiotic (OS) approach to investigate organisations based upon Morris [29], shaping most of the work with the realm of OS.

Stamper's Semiotic Ladder distinguishes between organisational and IT domains. It says the IT domain supports organisations and gives technology a particular flavour according to 'social worlds'. Social worlds comprise beliefs, law and culture feeding into Giddens legitimation and domination as intentional communication. OS offers a wealth of research to develop further Normative Statements.

References

1. Agile: Agile Alliance (2018). http://www.agilealliance.org/. Accessed Dec 2018
2. Atkin, A.: Peirce's Theory of Signs (2013). http://plato.stanford.edu/archives/sum2013/entries/peirce-semiotics/. Accessed Nov 2016
3. Avison, D., Fitzgerald, G.: Information Systems Development: Methodologies, Techniques and Tools. McGraw Hill, New York (2006)
4. Bharadwaj, A., El Sawy, O., Pavlou, P., Venkatraman, N.: Digital Business Strategy: Toward a Next Generation of Insights (2013)
5. Bano, M., Zowghi, D.: A systematic review on the relationship between user involvement. Inf. Softw. Technol. **58**, 148–169 (2015)
6. Beck, K.: Extreme Programming Explained. Addison-Wesley, Boston (2000)
7. Boella, G., van der Torre, L., Verhagen, H.: Introduction to normative multiagent systems. Comput. Math. Organ. Theory **12**(2–3), 71–79 (2006)
8. Brennan, A.: The Stanford Encyclopaedia of Philosophy (Winter 2012 Edition) (2012). http://plato.stanford.edu/archives/win2012/entries/necessary-sufficient/. Accessed June 2015
9. Chandler, D.: Semiotics – The Basics, 1st edn. Routledge, Abingdon (2002)
10. Charaf, C.M., Rosenkranz, C., Holten, R.: The emergence of shared understanding: applying functional pragmatics to study the requirements development process. Inf. Syst. J. **23**, 115–135 (2013)
11. Charlton, B., Andras, P.: The modernization imperative. Imprint Academic, Exeter (2003)
12. Chen, P.: The entity-relationship model - toward a unified view of data. ACM Trans. Database Syst. **1**, 9–36 (1976)
13. Durkheim, E.: Socialism. Collier-Macmillan, New York (1962)
14. Eco, U.: A Theory of Semiotics. Indiana University Press, Bloomington (1976)
15. Fernández, D.M., Wagner, S.: Naming the pain in requirements engineering: a design for a global family of surveys and first results from Germany. Inf. Softw. Technol. **57**, 616–643 (2015)
16. Giddens, A.: Central Problems in Social Theory: Action, Structure, and Contradiction in Social Analysis. University of California Press, Berkeley and Los Angeles (1979)
17. Giddens, A.: The Constitution of Society: Outline of the Theory of Structuration. University of California Press, Berkeley and Los Angeles (1984)
18. Giddens, A.: Modernity and Self-Identity, Self and Society in the Late Modern Age. Stanford University Press, Palo Alto (1991)
19. HBR Analytics Services: Accelerating the Pace of Digital Transformation; Harvard Business Review (2016)
20. Inayat, I., Salim, S.S., Marczak, S., Daneva, M., Shamshirband, S.: A systematic literature review on agile requirements engineering practices and challenges. Comput. Hum. Behav. **51**(2015), 915–929 (2015). https://doi.org/10.1016/j.chb.2014.10.046
21. ITIL: Best Practice Solutions (2015). https://www.axelos.com/best-practice-solutions/itil/what-is-itil. Accessed Nov 2015

22. Kane, G.C., Palmer, D., Phillips, A.N., Kiron, D., Buckley, N.: Strategy, Not Technology, Drives Digital Transformation. MIT Sloan Management Review and Deloitte University Press, July 2015
23. Krasner, G.E., Pope, S.T.: A description of the model-view-controller user interface paradigm in the smalltalk-80 system. J. Object Oriented Program. **1**(3), 26–49 (1988)
24. Liu, K.: Semiotics in Information Systems Engineering, 1st edn. Cambridge University Press, Cambridge (2000)
25. Liu, K., Li, W.: Organisational Semiotics for Business Informatics. Routledge, Abingdon (2014)
26. Loucopoulos, P., Karakostas, V.: System Requirements Engineering. McGraw-Hill, Inc., New York (1995)
27. Luhmann, N.: Introduction to Systems Theory. Polity Press, Cambridge (2012)
28. Marx, K.: 'Preface', to a contribution to the critique of political economy. In: Marx, K., Engels, F. (eds.) Selected Writings. Lawrence and Wishart, London (1968)
29. Morris, C.W.: Foundations of the theory of signs. In: International Encyclopedia of Unified Science, pp. 1–59. Chicago University Press (1938)
30. Nuseibeh, B., Easterbrook, S.: Requirements engineering: a roadmap. In: Proceedings of the Conference on the Future of Software Engineering, pp. 35–46. ACM, May 2000
31. Patton, J.: User Story Mapping: Discover the Whole Story, Build the Right Product. O'Reilly, Sebastopol (2014)
32. Peirce, C.: The Essential Writings: Selected Philosophical Writings (1893-1913), 1st edn. Indiana University Press, Bloomington (1998)
33. Pohl, K.: Requirements Engineering: Fundamentals, Principles, and Techniques. Springer, Heidelberg (2010)
34. Rosenkranz, C., Corvera Charaf, M., Holten, R.: Language quality in requirements development: tracing communication in the process of information systems development. J. Inf. Technol. **28**, 198–223 (2013)
35. de Saussure, F.: Course in General Linguistics (trans. R. Harris). Duckworth, London (1983)
36. Schwarz, A., Chin, W.W., Hirschheim, R., Schwarz, C.: Toward a process-based view of information technology acceptance. J. Inf. Technol. **29**, 73–96 (2014)
37. Short, T.: Peirce's Theory of Signs, 1st edn. Cambridge University Press, Cambridge (2007)
38. Sowa, J.: Knowledge Representation: Logical, Philosophical, and Computational Foundations. Brooks/Cole Thomson Learning, Pacific Grove (2000)
39. Stamper, R.: Signs, information, norms and systems. In: Signs of Work, pp. 349–399 (1996)
40. Thøgersen, J.: Social norms and cooperation in real-life social dilemmas. J. Econ. Psychol. **29**, 458–472 (2008)
41. UK GOV (2017). https://www.gov.uk/government/publications/made-smarter-review. Accessed Feb 2018
42. UML, 2.5: Unified Modelling Language Resource Page (2018). http://www.omg.org/spec/UML/2.5/PDF/. Accessed Dec 2018
43. VersionOne: 10th Annual state of agile survey (2016). https://versionone.com/pdf/VersionOne-10th-Annual-State-of-Agile-Report.pdf. Accessed Dec 2016

Getting it Right: A Model for Compliance Assessment

Kwasi Dankwa[✉] and Keiichi Nakata[✉]

Informatics Research Centre, Henley Business School, University of Reading,
Reading, UK
k.d.dankwa@pgr.reading.ac.uk, k.nakata@henley.ac.uk

Abstract. Compliance is important for organisations but models and tools to aid understanding of compliance behaviour is limited. This paper argues that the understanding of the interaction between subjects and objects and their intention to comply with requirements of rules and regulations may be a predictor of compliance behaviour. Thus, a Conceptual Compliance Assessment Model (CAM) is developed by extension of Technology Acceptance Model and Activity theory for assessment of compliance behaviour. Data collected and evaluated showed that the awareness and understanding of the mediational tool is critical in realizing the outcome. It also showed that other factors like the perceived usefulness, perceived ease of use, the community and the management set up also affected compliance behaviour. Essentially, the use of CAM will be useful in assessing the compliance activities of subjects which may aid in formulation of behaviour support systems to improve compliance behaviour.

Keywords: Compliance Assessment Model · Quality Management System
Activity theory · Technology Acceptance Model

1 Introduction

The quest for organisations to produce safety critical products and to meet customer needs has led to ubiquitous implementation of systems and processes that supports compliance. To these organisations, compliance is a way of ensuring that they get it right at the first time to reduce reworking processes and wastage of resources. Thus, compliance to rules, regulations, policies and standard is essential.

Consequently, tools, frameworks and models have been put in place to assess practice and to ensure that compliance requirements are met. Some of these tools include Compliance Action Framework [1], Analytical Framework for Behaviour Analysis [2] and ICT Approach [3]. However, non-compliances have been reported as most of the existing systems have failed to assess the reasons behind the non- compliance behaviour or the compliance intention. There is therefore the need to consider other tools and approaches that incorporates compliance intentions of agents to aid in the management of non-compliance. The purpose of this research is therefore to develop a conceptual model for the assessment of compliance behaviour that considers the reasons behind the non-compliance behaviour. The paper starts by reviewing tools and models that have been applied in information systems, develop a conceptual model

K. Liu et al. (Eds.): ICISO 2018, IFIP AICT 527, pp. 228–237, 2018.
https://doi.org/10.1007/978-3-319-94541-5_23

based on the literature review and evaluate the new conceptual model by assessing compliance behaviour to a Quality Management System (QMS).

2 Rational for the Model

2.1 Compliance Behaviour

The study of agents' attitudes and behaviour has a long history in information systems research and compliance behaviour is no exception. Compliance behaviour have been shown to be impacted by many factors which may include incentives, governance, controls, culture and behavioural issues. Because of this, researches in different disciplines have looked at compliance effects (for example, [1–3]) but there are still some gaps in theories and models to support compliance assessment. According to [4], management of compliance relies on the agents' behaviour to either follow requirements or not. Others [5] indicate that norms within the organisation influence human behaviour which in turn influence compliance to QMS. Accordingly, understanding factors that influences adoption of the rules and regulations and the effects of norms will be useful in understanding non-compliance behaviour. The next sections will therefore review two models that considers acceptance and use of IS and the interaction that exist between the subjects and the objects in the organisation.

2.2 Extension of Technology Acceptance Model (TAM)

Over the year's researchers have worked to gain a better understanding of technology acceptance and implementation success in order to make the most of technology investments. User acceptance of technology is seen as the demonstrable intention on the part of the user group to employ information technology for the purpose it is set to be used for [6]. Technology Acceptance Model (TAM) is one of the models which has captured the attention of the Information Systems (IS) community. It proposes that the behavioural intention by a user to use a system is influenced by perceived usefulness and perceived ease of use of the system which influences the actual use. Application and extension of TAM will aid the assessment of compliance behaviour because of its use in explaining and predicting acceptance behaviour of agents. Moreover, most of the compliance requirements are formulated into IS, as such the extension of TAM is considered as appropriate; we argue that the factors that influence user behaviour to accept and use technology for the purpose it was introduced can be applicable in assessment of compliance activities. This is because, for a staff to exhibit compliance behaviour, they must accept to follow the rules and regulations as required in consonance with TAM. We further argue that, because compliance is influenced by intention of the user, the success in using TAM to predict acceptance and use of technology can be extended to the analysis of compliance behaviour. According to [7], behavioural intention is the formulated conscious plans to perform or not to perform certain specified future behaviour. Since adherence to set of rules or regulations is a behavioural manifestation of compliance, we argue that understanding the factors that influence behavioural intention is relevant in analysing compliance behaviour. Consequently, by understanding user's acceptance of compliance requirements, assessment of the reasons for the compliance behaviour can be made. Essentially, use of TAM to assess acceptance of technology may be extended to assess acceptance and compliance to rules and regulations.

2.3 Extension of Activity Theory

Activity theory is a conceptual framework with "activity" being the foundational concept. This is understood as useful as it develops interaction between the subjects and the world objects [8]. An activity is defined by an object and this may be material thing, a plan or a common idea which is manipulatable by the participants of the activity [9]. According to [10] activity theory has been found to be effective in providing insights into all aspects of interactions and contradictions in processes. Its application in this research is therefore relevant as the processes within the organisation involves activities. As the subjects interact with the object by use of the tools and rules [11], the outcome of the interaction may be assessed. This interaction between the subject and the object is mainly characterized by two key aspects; the subjects of activities have needs which should be met. With organisations having needs, we argue that this theory will allow for the activities of the subjects to meet these needs to be assessed. It affords a process of reviewing the factors that are critical to the interaction between the subject and the object.

The next sections describe the conceptual model development, collection of data and evaluation of data.

3 Methodology

To meet the objective of the research, a design is considered that seek to understand the subjects view of a QMS. To do this, a conceptual model was developed by an extension of TAM with constructs in Activity Theory. Questions were formulated from the factors of the model and staff were interviewed to ascertain their views on the reasons behind non-compliance behaviour to a QMS.

3.1 Compliance Assessment Model

The proposed conceptual model, called Compliance Assessment Model (CAM) was developed as a synthesis of TAM and Activity Theory (Fig. 1). CAM is based on the premise that; the subject has a need and interacts with the object to attain the outcome. This interaction by the subject is achieved by use of mediational means; tools, rules and division of labour. The compliant use of the tools by the subject is influenced by the perceived usefulness and perceived ease of use of the tools.

3.2 Data Collection

The purpose of this section was to facilitate the collection of data for analysis. The data collection process enabled collection of information from all the relevant sources in the

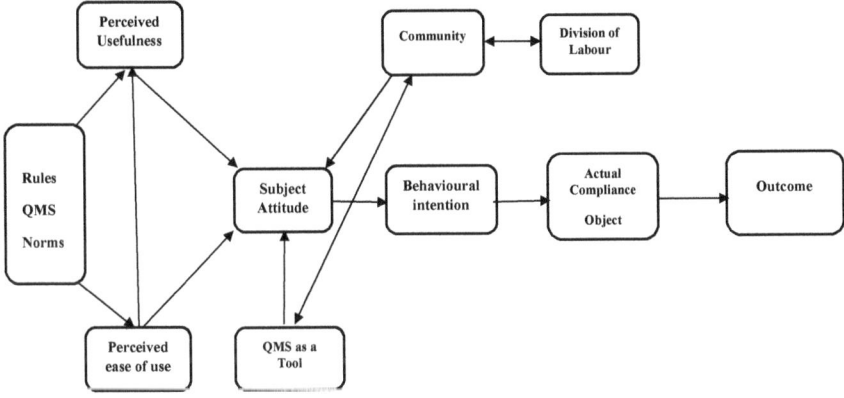

Fig. 1. Compliance assessment model

sample population. This was to allow for the answering of the research problem and to aid evaluation of the outcomes. To do this, the data collection was performed by use of purposeful sampling method. Seven staff members (Table 1) from different departments and staff grades in "a healthcare product provider" were selected for the interview. The selection of staff was based on their interaction with QMS and interviews were conducted over a period of 1 month with each interview lasting between 1–2 h using questions generated from the constructs of the conceptual model.

Thematic analysis was then used to analyze the data gathered from the interviews.

Table 1. Showing job titles of staff interviewed

Staff	A	B	C	D	E	F	G
Job title	Deputy head of lab	Lab manager	Biomedical scientist team manager	Trainee biomedical scientist	Director of lab	Assistant QA manager	Team supervisor in lab

3.3   Summary of Interview Data

The data collected from the interviews are summarized below.

Tool/Mediation. The criticality of the QMS was expressed by staff. Staff E stated, *"QMS is critical to the process and used to manage the quality of the products in the organisation. It has contributed to increasing the quality of patient output and has helped to improve patient engraftment outcome and failed engraftment is now very rare"*. Also, staff B indicated *"I see it as a fundamental part of the provision of healthcare services and products"*.

Subject Attitude. Most of the staff indicated that they have accepting attitude towards the QMS, but some had reservations about the QMS in routine use (practice). *"Is good and am open to the use of QMS even though I have occasions where I don't want to* *face using it" (staff B). "I find it useful at times when making decisions but at times I find it too picky as things that might not be as important in most cases (staff C)".*

Community. There was expression that the community of staff influence each other in the way they behave towards the QMS. Staff F stated: *"The collective attitude of staff in the department impacts on QMS and staff B indicated that "general shared frustration with the QMS within the Lab".*

Division of Labour. There was expression by staff that department structure (hierarchy) and stakeholders in other departments influences the way they related to the QMS. *"My staff in the department are influenced by me and they take QMS seriously, but Senior management team do not influence me positively" (staff A). "The managers in the department see the QMS and the QA staff as police and as such this notion is transferred across" (staff D).*

Perceived Usefulness. Staff expressed that if the QMS is perceived as useful for the task, then they may be inclined to comply all the time. *"Yes, I see QMS to be a useful tool as such I use it" (staff G). "I don't think I need the QMS to do my routine process" (staff D).*

Perceived Ease of Use. Staff expressed that if the QMS is perceived as easy to use, then staff compliance may increase as they will be more inclined to follow always. *"I see it as easy to use but again application is varied across staff and department" (staff C). "If QMS is simple, accessible, easy to learn and readily available then it will be followed" (staff G).*

Behavioural Intention. Some of the staff expressed that they intend to follow QMS always, but others had reservations in following QMS all the time. *Staff F indicated "Yes. I see it as part of my day to day stuff, I see QMS as part of the process and so the intention is to use it".* Staff B also asserted that they *"I intend to comply in all cases but may not be happy doing that".*

Actual Behaviour. Staff expressed mix-feelings that although they intend to follow the QMS, they do not follow always. *"I am more likely to follow the QMS in emergency situation than in less little things due to the clunky nature of the QMS" (staff A). "I generally do but the timing may be the main non-compliance. This is because I know is important and required for the output of our process but following sequential process of the QMS may be difficult" (Staff B).*

4   Findings and Discussion

4.1   Findings

Through the data collection and evaluation, three more constructs were noted: *KPI's verses QMS*, *Resource and time allocation* and *Misunderstanding/misplaced roles*. Summary of the 3 new constructs are stated below:

KPI's vs. QMS. Staff expressed that some of the KPIs tends to contradict the requirements of QMS and as such negatively influences compliance to QMS. Staff B indicated, *"Some of the KPI's are to reduce number of quality incidents raised and as such staff will prefer not to raise a lot to meet the KPI"*. Staff G also stated, *"Failure of management structure in line with KPIs etc. have also contributed to the failures in QMS"*.

Resource and Time Allocation. Staff expressed that the resource and time allocations are not always enough to achieve required outcome. *"Not enough time given to do the work, but you are expected to do it; only interested in statistics and not the actual process been done effectively" (staff A). "Staff always rushing off their feet (very busy) which leads to the mistakes/errors and to ask them to then complete QI and all related QMS paperwork, they will prefer not to report it" (staff E).*

Misunderstanding/Misplaced Roles. Staff expressed that there seem to be misunderstanding of roles within the department. *Staff E stated, "Frontline people think that they are doing QA work as people in production will expect QA to be raising Qis dealing with issues and not them"*.

Also, some of the staff indicated that actions of stakeholder's in other departments may impact negatively on them which may lead to non-compliance. "The department is like a hub so other department not conforming to the QMS will have an impact on our services as we can't be reliant on their report/results" (staff B).

Figure 2 shows the updated CAM model with the additional constructs based on the findings.

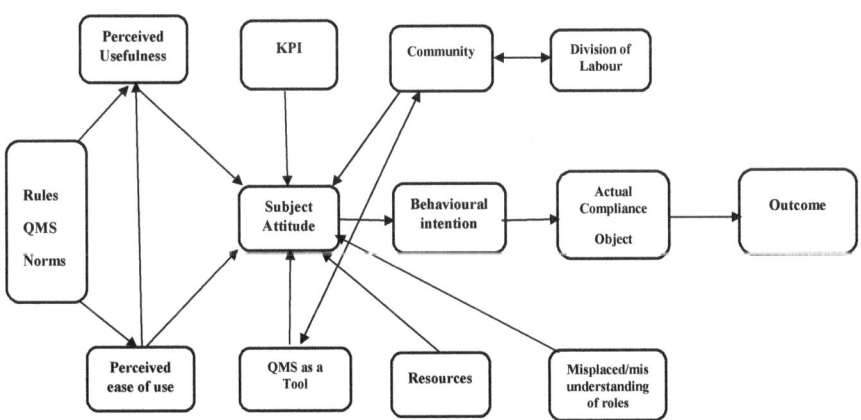

Fig. 2. Updated CAM model

4.2 Discussion

The model was developed to assess the adoption and compliant use of the QMS in place. Data collected and analyzed showed that the tool was seen as relevant by the staff: "QMS is critical to the process and used to manage the quality of the products in the organisation" (Staff E). This showed that in order to attain the required outcome, the awareness of the tool is critical. This supports [11] who indicated that the tool is relevant to attain the desired transformation. Consequently, the availability and awareness of the tool is important for compliant behaviour. Although all the agents showed awareness of the importance of the QMS, there were some reservations. This may be attributed to the presentation of the QMS as a sign in the form of; standard operating procedures, equipment manuals and policies. The use of the QMS may therefore be dependent on the interpretation by the agents. As such the training, experience, participation in workshop, knowledge and social setup etc. of the department is relevant for the outcome. Moreover, because the subjects have needs [12] they will require the tools to attain their needs. Because of this their awareness of the tool is important. Essentially, as the subject aligns their values with the organisation [13], a positive compliance culture is created that supports compliance behaviour. This was evident in the data collected as staff who accepted the values of the organisation were more willing to compliantly use the QMS. In using the QMS, the perceived usefulness of the tool was shown to influence the intention of the subjects. As stated by Staff G, "they see the QMS to be useful and as such they use it". This is consistent with [14], who indicated that perceived usefulness exhibited stronger and more consistent relationship to adoption and use. Essentially, the acceptance by the subjects that they perceive the QMS to be useful, the more incline they are to exhibit compliance behaviour. Also, the ease of use of the QMS was shown to influence the outcome. Staff C indicated that "compliance behaviour may be enhanced if there is ease of interpretation of the QMS". This supports [15], the possibility of non-compliance behaviour will increase if the procedures are so complicated that the operators cannot clearly understand the context of required actions specified in the procedures. As such, if the QMS is complicated and not easily understood then it will not be compliantly followed.

Data analysis showed that the community in which the subject operated influenced their behaviour. As stated by staff F, "there is collective attitude by staff to follow the QMS compliantly." This is consistent with [16] who stressed that community creates "collective programming of the mind" that makes groups unique and this can influence the pattern on thinking, feeling and potential interactions. As such, although the subjects may have diverse needs, they were all united by the norms within the department which influenced their compliance behaviour. Consequently, the social interactions act as the 'force behind' the observed activities. Importantly, social influence and interaction has a significant impact on the intention to use information systems [7]; in this case the intention to compliantly use the QMS. Thus, the subjects exhibited confidence in their actions through similar activities of peers within the departments which likely influenced the compliance behaviour. Furthermore, as the subjects look up to their managers on a routine basis, their behaviour is shaped by them. The hierarchy influenced the behaviour of staff either negatively or positively. Also, because of the reliance of the subjects on other stakeholders in the 'process chain', the data showed that there was stakeholder influence on compliance behaviour. Here, the subject relied on the output of the processes from their stakeholders. As such the negative output from the stakeholders subsequently influence the subject's behaviour. This is consistent with [5] who stressed that the reliance on the initiator in the 'life cycle' of responsibility ultimately influences the compliance behaviour; positively or negatively. Again, this was extended to stakeholders not fully understanding their roles which influence the interactions between the subjects and the object. Moreover, the resources in place (time, material) was essential in the subject's behaviour in that they influenced their approach to the process. There was evidence in the data as subjects indicated that they may not have enough time and as such may not compliantly follow the QMS. Another factor is the KPI's in place which were also seen to compete with the requirements of the QMS. As the staff strive to meet some of the KPI's they indicated that it affected their compliant use of the QMS. There is indication that staff intention to comply, was critical in their actual compliance behaviour. Staff who indicated that they always intend to comply also indicated that they actually comply to the use of the QMS. This is because the increased intentions may yield increased effort which may increase likelihood of the subject undertaking the behaviour [14]. Importantly, the data collected based on the model demonstrated its utility in assessing compliance behaviour.

4.3 Suitability and Benefit of the Updated CAM

From the evaluation of the updated CAM, the following suitability and benefits were observed.

1. The model will be useful in assessing subject intention to use the tool as prescribed which will be useful in predicting the actual use.
2. Because the model assesses the impact of the KPI against the tool, it will be useful in helping to set clear KPI's that supports compliance behaviour.
3. The model will be suitable in assessing acceptance and adoption of a new tool and aid subsequent 'in use' evaluation of the tool.
4. The model will be useful in assessing and understanding resources required for interaction between the subject and the object to achieve the outcome.
5. The model will be useful in understanding and defining roles of subjects. This will also help in reviewing the impact of the leadership team on subject behaviour.
6. The model will be suitable in assessing the reasons behind non-compliance behaviour. This will be useful in setting clear actions which will help safety critical organisations to meet regulatory requirements.

4.4 Limitations of the Updated CAM

Although the analysis has shown that actual behaviour and as such compliance behaviour can be assessed by use of the conceptual model, the findings cannot be generalised due to the interpretive nature of the research. It is recommended that further research be repeated in other organisations and situations, and an alternative research design (e.g., a quantitative study) be used to enable triangulation.

5 Conclusion

This research was set up to develop a Compliance Assessment Model that assesses reasons behind the non-compliance behaviour of agents. The model was developed by synthesis of TAM and Activity Theory. The data collection and evaluation indicated that, the factors from the updated model will be useful in predicting compliance behaviour. This model will be useful in assessing adoption of the compliance requirements and aid observation of the interaction between the subject and object to realise the outcome. Essentially, the use of the CAM model may aid in assessment of compliance behaviour which will be useful in formulating behaviour change support systems to aid compliance.

Acknowledgement. The authors would like to thank the Quality Assurance Department at the Blood Establishment for their cooperation and all the staff who took part in the interviews.

References

1. O'Neill, A.: An action framework for compliance and governance. Clin. Gov. Int. J. **19**(4), 342–359 (2014). https://doi.org/10.1108/CGIJ-07-2014-0022
2. Hirschauer, N., Bavorova, M., Martino, G.: An analytical framework for a behavioural analysis of non-compliance in food supply chains. Br. Food J. **114**(9), 1212–1227 (2012). https://doi.org/10.1108/00070701211258781
3. Governatori, G.: ICT Support for Regulatory Compliance of Business Processes (2014). http://arxiv.org/abs/1403.6865
4. Warkentin, M., Willison, R.: Behavioral and policy issues in information systems security: the insider threat. Eur. J. Inf. Syst. **18**(2), 101–105 (2009)
5. Dankwa, K., Nakata, K.: Making sense of non-compliance: a semiotic approach. In: Baranauskas, M.C.C., Liu, K., Sun, L., de Almeida Neris, V.P., Bonacin, R., Nakata, K. (eds.) ICISO 2016. IAICT, vol. 477, pp. 97–106. Springer, Cham (2016). https://doi.org/10.1007/978-3-319-42102-5_11
6. Dillon, A., Morris, M.: User acceptance of new information technology: theories and models. In: Williams, M. (ed.) Annual Review of Information Science and Technology, vol. 31, pp. 3–32. Information Today, Medford (1996)
7. Venkatesh, V., Morris, M.G., Davis, G.B., Davis, F.D.: User acceptance of information technology: toward a unified view. MIS Q. **27**, 425–478 (2003)
8. Kaptelinin, V.: Activity theory. In: Soegaard, M., Dam, R.F. (eds.) The Encyclopedia of Human-Computer Interaction, 2nd edn. The Interaction Design Foundation, Aarhus (2014). https://www.interaction-design.org/encyclopedia/activity_theory.html. Accessed 15 Apr 2018
9. Kuuti, K.: Activity theory as a potential framework for human-computer interaction research. In: Nardi, B. (ed.) Context and Consciousness: Activity Theory and Human-Computer Interaction, pp. 17–44. MIT Press, Cambridge (1996). Chap. 2
10. Abdullah, Z.: Activity theory as analytical tool: a case study of developing student teachers' creativity in design. Procedia – Soc. Behav. Sci. **131**(2010), 70–84 (2014). http://www.sciencedirect.com/science/article/pii/S1877042814029929
11. Engestrom, Y.: Learning by expanding: an activity–theoretical approach to developmental research (Helsinki, Orienta – Konsultit) (1987)
12. Kaptelinin, V., Nardi, B.A.: Acting with Technology: Activity Theory and Interaction Design. MIT Press, Cambridge (2006)
13. Jenkinson, D.: Compliance culture. J. Finan. Regul. Compliance **4**(1), 41–46 (1996). https://doi.org/10.1108/eb024866
14. Davis, F.D.: Perceived usefulness, perceived ease of use, and user acceptance of information technology. MIS Q. **13**(3), 319–340 (1989)

15. Park, J., Jung, W.: The operators' non-compliance behaviour to conduct emergency operating procedures - comparing with the work experience and the complexity of procedural steps. Reliab. Eng. Syst. Saf. **82**(2), 115–131 (2003). https://doi.org/10.1016/S0951-8320(03)00123-6
16. Hofstede, G.: Culture's Consequences: Comparing Values, Behaviours, Institutions, and organizations across nations, vol. 2. Sage Publications, Inc., Thousand Oaks (2001)

First Steps in Developing Tangible Artifacts for All: Enabling Ideation and Discussion Processes

Vanessa R. M. L. Maike[(⊠)] and M. Cecília C. Baranauskas

Institute of Computing, University of Campinas (UNICAMP),
Campinas, SP, Brazil
{vanessa.maike, cecilia}@ic.unicamp.br

Abstract. Including *everyone* in the process of designing information systems is a challenge, especially considering that techniques and tools traditionally used in this process are written documents. This can make them non-accessible to people in special conditions, e.g., the visually impaired. Therefore, in this paper we present the first steps we took towards redesigning some of these techniques and tools, turning them into tangible digital artifacts. These initiatives are presented as two case studies. One intends to tackle the problem of materializing an idea discussion tool that has an existing graphical representation. The other, takes on the challenge of re-interpreting an ideation technique with well-defined dynamics. In the end, they point towards how to redesign other artifacts.

Keywords: Universal Design · Tangible User Interface · TUI
Organizational Semiotics · Participatory Design · Human-Computer Interaction

1 Introduction

The design of information systems that consider the uniqueness of each person represents a challenge. However, it is also the principle behind *Design for All* or *Universal Design (UD)*. Here considered synonyms, both represent an approach to the design of environments or products that suit the broadest possible range of people, regardless of age or ability [13]. This has major importance in our current *information society* [12], which is based on the production and exchange of information, and a place for a variety of computer-mediated activities that everyone should have access to.

Universal Design is the core philosophy behind this work. In particular, we propose to take ideation and discussion tools and techniques which are usually based on written documents, and make them accessible to all, by turning them into digital artifacts. This way, we are creating technology that is inclusive and, at the same time, making more accessible the process of designing technology.

The technological approach we chose for such task was *Tangible User Interface (TUI)*, which is the coupling of digital information with tangible objects, with the goal of materializing the digital. Ishii [4] proposed the concept of TUI to push beyond the paradigm of Graphical User Interfaces (GUI) and its restriction to flat displays, mouse and keyboard. Inspiration came from the work of Weiser [15], who described ubiquitous

© IFIP International Federation for Information Processing 2018
Published by Springer International Publishing AG 2018. All Rights Reserved
K. Liu et al. (Eds.): ICISO 2018, IFIP AICT 527, pp. 238–247, 2018.
https://doi.org/10.1007/978-3-319-94541-5_24

computing as a new paradigm where computers were everywhere, invisible. In essence, TUI provides a new interaction paradigm, that intends to create a closer relationship between the physical and the virtual worlds. For the purpose of our work, i.e., bringing artifacts and techniques from the paper to the digital, this paradigm provides a good middle-term.

In this paper, we present the first steps we took in this direction. We do so in the form of two case studies. The first takes on the challenge of turning a paper-based discussion tool, the *Stakeholders Identification Diagram (SID)*, into a tangible, electronic artifact. The second case study is about reinterpreting a writing ideation technique, called BrainWriting, to make it accessible. Hence, this paper is organized as follows: Sect. 2 describes the theoretical foundation for this work, Sect. 3 presents the techniques and tools we intend to redesign, Sect. 4 contains the two case studies, and, finally, Sect. 5 highlights our concluding remarks and future steps.

2   Theoretical Foundation

We built this work upon two main pillars: **Participatory Design (PD)** and **Organizational Semiotics (OS)**.

On one hand, **PD** is an approach to the design of computer systems that brings people who are prospective users of the system into the design process, as active participants. PD started out in Scandinavia and the main principle behind it is that the people who will use the system are the experts in their domain [9]; as so, they have much to contribute to the design of products that will affect them. In other words, they hold the knowledge about their tasks and how to perform or improve them. Designers, then, should act as technical consultants. Hence, there is cooperation in the sense of a "mutual learning" [5], so that users can learn about the technical possibilities, and designers can learn about the application domain.

While working with participatory approaches, it is necessary to accept that they involve dealing with conflict [5], since different groups within the organization have their own interests and visions of what the system should do, and how it should do it [9]. Ignoring this fact can lead to a poor understanding of the organizational reality, or to systems that are for a few group of users [5]. To properly deal with this, [5] suggests applying different activities, ranging from individual ones to others that involve group negotiation and cooperation. In this sense, [8] describes sixty-one PD practices, applicable within different moments in the design process, and adequate for varied objectives and group sizes. These practices, however, are not meant to be linear step-by-step guides towards predictable and safe outcomes. Instead, they should be seen as scaffolds for complex, non-linear group processes.

On the other hand, **OS** involves the application of **Semiotics** to the study of organizations [6]. In this context, **organization** refers to when a group of people work together to accomplish a task [10]. However, the more elaborate its product, the more difficult is for all the involved to fully realize the secondary consequences of decisions they make. For example, a road is a product that reduces travel time, but at the same time it might increase air pollution and noise.

In this sense, organizations can be seen as **information systems**, i.e., they can create and convey information, as well as define and change meanings [6]. Here enters **Semiotics**, the study of *signs*, i.e., the triad of *representamen* – concrete form of the sign, *object* – what the sign represents, and *interpretant* – who is doing the sense-making. Therefore, looking at organizations as information systems and using the lens of Semiotics to their design, might allow that quality and accurate information gets to the right people, improving the decision-making process.

One useful way of looking at information systems is the organizational onion representation [6]. First proposed by [11], it shows an understanding of organizations as three sequential layers, one containing the other, like an onion. The outermost layer is called "informal information system", and it refers to the values, beliefs, intentions, habits, meanings and other cultural manifestations that can be established or changed. The intermediate layer is called "formal information system", where are the well-established aspects of culture such as rules, laws and social conventions. The innermost layer is called "technical information system", and it contains the parts of the formal system that can be automated by machines. Based on the organizational onion, [1] extended the idea to think about a design process. The basic idea is that there are three main stages of design – Analysis, Synthesis and Evaluation – and on each design iteration, these stages cut through the three layers – informal, formal and technical – in a non-linear order. The iterations persist until there is an acceptable product. In addition, for each stage there are different artifacts, techniques and tools to support the design process. This, in part, comes from a strong relationship between this design process and PD.

In fact, the common grounds PD and OS share show the importance of communication and of quality of information in the decision-making process. Hence, while PD emphasizes the role of *egalitarian participation* in system design, OS brings out the importance of *information*, not just the meanings it carries, but also the channels it travels through.

3   The Objects of Redesign

The techniques and tools we intend to redesign to become tangible (concrete) digital artifacts are separated into two categories: those for *ideation* (i.e. generation of ideas), and those for supporting *discussion* in three artefacts of OS (Stakeholders Identification Diagram, Evaluation Frame and Semiotic Framework).

3.1   Tangible Ideation Tools

We will focus our attention in two ideation methods, the *BrainWriting* [14] and the *BrainDraw* [8]. They are alternatives for *brainstorming*, the method for oral raising of ideas by a group of people. BrainWriting and BrainDraw follow a round-robin dynamics, where each participant starts with their own idea on a piece of paper and, after a predetermined amount of time, they pass the paper to another person and receive someone else's sheet. Then, they must complement the other person's idea until time runs out. The procedure is repeated until at least one cycle is completed, i.e., until everyone receives their sheet back. This style of brainstorming solves some problems of having an influencer among the participants, and leads to a more distributed discussion and proposition of ideas.

Both BrainWriting and BrainDraw are usually done in a silent manner, using pen and paper. The difference between them is that BrainWriting is the generation of *written* ideas, while BrainDraw consists of *drawings* of interface design ideas. They both are good options for groups of people where status differences are evident, or where conflict is likely to happen. Since everyone has an equal chance to show their own ideas and also to contribute with the ideas of all others, the democratic aspect of Participatory Design is strongly present in both techniques.

3.2 Tangible OS Tools

We chose to work on three artifacts from Organizational Semiotics. The first is the *Stakeholders Identification Diagram (SID)*, and it is used for pointing out all who are involved in a design process [7], which can be either groups of people (e.g. developers, users), or entities (e.g. universities, corporations). The traditional graphical representation of the artifact organizes the stakeholders into five sequential layers that contain each other, like an onion: Operation (innermost layer), Contribution, Source, Market, and Community (outermost layer). The idea is that, the closer to the center, the more directly involved with the design product the stakeholder is. Hence, towards the edge are the stakeholders who are not actively involved in the design process, but who somehow affect or are affected by it.

The second artifact is the *Evaluation Frame (EF)*, and it is used to support the reasoning of problems and solutions associated with each stakeholder identified in the SID [2]. It is represented as a table, with a column for raising issues, a column for solutions or ideas, and five rows, one for each SID category. Therefore, this artifact allows the identification of requirements, as well as the anticipation of issues that may affect the design.

The third and last artifact is the *Semiotic Framework (SF)*. In the context of our work, it is used for identifying and organizing requirements, in six levels of knowledge [10]. The graphical representation of the SF shows these levels stacked on top of each other, in a progressive manner, similar to a ladder. From bottom to top, they are the following: Physical, Empirical, Syntactic, Semantic, Pragmatic and Social World. The bottom three levels are related to the structure of signs, how they are organized and transmitted. In turn, the upper three levels are related to how signs are used, in terms of meanings, intentions, and social impact they have. Hence, the SF, as we use it, allows for a view of the system requirements, going from their technical infrastructure (bottom), to their information system (top).

The three artifacts are shown in Fig. 1. They are meant to be used by a group of people, preferably representatives from the stakeholders, in participatory practices. In the practices we have conducted [3], for the SID and the EF, the idea is to fill in the layers collectively. To do so, participants are given post-its and can freely place them where they see fit, in a large printed version of the artifact's graphical representations, in workshops planned for this. During this process, participants are encouraged to discuss amongst themselves what to write on the post-its and where to place them. This way, they can all contribute to the decision-making process, and collectively reach an

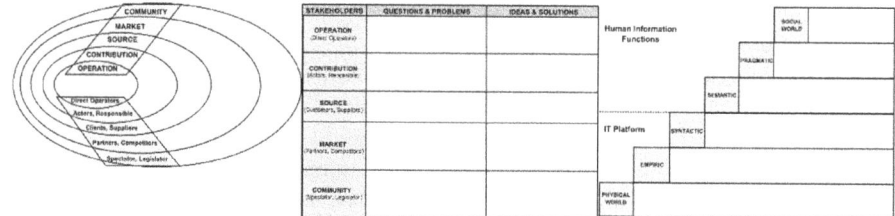

Fig. 1. To the left, the SID. In the middle, the EF. To the right, the SF.

understanding of the problem at hand. The SF, in turn, uses the results from the other two artifacts to allow stakeholders to discuss the system requirements and, at the same time, gain an understanding of its different dimensions.

4 Preliminary Case Studies

The first case study is about taking a discussion artifact – the *Stakeholders Identification Diagram (SID)* – and redesigning it to become a tangible digital artifact. To do so, we adopted a work method, so that the prototype follows Universal Design principles. Then, in the second case study we take an ideation method – the BrainWriting – propose and explore a new dynamics with digital tools, so that it becomes accessible to all.

4.1 The SID Case Study

In this case study, to design the digital artifact, we divided it into three independent tiers: *Hardware*, *Aesthetics*, and *Software*. This separation provides us with the flexibility to make changes in a tier without affecting the others. In turn, this reduces costs of future alterations, and allows compatibility with multiple forms of input and output – an important feature for Universal Design.

The *Hardware* tier is where we work on the electronic components of the artifact, such as micro-controllers, buttons, wires and sensors. It involves the technology the user will not see, because it is covered by the *Aesthetics* tier. This, in turn, is where are the tangible materials that people interact with. They make the interface between the hardware, the person, and the software. In addition, it constitutes a major part of what the user sees, so, as the name suggests, it aims to be visually pleasant. Finally, the *Software* tier contains the virtual interface of the artifacts. We chose the web platform due to its multi-device capabilities, and to its easy integration with several micro-controllers currently available. This tier receives the signals from the Hardware tier and provides the appropriate feedback, either to the hardware or to the person.

Therefore, to make the SID a tangible and digital artifact, we started out by the Aesthetics tier. We drew its five onion-like layers on cardboard, and cut out each layer, making them five independent pieces. We trimmed the edges of each piece so that, when they were laid out inside each other, there would not be friction. This way, it is easier to make each layer interactable, and they can be differentiated by touch – an important feature for the visually impaired. To add on to that differentiation, we also made the inner layers progressively taller than the outer layers.

Next, we worked on the Hardware tier. Behind each cardboard piece, we placed a push-button switch, and also an extra one outside the SID layers, to act as a control button. They were all connected to an Arduino micro-controller. The push-buttons we chose are simple but provide good accessibility, since they make a relatively loud click sound when pressed (an useful cue for the visually impaired), and they are neither too hard nor too soft to press, so even if who is pushing the button cannot hear the click (e.g. a deaf person), they can still feel the press. When a button is pushed, it sends a signal to the micro-controller, allowing us to program responses for each button.

Finally, the Software tier is composed by a web page with the graphical SID representation. The micro-controller communicates with the page so that, when a button is pushed, the page can provide the appropriate response. If one of the five SID layer buttons is pushed, the web page will visually highlight that layer on the graphical representation. It will also provide a text and sound feedback, listing all the stakeholders that were identified for that layer. Otherwise, if the separate control button is pushed, then the web page will ask (through sound and text) for a layer to be chosen, i.e., for one of the other five buttons to be pressed. When one of them is pushed, then the web page will prompt an input, either through voice or text, for a stakeholder to be added to that layer.

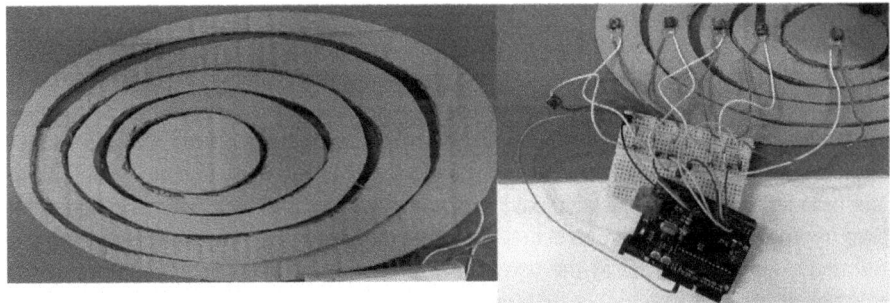

Fig. 2. To the left, the Aesthetics of the SID digital artifact. To the right, its Hardware.

Figure 2 shows the Aesthetics and the Hardware tiers of our SID prototype. The separation between the tiers allowed us to design the digital artifact in modules, starting from the known part (its looks), and then thinking about the interactions with it based on how the paper artifact has been used. For the next case study, we need to start from the interaction itself, since the ideation methods we chose are not based on specific graphic representations.

4.2 BrainWriting Case Study

The main challenge in adapting the BrainWriting technique lies on its very description: it is a silent and written method for generating ideas. In particular, if we consider a visually impaired person, both of these aspects are issues. So the first step was to figure out how to substitute the written input for another form of non-visual input that would not violate the silence requirement. This led to reasoning that the silence is necessary so that people can work in parallel, without affecting each other's ideas. So, for a pilot test, the solution we came up with was to substitute writing for speaking. This, in turn, meant that, at least for a trial run, the creation of ideas would be in series, not in parallel. Hence, the dynamics we did was the following: (1) the problem statement is explained to all participants at the same time; (2) on the first round, one by one participants leave the room and record, in private, their initial idea in a 30-s audio file; (3) on the next round, each participant listens, in private, to the audio with someone else's original idea and records another 30-s audio, complementing that idea; (4) on the subsequent rounds, participants listen to the audio with someone else's original idea, as well as all the audios others recorded to complement that idea. The process stops when all participants have complemented everyone else's ideas.

Of course, the activity had a limitation that does not happen in the original BrainWriting: between recordings, participants had time to reflect while they waited their turn. However, this can be solved if, for instance, participants are not in the same room, and each one uses a device (e.g. smartphone), and records and listens to ideas through the web. Another limitation is low anonymity, since it is easy to recognize someone's voice – perhaps easier than identifying their handwriting. However, this can also be solved by using voice recognition to translate the original audio into text, and then using text-to-speech to read it with a synthesized voice.

At the end of the dynamics, which involved four participants, we had four different ideas, each with four audio files – one from its creator and three from the other participants. Then, the first problem at hand is how to consolidate this data, i.e., how to allow participants to have a general picture of what they accomplished and, together, find the best ideas. Using voice recognition to translate audio into text can also be a solution here as well, since text makes it easier to create a bigger picture than audio. This broader view could be achieved in several ways. One would be creating a tag cloud of words, a graphical representation where the size of the words is proportional to how much they were used in the text. In turn, this cloud of word can also be represented by sound, i.e., the higher its frequency of use, the louder a term is read. Another method would be creating a vocabulary with the most important terms that showed up in the audios. To come up with these terms, it would be necessary either a group discussion or the work of a curator, i.e., someone to look at the ideas and select the most relevant information. This curator could be either a person or a machine.

4.3 Extending to Other Artifacts

In the first case study, we were able to take a discussion tool, the SID, and use its graphical representation as a starting point for the design of the digital artifact. The prototype we built, made with buttons and a micro-controller, is a good template for the other two OS artifacts, the EF and the SF, since they also already have graphical representations. For the design of their tangible digital artifacts, we will need to consider what could be a button, and what actions the buttons trigger. For instance, for the EF, there could be a button for each cell on the table, and for the SF, a button for each step on the ladder. They would each also need a confirmation button, to trigger the action of adding new information. Once we have a prototype for each OS artifact, the next step is to experiment with them in real problem discussions, to see if changes need to be made and how they can be improved.

From the second case study we learned that it is possible to adapt the round-robin dynamics in a way that preserves the individuality of contributions and, at the same time, fosters collaboration. The success in this adaptation encourages us to make similar reflections upon the OS artifacts, and how their use could be redesigned. We also learned that, to strive towards Universal Design, it is necessary for the data to be *transmitted* and *collected* through multiple channels, e.g., sound and text. In our experimentation with the BrainWriting, we only used audio because we were thinking about visual impairments, but if we were to consider, for instance, deafness, another form of input (e.g. text or sign language) would be required.

As for the BrainDraw, how to make "tangible drawings" is still an open question. Considering the round-robin dynamics, in parallel or in series, how could people use tangible materials to propose interface ideas? One solution would be to use LEGO pieces, since they provide an easy way to make well-defined shapes, and the pieces have a good fit with electronic components such as push-buttons. Therefore, it would be possible to wire some pieces with electronics, and let participants use them along with normal pieces to build their interface ideas. In addition, we could pre-program some behaviors so that participants could test their ideas in real-time. Also, if a vocabulary is formed during a BrainWriting activity, it could be reused in the Brain-Draw. For instance, with the BrainWriting, participants agree "clock" is essential for solving the problem at hand. For the BrainDraw, we provide pieces of interface that contemplate "clock" representations.

5 Conclusion

Including people in especial conditions, to the widest possible sense, in the process of designing a product was the challenge we took on. More specifically, in this paper we presented our initial efforts towards the redesign of some traditional techniques and artifacts from this context, to make them accessible to all people. We described the theoretical foundation for our work, the techniques and tools we intend to redesign, and then we presented two preliminary case studies. In the first case study we redesigned a tool for idea discussion – the SID – to become a digital artifact. We began from its graphical representation to create the aesthetics of our prototype, then we designed the interaction along with the hardware and the software. The method we applied to the SID serves as a template to design the digital artifacts of the EF and the SF as well.

In the second case study, we did a pilot experiment with an adaptation of the BrainWriting technique. This entailed understanding the meanings of its core definitions, and reinterpreting them in ways that make them more accessible, while maintaining their essence. Despite limitations that we can overcome, the dynamics worked and gave us indications as to how to promote discussion and deliberation. In this sense, one of the lessons was that it is necessary to work the data so that it can be available in multiple formats (e.g. sound and text). This facilitates collaboration and, at the same time, is coherent with Design for All.

The efforts we presented in this paper contribute to the practice of Organizational Semiotics and of Participatory Design because they bring the possibility of including in the ideation and discussion processes people who were left out before. We proposed to rethink the techniques and tools used in these areas through the lens of Universal Design, a process for including as many people as possible in the design of a product. Hence, we showed the initial stages of such process, the prototypes and explorations that will open the path for further steps. Future work, then, involves studying what the digital artifacts have to offer in terms of meaning construction, and what are their limitations. We have to see if they maintain the original idea of their written counterparts, or if they have somehow altered the process, especially with a large group of people.

Acknowledgements. This work is financially supported by the São Paulo Research Foundation (FAPESP) through grants #2015/16528-0 and #2015/24300-9, by Coordenação de Aperfeiçoamento de Pessoal de Nível Superior (CAPES) through grant #01-P-04554/2013 and by National Council for Scientific and Technological Development (CNPq) through grants #160911/2015-0 and #306272/2017-2.

References

1. Baranauskas, M.C.C., Bonacin, R.: Design – indicating through signs. Des. Issues **24**(3), 30–45 (2008). https://doi.org/10.1162/desi.2008.24.3.30
2. Baranauskas, M.C.C., Schimiguel, J., Simoni, C.A., Medeiros, C.B.: Guiding the process of requirements elicitation with a semiotic-based approach – a case study. In: Proceedings of the 11th International Conference on Human-Computer Interaction, pp. 100–111 (2005)
3. Buchdid, S.B., Pereira, R., Baranauskas, M.C.C.: Creating an iDTV application from inside a TV company: a situated and participatory approach. In: Liu, K., Gulliver, S.R., Li, W., Yu, C. (eds.) ICISO 2014. IAICT, vol. 426, pp. 63–73. Springer, Heidelberg (2014). https://doi.org/10.1007/978-3-642-55355-4_7
4. Ishii, H., Ullmer, B.: Tangible bits: towards seamless interfaces between people, bits and atoms. In: Proceedings of the ACM SIGCHI Conference on Human Factors in Computing Systems, pp. 234–241. ACM (1997)
5. Kyng, M.: Designing for cooperation: cooperating in design. Commun. ACM **34**(12), 65–73 (1991). https://doi.org/10.1145/125319.125323
6. Liu, K.: Semiotics in Information Systems Engineering. Cambridge University Press, New York (2000)
7. Liu, X.: Employing MEASUR Methods for Process Reengineering in China (2001)
8. Muller, M.J., Haslwanter, J.H., Dayton, T.: Participatory practices in the software lifecycle. In: Helander, M.G., Landauer, T.K., Prabhu, P.V. (eds.) Handbook of Human-Computer Interaction, 2nd edn, pp. 255–297. North-Holland, Amsterdam (1997). Chap. 11
9. Schuler, D., Namioka, A.: Participatory Design: Principles and Practices. CRC Press, Boca Raton (1993)
10. Stamper, R.K.: Information in Business and Administrative Systems. Wiley, New York (1973)
11. Stamper, R.K.: Language and computer in organised behaviour. In: Riet, R.P.V.D., Meersman, R.A. (eds.) Linguistic Instruments in Knowledge Engineering, pp. 143–163. Elsevier Science Inc., Amsterdam (1992)

12. Stephanidis, C., Salvendy, G., Akoumianakis, D., Arnold, A., Bevan, N., Dardailler, D., Emiliani, P.L., Iakovidis, I., Jenkins, P., Karshmer, A., Korn, P., Marcus, A., Murphy, H., Oppermann, C., Stary, C., Tamura, H., Tscheligi, M., Ueda, H., Weber, G., Ziegler, J.: Toward an information society for all: HCI challenges and R&D recommendations. Int. J. Hum.-Comput. Interact. **11**(1), 1–28 (1999). https://doi.org/10.1207/s15327590ijhc1101_1
13. Story, M.F., Mueller, J.L., Mace, R.L.: The Universal Design File: Designing for People of all Ages and Abilities. ERIC (1998)
14. VanGundy, A.B.: Brain writing for new product ideas: an alternative to brainstorming. J. Consum. Mark. **1**(2), 67–74 (1984). https://doi.org/10.1108/eb008097
15. Weiser, M.: The computer for the 21st century. Sci. Am. **265**(3), 94–104 (1991)

Does It Pay to Be Socially Responsible for Construction Companies?

Anupam Nanda[(⊠)] [iD]

Henley Business School, University of Reading, Reading RG6 6UD, UK
a.nanda@henley.reading.ac.uk

Abstract. Within the built environment, the Engineering and Construction (E&C) companies are very natural resource-intensive in terms of their business operations. In this paper, we focus on publicly listed E&C companies and analyse the role of Corporate Social Responsibility (CSR) activities on their corporate financial performance. The analytical framework is built around the economic theory of private provision of public goods. A basic Capital Asset Pricing Model (CAPM) is used to empirically examine the testable hypothesis with a panel data comprising 17 major E&C companies with monthly data over 2000-13. The results indicate that CSR activities can influence financial performance significantly after controlling for the firm size variable. We make use of several measures of CSR activities to test robustness. The broad results are robust to a range of alternative model specifications.

Keywords: Built environment · Corporate social responsibility
CAPM

1 Introduction

The role of Corporate Social Responsibility (CSR) in corporate performance has been explored extensively in the literature. While our understanding has improved, it is far from being definitive as findings remain mixed and new issues and challenges have emerged in recent years. With growing concerns around climate change and increasingly loud calls for sustainable business practices from all corners of the society, the role of a corporation is being redefined and broadened to include a stronger commitment to the sustainability issues of respective businesses. Therefore, the companies need to look beyond the Corporate Financial Performance (CFP) and focus on Corporate Social Performance (CSP). A natural question arises: how CSR activities are associated with corporate performances? A substantial share of the economic activities that directly comes under the sustainability scanner is channeled through the built environment. Within built environment, the Engineering and Construction (E&C) companies are perhaps the most natural resource intensive in terms of their business operations. The E&C companies, being unavoidably resource-intensive, are often subject to public dissent and face government controls and restrictions. Across the world, the E&C companies are expected to contribute to the society. Often such activities include mitigation of environmental impacts, sustainability goals, investment into social activities, improvement of working conditions, commitment to employee

K. Liu et al. (Eds.): ICISO 2018, IFIP AICT 527, pp. 248–256, 2018.
https://doi.org/10.1007/978-3-319-94541-5_25

wellbeing etc. The investment community is also very active in terms of prioritizing investible resources in companies with high CSR activities and performance. As a result, the marketplace may recognize the value that CSR activities can bring in terms of enhanced image or brand equity, increased revenue and ease of access to socially responsible funds.

Many studies have contested whether the CSR profile of a company influences its financial performance. This paper focuses on seventeen major E&C companies in order to identify and evaluate the relationship between their Corporate Social Responsibility (CSR) and their financial performance by using publicly available data and a Capital Asset Pricing Model (CAPM). A number of econometric techniques are employed to extract best possible information from the data in order to inform the research question. To this end, we firstly present the context of our research question with a brief overview of the extant literature. Then, the empirical framework is discussed, followed by data description and results. Finally, some concluding remarks are provided.

2 Context and Related Literature

The idea of corporate social responsibility (CSR) came through concerns coming out of sustainable future, global warming and environmental risks. This means, companies will need to invest a part of their hard-earned profit back into society. The argument is: since companies use resources from the society (i.e. people/human capital and natural resources) to fulfil their profit motive, they also need to give back to the society. However, this may also go against the promises to the shareholder of increasing profit/dividend. Milton Friedman famously argued that 'the sole social responsibility of business is to increase its profits'. So, why should a company engage in such activities, which are apparent net draws to their surplus cash?

This question has been repeatedly asked over the last few decades and therefore, the literature is rather extensive. It can be argued that CSR activities should also lead to increased revenue and performance of the company. It can be claimed that CSR activities can improve firms' competitive advantage by attracting socially responsible consumers and as a result of being a 'good corporate citizen', firms can enjoy enhanced image and reputation. Indeed, it is often argued that such brand enhancement and strategic positioning can successfully yield additional advantages linked to insulation from regulatory risk, public dissent, government sanctions and disruptions in activities, due to negative campaigns by social and environmental activists and non-governmental organisations [1, 2].

The empirical literature examining the effect of CSR activities on firms' financial performance is long and it is fraught with mixed and inconclusive results [3–5]. The main reason is our inability to understand the mediating factors and data constraints proving significant in creating estimation biases (for reviews see, [6–9] and see Fig. 1). In appraising the literature of CSR across the construction industry, Jones et al. [10] investigated the CSR issues of the UK's biggest construction companies. In their paper, they discussed the main characteristics of the CSR and the construction sector challenges by using the CSR reports and online published information of the leading construction companies of the UK. Their findings revealed very significant variations in the CSR reporting mainly focusing on environmental issues, but also, their research addressed issues related to health and safety, supply chain management, human resources, the communities, the government, ethics, etc. The authors suggested that although construction companies are taking the CSR principles into consideration, however, their performance indicators show poor evidence towards this direction as well as having low participation rates in the general benchmarking exercises. Moreover, Zhao et al. [11], by taking into consideration the CSR factor and especially its significance in the construction industry, developed a framework for CSR indicators for the construction enterprises globally as a tool for CSR performance. They considered the CSR stakeholders who are involved in the construction sector and proposed a CSR indicator system based on the stakeholders' theory.

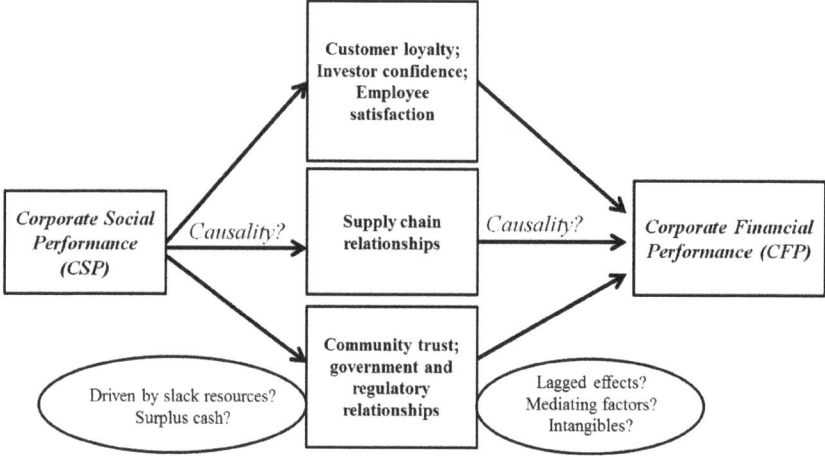

Fig. 1. Conundrum of CSR and financial performance

Above literature review indicates that there is a wide-spread recognition of the impact of CSR/sustainability activities on firm-level performances. However, the effect is lot less clear when we try to quantify it. Robust empirical analysis of the dynamic relationship between CSP and CFP requires some consideration of a number of potential issues. Any empirical investigation is fraught with significant data constraints and estimation biases. With these caveats, we move on to an empirical investigation of the relationship between CSP and CFP for seventeen E&C companies.

3   Empirical Framework

In terms of empirical modelling, there are several approaches that have been tried in the literature. Ever since the CSR ratings data became available across a number of companies over time, some studies have modelled the effect of the CSR rating on Tobin's q and total returns. While all modelling approaches are contested on some grounds, there is no definitive agreement in the literature on the best empirical framework. In this paper, we employ a tested and long-established asset pricing model – Capital Asset Pricing Model (CAPM). Sharpe's [12] and Lintner's [13] pioneering works, among others, have established the CAPM model as one of the most well-known and most frequently used models. The basic framework is represented as follows:

$$(r_{it} - rf_t) = \alpha + \beta_1(rm_{it} - rf_t) + u_{it} \tag{1}$$

r_{it} is the return rate of firm i's stock in time t; rf_{it} is the return of a risk-free asset in time t that may correspond to firm i; rm_{it} is the market's (benchmark index) return rate in time t that may correspond to firm i. The coefficient *beta* reflects the systematic risk or sensitivity of the expected excess asset returns to the expected excess market returns.

The most stringent criticism against CAPM model has been the low explanatory power or r-squared and strong assumptions regarding equal and symmetric information processing by all economic agents. However, the ability to control for other confounding factors into the Eq. (1) is very useful and can aid in answering many questions. Much like the approach in Cardebat and Sirven [14], we can add other control variables such as CSR and firm size as in Eq. (2) below.

$$(r_{it} - rf_t) = \alpha + \beta_1(rm_{it} - rf_t) + \beta_2 csr_i + \beta_3(other\ controls) + u_{it} \tag{2}$$

In Eq. (2), we also add other controls that may potentially impact the firm's performance such as number of employees, market cap and productivity (calculated as market cap per employee). We also try several alternative measures of CSR (see Table 1 for description of variables).

Since our dataset covers 17 firms observed over 157 months (Dec. 2000–Dec. 2013), we can model Eq. (2) within panel data framework. The advantage of this method is that it allows us to use both time series and cross sectional variations in the data, which increases the efficiency of the OLS estimates. A typical feature of panel data framework is the presence of unobserved heterogeneity. A potential bias in estimating Eq. (2) is the presence of correlation between unobserved heterogeneity at the firm level and the observables, which would otherwise violate standard assumptions of OLS estimation. Therefore, the disturbance term in Eq. (2) is specified as a two-way error component capturing firm-specific fixed effects and time-specific effects.

$$u_{it} = \gamma_i + \delta_t + \in_{it} \tag{3}$$

In this specification, heterogeneity is assumed to be constant over time and correlated with independent variables. The constant effect is removed by mean-differencing the data. This estimation strategy may be consistent with theoretical expectations that firm-specific unobserved characteristics can bring in permanent differences in individual firm's financial and corporate situation.

Finally, due to presence of large variation in firm size, type of business and corporate structure, it is quite likely that the variance of the error term in regression models may be non-constant, which would violate one of the key assumptions of OLS modelling. To address this inherent heteroscedasticity problem, we estimate all models with heteroscedasticity-robust standard error.

4   Data, Results and Analysis

Our data comprises monthly returns across seventeen E&C companies over 157 months of December 2000–December 2013 i.e. 2669 panel observations. The time period covered in this study is interesting as we can observe two economic cycles and moreover, the CSR activities and awareness took considerable prominence during this time period. The seventeen companies are:

Fluor Corporation, KBR Inc., URS Corporation, McDermott International, Tutor Perini Corporation, CB&I/Shaw Group, Jacobs Engineering Group, Granite Construction Inc., Willbros Group Inc., Babcock & Wilcox Company, Orion Marine Group Inc., Layne Christensen Company, Foster Wheeler AG, First Solar Inc., Matrix Service Company, Great Lakes Dredge & Dock Corporation and Sterling Construction Company.

Some companies have missing observations over certain period i.e. the regression dataset is an unbalanced panel. The stock price variable is obtained from Google finance (listed in NYSE and NASDAQ) and we use year-over-year return in excess of risk-free rate (10-year US Treasury bond) as the dependent variable. The market benchmark is the Dow Jones Sustainability Index (DJSI). DJSI is very appropriate as a benchmark for our question since it is most well-established and keenly followed market index measuring sustainability performance. The Dow Jones Sustainability World Index was launched in 1999 as the first global sustainability benchmark. The index family tracks the stock performance of the world's leading companies in terms of economic, environmental and social criteria.

The most important variable in question is the CSR measure. We use the CSRHub rating (*CSR rating*) as a starting point. We have also used the firm's rating compared to all company average of CSR rating (*CSR excess*). Since there have been significant criticism of such ratings, we have created our own subjective measure of website content on CSR activities to rate companies (*CSR web*) as follows (as in 2014).

5 = fully dedicated and prominent link in home page with full details across ESG parameters with visible sustainability reports;

4 = dedicated and prominent link in home page with some details across ESG parameters with visible sustainability reports;

3 = webpage with few details across ESG parameters with few visible sustainability reports;

2 = webpage with little details across ESG parameters with no visible sustainability reports;

1 = no webpage with poor details across ESG parameters with no visible sustainability reports;

Other controls that we have examined are: number of employees obtained from Google Finance and company websites; market cap sourced from Google Finance; productivity calculated as market cap divided by number of employees.

Table 1. Variable description and sources of data

Variable	Description	Sources
Stock return	Year-over-Year return	Google finance
Market return	Year-over-Year benchmark return	Dow Jones sustainability index - http://www.sustainability-indices.com/
Risk free rate	10 Year treasury yield	US federal reserve
Employees	log(no. of employees)	Company websites, Google finance
Market cap	log(market cap)	Google finance
Productivity	log(market cap divided by no. of employees) – proxy for productivity	
CSR rating	Rating of individual companies	CSRHub - https://www.csrhub.com/
CSR excess	CSR rating compared to the all company average	CSRHub - https://www.csrhub.com/
CSR web	Author' subjective evaluation (scale of 1–5, 5 being best) based on content on individual company website	Company websites
CSR int	CSR rating interacted with month-to-month return of DJSI Sustainability Index with all ethical exclusions	

We first estimate Eqs. 1 and 2 with the full sample. Table 2 reports seven model specifications. Model 1 is the baseline CAPM model that incorporates the size variables that may explain firm's performance. The number of employees has significant negative effects on excess return and market cap has significantly positive effects. When we add CSR variables in model 2, these results remain qualitatively unchanged. The *CSR rating* variable is significantly positive, while the *CSR web* variable affects financial performance negatively. The growing importance of online materials and use of such material for marketing purposes are important and this may play a role in negative effect on firm's performance. To address the problem of estimation in various firm sizes, we have used productivity variable in model 3, replacing other two size variables. It is possible that CSR activities are mostly viewed in a comparative sense i.e. compared with the market or industry standards. Therefore, in model 3, we include *CSR excess* computed as (all company average minus the firm's CSR rating) and it turned out to be negative which implies that if a company is under-performing compared to the all company average, it can entail significantly negative effect on financial performance. It is also important to note that issues of multicollinearity can be problematic and therefore, we have maintained parsimony in model specification. We find that the multicollinearity issue is not severe in our framework.

Table 2. Full sample regression results

	(1)	(2)	(3)	(4)	(5)
Excess market return	1.421***	1.411***	1.416***	1.420***	1.422***
	(25.02)	(24.91)	(25.11)	(21.30)	(21.36)
CSR rating		0.009***			
		(3.30)			
CSR web		−0.042**			
		(−3.04)			
CSR excess			−0.006*		
			(−2.08)		
CSR int				0.006	0.037**
				(0.92)	(3.04)
Employees	−0.038**	−0.027*			
	(−2.94)	(−2.08)			
Market cap	0.056***	0.069***			
	(4.33)	(5.55)			
Productivity			0.055***	0.076***	0.083***
			(4.36)	(7.74)	(8.07)
Intercept	−0.408**	−1.051***	−0.238**	−0.387***	−0.402***
	(−3.17)	(−5.04)	(−2.89)	(−4.74)	(−5.56)
Model specification	OLS	OLS	OLS	Random effects	Company fixed effects
R-squared	0.198	0.204	0.198	0.189	0.241
N	1969	1969	1969	1969	1969

t statistics based on robust standard error in parentheses;
$\sim$p < 0.1; * p < 0.05; ** p < 0.01; *** p < 0.001.

Models 1 through 3 in Table 2 do not control for unobserved heterogeneity. As explained before, it is possible to model unobserved heterogeneity in two ways – random effects and fixed effects. In model 4, we assume random effects and we assume fixed effect structure in model 5. We have performed Hausman specification test considering both models 4 and 5, and the results consistently suggested that a fixed effects specification was more appropriate [15]. Therefore, we take model 5 forward. The explanatory power (24%) of model 5 is highest among all models in Table 2 while this level of r-squared is not ideal but compared to many studies this is reasonable. In models 4 and 5, our CSR measure is time-varying, CSR int. Specifically, we interact CSR excess with DJSI total return with all ethical exclusion tags such as alcohol, tobacco, gambling, armaments, cluster bombs, landmines, firearms, nuclear and adult entertainment. While a valid concern against such interaction term is multicollinearity, we have found very low correlation (negative 3.1%) between CSR int and Market return. Moreover, such measure is valid as it compares CSR activities with that of all company average and also with the stringent DJSI sustainability index. We find significant positive effect (0.037) of excess CSR activity on financial performance in model 5. In our modelling framework and hypothesis testing, sign and significance of the effect is more relevant than the size of the coefficient. In general, we find that the CSR measures have significant effect on financial performance according to the CAPM modelling framework.

5 Conclusion

Being resource-intensive, the E&C companies often face government sanctions, public dissent and disruption of operations. The outcry of complying with strict sustainability regulations is perhaps louder for E&C companies than many other sectors. Therefore, it is quite an interesting exercise to study whether a 'responsible' E&C company 'does well by doing good' to the society. The empirical investigation of this question is fraught with many challenges starting with lack of good quality data on CSR activities.

In this paper, we focus on seventeen publicly listed E&C companies and analyse the role of their CSR activities on their corporate financial performance. The analytical framework is built around the economic theory of 'private provision of public goods'. We use basic Capital Asset Pricing Model (CAPM) to empirically examine the testable hypotheses. The model is enhanced by adding firm size and productivity controls that can boost the explanatory power of the specifications. Fixed effect modelling approach has been adopted to mitigate any attenuation bias in estimates from unobserved heterogeneity. The analysis of monthly data over Dec. 2000–Dec. 2013 reveals that CSR activities can significantly influence financial performance after controlling for firm size variable. The broad results are robust to several alternative model specifications. More data and better estimates of CSR activities are some areas of future research.

References

1. Bagnoli, M., Watts, S.: Selling to socially responsible consumers: competition and the private provision of public goods. J. Econ. Manag. Strategy **12**(3), 419–445 (2003)
2. Maxwell, J., Lyon, T., Hackett, S.: Self-regulation and social welfare: the political economy of corporate environmentalism. J. Law Econ. **43**(2), 583–618 (2000)
3. McWilliams, A., Siegel, D.: Corporate social responsibility and financial performance: correlation or misspecification? Strateg. Manag. J. **21**(5), 603–609 (2000)
4. McWilliams, A., Siegel, D.: Corporate social responsibility: a theory of the firm perspective. Acad. Manag. Rev. **26**, 117–127 (2001)
5. McWilliams, A., Siegel, D., Wright, P.: Corporate social responsibility: strategic implications. J. Manag. Stud. **43**, 1–18 (2006)
6. Stanwick, P., Stanwick, S.: The relationship between corporate social performance, and organizational size, financial performance, and environmental performance: an empirical examination. J. Bus. Ethics **17**(2), 195–204 (1998)
7. Roberts, P., Dowling, G.: Corporate reputation and sustained superior financial performance. Strateg. Manag. J. **23**(12), 1077–1093 (2002)
8. Margolis, J., Elfenbein, H., Walsh, J.: Does It Pay to be Good? A Meta-Analysis and Redirection of Research on the Relationship Between Corporate Social and Financial Performance. Mimeo, Harvard Business School, Boston (2007)

9. van Beurden, P., Goessling, T.: The worth of values – a literature review on the relation between corporate social and financial performance. J. Bus. Ethics **82**(2), 407–424 (2008)
10. Jones, P., Comfort, D., Hiller, D.: Corporate social responsibility and the UK construction industry. J. Corp. Real Estate **8**(3), 134–150 (2006)
11. Zhao, Z., Zhao, X., Davidson, K., Zuo, J.: A corporate social responsibility indicator system for construction enterprises. J. Clean. Prod. **29–30**, 277–289 (2012)
12. Sharpe, W.: Capital asset prices: a theory of market equilibrium under conditions of risk. J. Finan. **19**, 425–442 (1964)
13. Lintner, J.: The valuation of risk assets and the selection of risky investments in stock portfolios and capital budgets. Rev. Econ. Stat. **47**, 13–37 (1965)
14. Cardebat, J., Sirven, N.: What corporate social responsibility reporting adds to financial return? J. Econ. Inter. Finan. **2**(2), 020–027 (2010)
15. Hausman, J.: Specification tests in econometrics. Econometrica **46**(6), 1251–1271 (1978)

Business Intelligence and Analytics

Method of Operational Activities and Processes Optimization Design in Architecture

Xiaoxue Zhang[1(✉)], Aimin Luo[1], Gang Liu[2], and Junxian Liu[1]

[1] Science and Technology on Information Systems Engineering Laboratory,
National University of Defense Technology, Changsha, China
snowing1124@126.com, amluo@nudt.edu.cn,
18674864900@163.com
[2] ChongQing Communication Institute, Chongqing, China
liugang1109@126.com

Abstract. As the foundation and basis for developing architecture products and data, designing operational activities and processes is the key in architecture design. Current research lacks the optimization design method about them. To solve this problem. Firstly, this paper analyzed the data meta-models related to operational activities, proposed the process of optimal design of the operational activities and processes. Secondly, the objective function of the optimization of operational activities and processes are studied considering the time, success rate and cost. Thirdly, the process of simulation evaluation of operational activities and processes is designed, then we propose the method of how to convert activity-related architecture data into object Petri-net simulation model. Finally, three means of improving the operational activities and processes are given to arrive the optimal design objectives.

Keywords: Architecture · Operational activities and processes
Optimization · Evaluation

1 Introduction

During the specific architecture design, the design of operational activities and processes includes many aspects, such as the decomposition of top-level tasks, the generation of operational activities and the optimization of the operational activities and processes. All of these mainly be conducted by operational commanders. The design of the operational activities and processes is the basis for the development of system view, service view and so on. Only after the operational activities and process has been established can systems and services supporting the operational activities and processes be followed. So, the design results are directly related to the completion of the entire operational objectives. In this way, the design of the operational activities and processes is the most basic and crucial issue in the design of the Information systems architecture.

Currently, in the field of Operational activities Process design, the research focuses on two aspects: operational task decomposition and the generation of Course of Action (COA). Literature [1, 2] studied a method of applying Hierarchy Task Net (HTN)

K. Liu et al. (Eds.): ICISO 2018, IFIP AICT 527, pp. 259–267, 2018.
https://doi.org/10.1007/978-3-319-94541-5_26

planning to combat task decomposition and combat operations. Literature [3] put forward the concept of meta-activity, take meta-activity as the activity of atomic transactions in combat operations. The current methods of generation of course of actions can be divided into calculation-based methods and simulation-based methods. The COA generation based on the calculation method is divided into two kinds. One kind is based on mathematical programming, the other kind is based on the use of Artificial Intelligence (AI) [4, 5]. The simulation-based COA generation method takes the generation of operational action plan as a simulation process, considers the factors that influence the plan when generation in the simulation process, and uses the simulation results to represent the COA plan [6, 7]. In current research, there is still a lack of method to optimize the design of operational activities and processes in specific architecture design. This paper supposed that the operational activities and processes has been preliminarily generated, explored the evaluation method of the Operational activities Process using simulation model based on object petri-net, then studied the method of improving the Operational activities Process to achieve the ultimate optimal design goal. In Sect. 2, we analyzes the data meta-models related to operational activities and puts forward that the optimal design of operational activities and processes includes three parts: the decomposition of operational tasks, the generation of operational activities and processes and the optimization of operational activities and processes. In Sect. 3, we put forward the goal of optimizing the design of operational activities and processes. Then, we study the simulation design of operational activities in Sect. 4. Finally, in Sect. 5, three means are given to optimize the process of operational activities.

2   Analysis Based on Activity Related Data Meta-Models

Architecture data meta-model standardizes the relationship between architecture logical data [8]. Among them, Activity is the core element, the design of other architecture data is closely related to Activity. Architecture operational activities Process design is mainly aimed at the optimization design of the data related to combat activities. Figure 1 constructs the activity-related data mate-model of the architecture. In Fig. 1, the arrow with a solid arrow indicates the relationship; the arrow with a hollow arrow indicates the inheritance relationship.

The data related to operational activities mainly include several types of information:

1. Performers of activity execution: including Activity, Performer, activityPerfomedbyPerformer, activityMapstoOperationalNode, etc. These data described that activities are performed by which combat command unit. Here, Performer can be the organizational unit, battle node, system or service that is responsible for the activity.
2. Conditions when activity executing: including Activity, Condition, activityExcutedUnderCondition. These data describes the information of state and condition when executing activities, including the preconditions described in the rules and the state of the activities will change after execution.

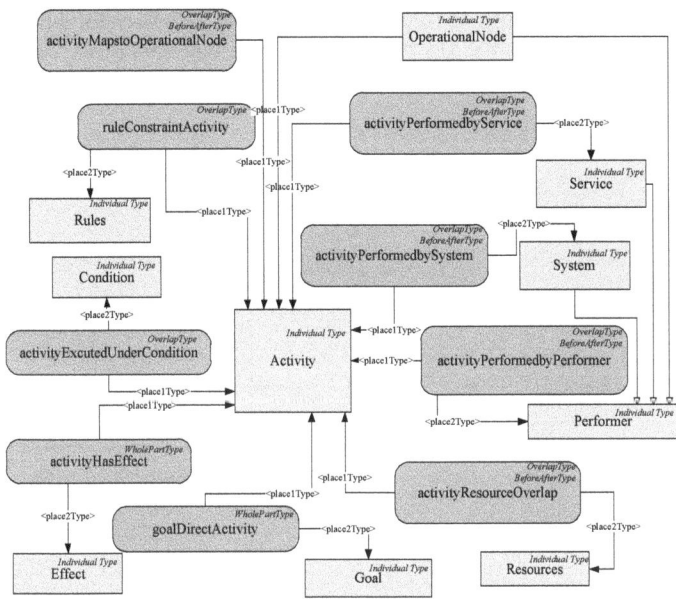

Fig. 1. Activity-related data meta-model in information systems architecture.

3. Rules of the activities: including Activity, Rule, ruleConstraintActivity. These data mainly describes the rules that activities need to fulfill when executing.
4. Goal of activity execution: including Activity, Goal, goalDirectActivity. These data mainly describe which mission objectives are fulfilled by the activity execution.
5. Consumption and output of Resource when activity executing: including Activity, Resource, activityResourceOverlap. These data mainly describes the relations between activities implementation and resource consumption or use. Resources can be divided into three types:

- Consumable resources: the execution of activities will consume such resources, such as missiles.
- Releasable resources: the execution of activities requires the use of such resources, but once the activity is completed, such resources will be released, such as missile vehicles.
- Sharable resources: Such as information resources, the implementation of activities has no effect on the resources themselves.

The process of operational activities and processes design includes three problems, as shown in Fig. 2, First is how to decompose the operational objectives and the mission into executable atomic activities. Second is how to generate the Operational activities Process, that is, considering the resource constraints, the conditions and the execution rules of each activity, how to generate the sequence of executable combat activities, called as preliminarily Operational activities Process. The third is to optimize the Operational activities Process that have been generated, we need to evaluate the existing operational activities and processes, analyze the existing problems in the design, and then optimize the operational activities and processes and modify the activities-related design.

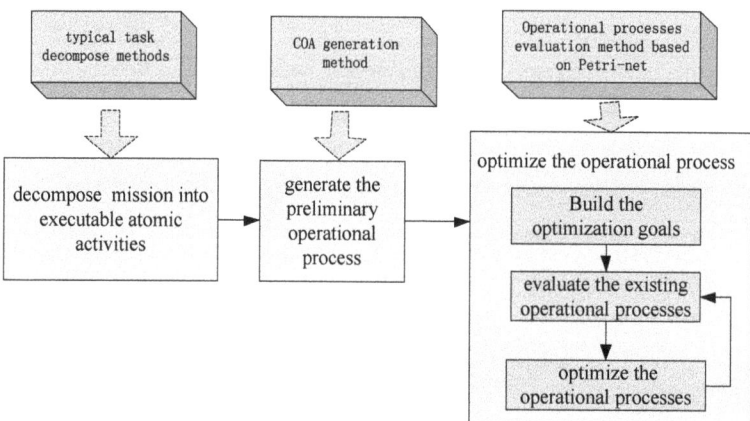

Fig. 2. The process of optimal design of the operational activities and processes.

3 The Optimization Goals of Operational Activities and Processes

After the operational preliminary process generation method is implemented, feasible operational activities and processes is obtained. How to improve the operational activities and processes is a problem that need to be solved in the optimization of operational activities and processes. In general, the indicators that optimize the design of the Operational activities Process include three factors: time, success rate and cost. For time and success rate, we can use the simulation method in Sect. 4. For the factors of cost. We can convert different types of resources into unified value.

The objective function value Z (BP) for a Operational activities Process includes a weighted composite of success rates, time, and costs, as shown in Eq. 1. If the target value satisfies the set threshold $Z(BP) > \theta$, the process solution is considered as feasible solution. If the optimization method can increase the value of Z (BP), then accept the optimization, otherwise, do not accept. The formula for calculating the objective function is as shown in Eqs. 2 to 4, where represents the weight of the indicator of number i. Before setting the weight of three factors, we need unified units and normalize each value. Relative to time and success rate of the indicator weights, the cost or resource consumption in the military information system has a lower weight value. The cost C in Eq. 3 is obtained by weighting the normalized resources. The success rate V in Eq. 2 and the time T in Eq. 4 can be simulated by the executable model. Section 3 describes the design of the executable model and the design of the simulation process.

$$Z(BP) = \sum_{i=1}^{3} wizi(BP) \tag{1}$$

$$z_1(BP) = V(BP) \tag{2}$$

$$z_2(BP) = 1/C(BP) \tag{3}$$

$$z_3(BP) = 1/T(BP). \tag{4}$$

4 Simulation Process Design of Operational Activities and Processes

In the architecture design, the design result of the Operational activities Process use architecture model to represent, and stored by the architecture data. This section explores how to translate architecture data into an object petri-net simulation model. After the simulation model is established, through the simulation experiment, the result of the time and success rate of the operational activities and processes design can be obtained.

In constructing the simulation model using object petri-nets, we need firstly define the mapping relationship between the architecture data and the object petri-nets simulation model. The hierarchy of activities decomposition can be represented by object classes, and the sub-activities formed by decomposition are the core components of the object class. During model construction of an object class, we can use transitions to represent activities, and resources are represented by the attributes of the tokens in the location, while the conditions and rules for the occurrence of the activity are represented by the transfer function. Table 1 shows the correspondence among the Operational activities Process elements, the architectural data elements and the object petri-net simulation model elements.

Table 1. The corresponding relationship among the operational activities process elements, architecture design elements and simulation model elements.

Operational activities process elements	Architecture design elements	Simulation model elements in object petri-net
The hierarchy of activities decomposition	Activity, WholePartType	Object class
Sub-activities	Activity	Transitions
Synchronization mechanism	Rule, ruleConstraintActivity	Transitions, transfer function
Resource	Resource, activityResourceOverlap, Information	Attributes of the tokens
Condition	Condition, activityPerformedUnderCondition	Transfer function
Effect	Condition, activityPerformedUnderCondition	Transfer function

Based on relationships between elements of logic data meta- model and elements of the object petri-net model, the process of constructing executable object petri-net is shown in Fig. 3.

- Step1: Build system model framework and OPN class library. Analyze Activity data items and the corresponding WholePart-Type, converted the activities that only have sub-activities without parent activities into the entire model framework; according to WholePartType and SuperSubType, abstract OPN model between Relationship, construct OPN class library framework.
- Step2: Determine the input and output ports. According to BeforeAfterType, determine the interaction relationships between different classes. According to activityProducesResource and activityConsumesResource, explicit interaction information. According to information and resource data items, clarify the characteristics of the interaction information, then determine the OPN model input and output ports.
- Step3: Establish the OPN framework model. According to BeforeAfterType description of activities, establish each OPN framework model. If one activity have sub-activities (judge by WholePartType), convert it to an object class, otherwise, convert it into switch. Then, connect the input and output ports in models with the corresponding transfers.
- Step4: Perfect the OPN model. Learn from the description of system performance parameters and information interaction by ruleConstraintActivity, masureOfTypeResource, activityPerformedUnderCondition, activityProduces- Resource and activityConsumes-Resource, combined with the description of Activity and transfer rules by BeforeAfterType and Rule, add the script function in the OPN framework, including Action function, delay function and event handling function to realize the related functions of each model.
- Step5: OPN model evaluation process. According to the established evaluation index system, add the relevant index data collection script to the model to complete the OPN model;
- Step6: Generate simulation cases and simulate. Add initialization function, instantiated function, instantiation of the top node model to generate the overall simulation case. According to the assessment acquirement, we can design simulation experiments, configure models for simulation, deal with the collected simulation data, and correlates these data with the evaluation index, then we can carry out the evaluation of the Operational activities Process according to the pre-determined evaluation model. For complex functions that are not easy to be implemented by scripts, dynamic link library algorithms can be compiled with VC and called in the OPN model.

According to plan generated by operational activities and processes, we can configure the action function of the simulation model according to the data of the architecture design, then run the simulation and get the simulation results. The simulation results include the execution time, success rate, and resource consumption over time of the solution.

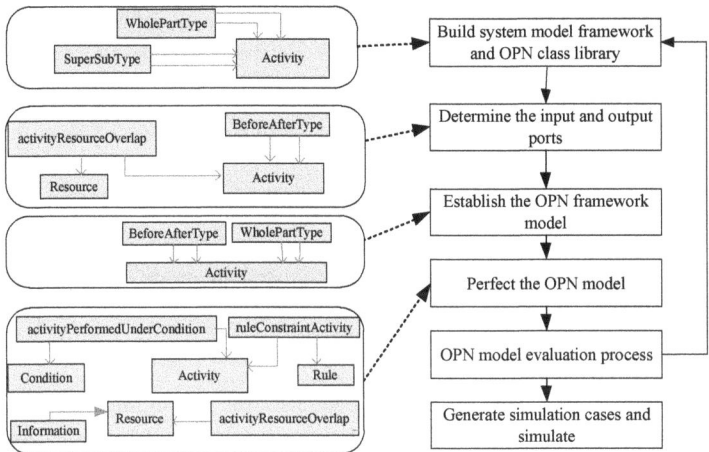

Fig. 3. Object petri-net simulation model constructing process based on data meta-model in DoDAF2.0.

5   Optimization Process of Operational Activities and Processes Plan

In the simulation experiment based on object petri-net, we got the execution time, success rate, and resource consumption over time of the solution. The optimization method is mainly aimed at the execution time, execution success rate and resource allocation in activities, so as to achieve the optimal objective function value of the entire operational activities and processes plan in Sect. 3. Drawing on the method of business process re-engineering, considering the characteristics of the operational activities and processes, the optimization methods of operational activities and processes mainly include the following three kinds:

- First method: shorten the execution time of key activities to shorten the completion time of the whole process.

After generating the initial operational activities and processes, key activities that affect the execution time of the entire Operational activities Process can be found. Compressing the execution time of critical activity can significantly reduce the overall execution time of the entire Operational activities Process.

- Second method: increase the parallel activities to improve the success rate of the completion of operational activities and processes.

Considering the uncertainty probability of a single activity, the total execution time of the processes can be obtained through simulation, and the impact of the success rates of different tasks on the program can be analyzed and compared. First, find activities that increase parallelism, as the number of resources allows. Then, based on the execution of the activities, execute the simulation, the simulation results show the sensitivity of each activity to the success rate. Find the most influential activity in the operational activities and processes, and try to improve the success rate of the influential activity.

- Third method: maximize the efficiency of resource use, to achieve the optimal allocation of resources.

In the case of spare resources are available, reallocate resources to various activities so as to maximize the use of resources in order to optimize the allocation of resources for operational activities. Under normal circumstances, there are two kinds of resource allocation situation:

- The resources required for activity are only one kind

After all operational activities have been met, the remaining resources can be optimal allocated. For example, if all the activities in a combat operations are satisfied, there are remaining reconnaissance resources A and firepower B, then we can search for activities that can be met by resources A and activities that can be met by resources B, then get the remaining resources A and B. Then we can obtain the optimal configuration of several feasible programs, choose the best feasible options to maximize the objective function, in this way, we can get the resource allocation program.

- When the activities can be completed using different types of resources

In this case, the resource allocation should be based on the success rate, time and cost of resource, then select the best matching solution. Under normal circumstances, the success rate of activities is the first factor to consider, followed by the completion time, and finally the cost of resource consumption.

The overall steps in the optimization of operational activities and processes are:

- Step1: Calculate the objective function value Z (BP) of the plan. If the Z (BP) > θ is satisfied, then accept the scheme. Otherwise, go to the next step.
- Step2: Calculate the objective function value Z1(BP), if Z1(BP) > Z(BP), then accept the optimization; otherwise, reject;
- Step3: Calculate the objective function value Z2(BP), if Z2(BP) > Z(BP), then accept the optimization; otherwise, reject;
- Step4: Calculate the objective function value Z3(BP), if Z3(BP) > Z(BP), then accept the optimization; otherwise, reject;
- Step5: Generate new Operational activities Process plan and calculate the objective function value Znew(BP). If Znew(BP) > θ, accept the new process; otherwise, redesign the Operational activities Process and go to Step1 until the objective function value satisfies the threshold θ requirement.

6 Conclusions

The design of operational activities and processes is the key issue in architecture design. In this paper, we take insight in the problems about the optimization design of operational activities and processes, and analyze the three problems involved in the process optimization of operational activities based on the data meta-model. We also study the objective function of the optimization of the operational activities and processes, the simulation evaluation of the operational activities based on object petri-net, and the methods of improving the operational activities. Finally, the objectives of the operational activities are optimized. The next step will be studying the specific case applications and other optimization method for services and organizations.

References

1. Kaelbling, L.P., Lozano-Perez, T.: Hierarchical task and motion planning in the now. Massachusetts Institute of Technology, Cambridge (2010)
2. Nau, D., Au, T., Ilghami, O., Kuter, U.: SHOP2: an HTN planning system. JAIR **20**(3), 379–404 (2003)
3. Dou, Y.: Study on method of generation requirement for weaponry and equipment capability for meta - activity decomposition. Master's thesis of National University of Defense Technology (2011)
4. Belfares, L., Guitouni, A.: Multi objective genetic algorithms for courses of action planning. In: Proceedings of IEEE Congress on Evolutionary Computation, pp. 1543–1551 (2003)
5. Freuder, E.C., Nareyek, A., Fourer, R., et al.: Constraints and AI planning. IEEE Intell. Syst. **20**(2), 62–72 (2005)
6. Cox, L., Popken, D.: A simulation-optimization approach to air warfare planning. J. Defense Model. Simul.: Appl. Methodol. Technol. **1**(3), 127–140 (2004)
7. Pooch, U.W., Surdu, J.R.: Simulation technologies in the mission operational environment. Simul. J. Soc. Comput. Simul. **74**(3), 138–161 (2000)
8. DoD Architecture Framework Working Group: DoD Architecture Framework Version 2.0 Volume II: Architectural Data and Models. Department of Defense, U.S. (2009)

Business Intelligence Architecture Informed by Organisational Semiotics

John Effah[1(✉)], Prince Kwame Senyo[1,2] (iD),
and Stephen Opoku-Anokye[2]

[1] Department of Operations and Management Information Systems,
University of Ghana Business School, Accra, Ghana
{jeffah,pksenyo}@ug.edu.gh
[2] Informatics Research Centre, Henley Business School,
University of Reading, Reading, UK
stephen.opoku-anokye@henley.ac.uk

Abstract. This study draws on organisational semiotics and design science methodology informed by abductive reasoning to develop a business intelligence (BI) architecture. Organisational semiotics research has so far paid limited attention to BI in general and its architecture in particular. Moreover, BI research in information systems (IS) focuses largely on either technical or social activities. Organisational semiotics offers frameworks and model which can be used to develop a BI architecture with combined technical and social views. This study therefore develops a BI architecture based on knowledge hierarchy, semiotic framework, and semiotic activity hierarchy. The paper uses a manufacturing company's BI experience as a case study to inform and evaluate the proposed architecture. The study's contribution stems from its development of the organisational semiotics informed BI architecture and its implications for research and practice.

Keywords: Organisational semiotics · Business intelligence
Knowledge hierarchy · Forma-informa-performa
Semiotic framework

1 Introduction

Following technological advancement in data infrastructure as well as tools and techniques for analytics and data mining, business intelligence (BI) has increasingly attracted research attention in information systems [5]. Recent conceptualizations view BI as the ability to acquire and apply actionable knowledge to make decisions [8]. As a multidisciplinary concept, BI lacks a consensual definition [7, 16]. However, in information systems, BI refers to the use of information and communication technologies (ICTs) for data gathering and storage to generate actionable knowledge for decision making [15, 17]. BI has generally been viewed as a process [15]. However, this study argues that beyond being a process, BI can also be an output as actionable knowledge.

K. Liu et al. (Eds.): ICISO 2018, IFIP AICT 527, pp. 268–277, 2018.
https://doi.org/10.1007/978-3-319-94541-5_27

Thus far, organisational semiotics research on BI remains limited. The few studies on the subject have focused largely on data visualization [11, 13], which is only a component of the final stage of the BI process. As a result, not much is known about BI process in organisational semiotics. A recent study on information architecture [21] makes a case for increasing the scope of BI research in organisational semiotics. The current study responds to such a call by developing a semiotic informed BI architecture.

The rest of the paper is structured as follows. Section 2 reviews related works on knowledge hierarchy and BI systems. Section 3 presents semiotic framework and semiotic activity hierarchy as the study's theoretical foundation. Section 4 presents BI experience of a manufacturing firm's human resource intelligence system as a case for developing and evaluating the BI architecture. Section 5 develops the BI architecture based on the related works, the theoretical foundation and the case study through an iterative process. Section 6 discusses the results of the study. Finally, Sect. 7 provides the conclusion with suggestions for future research.

2 Related Works

2.1 The Knowledge Hierarchy

Knowledge hierarchy [1, 18], also called information hierarchy or wisdom hierarchy, represents the structural and functional relationships between data, information, knowledge and sometimes wisdom [4, 18]. Figure 1 shows the knowledge hierarchy and its layers.

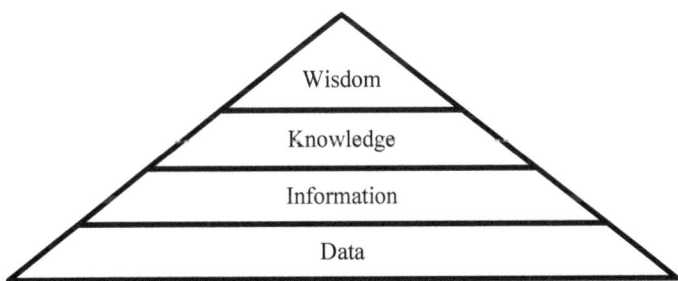

Fig. 1. Knowledge hierarchy [18]

Like knowledge itself, concepts within the hierarchy lack consensual definitions across disciplines. Table 1 however offers generic definitions as used in information systems [e.g., 4, 18]. Data refers to symbolic facts captured and stored in media; information constitutes statements with meanings; knowledge refers to true statements that are socially believed and verified; while wisdom refers to applied knowledge judged to be right and socially acceptable.

Table 1. Definitions of knowledge hierarchy concepts

Element	Meaning
Wisdom	Judgements that are socially desirable
Knowledge	Beliefs that have been socially verified to be true
Information	Meanings derived from processed data
Data	Symbolic facts that have been captured

The functional perspective shows the hierarchy as dynamic interactions between the elements. Thus, data undergoes processing to derive information, which is analyzed to generate knowledge, which is judged or assessed to get wisdom. Knowledge hierarchy has been applied with semiotic framework in organisational semiotics research [e.g., 2]. However, its relationship with BI remains limited. The current study therefore adapts the knowledge hierarchy to derive an intelligence hierarchy as part of the process for developing the BI architecture.

2.2 Business Intelligence Systems

Business intelligence systems [17] refer to a collection of technologies and techniques for capturing, preparing and transforming data into knowledge for decisions. Figure 2 shows a framework for BI system and related components.

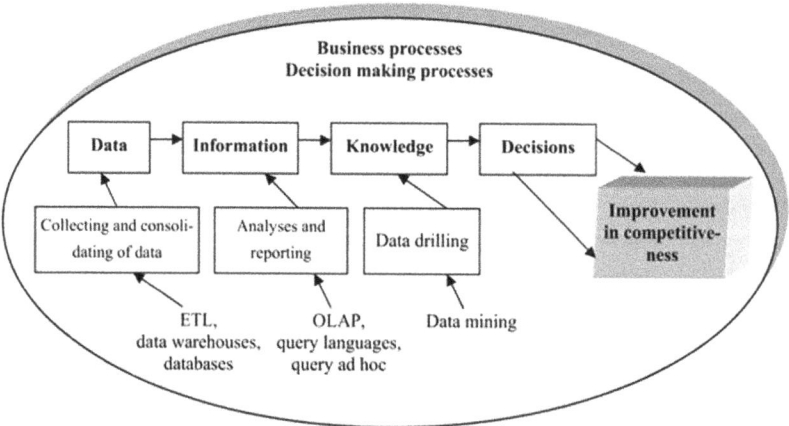

Fig. 2. Business intelligence system [17]

Figure 2 presents four stages of the BI system and an embedded three-layer model. The stages comprise data, information, knowledge and decisions. Each stage has underlying techniques supported by relevant tools. Thus, first data collection and consolidation techniques use ETL, data warehouse and database tools to generate data. Second, data analyses and reporting techniques depend on OLAP and query tools to generate information. Finally, data drilling uses data mining tools to generate knowledge to support decisions for improved business processes and competitiveness.

A key limitation of the intelligence system is the failure to conceptualise and incorporate intelligence as a fundamental component of the model. Thus, the model uses BI only as a process and not as an output that emerges at some point of the intelligence process. In simple terms, not all knowledge may be useful for decision making. To address this limitation, this study draws on the BI system to develop the organisational semiotics informed BI architecture in Sect. 4.2.

3 Organisational Semiotics

Organisational semiotics draws on signs to study information and communication systems in organisational context [10, 12]. A sign refers to whatever that stands to someone for something [9]. The current study draws on the semiotic frameworks and semiotic activity hierarchy as a combined theoretical foundation for the BI architecture.

3.1 Semiotic Framework

The semiotic framework (also called semiotic ladder) hierarchically structures sign systems into technical and social layers as shown in Fig. 3.

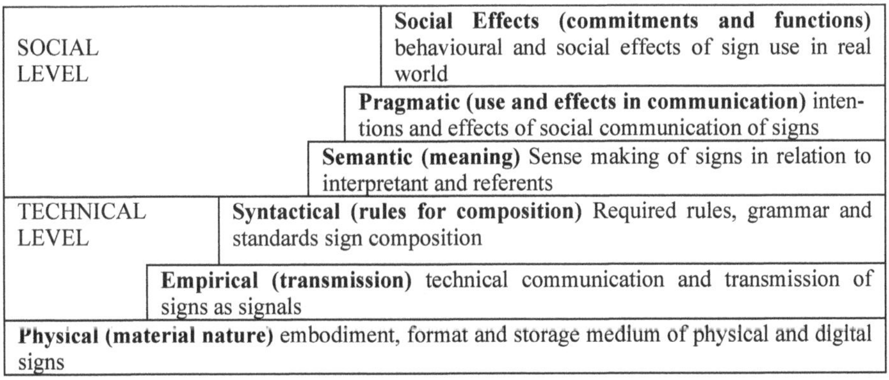

SOCIAL LEVEL		**Social Effects (commitments and functions)** behavioural and social effects of sign use in real world
		Pragmatic (use and effects in communication) intentions and effects of social communication of signs
	Semantic (meaning) Sense making of signs in relation to interpretant and referents	
TECHNICAL LEVEL	**Syntactical (rules for composition)** Required rules, grammar and standards sign composition	
	Empirical (transmission) technical communication and transmission of signs as signals	
Physical (material nature) embodiment, format and storage medium of physical and digital signs		

Fig. 3. Generic semiotic framework: Adapted from [14]

The technical layers comprise the physical, empirical and syntactic. First, the physical constitutes the material and digital components of signs. Second, the empirical concerns observable properties of signals as signs in transmission through a communication medium such as speed, capacity, efficiency and errors. Third, the syntactic concerns rules and standards regarding the physical composition and structure of a sign.

The social layers comprise the semantic, pragmatic and social effects. The semantic deals with meanings that signs convey. The pragmatic relates to the intentions as well as use and effects of signs in communication [10]. The social concerns change that communication and use of signs effect in the real world. Such effects include changes in the status quo that results from social activities such as agreements, norms and decisions. The next section presents semiotic activity hierarchy based on the semiotic framework.

3.2 Semiotic Activity Hierarchy

The notion of semiotic activity is introduced in this study as layers of formative, informative and performative activities based on the semiotic framework as shown in Fig. 4. The formative activity involves the physical, empirical and syntactic layers for composition and transmission of signs as data; informative activity relates to interpretation and communication of signs as information; finally, performative activity informs the use of actionable knowledge to make a decision that effect changes in the real world.

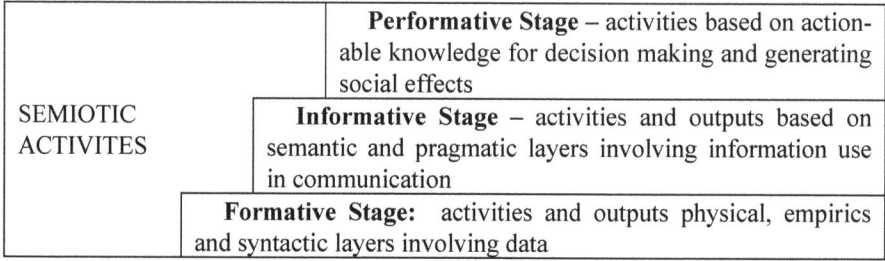

Fig. 4. Semiotic activities hierarchy

The layers of activities are based on the notions of forma, informa and performa as patterns of signs systems developed by Dietz [6] and related to the semiotic framework by Beynon-Davies [3] as semiotic acts. According to Dietz [6] forma refers to material or physical composition of a sign; informa deals with content and meaning of signs; while performa deals with communication and use of signs for making decisions for social actions.

4 Case Study

This section presents the BI experience of a multi-site manufacturing company in the UK, MSMC (pseudonym) involving human resource and diseases data warehousing and mining. In 2010, the company implemented a BI solution with a data warehouse for consolidating and restructuring operational data including that of human resources; metadata layer for providing meaningful data views from the data warehouse and marts; and presentation layer for reporting and analytics, including pre-built reports, ad-hoc queries and analysis as well as BI visualization.

In 2011, the Human Resource (HR) Director had a requirement to know monthly trends of sickness among the workforce across all sites. To do this, the BI team extended the existing data warehouse to include disease outbreak data in areas of the various sites. Subsequent data mining activities established associations between the health data and music festival data. Hence, additional data on music festivals were incorporated into the data warehouse and the HR data mart. The following section shows the semiotic activities that occurred at various stages of the BI architecture.

4.1 Formative Activities

The physical implementation of the data store layer of the BI solution included a consolidation and restructuring data warehouse (CRDW). The techniques used at the formative stage involved the use of extract, transform and load (ETL) tools to collect data from operational and external sources including HR data, transforming the data through restructuring and cleaning and loading data into the warehouse.

The HRM system primarily supported the operations of the HR Department. As such, it was developed to capture and store employee related data across the organisation, including data on sickness and sick leave. The organisation's policy on sick leave allows employees to self-certify if the sickness period is not more than 7 days in a single period or 10 days in total for a whole year. Within these periods, self-certified sick leave does not require a note from a medical practitioner or evidence of visit to a medical centre. As part of the formative activities, data were collected by the recording of sick leave taken using the organisation's Human Resource Management (HRM) System. Also, the data were extracted from the HRM System and loaded into an Organisation-wide integrated data warehouse. This was done to consolidate data on sick leave and from other sources, and to prepare the data for reporting and analytics.

Beyond the internal sources, ETL tools were used to capture and load NHS data on disease outbreaks and music festivals related to areas close various sites of the company. In sum, the BI formative activities made data available for the informative and performative activities.

4.2 Informative Activity

At the informative stage, a metadata set was setup with a prebuilt report for the monthly sickness trend to meet the information requirements of the HR director. In January 2012, the monthly trends report up to December 2011 highlighted August as the month with over 50% of recorded employee sickness, which had been consistent for the past 6 years. A further analysis of SiteX (pseudonym) of the company highlighted the 3rd week of August as accounting for over 75% of all reported employee sicknesses across the same 6-year period. Moreover, over 85% of all reported sickness in August for the 6-year period were self-certified, of which 90% were from one particular manufacturing site.

4.3 Performative Activity

Beyond the employee sickness data, health data from the National Health Service were analysed to identify any possible disease outbreaks in August, especially, the 3rd week. However, none was found. Analysis of data from the two water companies for the residential areas within commutable distance of 2-hours drive from SiteX also revealed no reported contamination in the periods concerned.

However, a search of local activities in the immediate surroundings of SiteX identified a music festival that starts on the 2nd weekend of August. Further investigations showed the festival has been running for over 50 years and has become very popular over the last 15 years. Further analysis revealed that over 70% of the people who attend this music festival as between the ages of 20 and 37 years.

Combining this external data from the organisers of the music festival with the internal HR data. Mining of the combined data revealed a strong correlation between the festival start date and the sick leave taken over the last 15 years. Also, the data revealed an exponential increase of sick leave taken during the 3rd week in August from 15 years ago to 6 years ago where it plateaued. Armed with this information, the senior management team decided to change the policy on self-certified sick leave from 7 days to 2 days in any single period.

5 Business Intelligence Architecture

This section presents the organisational semiotic informed BI architecture, which was developed through design science methodology informed by abductive reasoning [20]. The process began with the third author's observation of challenges that were associated with lack of a BI model to support the case organisation's decision and policy evaluation on sick leave. Following this, the study drew on the conventional knowledge hierarchy to develop an intelligence hierarchy as shown in Fig. 5.

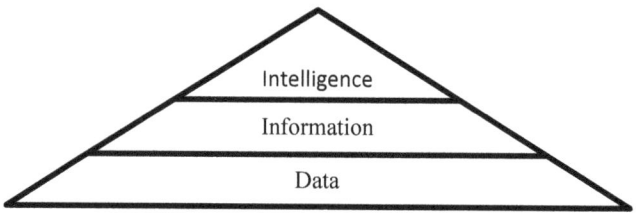

Fig. 5. Intelligence hierarchy

As Fig. 5 shows, the notion of intelligence replaces knowledge and wisdom. In this study, intelligence is considered as a form of knowledge that supports decision making and therefore actionable; hence the decision to use it to substitute knowledge and wisdom. In relation to the semiotic activity hierarchy, formative activity generates data, informative activity generates information while performative activity in the form of data mining generates intelligence to support decision making.

Subsequently, the study drew on the intelligence hierarchy and the semiotic framework with activity hierarchy to develop an initial BI architecture, which was validated and refined with the case study. Thus, the BI architecture process followed an iterative process whereby the BI experience in the case study served as a guide and evaluation criteria for refinement. Figure 6 shows the final architecture that emerged from the iterative process.

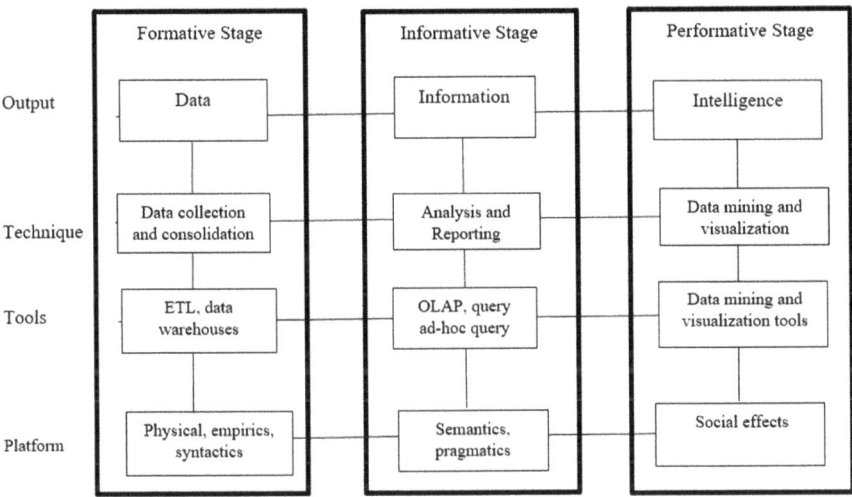

Fig. 6. Business intelligence architecture

The architecture shows 4 layers and 3 stages with their output and supporting activities, techniques and tools. The interconnecting lines show how the various components are intertwined to generate the required intelligence to support decision making for organisational activities. The intelligence generation process begins from the formative stage where the platform layer relies on the tool and technique layers to generate data as output. This stage supports the informative stage to generate information as output. Finally, the performative stage generates intelligence as output, in the form of actionable knowledge for organisational decision making.

6 Discussion

The case study shows the three stages of BI process and output as well as supporting techniques and tools of the proposed architecture. The formative activity corresponds to the data warehouse and ETL as tools, extraction and consolidation of internal as well as external data as techniques and the accumulated data as the output. In relation to the semiotic framework, the formative activity relies on the technical platform: physical, empirics and syntax.

The informative activity relates to metadata and reporting of monthly trend reports on sick leave. The underlying technique was analysis and reporting with OLAP, general query and ad-hoc query tools as supporting technologies. In terms of the semiotic framework, the informative activity relates to semantics and pragmatics in terms of sense-making and communication of information.

Finally, the performative activity involved the use of intelligence knowledge to make a decision by changing the policy on sick leave. The supporting technique involve data mining and data visualisation while the underlying tools were data mining and visualization software. In relation to the semiotic ladder, the performative activity relies on the social world effects.

The three activities show a clear distinction between data, information and intelligence in the architecture. Data is considered as symbolic facts that are accumulated to support informative and performative activities. Informative activity produces meaningful messages to provide answers to known questions through analytics as in the case of the HR director. Intelligence however presents actionable knowledge based on unknown and unexpected patterns, relationships, and associations as was the case with the sick leave and the music festival period. However, in practice, the three are not independent but highly related as demonstrated by the various intersecting line of the architecture.

Existing BI studies [e.g., 15, 19] largely portray the concept from a technical perspective and pays less attention to the social dimension. Also related organisational semiotic studies discuss some part of the subject in relation to knowledge management [e.g., 2] but does not link to BI. Our study therefore comes as the first to use organisational semiotics to develop a BI architecture with clear distinction between data, information and intelligence and their relationships at the semiotic, tools, techniques output and activity levels.

7 Conclusion

The purpose of the study was to develop a BI architecture based on the organisational semiotics framework. The study therefore presents a BI architecture founded on the organisational semiotic framework, intelligence hierarchy, semiotic activity framework based on formative, informative, and performative activity levels. Viewing intelligence as an actionable knowledge for decision making, the study contributes to organisational semiotics research by extending it to the domain of BI. It also contributes to BI research by basing the architecture on semiotic principles and frameworks.

For contribution to practice, the findings present a clearer BI process that intelligence analysts, developers and users can draw on to identify relevant technologies, techniques and activities that are required to develop and deploy a BI system in an organisational setting. In addition, the architecture presents a clearer network between data, information and intelligence to inform practices on how to develop such a system.

The limitation of the study stems from its exploratory nature and single case illustration in a human resource intelligence system. Given that BI does not focus on a single domain or problem area as does decision support systems, future research will evaluate the architecture in a multi-domain environment such as supply chain and customer relationship management.

References

1. Ackoff, R.L.: From data to wisdom. J. Appl. Syst. Anal. **16**(1), 3–9 (1989)
2. Baskarada, S., Koronios, A.: Data, information, knowledge, wisdom (DIKW): a semiotic theoretical and empirical exploration of the hierarchy and its quality dimension. Australas. J. Inf. Syst. **18**(1), 5–24 (2013)

3. Beynon-Davies, P.: Formatics. In: Americas Conference on Information Systems, Seattle, Washington, 9–12 August 2012 (2012)
4. Boell, S.K., Cecez-Kecmanovic, D.: What is "information" beyond a definition? In: Thirty Sixth International Conferences on Information Systems, Forth Worth, pp. 1–20 (2015)
5. Chen, H., Storey, V.C.: Business intelligence and analytics: from big data to big impact. MIS Q. **36**(4), 1165–1188 (2012)
6. Dietz, J.: The deep structure of business processes. Commun. ACM **49**(5), 59–64 (2006)
7. Grossmann, W., Rinderle-Ma, S.: Fundamentals of Business Intelligence. Springer, Heidelberg (2015). https://doi.org/10.1007/978-3-662-46531-8
8. Leismeister, J.: Collective intelligence. Bus. Inf. Syst. Eng. **4**(2), 245–248 (2010)
9. Liu, K.: Requirements reengineering from legacy information systems using semiotic techniques. Syst. Signs Actions Int. J. Commun. Inf. Technol. Work **1**(1), 38–61 (2005)
10. Liu, K.: Semiotics in Information Systems Engineering. Cambridge University Press, Cambridge (2000)
11. Liu, K.: Semiotics in visualisation. In: 2014 9th International Conference on Evaluation of Novel Approaches to Software Engineering (ENASE), pp. 1–3 (2014)
12. Liu, K., Li, W.: Organisational Semiotics for Business Informatics. Routeledge, London (2015)
13. Liu, K., Tan, C.: Semiotics in digital visualisation. In: Cordeiro, J., Hammoudi, S., Maciaszek, L., Camp, O., Filipe, J. (eds.) ICEIS 2014. LNBIP, vol. 227, pp. 3–13. Springer, Cham (2015). https://doi.org/10.1007/978-3-319-22348-3_1
14. Mingers, J.: Guidelines for Conducting Semiotic Research in Information Systems (2014)
15. Negash, S.: Business intelligence. Commun. Assoc. Inf. Syst. **13**, 177–195 (2004)
16. Olszak, C.: Toward better understanding and use of business intelligence in organizations. Inf. Syst. Manag. **33**(2), 105–123 (2016)
17. Olszak, C., Ziemba, E.: Approach to building and implementing business intelligence systems. Interdiscip. J. Inf. Knowl. Manag. **2**, 135–148 (2007)
18. Rowley, J.: The wisdom hierarchy: representations of the DIKW hierarchy. J. Inf. Sci. **33**(2), 163–180 (2007)
19. Sahay, B.S., Ranjan, J.: Real time business intelligence in supply chain analytics. Inf. Manag. Comput. Secur. **16**(1), 28–48 (2008)
20. Tan, C., et al.: Information architecture for healthcare organizations: the case of a NHS hospital in UK. In: ICIS 2013 Proceedings, pp. 1–11 (2013)
21. Tan, C., Liu, K.: An organisational semiotics inspired information architecture: pervasive healthcare as a case study. In: ICISO 2013 – Proceedings of the 14th International Conference on Informatics Semiotics in Organisations IFIP WG8.1 Working Conference, pp. 35–44 (2013)

Chaotic Time Series for Copper's Price Forecast

Neural Networks and the Discovery of Knowledge for Big Data

Raúl Carrasco[1,2](✉) ⓘ, Manuel Vargas[3,4] ⓘ, Ismael Soto[5] ⓘ,
Diego Fuentealba[6,7] ⓘ, Leonardo Banguera[8] ⓘ,
and Guillermo Fuertes[4] ⓘ

[1] Facultad de Administración y Economía, Universidad de Santiago de Chile,
Santiago 9170022, Chile
raul.carrasco.a@usach.cl
[2] Facultad de Ingeniería, Ciencia y Tecnología,
Universidad Bernardo O'Higgins, Santiago 8370993, Chile
[3] Departamento de Ingeniería Industrial, Universidad San Sebastián,
Santiago 8420524, Chile
manuel.vargasg@usach.cl
[4] Departamento de Ingeniería Industrial, Universidad de Santiago de Chile,
Santiago 9170124, Chile
guillermo.fuertes@usach.cl
[5] Departamento de Ingeniería Eléctrica, Universidad de Santiago de Chile,
Santiago 9170124, Chile
ismael.soto@usach.cl
[6] Informatics Research Centre, University of Reading, Reading, UK
d.a.fuentealbacid@pgr.reading.ac.uk
[7] School of Informatics and Telecommunications,
Universidad Tecnológica de Chile-INACAP, Santiago, Chile
[8] Department of Industrial Engineering, University of Guayaquil,
Guayaquil, Ecuador
leonardo.banguera@usach.cl

Abstract. We investigated the potential of Artificial Neural Networks (ANN), ANN to forecasts in chaotic series of the price of copper; based on different combinations of structure and possibilities of knowledge in big discovery data. Two neural network models were built to predict the price of copper of the London Metal Exchange (LME) with lots of 100 to 1000 data. We used the Feed Forward Neural Network (FFNN) algorithm and Cascade Forward Neural Network (CFNN) combining training, transfer and performance implemented functions in MatLab. The main findings support the use of the ANN in financial forecasts in series of copper prices. The copper price's forecast using different batches size of data can be improved by changing the number of neurons, functions of transfer, and functions of performance s. In addition, a negative correlation of -0.79 was found in performance indicators using RMS and IA.

Keywords: Big Data · Copper price · Chaos theory · Neural network
Nonlinear systems · Time series forecasting

K. Liu et al. (Eds.): ICISO 2018, IFIP AICT 527, pp. 278–288, 2018.
https://doi.org/10.1007/978-3-319-94541-5_28

1 Introduction

Copper is one of the basic metal products listed on major exchanges in the world: the LME, Commodity Exchange of New York (COMEX) and Shanghai Futures Exchange (SHFE). Prices in these exchanges reflect the balance between the supply and demand of copper worldwide, although they may be strongly influenced by the rates of currency exchange and investment flows, factors that may cause fluctuations of volatile prices partially linked to changes in the economic cycle activity [1].

The price of copper is a sensitive issue for major producers such as Codelco, Freeport-McMoRan Copper & Gold, Glencore Xstrata, BHP Billiton, Southern Copper Corporation, American Smelting and Refining Company. Economies such as those of Chile and Zambia rely heavily on copper production and, subsequently, in the evolution of the prices of the same [2], being Chile the largest producer and exporter of the world.

Several studies include copper as one of the products of interest in the evaluations of the forecast to improve the prediction of prices. They employ a variety of different methods and mathematical models: time series [3–5], combined with wavelet [6, 7], transformed of Fourier [8], swarm optimisation algorithm [9], and models of multi-products [10].

A fairly accurate time series model could predict several years forward, whose skill is an advantage for the planning of future requirements. Research on nonlinear dynamical systems has allowed in recent years significantly improve the impact of the predictive capacity of the times series. Chaos is a universal complex dynamic phenomenon that exists in different natural and social systems such as communication, economics and biology. The auto-correlation of chaotic behaviour in the economy began in the decade of 1980, applied to macroeconomic variables such as the gross domestic product (GDP) and monetary aggregates [11]. Since then, several studies have been conducted to search chaotic behaviour in economic and financial series [12, 13].

In this context, amongst the most used techniques and tools are graphics analysis of recurrence, Temporal Space Entropy (STE) Hurst coefficient and exponent of the Lyapunov dimension of correlation for the matching of chaotic behaviour in these series [14]. Additionally, the existence of chaotic behaviour in the commodities of copper was corroborated in [15].

The motivations and the need to carry out this research is to evaluate the ANN by different dimensions, type of networks, functions and structures.

2 Methodology

The continuous increase of the power of calculation and availability of data has grown the attention in the use of ANN in many types of problems of prediction. The ANN can model and predict linear and nonlinear time-series with a high degree of accuracy, to capture any relationship between the data without prior knowledge of the problem which is modelled [16].

The methodology used for visual and statistical analysis is summarised according to the Fig. 1 adapted the Loshin [17].

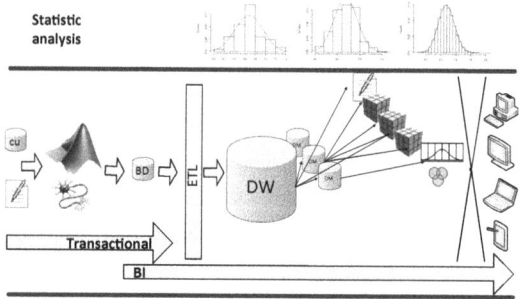

Fig. 1. Methodological graph based on methodology of Business Intelligence (BI).

The closing prices of copper traded on the LME were used with the different functions of learning, optimisation and transfer as input. Then, the quality of the forecast of the ANN performed in MatLab R2014a simulation tool was evaluated with Root Mean Square (RMS) and the Adequacy Index (IA). The saved data goes through the process of Extract, Transform and Load (ETL) to be stored in the Data Warehouse (DW) in a multi-dimensional form, using SQL Server 2008. The visual analysis of the results is done by the software BI Tableau Desktop 8.3 as Frontend, and the R version 3.1.2 software to perform the corresponding statistical analysis.

2.1 Segmentation of Data

Data were segmented into two sizes of batches. The former with 100 and the later with thousand data. Periods from 22/01/2015 to 16/06/2015 and the 01/07/2011 to 16/06/2015 respectively.

Segmentation according to the evaluated batch records is according to the Table 1.

Table 1. Segmentation's records.

Batch	Training	Testing	Verification
Theoretician	First 70% of the data	15% next data	15% of the final data
100	[1;70]	[71;85]	[86;100]
1000	[1;700]	[701:850]	[851;1000]

2.2 Artificial Neural Networks

Represented FFNN has been taken to this work in the Fig. 2(a) and the represented CFNN in the Fig. 2(b). We have selected some of the features available in the toolbox of Matlab software.

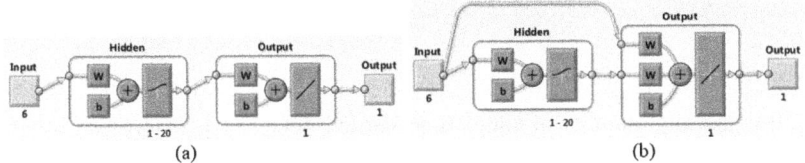

Fig. 2. (a) FFNN of 1–20 neurons in the hidden layer. (b) CFNN of 1–20 neurons in the hidden layer [18].

The inputs used in the system correspond to $t_{-1}, t_{-2}, t_{-3}, t_{-4}, t_{-1}, t_{-6}$ and target t_0 the copper price time series.

2.3 Alternatives of Evaluation

The different alternatives of a network are given according to different combinations between their functions as shown in Eq. (1).

$$M = E * R * F * n \tag{1}$$

where,

M, It is an alternative for a network number.
E, It is the number of training functions.
R, It is the number of performance functions.
F, It is the number of transfer functions.
n, It is the number of neurons in the hidden layer.

Replacing values in the Eq. (1) gets the number of alternatives for a network.

$$M = 9 * 2 * 3 * 20 = 1080$$

To calculate the total number of alternatives evaluated in this work is obtained from the Eq. (2).

$$T = M * N * L \tag{2}$$

where,

T, It is the number of evaluated alternatives.
N, It is the number of networks (structure of similar functions).
L, It is the number of batches of data.

Replacing values in the Eq. (2) obtained 4320 alternative evaluated in this work.

$$T = 1080 * 2 * 2 = 4320$$

Were 27 simulations for each of the 4320 alternatives evaluated in this work with a total of 116640 simulations according to the Eq. (3).

$$T_s = T * S \tag{3}$$

Where,

T_s, It is the total number of simulations carried out.
S, It is the number of simulations for each alternative.

2.4   Multidimensional Model

This research focuses on the evaluation of two networks simultaneously from different dimensions. The FFNN and the CFNN in dimRed, training features (trainbfg, traincgb, traincgf, traincgp, traingd, traingdm, traingda, traingdx, trainlm) in dimFuncTrain, in dimFuncTransfer (logsig, tansig, purelin) transfer functions, functions (mse, sse) performance in dimFuncPerform. Number them 1 to 20 neurons, with batches of 100 and 1,000 data. The function of learning was the learngdm and the metrics of evaluation [RMS, IA, bestEpoch, duration] in fact table.

Figure 3 shows the "star model" [19] used to perform multidimensional analysis according to the methodology proposed by Kimball [20]. The construction of the DW was based on multidimensional modelling, in which the structures of the information on table are facts and dimensions [21].

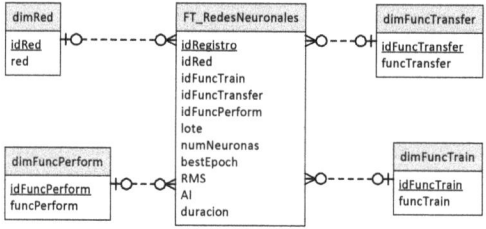

Fig. 3.   Star model for multidimensional analysis of project.

2.5   Performance Measures

$$RMS = \sqrt{\frac{\sum_{i=1}^{n}(o_i - p_i)^2}{\sum_{i=1}^{n} o_i^2}} \tag{4}$$

$$IA = 1 - \frac{\sum_{i=1}^{n}(o_i' - p_i')^2}{\sum_{i=1}^{n}(|o_i'| - |p_i'|)^2} \tag{5}$$

The results were validated using performance measures that allow indicating the degree of generalisation of the model used. The indexes are the average quadratic Error (RMS), and the index of adequacy (IA). Both are shown in the Eqs. (4) and (5), respectively, where o_i and p_i are the values observed and predicted respectively at the time i, and N is the total number of data. In addition, $p'_i = p_i - o_m$ and $o'_i = o_i - o_m$, being o_m value average of the observations [22].

IA indicates the degree of adjustment that has the values estimated with the actual values of a variable. A value close to 1 indicates a good estimate. On the other hand, near-zero RMS indicate a good quality setting.

3   Results

3.1   Knowledge Discovery

The knowledge is in the data, however, must be extracted and built for the consumption of the users. New technological solutions are required for data management. The new software and methodologies are the solution to make sense of the data, allowing to extract useful information for the construction of knowledge, supporting decision making. Data from markets together with the new data generated from different data mining techniques, can help to the analysis and the management of Big Data [23, 24]. In this case, the business intelligence tool enables the discovery of knowledge.

Figure 4 shows the best results obtained in the average assessment (RMS)$^-$in lots of 100 data FFNN. The indexes are shown in a scale of colors, where the blue colour indicates better value performances corresponding to the minimum of the RMS and the red colour lower performance. After several iterations were obtained the best results to correspond to functions purelin, traincgb, traincgf, traincgp, mse and sse between 1 and 5 neurons.

Red / Lote / Train Fcn / Perform Fcn

Feed-Forward Neural Network

100

Transfer Fcn	Num Neuron..	traincgb		traincgf		traincgp	
		mse	sse	mse	sse	mse	sse
purelin	1	0,008099	0,008925	0,008181	0,008422	0,008019	0,008118
	2	0,008526	0,009139	0,008679	0,008363	0,008532	0,008523
	3	0,008295	0,008499	0,008248	0,008521	0,008938	0,008595
	4	0,008201	0,008532	0,008576	0,008494	0,008379	0,008865
	5	0,008927	0,008471	0,008495	0,008650	0,008305	0,008040

Fig. 4. Final result and visual analysis of the FFNN, batch = 100. (Color figure online)

(AI) in the FFNN average assessment indicates a better fit in the curves, for this case are kept the same functions and expands the range of neurons from 1 to 20.

In the case of the FFNN network for batches of 1000 data, the best results of $\overline{RMS}$ and $\overline{AI}$ they correspond to the functions purelin, trainlm, mse and sse with ranges of neurons from 6 to 10 in Table 2.

Table 2. FFNN for batches of 1000, functions purelin, trainlm, mse and sse with ranges of neurons from 6 to 10.

Perform	Neurons	$\overline{RMS}$	$\overline{IA}$
mse	6	0.007682365	0.97249718
mse	7	0.007676144	0.972600372
mse	8	0.007686618	0.972512072
mse	9	0.007678558	0.972517947
mse	10	0.007682348	0.972498224
sse	6	0.007680212	0.972510564
sse	7	0.00768904	0.972449236
sse	8	0.007678767	0.972536585
sse	9	0.007675839	0.972631146
sse	10	0.00768069	0.972486787

In the case of CFNN for batches of 100 data, the best results for the averages of $\overline{RMS}$ and $\overline{AI}$ they correspond to the functions purelin, traincgb, traincgf, traincgp, mse and sse between 1 and 2 neurons in Table 3.

Table 3. CFNN for batches of 100, purelin, traincgb, traincgf, traincgp, mse and sse between 1 and 2 neurons functions.

		Mse	mse	sse	sse
trainFcn	n	$\overline{RMS}$	$\overline{IA}$	$\overline{RMS}$	$\overline{IA}$
traincgb	1	0.008416036	0.999978052	0.008722153	0.999976384
traincgb	2	0.008596207	0.999977127	0.008489567	0.999977647
traincgf	1	0.008737803	0.999976242	0.008464134	0.99997776
traincgf	2	0.008556195	0.999977299	0.008739409	0.999976321
traincgp	1	0.008581721	0.999977098	0.008644758	0.999976784
traincgp	2	0.008634526	0.999976813	0.008536383	0.999977431

CFNN batches of 1000 data, for best results unemployment averages $\overline{RMS}$ and $\overline{AI}$ they correspond to the functions purelin, trainlm, mse and sse with ranges from 3 to 4 neurons in Table 4.

We found that FFNN and CFNN for batches of 100 data obtained the best results with the training functions named traincgf, traincgb, and traincgp. On the other hand, for batches of 1000 data, the best function of training was the trainlm in FFNN and CFNN.

Table 4. CFNN for 1000 batches, functions purelin, trainlm, mse and sse with ranges from 3 to 5 neurons.

Perform	Neurons	$\overline{RMS}$	$\overline{AI}$
mse	3	0.007678561	0.972558102
mse	4	0.007684607	0.972423949
mse	5	0.007675506	0.972534376
sse	3	0.007670738	0.972539376
sse	4	0.007681384	0.972468666
sse	5	0.007683084	0.97254968

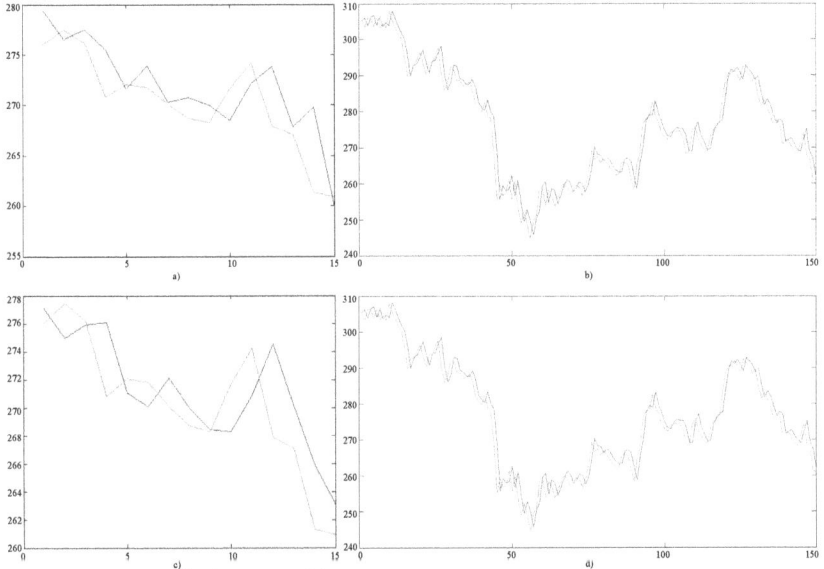

Fig. 5. (a) Forecast of the FFNN for data verification with lot of 100, purelin, traincgp and sse of 5 neurons functions; (b) Forecast of the FFNN for data verification with lot of 1000, purelin, trainlm and sse of 7 neurons functions; (c) Forecast of CFNN for data verification with lot of 100, purelin, traincgb and sse of 1 neurons functions; (d) Forecast of CFNN for data verification with lot of 1000, purelin, trainlm and mse of 3 neurons functions.

3.2 Forecast

The charts show the forecast made by the FFNN and chaotic CFNN in series of the copper's price (Fig. 5a, b, c and d). FFNN and CFNN show similar values in his performance's ratings.

3.3 Statistic Analysis

The CFNN (trainFcn = trainlm, performFcn = sse, transferFcn = purelin, learnFcn = learngdm, lot = 1000, numNeuronas = 3) simulo up to 10000 simulations, where obtained good results in the performance of the network, with average measures of RMS of 0.00767957, IA of 0.9725127 and best_epoch of 3.1376; minimum values of 0.007535554; 0.9698627 and 1 respectively, maximum values of 0.007712344; 0.9731063 and 11 respectively, in the Table 5 the statistical summary of the simulation.

Table 5. Statistical simulation.

Perform	RMS	IA	best_epoch
mean	0.00767957	0.9725127	3.1376
sd	0.00002461	0.000225216	1.417486
min	0.007535554	0.9698627	1
25%	0.007671562	0.9723753	2
50%	0.007693985	0.9723813	3
75%	0.007694727	0.9726121	4
max	0.007712344	0.9731063	11
n	1000		

To review the distribution of RMS performance measures is observed which is skewed to the left Fig. 6a, Therefore, the bias is negative (less than the median average); Instead the IA is skewed to the right index Fig. 6b, therefore, the bias is positive (greater than the median average) and the best_epoch this biased right in Fig. 6c. On the other hand the correlations (Pearson) graph shows a high negative correlation of −0.79 between RMS and the IA which shows the good performance of the ANN indicated by RMS will also be it according to the IA. On the other hand presents a negative correlation of −0.49 between IA and best_epoch; and a positive correlation of 0.52 between RMS and best_epoch.

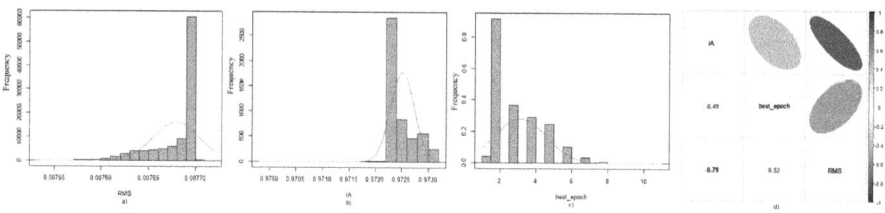

Fig. 6. (a) Distribution of RMS, (b) distribution of IA, (c) distribution of best_epoch and (d) plot of correlations between IA and RMS best_epoch.

4   Conclusions

Forecasts based on neural network, nonlinear models achieved better results compared with linear forecasting models. Combinations of two neural network models, with nine training functions, two functions of performance, lots of 100 to 1000 data and ranges from 1 to 20 neurons and three transfer functions have been studied.

For different batch size of data it is to be more sensitive to the functions of training on the functions of transfer, performance, number of neurons.

The results of the simulations predict in the case of the copper price series; the best combinations of functions are vector (trainFcn = trainlm, performFcn = sse, transferFcn = purelin, learnFcn = learngdm, lot = 1000, number neurons = 3) for batch 1000 network CFNN and vector (trainFcn = traincgp, performFcn = mse, transferFcn = purelin, learnFcn = learngdm, lot = 100, numNeuronas = 1) to the FFNN.

Found a high negative correlation of −0.79 in the performance indicators used RMS e IA.

In future work, it is necessary to review the contribution of other macroeconomic variables in the performance of the model, in particular, market of capitals of other commodities.

Finally, the characteristics of these time series, should be analysed the same set of combinations of functions in other economic series of price, to assess the possible relationships of the systems involved.

Acknowledgment. The authors are acknowledgment the financing of the project "Multiuser VLC for underground mining", code: IT17M10012 and this research has been supported by DICYT (Scientific and Technological Research Bureau) of The University of Santiago of Chile (USACH) and Department of Industrial Engineering.

References

1. Roberts, M.C.: Duration and characteristics of metal price cycles. Resour. Policy **34**, 87–102 (2009)
2. Sánchez Lasheras, F., de Cos Juez, F.J., Suárez Sánchez, A., Krzemień, A., Riesgo Fernández, P.: Forecasting the COMEX copper spot price by means of neural networks and ARIMA models. Resour. Policy **45**, 37–43 (2015)
3. Dooley, G., Lenihan, H.: An assessment of time series methods in metal price forecasting. Resour. Policy **30**, 208–217 (2005)
4. Carrasco, R., Astudillo, G., Soto, I., Chacon, M., Fuentealba, D.: Forecast of copper price series using vector support machines. In: 2018 7th International Conference on Industrial Technology and Management (ICITM), pp. 380–384. IEEE (2018)
5. Seguel, F., Carrasco, R., Adasme, P., Alfaro, M., Soto, I.: A meta-heuristic approach for copper price forecasting. In: Liu, K., Nakata, K., Li, W., Galarreta, D. (eds.) ICISO 2015. IAICT, vol. 449, pp. 156–165. Springer, Cham (2015). https://doi.org/10.1007/978-3-319-16274-4_16
6. Kriechbaumer, T., Angus, A., Parsons, D., Rivas Casado, M.: An improved wavelet–ARIMA approach for forecasting metal prices. Resour. Policy **39**, 32–41 (2014)

7. Goss, B.A., Avsar, S.G.: Simultaneity, forecasting and profits in London copper futures. Aust. Econ. Pap. **52**, 79–96 (2013)
8. Khalifa, A., Miao, H., Ramchander, S.: Return distributions and volatility forecasting in metal futures markets: evidence from gold, silver, and copper. J. Futures Marks **31**, 55–80 (2011)
9. Ma, W., Zhu, X., Wang, M.: Forecasting iron ore import and consumption of China using grey model optimized by particle swarm optimization algorithm. Resour. Policy **38**, 613–620 (2013)
10. Cortazar, G., Eterovic, F.: Can oil prices help estimate commodity futures prices? The cases of copper and silver. Resour. Policy **35**, 283–291 (2010)
11. Lebaron, B.: Chaos and nonlinear forecastability in economics and finance. Philos. Trans. Phys. Sci. Eng. **348**, 397–404 (1994)
12. Los, C.A.: Visualization of chaos for finance majors. EconWPA (2004)
13. Los, C.A., Yu, B.: Persistence characteristics of the Chinese stock markets. Int. Rev. Financ. Anal. **17**, 64–82 (2008)
14. Espinosa, C.: Caos en el mercado de commodities. Cuad. Econ. **29**, 155–177 (2010)
15. Carrasco, R., Vargas, M., Alfaro, M., Soto, I., Fuertes, G.: Copper metal price using chaotic time series forecasting. IEEE Lat. Am. Trans. **13**, 1961–1965 (2015)
16. Kourentzes, N., Barrow, D.K., Crone, S.F.: Neural network ensemble operators for time series forecasting. Expert Syst. Appl. **41**, 4235–4244 (2014)
17. Loshin, D.: The business intelligence environment, Chap. 5. In: Loshin, D. (ed.) business intelligence, pp. 61–76. Morgan Kaufmann, Boston (2013)
18. MathWorks: MatLab 2014a (2014)
19. Howson, C.: Successful Business Intelligence: Secrets to Making BI a Killer App [Hardcover]. McGraw-Hill Osborne Media, New York (2007)
20. Sherman, R.: Data architecture, Chap. 6. In: Business Intelligence Guidebook, pp. 107–142. Morgan Kaufmann, Boston (2015)
21. Soler, E., Trujillo, J., Fernández-Medina, E., Piattini, M.: Building a secure star schema in data warehouses by an extension of the relational package from CWM. Comput. Stand. Interfaces **30**, 341–350 (2008)
22. Zambrano Matamala, C., Rojas Díaz, D., Carvajal Cuello, K., Acuña Leiva, G.: Análisis de rendimiento académico estudiantil usando data warehouse y redes neuronales. Ingeniare. Rev. Chil. Ing. **19**, 369–381 (2011)
23. Xhafa, F., Taniar, D.: Big data knowledge discovery. Knowl.-Based Syst. **79**, 1–2 (2015)
24. Lagos, C., Carrasco, R., Fuertes, G., Gutiérrez, S., Soto, I., Vargas, M.: Big data on decision making in energetic management of copper mining. Int. J. Comput. Commun. Control **12**, 61–75 (2017)

An Abductive Process of Developing Interactive Data Visualization: A Case Study of Market Attractiveness Analysis

Qi Li[(⊠)] and Kecheng Liu

Informatics Research Center, Henley Business School, University of Reading,
Reading RG6 6UD, UK
q.li5@pgr.reading.ac.uk, k.liu@henley.ac.uk

Abstract. Data visualization has been widely utilized in various scenarios in data analytics for business purposes, especially helping novice readers make sense of complex dataset with interactive functions. However, due to an insufficient theoretical understanding of the process of developing interactive functions and visual presentations, interactive data visualization tools often display all available automatic graphing functions in front of users, instead of guiding them to choose a visualization based on their demands. Thus, this paper is intended to construct a process of developing interactive visualization with a specific focus on enabling the interoperation between design and interpretation. Stemmed from organizational semiotics, an abductive process will be portrayed in this paper to interpret the process of developing interactive data visualization. Especially the interactive functions will be employed in an iterative process, where producers can be aware of and respond to readers' information demands on semantic, pragmatic and social levels.

Keywords: Interactive data visualization · Organizational semiotics
Abductive reasoning process

1 Introduction

Data visualization plays an important role in business analytic intelligence, in terms of helping users make sense of a large amount of data, by using visual aids in order to convey a message to its readers [1]. Other scholars further extend the scope of contributions of data visualization to communication between readers and producers, exploration of the complex dataset and making sense of the information demanded decision-making [2, 3]. With the development in-memory computing and cloud techniques, data visualization can be more agile to adapt to users' demands, in other words, quickly responding to users' requests by the embedded interactive functions. In addition, the collaboration among different users will be promoted based on web-based visualization application, where different views from multiple users, producers and experts can be incorporated into the process of developing data visualization [4]. In short, other than supporting individual's exploration and sense-making of the dataset, data visualization facilitates the communication by interactive functions. [26]

© IFIP International Federation for Information Processing 2018
Published by Springer International Publishing AG 2018. All Rights Reserved
K. Liu et al. (Eds.): ICISO 2018, IFIP AICT 527, pp. 289–298, 2018.
https://doi.org/10.1007/978-3-319-94541-5_29

However, according to the observation on the leading visualization tools, such Tableau, QlikView, and PowerBI, although 'interactive visualization exploration' has been listed as a critical capacity of business intelligence, the focus remains on the generation of various visual representations with automatic graphing and enabling users to analyze and manipulate data by interacting with the visual representations [5]. This observation is also echoed by the prior research, which points out that the concept of interactive data visualization remains unclearly defined and its development process is still vaguely portrayed, even though the diverse technique is available and able to support users to interact with data [6, 7].

This paper will construct a process for developing interactive data visualization with a specific focus on understanding readers' multi-levels of information demands and guiding the producers to fulfil the demands by using interactive functions. Organizational semiotics, the doctrine of sign research, which has been applied to various prior research for understanding the process of information transfer among different parties, will be utilized at the theoretical foundation to the understanding of levels of interpretation. Also, the logical reasoning process will be referred to, to explain how a visualization will be interpreted and to discover the key interactions demanded during this process. In the illustrative case study, the abduction process will be applied to help design a data visualization of market attractiveness analysis.

2   Abduction in Organizational Semiotics

Data visualization can be articulated as a process of communication with graphics means [1, 8, 9]. Semiotic is a theoretical ground of signs and signification. It can help interpret the process where a sign as a carrier to deliver information among different parties. It also guides the discovery of implicit and explicit factors impact the efficacy of information transferring [10]. By having an in-depth understanding of the process and the significant influencing factors, the producers can further work on improving the efficacy of communication, e.g. the right information can be communicated at the right time, by the right method and to the right people. Supported by organizational semiotics, the research can focus on application and usefulness of signs in a business context, where the communication among individuals and business objects are driven by business purposes, serving for business objectives and influenced by organizational environments [11].

2.1   Semiotics

Semiosis reveals the process of sense-making, where an individual understands a sign by interpreting it based on the link with a certain object [12]. It is a universal mechanism which can be utilized to all sign-processing activities, which helps people recognize the importance of creating and using signs. Interactive data visualization can be regarded as a typical sign-based communication, where visual representations act as signs to facilitate the communication between producers and readers.

The whole process of semiosis can be articulated into the following triangular model of semiosis [11]. The firstness is a sign or representation which is utilized as a sign vehicle linking to a secondness. The secondness is an object, which should be reflected by the sign in the firstness. However, the reflection might not be generic and spontaneous, where readers cannot perfectly receive the information sent by producers without any deviation. Instead, the reflection will be impacted by the readers' interpretation based on prior knowledge, various purposes of interpretation and pressures from the organisational and social environment.

In the context of interactive data visualization, the meaning of the three elements in semiosis framework can be further expanded [11].

Table 1. Elements in semiosis in the context of visualization

Elements [11]	Explanations in the context of visualization
The sign, which is considered as a signifier	Visual representations, including adiagram, chart, map and table [13]
The object, which is considered as the signified	Business reality reflected or implied by the visual representations, e.g. market size; sales trend
The interpretant, which is considered as the effect of signs on readers' action (incl. reading, interpreting and behaving upon)	A process and result of interpreting signs and identifying their reflection based on readers' subjective elements [14] e.g. knowledge, experience and perception of environmental pressures e.g. driven by the sales-oriented strategy, managers will focus more on the information related to current and potential sales

Even though the semiosis portrays a general framework for discovering the visualization process where readers make sense of visual representation, the interpretant can be explained further, especially identifying the factors influencing interpretant on both technical and social aspects.

2.2   Semiotic Ladder

Interpretant has a broader scope than interpretation, which covers not only signifying a sign and identifying the meaning associated with the sign, but also involving readers' background knowledge, intentions and influences (incl. support and restrain) from social norms [15]. Thus, the semiotic ladder offers a framework of taxonomy to categorize the various influencing factors towards interpretant to 6 levels. By understanding the concepts and characteristics of different levels, visualization producers can have an in-depth understanding in terms of the barriers which hinder readers from making sense of visual representations.

Stemmed from the theory of organizational semiotics, which suggests understanding the barriers hindering the communication in the context of business through the lens of semiotics, Stamper [10] suggests analyzing the sign effect through 6 levels, consisting of two aspects of human information function and IT platform. IT platform is closely related to the infrastructure, physical quality and structure of sign. Different from the traditional semiotic framework which mostly focuses on the meaning and interpretation, Stamper points out that the physical quality and construction of sign will impact on humans understanding of sign. On the aspect of human information function, the semiotic framework is intended to address the challenges on signifying signs in terms of transferring their meaning, fulfilling readers' intentions and responding to the social norms [12].

When it comes to interactive data visualization, the lower three layers encourages producers to incorporate the Gestalt Law and pre-attentive attributes into visualization design, in order to assist human brain perceptive system to visually identify the patterns e.g. size, proximity and colours [16]. On the upper three layers of the semiotic framework, the focus shifts from visual representation (signs) to interpretant of visual representation (sign effect). As it is implied from the comment 'featureless data is equivalent to noise' [17], there is a big challenge on the cognition aspect of interactive data visualization: to enable users to capture the pattern of dataset, to make sense of them based on their background knowledge, intentions and to cope with social pressure. Since this paper mainly focuses on the sense-making aspect of interactive data visualization, the process framework will focus more on the key questions and norms on the upper three layers (Table 2). However, the semiotic framework might have offered a comprehensive guideline for producers to recognize a series of social and technical factors which might affect the interpretation of signs – making sense of visual representations, but it does not offer a set of tangible methods to elicit and document the elements and produce a practical solution.

Table 2. Upper three levels of semiotic ladder

Factors	Explanation [12]	In the context of interactive data visualization
Semantics	Meaning indicted by signs: the relationship between signs and objects	Do readers have a statistic or mathematics background to understand the algorithms for data analytics? What factors will readers mainly consider for measuring market?
Pragmatics	Intentions of readers to make sense of the dataset	What is the motivation(s) for readers to interpret the visual representations? What is the business purposes?
Social world	Context or environment where some factors might impact readers' focus and interpretation of visual representations	Based on what a reader can recognise, what are the major social and environmental factors which might impact on readers' opinions or focus? E.g. corporate strategy, tones from the top

2.3   Abduction

Tan and Liu [3] state that the process of developing data visualization can be depicted as a shared semiosis where the visual representation is used as a carrier to facilitate the communication between the producers and readers. Not only is it focusing on the artefact which carries the visual representation in the final stage, but also focusing on the process where a reader interprets the visualization. Also, norm centric activities where norm can be used as a powerful tool to help make producers and document readers' aware of theexplicit and implicit demands of the various levels of interpreting.

Thus, this research, inspired by the three principles from Liu [14], is intended to construct a framework for producing data visualization, especially empowering readers to implement abductive reasoning, guiding producers to place interactive functions based on norms and specifying the process of developing data visualization to steps.

The concept of abduction can be traced back to Peirce, 1930s, which can be demonstrated in semiosis where people explore signs with their prior knowledge, spots new (unmatched patterns with their prior knowledge) and refine the prior knowledge by proposing new propositions and hypothesis which might result in further actions, e.g. further discovery by other means [18]. Dubois and Gadde [19] claim that abduction can be used as an approach to push creativity and help the reader form a proposition by making sense of what They have observed and how it differs from their own understanding. Other than abduction, induction and deduction are two other main-stream reasoning processes.

In contrast, deduction encourages people to extract the logical conclusion from the prior theories, to form new hypotheses and propositions, and to test them in the form of empirical study. Induction follows the opposite way compared with deduction [20]. Instead of obtaining knowledge from prior literature, induction will guide people to generalize a theoretical form based on an observation [21].

Different from induction and deduction, the method of abduction supports humans to develop or refine their knowledge by systematizing the creativity and intuition into their logic reasoning process [22]. The factors, such as prior knowledge and context, is also recognized to be influencedby the people's understanding, instead of purely relying on what people can observe in the empirical study [23]. Therefore, the aim of abduction is more than to spot the difference between empirical studies and prior understanding, but also tounderstand the new phenomenon and re-frame the prior knowledge based on the fresh inputs.

3   Constructing a Process for Developing Interactive Data Visualization

In this research the logical reasoning process of abduction can be depicted as follows, consisting of 5 steps (Fig. 1).

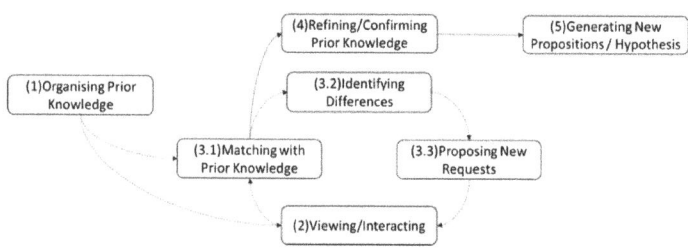

Fig. 1. Abductive process of developing data visualization

3.1   Step One: Capturing and Organizing Readers' Prior Knowledge

Stemmed from the framework of the semiotic ladder, readers' interpretant of signs can be influenced by their prior knowledge (semantic level), intentions (pragmatic level) and social context (social world level). Also, based on the concept of abduction, readers always intend to observe any phenomenon with a series of hypotheses generated from their prior knowledge. Thus, during the primary stages of developing the concept of data visualization, producers are encouraged to grasp readers' requirements and prior understanding by incorporating six interrogatives [24]. It is only when after these interrogatives have been considered that further investigations can take place as a way of guiding the design of interactive functions.

3.2   Step Two: Viewing the Initial Data Visualization

Based on the information obtained from the previous step and dataset available on hand, the producer can draft the initial version of data representation and present it to the user. The user can then have the initial view of the data representation and try to extract the demanded information. The design of interactive function at this stage is based on the initial input of users' demand and data availability. Thus, the user can explore the dataset based on its initial understanding.

3.3   Step Three: Entering Iteration Loop

Once readers have found that the information revealed from the initial data visualization is different from their prior understanding, the readers might enter into an iterative process (Sects. 3.1, 3.2 and 3.3), in which they can request further questions based on their information demands to interpret the differences.

Based on the observation in step two, readers would compare the information derived from viewing the data visualization with their prior knowledge (Sect. 3.1). In other words, they will compare what they have seen from the visualization with what they have understood from their prior experience and identify the differences (Sect. 3.2), where they can further address new questions related to data visualization by its interactive functions (Sect. 3.3).

3.4   Step Four: Refining the Prior Knowledge

Through continuously addressing different information demands, readers will eventually be able to gain an in-depth understanding of the domain question(s). They can then add the information learnt via the interaction with data visualization into the prior knowledge, and generate a new understanding for the specific domain questions, which can then guide their behaviors.

3.5   Step Five: Generating New Hypothesis

After refining the prior understanding, the readers can further generate a new proposition for their domain questions, which can be further articulated to be a solution for the domain questions they raised up at the very beginning. Also, the readers might generate a further hypothesis which can be tested in the reality or in different scenarios. By this way, they might enter another abductive process by other means to further refine their knowledge.

4   Illustrative Case Study: Market Attractiveness Analysis

In this research, an analysis of global market attractiveness of energy drink industry will be referred to as an illustrative case study. The key domain question raised up by the target readers is to identify the most attractive market(s) to develop a new brand of energy drink, and they expect the delivery to be able to reveal the answer by graphics that they can easily understand. Thus, this case study illustrates all 5 steps of the abductive process of developing interactive data visualization.

4.1   Step One: Capturing and Organizing Readers' Prior Knowledge

A semi-structured interview with the target readers takes place at the very beginning of capturing the initial requests of developing data visualization. Information obtained from the interview will be mapped based on the framework of six interrogations, and then migrate to the 3rd-level of the semiotic framework.

4.2   Step Two: Viewing the Initial Data Visualization

Based on the information obtained in step one, two bar charts are drawn-up for fulfilling the initial information requests – showing the market with the highest/lowest sales and volume. The advantage of bar charts, is that it enables readers to easily compare the data by bar length and to identify the highest/lowest data by ordering.

After viewing the initial presentation of data visualization, the target readers confirm some of their initial hypothesis, by focusing on countries with a high population, which as a result will allow for an increase in sales and volume. These countries include China, Japan and the United States. However, they also discovered that the information differed from the prior experience. For example, some markets like Brazil and UAE might not rank high in terms of sales butranked in the top tier of sales due to the high unit price.

4.3   Step Three: Entering in Iteration Loop

Based on the questions generated from the initial view of data visualization in step two, the target readers enter the iterative loop where they can address further requests for information based on their new hypothesis. A round of interviews took place to allow the target readers to compare the information from data visualization and prior experience, to articulate the specific gaps and to reveal more details of their new requests and hypotheses. During the interview, the target readers expressed the idea of taking more variables from the non-sales aspects into the measurement of market attractiveness, since an attractive market should not merely be identified by the sales data in a short period. Instead, incorporating non-sales data might help reveal a view of long-term market development.

4.4   Step Four: Refining the Prior Knowledge

Once the target readers find the data visualization provides sufficient information for them to justify the prior hypothesis, they decided to end the iteration and tried to refine the prior understanding. The information grasped from the data visualization would be added to the prior knowledge. For example, the target readers had thought to put the focus on the western European market since it seems to be a mature market. However, with the aid of data visualization, they found that the new brand is likely to be launched in Brazil and the Middle East. The reason for this being is that there tends to less competitiveness, which lends itself to more room for a new brand to set up and grow. Also, instead of merely focusing on a single market, Hub-and-Spoke can be considered to apply in Middle Eastern markets since some similarities can be found on data patterns of their energy drink consumption and market competition, e.g. setting UAE as the Hub and gradually expand the brand influence on its neighbor countries (spokes) via a new fashion.

4.5   Step Five: Generating New Hypotheses

During the final step, a workshop took place to finalize the interactive data visualization based on documents of all hypothesis and information requests provided by the target readers. The format of 'context-content-conclusion' has been used for the final presentation, which can demonstrate the key questions and hypothesis (context), the filtered data in a graphic format with interactive function (content), and summary of data pattern (conclusion). The target readers can take the interactive data visualization as an input to their business strategy formation or a document to provoke a discussion of strategic decision.

5   Discussion and Conclusion

This paper portrays an abductive process of developing interactive data visualization, where different mechanisms have been used to facilitate the communication and interoperation between producers and target readers. The information demands from target readers have been be analyzed by different levels based on the semiotic framework, including semantic, pragmatic and social levels. Also, the iteration loop allows target readers to continuously address the requests for more information to justify their hypothesis, which can be documented and analysed in the format of the norm and eventually lead the design of interactive functions. In the end, a case study of global market attractiveness analysis has been used to illustrate the proposed process of developing interactive data visualization.

In terms of contributions of this research, it further develops the statement from [3] - visualization as a process of abduction, by demonstrating a detailed process where visualization producers can capture targets' multi-level information demands and elicit them into the design of interactive function. Also, by further developing the idea of enabling the interoperation between producers and readers, the iteration loop enables both two parties to continuously synergize the understanding of information request, targets', purposes, and potential influence from the corporate strategy (social environment). [26]

However, there are two limitations which should be addressed in order to inspire further studies. Firstly, this research does not set criteria to measure the satisfaction of target readers about fulfilling their information demands. Without the criteria, the target readers might be trapped by 'confirmation bias' where they think they might have had sufficient information but actually, this is not the case [25]. Therefore, the following research can further work on specifying the criteria for measuring readers' satisfaction of information fulfilment. Secondly, this research does not compare the proposed process with the traditional way of developing visualization from the readers' perspective about the extent in which the new process helped them understand data better than the traditional approach. Thus, a comparative research between the abductive process and non-abductive process of developing interactive data visualization should be conducted to justify the helpfulness of the abductive process.

References

1. Chen, M., Ebert, D., Hagen, H., et al.: Data, information, and knowledge in visualization. Comput. Graph Appl. IEEE **29**, 12–19 (2009). https://doi.org/10.1109/tvcg.2010.179
2. Segel, E., Heer, J.: Narrative visualization: telling stories with data. Vis. Comput. Graph **16** (6), 1139–1148 (2010). https://doi.org/10.1109/TVCG.2010.179
3. Liu, K., Tan, C.: Semiotics in visualisation. In: 16th International Conference on Enterprise Information Systems, ICEIS 2014, Lisbon, Portugal, pp. 5–7 (2015)
4. Tableau: Visual Analysis Best Practices, p. 41 (2014)
5. Gartner: Magic quadrant for business intelligence and analytics platforms, pp. 1–126. Gartner (2017). https://doi.org/10.1017/cbo9781107415324.004
6. Shneiderman, B.: The eyes have it: a task by data type taxonomy for information visualizations. In: Proceedings of the 1996 IEEE Symposium Visual Language, pp. 336–343 (1996). https://doi.org/10.1109/vl.1996.545307
7. Strecker, J.: Data visualization in review: summary. In: Evaluating IDRC results-communicating research for influence, IDRC (2012). https://idlbnc.idrc.ca/dspace/bitstream/10625/49286/1/IDL-49286.pdf

8. SAS: Data visualization: making big data approachable and valuable. Whitepaper, Source IDG Research Services, April 2012

9. Wang, Y., Liu, D., Qu, H., et al.: A guided tour of literature review: facilitating academic paper reading with narrative visualization. In: Proceedings of the 9th International Symposium Visual Information Communication Interact - VINCI 2016, pp. 17–24 (2016). https://doi.org/10.1145/2968220.2968242

10. Stamper, R.K.: Information, Organisation and Technology: Studies in Organisational Semiotics. Springer, Boston (2001). https://doi.org/10.1007/978-1-4615-1655-2

11. Liu, K., Li, W.: Organisational Semiotics for Business Informatics. Taylor & Francis, London (2014)

12. Stamper, R., Liu, K., Hafkamp, M., Ades, Y.: Understanding the roles of signs and norms in organizations - a semiotic approach to information systems design. Behav. Inf. Technol. **19**, 15–27 (2000). https://doi.org/10.1080/014492900118768

13. Friendly, M.: Brief history of data visualization. Handbook of Data Visualization. Springer Handbooks of Computational Statistics, pp. 15–56. Springer, Berlin (2006). https://doi.org/10.1007/978-3-540-33037-0_2

14. Liu, K., Tan, C.: Semiotics in digital visualisation. In: Cordeiro, J., Hammoudi, S., Maciaszek, L., Camp, O., Filipe, J. (eds.) ICEIS 2014. LNBIP, vol. 227, pp. 3–13. Springer, Cham (2015). https://doi.org/10.1007/978-3-319-22348-3_1

15. Stamper, R.K.: Information in Business and Administrative Systems. Wiley, New York (1973)

16. Tufte, E.R.: Envisioning Information. Graphics Press, Cheshire (2001)

17. Chi, E.H., Riedl, J.T.: An operator interaction framework for visualization systems. In: 1998 Proceedings of the IEEE Symposium on Information Visualization, pp. 63–70 (1998)

18. Kovács, G., Spens, K.M.: Abductive reasoning in logistics research. Int. J. Phys. Distrib. Logist. Manag. **35**, 132–144 (2005). https://doi.org/10.1108/09600030510590318

19. Dubois, A., Gadde, L.E.: Systematic combining: an abductive approach to case research. J. Bus. Res. **55**, 553–560 (2002). https://doi.org/10.1016/S0148-2963(00)00195-8

20. Ho, Y.C.: Abduction? Deduction? Induction? Is there a logic of exploratory data analysis? In: Proceedings of the Annual Meeting American Educational Research Association, p. 28 (1994). http://citeseerx.ist.psu.edu/viewdoc/download?doi=10.1.1.135.3507&rep=rep1&type=pdf

21. Sowa, J.F.: Knowledge Representation: Logical, Philisophical, and Computational Foundations, p. 594. Brooks/Cole, Belmont (2000)

22. Kolko, J.: Abductive thinking and sensemaking: the drivers of design synthesis. Des. Issues **26**, 15–28 (2010). https://doi.org/10.1162/desi.2010.26.1.15

23. Arrighi, C., Ferrario, R.: Abductive Reasoning, pp. 1–16. Interpretation and Collaborative Processes. Kluwer Academic Publishers, Dordrecht (2005)

24. Tan, C., Liu, K.: An organisational semiotics inspired information architecture: pervasive healthcare as a case study. In: ICISO 2013 - Proceedings of the 14th International Conference Informatics Semiotics Organisation IFIP WG81 Work Conference, pp. 35–44 (2013)

25. Kodagoda, N., Attfield, S., Wong, B.L., et al.: Using interactive visual reasoning to support sense-making: implications for design. IEEE Trans. Vis. Comput. Graph **19**, 2217–2226 (2013). https://doi.org/10.1109/TVCG.2013.211

26. Li, Q., Liu, K.: Interactive data visualisation: facilitate the accountability disclosure through the lens of organisational semiotics. In: International Conference on Informatics and Semiotics in Organisations, pp. 133–142. Springer, (2016)

Local Government Open Data (LGOD) Initiatives: Analysis of Trends and Similarities Among Early Adopters

Eric Afful-Dadzie[(✉)] [iD] and Anthony Afful-Dadzie [iD]

OMIS Department, University of Ghana Business School, LG 78, Accra, Ghana
{eafful-dadzie, aafful-dadzie}@ug.edu.gh

Abstract. This paper focuses on developments of open government data (OGD) at city, municipal, county, federal state, regional and provincial levels around the world. This is in line with recent OGD trends where local government authorities, especially in developed countries, are launching separate OGD web portals to complement central governments' efforts at liberating public data. Focusing on early LGOD adopters, an inventory audit of contents and functionalities in use at LGOD web portals was conducted. The data generated was analyzed for trends and (dis)similarities among early LGOD adopters. The results of the study points to a general sense of heterogeneity among LGODs across the world in terms of adherence to OGD web publishing standards. There is also a lack of uniformity in terms of OGD web portal functionalities and contents even among local government authorities within a same country.

Keywords: Open government data (OGD)
Local government open data (LGOD) · Open data · Early adopters
Clustering

1 Introduction

Though relatively new, there is a growing interest in Open Government Data (OGD) from governments, civil society groups, the media, researchers, among others. OGD which primarily seeks the liberation of government controlled data, began with President Obama's open data initiative of 2009 and was subsequently strengthened by the 2013 G8 Open Data Charter [1–3]. These initiatives sought to encourage countries to make open and for free, public data to the citizenry. To further facilitate the adoption of OGD, the Open Government Partnership (OGP) was created to bring together countries that have affirmed their willingness to provide easy and free access to public data. Typically, countries are admitted as members of OGP when they submit to a number of processes including, formal expression of interest by heads of sovereign states, endorsement of open government declaration, submission of a country action plan and finally, a commitment to an independent reporting mechanism. Member countries are then expected to launch an OGD web portal as a public data repository. Both the initial processes together with the opening of OGD web portals, often occur at the instance of central governments. That is to say that, central government politicians and administrators are often the visible faces in these OGD projects. Such roles played

© IFIP International Federation for Information Processing 2018
Published by Springer International Publishing AG 2018. All Rights Reserved
K. Liu et al. (Eds.): ICISO 2018, IFIP AICT 527, pp. 299–308, 2018.
https://doi.org/10.1007/978-3-319-94541-5_30

by central governments have partly made central government open data (COGD) the main focus, often at the neglect of other variants.

Recently however, local governments through cities, municipalities, counties, federal states, regions and provinces have been launching their own independently operated OGD web portals. This is welcoming, since it complements central governments' efforts at releasing public data to entrench democracy and spur economic growth and innovation among citizens [4]. The idea of an independently-run local government open data (LGOD) is fast gaining momentum especially in the developed world. For instance, as of 2016, there are as many as 290 local authorities comprising of cities, counties, federal states, regions and provinces that are actively running independent OGD web portals at their local administrative levels. It must be noted that though central governments' role in OGD is crucial, local governments are the real policy actors when it comes to both the supply and demand sides of OGD implementation. This is true since most public datasets are first generated at the level of local authorities or agencies, while a functional OGD system also assists local governments to transform service deliveries through significant cost savings and regular evaluation of local services performance [5, 6]. This helps to actualize the value creation potential of OGD. We therefore argue in this paper, that an equal measure of attention should be given to local government open data (LGOD) as given to central government open data (CGOD). To generate more research and advocacy interests in LGODs, this paper focuses on activities of LGOD early adopters around the world. The paper first audits technical standards in use at LGOD web portals around the world. Data derived from the web content and functionalities audit are analyzed for trends and (dis)similarities among early local government-based OGD adopters.

Though researchers continue to report on OGD activities and initiatives at the level of central governments, very few works have focused on local government open data initiatives. None of the few published works on LGODs comprehensively reviews technical features of web portals for trends and similarities. The closest works in terms of the OGD web audit approach, came from [7, 8]. The work by Chatfield and Reddick audited open data portals of twenty local governments in some of Australia's large cities. In [8], an audit of the content and functionalities of OGD web portals in seven countries in Africa was conducted. The work by [9], looked at the quality of open data web portals but only focused on CGODs. Similarly, [10] also looked at open data at local government levels but focused on determining factors that influence the success or failure of open data initiatives. This paper fills the gap by auditing web portals of 'independent' LGOD early adopters and further analyze the data to glean vital information regarding trends and (dis)similarities among them.

2   Methodology

The methodology is divided into two stages. In the first stage, an inventory audit of LGOD web portals was carried out benchmarked against widely accepted technical standards for publication of OGD. Two of such technical recommendations come from the World Wide Web Consortium (W3C) authored by [11] and the World Bank's open data toolkit [12]. In the second part, the data generated from the inventory audit was analyzed using association rules mining and K-Means clustering techniques to determine frequent trends and natural groups among the early LGOD adopters. The following sections present brief introduction to the audit and the techniques used in the analysis.

Table 1. Attribute selection for inventory strategy.

	Feature	Audit strategy
LGOD web portal content and services	Data format	Open government data requires public organizations to publish data in a form that is easily accessible by data users. In particular, the W3C and the World Bank strongly recommend that public data are published in machine-readable non-proprietary electronic format. Non-proprietary machine-readable data formats ensure easy access and processing by data users. In the audit however, most web portals were found to provide both non-proprietary and some proprietary formats. Some of the common list of data formats audited were RDF, CSV, PDF, XLX(S), JSON, XML, KML, GeoJSON, ODS/ODF etc.
	Metadata	This is one of the essential OGD publication features which requires public organizations to accompany datasets with relevant information that describe the dataset. Some relevant metadata features could be the publication date of data, author attribution, and unit of measurements of data attributes among others. The audit checked for the presence or otherwise of metadata on LGOD web portals by randomly scanning through 5 datasets on each subject (category)
	Data currentness	Here, the audit sought to find the age of the most current data published on the portal. If the latest data is less than 30days old, it is regarded in this research as "current". However, if the latest dataset is more than 30 d old, then it regarded as "not current". In the data collection, LGOD portals exhibiting current datasets were assigned the code 1 while a 0 for not current data sets
	Data visualization	Another requirement of OGD web portals is the provision of a data visualization tool. Such tools help data users to preview datasets before download. Visualization features come in various forms including tables, graphs, maps etc. The audit strategy checked whether the OGD portals provided this feature in the design or not. If this functionality was provided, the local authority is a 1 in the data collection stage. However, if not available, it is assigned a 0
	Data search	This OGD attribute seeks a data functionality that makes it easier for users to search specific information. Supported by the W3C and the World Bank, OGD web portals are expected to be searched by data types, subject and organization. The audit looked for the presence of this feature and scored a 1 for availability and a 0 for a non-availability of the functionality

(continued)

Table 1. (*continued*)

	Feature	Audit strategy
LGOD web portal functionalities	Links to external sites	OGD web portals are additionally required to embed links to external data sources. This serves as a guide to data users to access related data stored on other public servers. If an OGD web portal does not have an ownership right to a data, providing the external link aids data users to access it on a platform that holds the valid license
	Social media integration	This World Bank Technical Option recommends the integration of social media plugins in OGD web portals. This in line with contemporary ways of engaging with people, ensures that users are able to share their views, experiences and general concerns on the web platform to be subsequently addressed. The feature therefore checks for the inclusion of at least one social media plugin. If this criterion is satisfied, the value 1 is assigned, otherwise a 0 indicates an absence
	License	The World Bank's technical option on open data stipulates that OGD web portals display license for each dataset. In view of this, this feature checks for the existence of an open data license on the web platform. Typically, most OGD portals are licensed either under Creative Commons or the open data license. Some other standards are used by some LGODs

2.1   Data Collection - LGOD Web Portal Audit Criteria

Attributes used in the study as shown in Table 1 were guided by requirements put forward by the W3C and the World Bank regarding OGD web data publication. Some common standards shared by the two bodies are (1) the need for datasets to be released or published in their raw forms (2) a metadata supplied for each dataset (3) data to be published in machine-readable, non-proprietary electronic formats such as CSV, JSON, XML, KML etc. (4) an open license to be provided by each data web portals and (5) a data visualization tool to guide data users. The criteria (attributes) for the audit were divided broadly into two categories namely; web portal contents and functionalities and are shown in Table 1. This approach is similar to the one used in [8]. The list of local authorities (cities, counties, municipals, federal states, regions and provinces) were collected from open government data U.S. (https://www.data.gov/open-gov/) and Data Portals (http://dataportals.org/search). In all, 288 local governments were identified as operating independent OGD web portals different from their national portal. In this paper, local administrations around the world that have shown early interest in LGOD are classified as early adopters. During the web portal audit, about 15 LGODs were found to have nonfunctional Uniform Resource Locators (URLs) and therefore could not be accessed. This brought the total number of LGOD portals studied in this paper to 273. The data collection period was from November, 2016 to March, 2017. A web content analysis was carried out to determine how each local government authority faired on each of the criteria. To this effect, the web portal of each LGOD was examined to identify the features outlined in Table 1. Most of the functions and content of the portals were identified on the home page through visual examination. However, some required a thorough search through all the web pages as well as the html source codes to ascertain the presence or the absence of the feature in question. If a criterion is available on the web portal, the feature was assigned 1 to indicate its presence, otherwise, the feature was assigned a 0 to mean an absence.

2.2 K-Means Clustering

Clustering methods partition data points into homogenous groups called clusters. The K-Means clustering is an unsupervised algorithm that seeks to detect natural groups in unlabeled data. The term unlabeled is used to mean data that does not have pre-defined output [13]. In K-Means, the number of clusters are typically chosen apriori – meaning clustering intends to partition n objects into k clusters in which each object belongs to the cluster with the nearest mean. The goal of this algorithm is to find groups in the data, with the number of groups represented by the variable K. The algorithm works iteratively to assign each data point to one of K groups based on feature similarity. The rationale behind the use of the K-Means algorithm in this study was to find LGOD early adopters who share similar features in web content and functionality and to further determine whether they are in the same country or otherwise. The next section presents research questions to help elicit the right answers from the study.

3 Research Questions

The following research questions were used to guide the study. The questions are further analyzed in the result section.

RQ1. What are the global trends as far as local government open data initiatives are concerned?

RQ2. Which cities, federal states or provinces fall into unique natural groups and why?

RQ3. What do the similarities and dissimilarities among early LGOD adopters say about local government adherence to OGD web publication standards?

4 Results

This section provides answers to research question 1, which sought to understand the global trends as far as local government open data initiatives are concerned. Currently, as of 2016, there are about 27 sovereign countries around the world where local government authorities have launched completely separate OGD portals that are different from what their central governments operate. Conveniently referred to as 'early adopters' in this study, majority of them are in the U.S., Canada, Italy, Spain, United Kingdom, France and Australia (See Fig. 1). There are however three LGOD adopters in South America (Brazil, Argentina and Chile) and in Asia (Taiwan, South Korea and China). No African city or region is currently implementing an OGD web portal separate from its country-level portal as of the time of this paper. Preliminary audit report as seen in Fig. 1 shows that, the U.S. and Canada are currently the leading implementers of LGODs in the world.

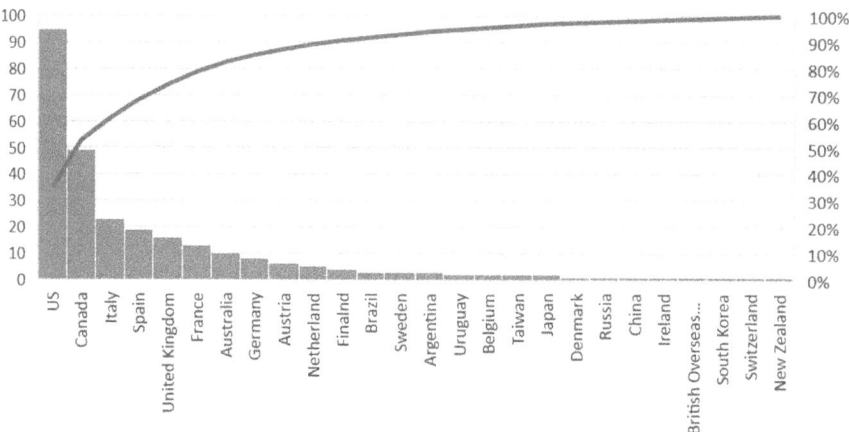

Fig. 1. Country representations of early LGOD adopters.

For instance, out of the 273 early LGOD implementers in the study, the US accounts for 95 of them, representing 34.8% while Canada accounts for 49 representing 17.95% as. The study further classified the early LGOD adopters into two main groups; cities/towns/counties on one hand, and provinces/federal states/regions onanother. The classification which was simply based on size and level of autonomy of the local administration, found 73 LGODs belonging to the category of provinces/federal states/regions while 195 of them were cities/towns/counties. In terms of content and functionalities provided on LGOD web platforms, the audit data showed that on the whole, most LGOD early adopters are providing adequate OGD web functionalities and content that meet most of the standards put forward by W3C and the World Bank. For instance, in terms of web functionalities, the study observed that most local authorities, representing 84.25% were providing data search features, 78.02% provided open data licenses and 63.7% had social media plugins integrated in their web portals. Similarly, in terms of web content, most LGODs representing 77.3% provided metadata to accompany datasets, 59.7% had up-to-date data sets and majority had a wide range of data formats on offer to help data users to easily access, share and redistribute data. In particular, it was observed that the most used data format on most LGOD web platforms was the comma separated value (CSV), which was present on 70.7% of the LGOD web portals audited. Other notable data formats heavily in use are XML, data APIs and JSON data formats as shown in Fig. 2. The use of the non-proprietary data formats is welcoming since it supports some of the ideals of OGD – to make public data progressively free and easily accessible. There are however other data formats that

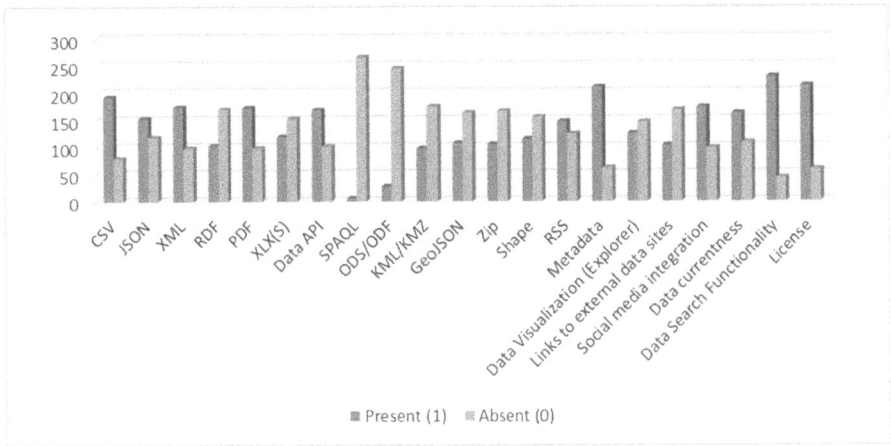

Fig. 2. Frequency count of web content and functionality features on LGOD portals

are not being giving much attention. For instance, majority of the LGODs were silent on geographical data formats such as GeoJSON, KML and shape files. The audit data further showed that, most of the geographical data formats were provided by local government authorities in Canada; mostly in the form of either KML of GeoJSON files. There were some equally important OGD web portal features that are not particularly being paid attention to. Some of these are data visualization (previews) and links to external data sites. These requirements are both suggested by the W3C and the World Bank as key to aiding data users in their search of public data. Data visualization for instance ensures that the user previews the data with graphical tools before download. In spite of some of the short comings with LGOD web portals, there is a general satisfiable trend by most of the early adopters to adhere to the international standards for publishing OGD. Overall, the level of adherence to international standards as far as LGOD's are concerned can be described as high.

The analysis further focused on detecting natural groups or clusters within the LGOD early adopters as stipulated in RQ2. The study sought four groups ($k = 4$) in the data, separately for OGD content and OGD functionalities. In all, there were 73 LGODs in cluster 1, 63 in cluster 2, 66 in cluster 3 and 71 in cluster 4. The U.S. and Canada dominated in all the clusters contributing a total of 94 and 49 local government authorities out of the 273 in our study.

Overall, LGODs in clusters 3 and 4 respectively provide the most OGD features in terms of content and functionalities. Contributing to 16.67% of the local authorities in cluster 3, Canada leads in terms of the provision of OGD content benchmarked in the study. The U.S., Spain, Italy and France follow Canada in cluster 3. Similarly, in cluster 4, the U.S. contributes to about 63.4% of the total LGODs, and therefore provides far richer OGD functionalities and services than all other countries observed in the study. Canada, Italy, Spain and France follow in that order in terms of OGD functionalities. Specific to OGD contents, the strength of LGODs in cluster 4 as shown in Fig. 3, is the provision of features such as metadata, non-proprietary data formats

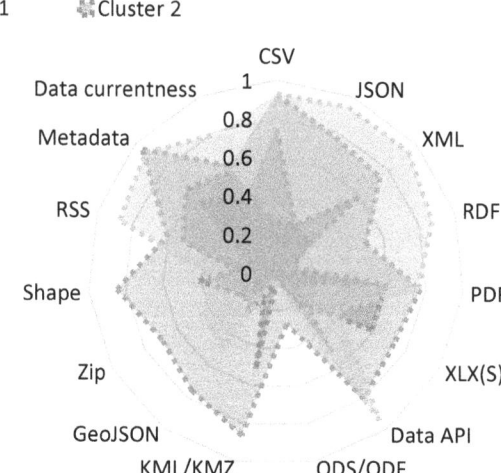

Fig. 3. Strength of LGODs in terms of OGD web contents

and current datasets. For instance, in terms of data formats, LGODs in cluster 4 provide most of the recommended non-proprietary formats such as CSV, JSON, XML, RDF, as well as RSS and data APIs. However, LGODs in cluster 3 of which Canada dominates, focus more on geographic data formats such as Shape, GoeJSON and KML/KMZ. Geographic data is increasingly becoming one of the sought after data on OGD web portals and therefore adequate provision of appropriate Geo data formats would ease access of such data. Though overall, the clustering shows that, LGODs in clusters 1 and 2 lag behind their counterparts in clusters 3 and 4, one significant observation seen in cluster 2, is the provision of the XLX(S) data format. This spreadsheet data format is proprietary, and therefore not recommended highly by OGD web publishing standards. In terms of provision of OGD web functionalities, clusters 3 and 4 again provided more OGD functionalities than the other clusters. For instance, the strength of LGODs in cluster 3 can be seen in the provision of open data licenses and links to external data sites. LGODs in cluster 4 on the other hand, provided more of data visualization and data search functionalities. LGODs in cluster 1 urged slightly above clusters 3 and 4 in terms of provision of social media integration plugins.

5   Discussion and Conclusion

The results of the LGOD web portal inventory audit give a general insight into the trends, relationships and similarities among LGOD implementers around the world. In terms of geographical distribution of LGODs, the apparent trend shows early adopters are mostly found in the global north. Significantly, North America represented only by the U.S. and Canada have a combined share of 41.4% of the total LGODs in the world. There are no cities, federal states, provinces or regions in Africa currently implementing the concept of a decentralized open government data. In Asia, one city each in

China and South Korea and two in Taiwan are the early LGOD implementers. In South America, Brazil leads in terms of the number of early LGODs, followed by Argentina and Uruguay. Front runners of LGODs in Europe are Italy, Spain, U.K, France, Germany, Austria, Netherland, Finland, Sweden and Belgium in the order of number of local authorities involved. Australia represents the Oceania as the only implementer of LGODs. The LGOD web audit afforded the opportunity to find clusters or natural groups into which LGOD early adopters belong. The clustering scheme though not meant to be a score card of performance of the LGODs, give an indication of the strength of each cluster in terms of which OGD features they provide to data users. This approach is to aid policy makers to support seemingly struggling LGODs in terms of technical support and resources. For instance, local authorities in cluster 1, lag far behind in terms of provision of standard OGD features. Therefore, though a welcoming attempt by local authorities in cluster 1, it is observed that they are not adhering to international OGD publishing standards. Such cities, towns, federal states, provinces etc. would need to be supported to attain the right standards. There is a general lack of uniformity by LGODs in terms of the content and features they publish for their data users. The seeming heterogeneity among LOGD web portals is affirmed by [9, 14]. For instance, even within the same country, the web template as well as the OGD features used tend to be different at the national, state and city levels. Apart from the U.S. which for the most part provides a common OGD web template for both its national as well as local authorities (federal states, cities, towns and counties), most of the 27 countries have their OGD web architecture different from their local authorities.

References

1. Tauberer, J.: History of the Movement. Open Government Data: The Book (2012). https://opengovdata.io/2014/history-the-movement/
2. Attard, J., Orlandi, F., Scerri, S., Auer, S.: A systematic review of open government data initiatives. Gov. Inf. Q. **32**(4), 399–418 (2015)
3. Castro, D., Korte, T.: Open Data in the G8: A Review of Progress on the Open Data Charter (2015). http://www.datainnovation.org/2015/03/open-data-in-the-g8. Accessed 25 Mar 2015
4. Janssen, M., Charalabidis, Y., Zuiderwijk, A.: Benefits, adoption barriers and myths of open data and open government. Inf. Syst. Manag. **29**(4), 258–268 (2012)
5. Rahily, L.: Innovation in Local Government: Open Data and Information Technology. McKinsey Publications, New York (2014)
6. Hammell, R.: Open data–driving growth, ingenuity and innovation. Deloitte White paper (2012)
7. Chatfield, A.T., Reddick, C.G.: A longitudinal cross-sector analysis of open data portal service capability: the case of Australian local governments. Gov. Inf. Q. **34**, 231–243 (2017)
8. Afful-Dadzie, E., Afful-Dadzie, A.: Open government data in Africa: a preference elicitation analysis of media practitioners. Gov. Inf. Q. **34**(2), 244–255 (2017)
9. Sáez Martín, A., Rosario, A.H.D., Pérez, M.D.C.C.: An international analysis of the quality of open government data portals. Soc. Sci. Comput. Rev. **34**(3), 298–311 (2016)

10. Susha, I., Zuiderwijk, A., Charalabidis, Y., Parycek, P., Janssen, M.: Critical factors for open data publication and use: a comparison of city-level, regional, and transnational cases. JeDEM-eJournal eDemocracy Open Gov. **7**(2), 94–115 (2015)
11. Bennett, D., Harvey, A.: Publishing Open Government Data. World Wide Web Consortium (2009). https://www.w3.org/TR/gov-data/
12. Herzog, T.: Technology Options for Open Government Data Platforms. World Bank Working paper (2014). http://opendatatoolkit.worldbank.org/en/technology.html
13. Rai, P., Singh, S.: A survey of clustering techniques. Int. J. Comput. Appl. **7**(12), 1–5 (2010)
14. Zuiderwijk, A., Janssen, M.: Open data policies, their implementation and impact: a framework for comparison. Gov. Inf. Q. **31**(1), 17–29 (2014)

Poster Papers

Information Systems Governance and Industry 4.0 - Epistemology of Data and Semiotics Methodologies of IS in Digital Ecosystems

Ângela Lacerda Nobre[1]([✉]), Rogério Duarte[2], and Marc Jacquinet[3]

[1] Escola Superior de Ciências Empresariais do Instituto Politécnico de Setúbal ESCE-IPS, Campus do IPS Estefanilha, 2910-761 Setúbal, Portugal
angela.nobre@esce.ips.pt
[2] Escola Superior de Tecnologia do Instituto Politécnico de Setúbal ESTS-IPS, Campus do IPS, Estefanilha, 2910-761 Setúbal, Portugal
rogerio.duarte@estsetubal.ips.pt
[3] Universidade Aberta Rua da Escola Politécnica, 141-147, 1269-001 Lisbon, Portugal
mjacquinet@uab.pt

Abstract. Contemporary Information Systems management incorporates the need to make explicit the links between semiotics, meaning-making and the digital age. This focus addresses, at its core, pure rationality, that is, the capacity of human interpretation and of human inscription upon reality. Creating the new real, that is the motto. Humans are intrinsically semiotic creatures. Consequently, semiotics is not a choice or an option but something that works like a second skin, establishing limits and permeable linkages between: (i) human thought and human's infinite world of imagination; and (ii) human action, with its correspondent infinite world of intentionality, of desire and of unexplored possibilities. Two instances are contrasted as two reading lenses of current business reality: IS governance and industry 4.0. These phenomena correspond to the need to take accountability, transparency and responsibility into account, when designing IS and when using such systems through the ecology of connectivity, Big Data and the Internet of Things. Political, social and cultural dimensions are brought into the equation, when addressing the question of the relevance and adequateness of IS theory and practice to respond to contemporary challenges. The message is that what has already been achieved is but a shadow, a pale vision, of what might be achieved in the age of the new Renaissance.

Keywords: Semiotic learning · Social semiotics · Material phenomenology
Poetic rationality · Data epistemology

1 Epistemology of Data and Semiotics

Challenging times call for challenging thought and action. The multitude of factors involved in addressing the relationship between technology and society is paramount. Semiotics enables addressing such complexity because semiotics analysis captures the

K. Liu et al. (Eds.): ICISO 2018, IFIP AICT 527, pp. 311–312, 2018.
https://doi.org/10.1007/978-3-319-94541-5

value chain of signification and of meaning-making (Nobre 2007). Artificial Intelligence (AI) is a central knowledge area to take into account in order to situate, position and interpret contemporary societies. From understanding the power of AI it is possible to acknowledge the need for semiotic-based information systems' theories, such as Ronald Stamper's Organisational Semiotics (OS).

Bernard Stiegler and Bruno Bachimont (1996) are interesting authors whose contributions have helped to understand the importance of the epistemology of data. There are four paradigms that help to explain current contexts, in terms of historical evolution: first, the empirical age, where meaning emerged from practice; second, the theoretical age, where meaning emerged from ideas, such as Descartes' contribution to modern science; third, the period between 1950 and 1990, forty years of development of applied calculus; and forth, the present age of data manipulation.

Pédauque (2006) addresses the role of documentation in the context of postmodernity. The digital world and its capacity to cut the connection to the heterogeneous nature of reality, is both its strength and its weakness. Whilst digital media agglomerates everything creating an homogeneous set of data, semiotics maintains the heterodox nature of reality, therefore it does not loose meaning neither the meaning-making capacity.

Epistemological and phenomenological perspectives are needed in order to trace, to map and to explore the different dimensions of the complexity of IS contexts. Baranauskas and Bonacin (2018) address the role of design and of its relation to signs. IS governance will be part of business leaders' agendas once the full impact of their power to bring much needed change at global level is understood. Issues related to sustainability and to human development have much to gain from IS engagement in social innovation and in global change. The digital era has found in manufacture a stronghold for the creation of new possibilities of human realization. Lu (2017) calls attention to the open research importance of industry 4.0. The core idea is that new categories of thought and action, new cognitive structures, are the product of technological evolution. Such technical change, visible through realities such as industry 4.0 or augmented reality, is understood as an enabler of human capacity to read, to interpret and to intervene upon the world. This new digital world is both a product of human endeavors and a process through which humans create new realities, the new real.

References

1. Bachimont, B.: Herméneutique matérielle et artéfacture. Thèse en épistémologie (1996)
2. Baranauskas, C., Bonacin, R.: Design: indicating through signs. Des. Issues **24**(3), 30–45 (2018). MIT Press
3. Lu, Y.: Industry 4.0: a survey on technologies, applications and open research issues. J. Ind. Inf. Integr. **6**, 1–10 (2017)
4. Nobre, A.L.: Knowledge processes and organizational learning. In: McInerney, C.R., Day, R.E. (eds.) Rethinking Knowledge Management. Information Science and Knowledge Management, vol. 12. Springer, Heidelberg (2007)
5. Pédauque, R.: Document et modernités. Version finale dite «Pédauque 3» (2006)

Value Co-creation and Local Content Development: Transformation, Digitalization and Innovation in the Oil and Gas Industry

Irina Heim$^{(\boxtimes)}$ (iD)

Henley Business School, University of Reading,
Whiteknights, Reading RG66UR, UK
i.heim@pgr.reading.ac.uk

Abstract. This study explains how the co-creation of value in networks can lead to technological upgrades in a local industry (local content development) through transformation of business processes, digitalization of drilling rigs and innovation in oil extraction in the oil and gas industry of Kazakhstan. Theoretical perspectives on local content development (LCD) are predominantly informed by economic and political perspectives. The aim of this paper is to develop a strategic perspective on LCD in clusters. This is qualitative research which uses a case study approach.

Keywords: Oil and gas industry · Value Co-creation
Local content development · Digitalization · Clusters

1 Introduction

The broad definition of local content policy (LCP) assumes that it is - "an industrial tool that can enable domestic producers to expand their activities, at least partially with domestic inputs, and gain access to international technological and managerial expertise... [in order to] enhance their competitiveness" [3, 4]. While literature on this topic is currently emerging, this research agenda is predominantly informed by economic and political perspectives, strategic perspectives are virtually absent [3]. This is in itself problematic, because the reason why LCPs may fail is that they are based on an insufficient understanding of stakeholders' strategies and interests. This paper fills this gap in theory by embracing the role of LCPs in technological upgrade. Technological upgrade is defined as increased organizational performance and competitiveness as a result of improved technology capabilities.

2 Collaborative Approach to LCP

Shapiro and Rabinowitz [5] provided an explanation for cooperative approach to regulation in economics, suggesting that collaborative techniques have to be combined with punishment. A collaborative approach to LCPs that defines the expectations of the government, while providing the international oil companies with flexibility to develop its own local content plans and procurement procedures can achieve greater results. The reason why companies collaborate is joint creation of value, or value co-creation. In the management literature, value co-creation is a paradigm that has emerged from the service management field, innovation management studies, and marketing and consumer research [1]. It states that organizations interact with each other for the development of new business opportunities. Purposeful interaction creates benefits – driving dialogue, learning, and resource transfer. Firms act as resource integrators, as specialization forces them to access existing knowledge, skills, competences, people, products, and available investment [2]. This interaction which technological platforms often mediate, leads to innovation, participation, and improved services [1]. Therefore, ICT technologies has effect on performance of local companies in the oil and gas cluster, a network of interconnected international and local companies, including small and medium enterprises, specialized suppliers, service providers, firms in related industries, associated institutions (universities, standard agencies, and trade associations), government and citizens that co-create value and develop local content through interactions and exchange of resources, technology and management skills with each other. The role of LCP is to support value co-creation in clusters. This can lead to the technological upgrade, i.e. organizational performance and competitiveness based on improved technology capabilities and further local content development.

References

1. Galvagno, M., Dalli, D.: Theory of value co-creation: a systematic literature review. Manag. Serv. Qual. **24**(6), 643–683 (2014)
2. Gummesson, E., Mele, C.: Marketing as value co-creation through network interaction and resource integration. J. Bus. Mark. Manage. **4**(4), 181–198 (2010)
3. Hansen, M.W.: Toward a strategic management perspective on local content in African extractives. In: Proceedings of 2017 EIBA Conference in Milan, 14–17 December (2017). http://openarchive.cbs.dk/handle/10398/9564
4. Kalyuzhnova, Y., Nygaard, C., Omarov, Y., Saparbayev, A.: Local content policies in resource-rich countries. Palgrave, London (2016)
5. Shapiro, S.A., Rabinowitz, R.S.: Punishment versus cooperation in regulatory enforcement: a case study of OSHA. Adm. Law Rev. **49**(4), 713–762 (1997)

The Interplay of FDI and R&D: A Study in the Seven Developed Countries

Yutong Li[(✉)]

University of Reading, Berkshire RG6 6AE, UK
y.li8@pgr.reading.ac.uk

Abstract. With the globalization process in the recent two decades, more and more countries are focusing on improving their technology to get more comparative advantages than other countries. The purpose of this paper is trying to explain the causality between foreign direct investment and R&D. We will analysis seven developed countries (Denmark, Finland, Ireland, Japan, the Netherland, the United Kingdom, and the United States) and use pooling data analysis to investigate this causality during the last 35 years.

Keywords: FDI · R&D · Developed countries

1 Introduction

The purpose of this poster paper is to investigate the causality of foreign direct investment and R&D in the developed countries. One of the motivations in the globalisation foreign direct investment, called knowledge, which means the company may separate their headquarters and R&D activities. For example, the headquarters may be in one market, but served the knowledge generated from another market. Therefore, the research question in this paper set as what is the role of research and development played in the foreign direct investment flow? More specifics of this research question could be if one country had high technology, whether that country would like to produce new products in their own country and to attract foreign country investment inward flow; or this country will 'sell' this new technology and conduct investment into other countries?

For example, the United States had the latest technology in the world, which makes it has a more comparative advantage than other countries. Thus, the United States could conduct investment into other countries in some specific area, like agriculture and labour-intensive industry. Therefore, there is a mutual partner relationship between the United States and the other countries. The same situation also could exist in the other nations. We use seven developed countries as an example to estimate if there is a significant relationship between foreign direct investment and local R&D activities.

2 Pooling Data Analysis

Table 1 indicates a brief regression result in individual countries, which is including three pair relationships between, FDI, local R&D activities, and economic growth. According to the Table, the first causality is about the FDI inward flows and R&D.

© IFIP International Federation for Information Processing 2018
Published by Springer International Publishing AG 2018. All Rights Reserved
K. Liu et al. (Eds.): ICISO 2018, IFIP AICT 527, pp. 315–317, 2018.
https://doi.org/10.1007/978-3-319-94541-5

Table 1. Regression result in seven countries

Country	FDIN to RD	RD to FDIN	FDIO to RD	RD to FDIO	GDP to RD	RD to GDP
Denmark	−	+	+*	−	+	+
Finland	+	+	+***	+***	−	−
Ireland	−*	−	−	+	+	+
Japan	−	−	−	+	−	−
Netherland	+	+***	+**	−	−	−***
The United Kingdom	+	−***	−	−*	−	−***
The United States	+	−	−**	−***	+*	−***

* p < 0.1, ** p < 0.05, *** p < 0.01

In Ireland, FDI inward flows shows a significant negative influence on its R&D. That means in Ireland if they hold a high technology, the most thing they would like do is to conduct foreign investment in the developing country, which is their efficiency seeking motivation, rather than attract foreign investment from another developed country. On the other hand, the R&D in the Netherland displays a positive effect of FDI inward flows, but an antagonistic relationship in the United Kingdom.

For the second causality between FDI outward flows and R&D activities, in Finland, which illustrate a complementary relationship and also they have a positive influence on each other. That means the government prefer to spend more money on their innovation and to improve their unique technology, to have a comparative advantage; rather than conduct foreign investment into other countries. For the last causality, there is only one country, the United States, indicates the economic growth will support the R&D development. However, on the other side of this relationship, local R&D activities show a significant negative influence on GDP growth, which has the same result as the pooling data regression. Again, it has proved that in the short-run, the government could not get benefit from R&D Department.

3   Conclusion

In this paper, we have analyzed the relationship between foreign direct investment and technology in seven developed countries. In general, according to the pooling data regression (See Table 1), there is a bi-direction relationship between FDI flows and technology. However, the technology has a diminishing changed effect for both FDI inward flows and outward flows, which mean the technology, will not support FDI flows after few years. In another word, because the renewal of technology, the government have to update their technology frequently, to keep the high competition and comparative advantage in the global market.

References

1. Annan-Dlab, F., Filippalos, F.: Multinational firms' motivations and foreign direct investment decisions: an analysis of the software and IT and financial services sectors in the irish context. Thunderbird Int. Bus. Rev. **59**(6), 739–755 (2017)
2. Barrell, R., Pain, N.: Foreign direct investment, technological change, and economic growth within Europe. Econ. J. **107**, 1770–1786 (1997)
3. Choong, C.: Does domestic financial development enhance the linkages between foreign direct investment and economic growth? Empir. Econ. **42**, 819–834 (2012)
4. Harding, T., Javorcik, B.: foreign direct investment and export upgrading. Rev. Econ. Stat. **94**(4), 961–980 (2012)
5. Hymer, H.: The International Operations of Nation Firm: A Study of Direct Foreign Investment. Cambridge (1976)
6. Luiz, R., De Mello.: Foreign direct investment-led growth: evidence from time series and panel data. Am. Econ. Rev. **89**(3), 379–399 (1999)
7. Pradhan, R., Arvin, M., Bahmani, S., Bennett, S.: The innovation-growth link in OECD countries: could other macroeconomic variables matter? Technol. Soc. **51**, 113–123 (2017)
8. Tahir, M., Khan, I., Shah, A.: Foreign remittances, foreign direct investment, foreign imports and economic growth in Pakistan: a time series analysis. Arab Econ. Bus. J. **10**, 82–89 (2015)
9. Wooldridge, J.: Introductory Econometrics: A Modern Approach. United States: South-Western. Cengage Learning (2010)

The Pattern of Foreign Direct Investment and International Trade: A Study of 30 OECD Countries from 1981 to 2015

Yutong Li[✉]

University of Reading, Berkshire RG6 6AE, UK
y.li8@pgr.reading.ac.uk

Abstract. This paper is a macroeconomic study investigating the causality of foreign direct investment and international trade. The research is based on 30 OECD countries from 1981 to 2015 and using data collected from official annual time series data. To interpret the causality in each country, we added six country profile factors to cooperate analysis whether different country profile factors would change the causality. The main findings indicate that there is a bi-direction always exists if the country has either pure high-ranking level of all the country profile factors or they have a pure of the low ranking level of country profile factors.

Keywords: FDI · International trade · OECD

1 Introduction

The primary purpose of this working paper is to measure the causality of foreign direct investment and international trade: whether they are 'complementary' to each other, or they could 'substitute' for each other. We will analysis 30 countries in OECD by using vector autoregression model; the endogenous variables of VAR model consist of FDI inward, FDI outward, export, import; and the exogenous variable in this model will be GDP at a constant price in 2005. To interpret the relationship between foreign direct investment and international trade, we will separate it into two parts: one is to analyze the effect of global trade on FDI, and the other one is to measure the impact of FDI on international trade. There will be four key relationships are including the effect of import on FDI inward, the impact of FDI inward on import, the effect of export on FDI outward, and the effect of FDI outward on export. The model will use in the paper showed below:

$$
\begin{pmatrix} FDIN_t \\ FDIO_t \\ X_t \\ M_t \end{pmatrix} = C \begin{pmatrix} \phi_{11} \\ \phi_{21} \\ \phi_{31} \\ \phi_{41} \end{pmatrix} + \prod \begin{pmatrix} FDIN_{t-1} \\ FDIO_{t-1} \\ X_{t-1} \\ M_{t-1} \end{pmatrix} + Exogenous\,Variables + \begin{pmatrix} \mu_{1t} \\ \mu_{2t} \\ \mu_{3t} \\ \mu_{4t} \end{pmatrix} \quad (1)
$$

K. Liu et al. (Eds.): ICISO 2018, IFIP AICT 527, pp. 318–319, 2018.
https://doi.org/10.1007/978-3-319-94541-5

2 Contribution and Conclusion

The contribution of this paper is that we add five country profiles to analysis the regression result to explain the relationship between FDI and international trade. These profiles are including government institutions, market sophistication, knowledge input, knowledge and technology output, and product market regulations. We also use FDI regulatory restriction to divided 30 countries into two groups. There are 11 countries in the first group, which means they have a strict FDI restriction. The remaining 19 countries have a less FDI regulatory restriction is in the second group. Moreover, we use 'Y' indicate if one country has a strong comparative advantage in this sector; 'N' indicates if a country has a comparative weakness advantage than other OECD countries in this sector. Moreover, 'Y*' means this country has a relatively strong comparative advantage (the score above the average), and 'N*' means this country has a relative weakness comparative advantage (the score below the average). We found that the more factors the country has and also under the less FDI regulatory restriction, this country has a more robust relationship between FDI and international trade.

References

1. Harding, T., Javorcik, B.: Foreign direct investment and export upgrading. Rev. Econ. Stat. **94**(4), 964–980 (2012)
2. Markuson, R., Svensson, L.: Trade in goods and factors with international differences in technology. Int. Econ. Rev. **26**, 175–192 (1985)
3. Pain, N., Wakelin, K.: Export Performance and the Role of Foreign Direct Investment, vol. 66. University of Manchester (1998)
4. Rana, A., Keberwar, M.: The Political Economy of FDI Flows into Developing Countries: Does the Depth of International Trade Agreements Matter? University of Orleans (2014)
5. Tekin, R.: Economic growth, exports and foreign direct investment in least development countries: a panel granger causality analysis. Econ. Model. **29**, 868–878 (2012)
6. Vu, B., Noy, I.: Sector analysis of foreign direct investment and growth in the developed countries. J. Int. Financ. Markets Inst. Money **19**, 402–413 (2009)
7. Wacker, K.: Do Multinationals Deteriorate Developing Countries' Export Price? The Impact of FDI ON Net Barter Terms of Trade. The World Economy. (2015)
8. Wooldridge, J.: Introductory Econometrics: A Modern Approach. South-Western, Cengage Learning, United States (2010)

Author Index

Abdaless, Sara 33
Afful-Dadzie, Anthony 299
Afful-Dadzie, Eric 299
Ambalov, Vitaly 155
Ashok, Mona 145
Askool, Sanaa 43

Banguera, Leonardo 278
Baranauskas, M. Cecília C. 197, 208, 238
Benfell, Adrian 218
Berckhan, Sophie 177
Bonacin, Rodrigo 187

Caine, Jamie 136
Calado, Ivo 187
Carrasco, Raúl 278
Clarke, Alison 177
Cordeiro, José 105

da Hora Rodrigues, Kamila Rios 53
da Silva, José Valderlei 197, 208
Dankwa, Kwasi 228
de Almeida Neris, Vânia Paula 53
de Souza, Paula Maia 53
dos Reis, Julio Cesar 187
Duarte, Rogério 311

Effah, John 125, 268

Fuentealba, Diego 278
Fuertes, Guillermo 278

Galarreta, Daniel 63
Garcia, Franco Eusébio 53

Hayashi, Elaine C. S. 197, 208
Heim, Irina 155, 313
Hoy, Zoe 218

Ibañez, Vladimiro 3
Ibarra, Manuel 3
Ibarra, Waldo 3

Jacobs, Aimee 43
Jacquinet, Marc 311

Li, Enyun 12
Li, Qi 289
Li, Weizi 83, 117
Li, Yutong 315, 318
Liu, Gang 259
Liu, Junxian 259
Liu, Kecheng 33, 117, 125, 289
Liu, Shixiong 83
Luo, Aimin 259

Maike, Vanessa R. M. L. 238
Maksim, Belitski 117
Meesters, Kenny 22
Michell, Vaughan 73
Moran, Stuart 177

Ñahuinlla, Emerson 3
Nakata, Keiichi 228
Nanda, Anupam 248
Navarro, Angel 3
Nieuwenhuijsen, Ralf 94
Nobre, Ângela Lacerda 311

Opoku-Anokye, Stephen 268

Pan, Yu-Chun 43, 73
Pereira, Roberto 197, 208
Piccolo, Lara S. G. 22

Roberts, Shadrock 22

Sabine, Khalil 117
Senyo, Prince Kwame 125, 268
Soto, Ismael 278
Soto, Wilfredo 3

Tan, Chekfoung 33, 43
Tang, Yinshan 12
Tehrani, Jasmine 73

Valerie, Fernandez   117
van Breemen, Auke J. J.   94
Vargas, Manuel   278
von Rosing, Mark   136

Wheatman, Martin John   167

Zhang, Xiaoxue   259